Study Guide

Study Guide

to accompany

EXPLORING PSYCHOLOGY

David G. Myers

Richard O. Straub

University of Michigan, Dearborn

WORTH PUBLISHERS, INC.

Study Guide
by Richard O. Straub
to accompany
Myers: **Exploring Psychology**

Printed in the United States of America.
ISBN: 0-87901-443-1
   2 3 4 5—93 92 91 90

Worth Publishers, Inc.
33 Irving Place
New York, New York 10003

Preface

This Study Guide is designed for use with *Exploring Psychology* by David G. Myers. It is intended to help you evaluate your understanding of the text material, and then to review any problem areas. "How to Manage Your Time Efficiently and Study More Effectively" (p. ix) gives detailed instructions on how to use the Study Guide for maximum benefit. It also offers additional study suggestions based on principles of time management, effective notetaking, evaluation of exam performance, and an effective program for improving your comprehension while studying from textbooks.

I would like to thank all the students and instructors who used this Study Guide in its earlier editions and provided such insightful and useful suggestions. Special thanks to Betty Shapiro for her outstanding editorial work on this project and to Harry Schwirck for overseeing its completion. I would also like to thank Pam, Jeremy, Rebecca, and Melissa for their continuing love, support, and patience.

Richard O. Straub
January 1990

Contents

How to Manage Your Time Efficiently and Study More Effectively

How effectively do you study? Good study habits make the job of being a college student much easier. Many students, who *could* succeed in college, fail or drop out because they have never learned to manage their time efficiently. Even the best students can usually benefit from an in-depth evaluation of their current study habits.

There are many ways to achieve academic success, of course, but your approach may not be the most effective or efficient. Are you sacrificing your social life or your physical or mental health in order to get A's on your exams? Good study habits result in better grades *and* more time for other activities.

Evaluate Your Current Study Habits

To improve your study habits, you must first have an accurate picture of how you currently spend your time. Begin by putting together a profile of your present living and studying habits. Answer the following questions by writing *yes* or *no* on each line.

_____ 1. Do you usually set up a schedule to budget your time for studying, recreation, and other activities?

_____ 2. Do you often put off studying until time pressures force you to cram?

_____ 3. Do other students seem to study less than you do, but get better grades?

_____ 4. Do you usually spend hours at a time studying one subject, rather than dividing that time between several subjects?

_____ 5. Do you often have trouble remembering what you have just read in a textbook?

_____ 6. Before reading a chapter in a textbook, do you skim through it and read the section headings?

_____ 7. Do you try to predict exam questions from your lecture notes and reading?

_____ 8. Do you usually attempt to paraphrase or summarize what you have just finished reading?

_____ 9. Do you find it difficult to concentrate very long when you study?

_____ 10. Do you often feel that you studied the wrong material for an exam?

Thousands of college students have participated in similar surveys. Students who are fully realizing their academic potential usually respond as follows: (1) yes, (2) no, (3) no, (4) no, (5) no, (6) yes, (7) yes, (8) yes, (9) no, (10) no.

Compare your responses to those of successful students. The greater the discrepancy, the more you could benefit from a program to improve your study habits. The questions are designed to identify areas of weakness. Once you have identified your weaknesses, you will be able to set specific goals for improvement and implement a program for reaching them.

Manage Your Time

Do you often feel frustrated because there isn't enough time to do all the things you must and want to do? Take heart. Even the most productive and successful people feel this way at times. But they establish priorities for their activities and they learn to budget time for each of them. There's much in the saying "If you want something done, ask a busy person to do it." A busy person knows how to get things done.

If you don't now have a system for budgeting your time, develop one. Not only will your academic accomplishments increase, but you will actually find more time in your schedule for other activities. And you won't have to feel guilty about "taking time off," because all your obligations will be covered.

Establish a Baseline

As a first step in preparing to budget your time, keep a diary for a few days to establish a summary, or baseline, of the time you spend in studying, socializing, working, and so on. If you are like many students, much of your "study" time is nonproductive; you may sit at your desk and leaf through a book, but the time is actually wasted. Or you may procrastinate. You are always getting ready to study, but you rarely do.

Besides revealing where you waste time, your diary will give you a realistic picture of how much time you need to allot for meals, commuting, and other fixed activities. In addition, careful records should indicate the times of the day when you are consistently most productive. A sample time-management diary is shown in Table 1.

Plan the Term

Having established and evaluated your baseline, you are ready to devise a more efficient schedule. Buy a calendar that covers the entire school term and has ample space for each day. Using the course outlines

Table 1   Sample Time-Management Diary

| | Monday | |
Behavior	Time Completed	Duration Hours: Minutes
Sleep	7:00	7:30
Dressing	7:25	:25
Breakfast	7:45	:20
Commute	8:20	:35
Coffee	9:00	:40
French	10:00	1:00
Socialize	10:15	:15
Videogame	10:35	:20
Coffee	11:00	:25
Psychology	12:00	1:00
Lunch	12:25	:25
Study Lab	1:00	:35
Psych. Lab	4:00	3:00
Work	5:30	1:30
Commute	6:10	:40
Dinner	6:45	:35
TV	7:30	:45
Study Psych.	10:00	2:30
Socialize	11:30	1:30
Sleep		

Prepare a similar chart for each day of the week. When you finish an activity, note it on the chart and write down the time it was completed. Then determine its duration by subtracting the time the previous activity was finished from the newly entered time.

provided by your instructors, enter the dates of all exams, term paper deadlines, and other important academic obligations. If you have any long-range personal plans (concerts, weekend trips, etc.), enter the dates on the calendar as well. Keep your calendar up to date and refer to it often. I recommend carrying it with you at all times.

Develop a Weekly Calendar

Now that you have a general picture of the school term, develop a weekly schedule that includes all of your activities. Aim for a schedule that you can live with for the entire school term. A sample weekly schedule, incorporating the following guidelines, is shown in Table 2.

1. Enter your class times, work hours, and any other fixed obligations first. *Be thorough.* Using information from your time management diary, allow plenty of time for such things as commuting, meals, laundry, and the like.

2. Set up a study schedule for each of your courses. The study habits survey and your time management diary will direct you. The following guidelines should also be useful.

(a) Establish regular study times for each course. The 4 hours needed to study one subject, for example, are most profitable when divided into shorter periods spaced over several days. If you cram your studying into one 4-hour block, what you attempt to learn in the third or fourth hour will interfere with what you studied in the first 2 hours. Newly acquired knowledge is like wet cement. It needs some time to "harden" to become memory.

(b) Alternate subjects. The type of interference just mentioned is greatest between similar topics. Set up a schedule in which you spend time on several *different* courses during each study session. Besides reducing the potential for interference, alternating subjects will help to prevent mental fatigue with one topic.

(c) Set weekly goals to determine the amount of study time you need to do well in each course. This will depend on, among other things, the difficulty of your courses and the effectiveness of your methods. Many professors recommend studying at least 1 to 2 hours for each hour in class. If your time diary indicates that you presently study less time than that, do not plan to jump immediately to a much higher level. Increase study time from your baseline by setting weekly goals [see **(4)**] that will gradually bring you up to the desired level. As an initial schedule, for example, you might set aside an amount of study time for each course that matches class time.

Table 2 Sample Weekly Schedule

Time	Mon.	Tues.	Wed.	Thurs.	Fri.	Sat.
7–8	Dress Eat	Dress Eat	Dress Eat	Dress Eat	Dress Eat	
8–9	Psych.	Study Psych.	Psych.	Study Psych.	Psych.	Dress Eat
9–10	Eng.	Study Eng.	Eng.	Study Eng.	Eng.	Study Eng.
10–11	Study French	Free	Study French	Open Study	Study French	Study Stats.
11–12	French	Study Psych. Lab	French	Open Study	French	Study Stats.
12–1	Lunch	Lunch	Lunch	Lunch	Lunch	Lunch
1–2	Stats.	Psych. Lab	Stats.	Study or Free	Stats.	Free
2–3	Bio.	Psych. Lab	Bio.	Free	Bio.	Free
3–4	Free	Psych.	Free	Free	Free	Free
4–5	Job	Job	Job	Job	Job	Free
5–6	Job	Job	Job	Job	Job	Free
6–7	Dinner	Dinner	Dinner	Dinner	Dinner	Dinner
7–8	Study Bio.	Study Bio.	Study Bio.	Study Bio.	Free	Free
8–9	Study Eng.	Study Stats.	Study Psych.	Open Study	Open Study	Free
9–10	Open Study	Open Study	Open Study	Open	Free	Free

This is a sample schedule for a student with a 16-credit load and a 10-hour-per-week part-time job. Using this chart as an illustration, make up a weekly schedule, following the guidelines outlined here.

(d) Schedule for maximum effectiveness. Tailor your schedule to meet the demands of each course. For the course that emphasizes lecture notes, schedule time for a daily review soon after the class. This will give you a chance to revise your notes and clean up any hard-to-decipher shorthand while the material is still fresh in your mind. If you are evaluated for class participation (for example, in a language course), allow time for a review just *before* the class meets. Schedule study time for your most difficult (or least motivating) courses during times when you are the most alert and distractions are fewest.

(e) Schedule open study time. Emergencies, additional obligations, and the like could throw off your schedule. And you may simply need some extra time periodically for a project or for review in one or your courses. Schedule several hours each week for such purposes.

3. After you have budgeted time for studying, fill in slots for recreation, hobbies, relaxation, household errands, and the like.

4. Set specific goals. Before each study session, make a list of specific goals. The simple note "7–8 PM: study psychology" is too broad to ensure the most effective use of the time. Formulate your daily goals according to what you know you must accomplish during the term. If you have course outlines with advance assignments, set systematic daily goals that will allow you, for example, to cover fifteen chapters before the exam. And be realistic: can you actually expect to cover a 78-page chapter in one session? Divide large tasks into smaller units; stop at the most logical resting points. When you complete a specific goal, take a 5- or 10-minute break before tackling the next goal.

5. Evaluate how successful or unsuccessful your studying has been on a daily or weekly basis. Did you reach most of your goals? If so, reward yourself immediately. You might even make a list of five to ten rewards to choose from. If you have trouble studying regularly, you may be able to motivate yourself by making such rewards contingent on completing specific goals.

6. Finally, until you have lived with your schedule for several weeks, don't hesitate to revise it. You may need to allow more time for chemistry, for example, and less for some other course. If you are trying to study regularly for the first time and are feeling burned out, you probably have set your initial goals too high. Don't let failure cause you to despair and abandon the program. Accept your limitations and revise your schedule so that you are studying only 15 to 20 minutes more each evening than you are used to. The point is to *identify a regular schedule with which you can achieve some success*. Time management, like any skill, must be practiced to become effective.

Techniques for Effective Study

Knowing how to put study time to best use is, of course, as important as finding a place for it in your schedule. Here are some suggestions that should enable you to increase your reading comprehension and improve your notetaking. A few study tips are included as well.

Using SQ3R to Increase Reading Comprehension

How do you study from a textbook? If you are like many students, you simply read and reread in a *passive* manner. Studies have shown, however, that most students who simply read a textbook cannot remember more than half the material ten minutes after they have finished. Often, what is retained is the unessential material rather than the important points upon which exam questions will be based.

This Study Guide employs a program known as SQ3R (*Survey, Question, Read, Recite,* and *Review*) to facilitate, and allow you to assess, your comprehension of the important facts and concepts in *Exploring Psychology*, by David Myers.

Research has shown that students using SQ3R achieve significantly greater comprehension of textbooks than students reading in the more traditional passive manner. Once you have learned this program, you can improve your comprehension of any textbook.

Survey   Before reading a chapter, determine whether the text or the study guide has an outline or list of objectives. Read this material and the summary at the end of the chapter. Next, read the textbook chapter fairly quickly, paying special attention to the major headings and subheadings. This survey will give you an idea of the chapter's contents and organization. You will then be able to divide the chapter into logical sections in order to formulate specific goals for a more careful reading of the chapter.

In this Study Guide, the *Chapter Overview* summarizes the major topics of the textbook chapter. This section also provides a few suggestions for approaching topics you may find difficult.

Question   You will retain material longer when you have a use for it. If you look up a word's definition in order to solve a crossword puzzle, for example, you will remember it longer than if you merely fill in the letters as a result of putting other words in. Surveying the chapter will allow you to generate important questions that the chapter will proceed to answer. These questions correspond to "mental files" into which knowledge will be sorted for easy access.

As you survey, jot down several questions for each chapter section. One simple technique is to generate questions by rephrasing a section heading. For example, the "Concepts" heading could be turned into "What is a concept?" Good questions will allow you to focus on the important points in the text. Examples of good questions are those that begin as follows: "List two examples of . . . ?" "What is the function of . . . ?" "What is the significance of . . . ?" Such questions give a purpose to your reading. Similarly, you can formulate questions based on the chapter outline.

The *Guided Study* section of this Study Guide provides the types of questions you might formulate while surveying each chapter. This section is a detailed set of objectives covering the points made in the text.

Read   When you have established "files" for each section of the chapter, review your first question, begin reading, and continue until you have discovered its answer. If you come to material that seems to answer an important question you don't have a file for, stop and write down the question.

Using this Study Guide, read the chapter one section at a time. First, preview the section by skimming it, noting headings and boldface items. Next, study the appropriate section objectives in the *Guided Study*. Then, as you read the chapter section, search for the answer to each objective.

Be sure to read everything. Don't skip photo or art captions, graphs, or marginal notes. In some cases, what may seem vague in reading will be made clear by a simple graph. Keep in mind that test questions are sometimes drawn from illustrations and charts.

Recite   When you have found the answer to a question, close your eyes and mentally recite the question and its answer. Then *write* the answer next to the question. It is important that you recite an answer in your own words rather than the author's. Don't rely on your short-term memory to repeat the author's words verbatim.

In responding to the objectives, pay close attention to what is called for. If you are asked to identify or list, do just that. If asked to compare, contrast, or do both, you should focus on the similarities (compare) and differences (contrast) between the concepts or theories. Answering the objectives carefully will not only help you to focus your attention on the important concepts of the text, but it will also provide excellent practice for essay exams.

Recitation is an extremely effective study technique, recommended by many learning experts. In addition to increasing reading comprehension, it is useful for review. Trying to explain something in your own words clarifies your knowledge, often by revealing aspects of your answer that are vague or incomplete. If you repeatedly rely upon "I know" in recitation, you really *may not know*.

Recitation has the additional advantage of simulating an exam, especially an essay exam; the same skills are required in both cases. Too often students study without ever putting the book and notes aside, which makes it easy for them to develop false confidence in their knowledge. When the material is in front of you, you may be able to *recognize* an answer, but will you be able to *recall* it later, when you take an exam that does not provide these retrieval cues?

After you have recited and written your answer, continue with your next question. Read, recite, and so on.

Review   When you have answered the last question on the material you have designated as a study goal, go back and review. Read over each question and your written answer to it. Your review might also include a brief written summary that integrates all of your questions and answers. This review need not take longer than a few minutes, but it is important. It will help you retain the material longer and will greatly facilitate a final review of each chapter before the exam.

In this Study Guide, the *Chapter Review* section contains fill-in and short essay questions for you to complete after you have finished reading the text and written answers to the objectives. The correct answers are given at the end of the chapter. Generally to the fill-in questions, your answers should match exactly (as in the case of important terms, theories, or people). In some cases, particularly for the short essay questions, an answer that is close in meaning will suffice. You should go through the review several times before taking an exam, so it is a good idea to mentally fill in the answers until you are ready for a final pretest review. Textbook page references are provided with each sec-

tion title, in case you need to review any of the material.

Also provided to facilitate your review are two *Progress Tests* that include multiple-choice questions and, where appropriate, matching or true–false questions. These tests are *not* to be taken until you have read the chapter, written answers to the objectives, and completed the *Chapter Review*. Correct answers, along with explanations of why each alternative is correct or incorrect, are provided at the end of the chapter. The relevant text page numbers for each question are also given. If you miss a question, read these explanations and, if necessary, review the text pages. The progress tests do not test every aspect of a concept, so you should treat an incorrect answer as an indication that you need to review the concept.

Following the two tests is a list of *Key Terms* from the chapter, with space provided for you to write a brief definition, or explanation, of each term, theory, or concept. As with the *Guided Study* objectives, it is important that these answers be written from memory, and in your own words. The *Answers* section at the end of the chapter gives a definition of each term, sometimes along with an example of its usage and/or a tip to help you remember its meaning.

In this Study Guide, an additional section called *Focus on Psychology* is provided to enrich your understanding of the textbook material. This section expands upon the text coverage by providing provocative issues for you to think about or by summarizing relevant research articles. In addition to serving as refreshing study breaks from the other sections of the Study Guide, the *Focus* sections will enrich your understanding of the textbook's material by applying it to new information. Integrating the textbook material with this new information is an excellent way for you to learn by actively participating, rather than by merely repeating information from the text.

One final suggestion: Incorporate SQ3R into your time-management calendar. Set specific goals for completing SQ3R with each assigned chapter. Keep a record of chapters completed, and reward yourself for being conscientious. Initially, it takes more time and effort to "read" using SQ3R, but with practice, the steps will become automatic. More important, you will comprehend significantly more material and retain knowledge longer than passive readers do.

Taking Lecture Notes

Are your class notes as useful as they might be? One way to determine their worth is to compare them with those taken by other good students. Are yours as thorough? Do they provide you with a comprehensible outline of each lecture? If not, then the following suggestions might increase the effectiveness of your notetaking.

1. Keep a separate notebook for each course. Use $8\frac{1}{2} \times 11$-inch pages. Consider using a ring binder, which would allow you to revise and insert notes while still preserving lecture order.

2. Take notes in the format of a lecture outline. Use roman numerals for major points, letters for supporting arguments, and so on. Some instructors will make this easy by delivering organized lectures and, in some cases, by outlining their lectures on the board. If a lecture is disorganized, you will probably want to reorganize your notes soon after the class.

3. As you take notes in class, leave a wide margin on one side of each page. After the lecture, expand or clarify any shorthand notes while the material is fresh in your mind. Use this time to write important questions in the margin next to notes that answer them. This will facilitate later review of the material and will allow you to anticipate similar exam questions.

Evaluate Your Exam Performance

How often have you received a grade on an exam that did not do justice to the effort you spent preparing for the exam? This is a common experience that can leave one feeling bewildered and abused. "What do I have to do to get an A?" "The test was unfair!" "I studied the wrong material!"

The chances of this happening are greatly reduced if you have an effective time-management schedule and use the study techniques described here. But it can happen to the best-prepared student and is most likely to occur on your first exam with a new professor.

Remember that there are two main reasons for studying. One is to learn for your own general academic development. Many people believe that such knowledge is all that really matters. Of course, it is possible, though unlikely, to be an expert on a topic without achieving commensurate grades, just as one can, occasionally, earn an excellent grade without truly mastering the course material. During a job interview or in the workplace, however, your A in Fortran won't mean much if you can't actually program a computer.

In order to keep career options open after you graduate, you must know the material *and* maintain competitive grades. In the short run, this means performing well on exams, which is the second main objective in studying.

Probably the single best piece of advice to keep in mind when studying for exams is to *try to predict exam questions.* This means ignoring the trivia and focusing on the important questions and their answers (with your instructor's emphasis in mind).

A second point is obvious. How well you do on exams is determined by your mastery of *both* lecture and textbook material. Many students (partly because of poor time management) concentrate too much on one at the expense of the other.

To evaluate how well you are learning lecture and textbook material, analyze the questions you missed on the first exam. If your instructor does not review exams during class, you can easily do it yourself. Divide the questions into two categories: those drawn primarily from lectures and those drawn primarily from the textbook. Determine the percentage of questions you missed in each category. If your errors are evenly distributed and you are satisfied with your grade, you have no problem. If you are weaker in one area, you will need to set future goals for increasing and/or improving your study of that area.

Similarly, note the percentage of test questions drawn from each category. Although most courses involve exams that cover *both* lecture notes and the textbook, the relative emphasis of each may vary from instructor to instructor. While your instructors may not be entirely consistent in making up future exams, you may be able to tailor your studying for each course by placing *additional* emphasis on the appropriate area.

Exam evaluation will also point out the types of questions your instructor prefers. Does the exam consist primarily of multiple-choice, true–false, or essay questions? You may also discover that an instructor is fond of wording questions in certain ways. For example, an instructor may rely heavily on questions that require you to draw an analogy between a theory or concept and a real-world example. Evaluate both your instructor's style and how well you do with each format. Use this information to guide your future exam preparation.

Important aids, not only in studying for exams but also in determining how well prepared you are, are the *Progress Tests* provided in this Study Guide. If these tests don't include all of the types of questions your instructor typically writes, make up your own practice exam questions. Spend extra time testing yourself with question formats that are most difficult for you. There is no better way to evaluate your preparation for an upcoming exam than by testing yourself under the conditions most likely to be in effect during the actual test.

A Few Practical Tips

Even the best intentions for studying sometimes fail. Some of these failures occur because students attempt to work under conditions that are simply not conducive to concentrated study. To help ensure the success of your self-management program, here are a few suggestions that should assist you in reducing the possibility of procrastination or distraction.

1. If you have set up a schedule for studying, make your roommate, family, and friends aware of this commitment, and ask them to honor your quiet study time. Close your door and post a "Do Not Disturb" sign.

2. Set up a place to study that minimizes potential distractions. Use a desk or table, not your bed or an extremely comfortable chair. Keep your desk and the walls around it free from clutter. If you need a place other than your room, find one that meets as many of the above requirements as possible — for example, in the library stacks.

3. Do nothing but study in this place. It should become associated with studying so that it "triggers" this activity, just as a mouth-watering aroma elicits an appetite.

4. Never study with the television on or with other distracting noises present. If you must have music in the background in order to mask outside noises, for example, play soft instrumental music. Don't pick vocal selections; your mind will be drawn to the lyrics.

5. Study by yourself. Other students can be distracting or can break the pace at which *your* learning is most efficient. In addition, there is always the possibility that group studying will become a social gathering. Reserve that for its own place in your time schedule.

If you continue to have difficulty concentrating for very long, try the following suggestions.

6. Study your most difficult or most challenging subjects first, when you are most alert.

7. Start with relatively short periods of concentrated study, with breaks in between. If your attention starts to wander, get up immediately and take a break. It is better to study effectively for 15 minutes and then take a break than to fritter away 45 minutes out of an hour. Gradually increase the length of study periods, using your attention span as an indicator of successful pacing.

Some Closing Thoughts

I hope that these suggestions not only help make you more successful academically, but also enhance the quality of your college life in general. Having the necessary skills makes any job a lot easier and more pleasant. Let me repeat my warning not to attempt to make too drastic a change in your life-style immediately. Start by establishing a few realistic goals; then gradually shape your performance to the desired level. Good habits require time and self-discipline to develop. Once established they can last a lifetime.

Study Guide

Chapter **1** | # Introducing Psychology

Chapter Overview

Psychology's historical development and current activities lead us to define the field as the science of behavior and mental processes. Chapter 1 discusses the development of psychology and the range of behaviors and mental processes being investigated by psychologists in each of the various specialty areas. In addition, it explains how psychologists employ the methods of observation, correlation, and experimentation in order to describe, predict, and understand behavior. Chapter 1 concludes with a discussion of several questions people often ask about psychology, including whether laboratory experiments are ethical, why animal research is relevant, whether psychological theories aren't simply based on common sense, and whether psychology's principles don't have the potential for misuse.

Chapter 1 should not be too difficult for you; there are not very many difficult terms or theories to remember. However, the chapter does introduce a number of concepts and issues that will play an important role in later chapters. Pay particular attention to the section "Psychology's Methods and Aims." Make sure you understand the method of experimentation, especially the importance of control conditions and the difference between independent and dependent variables.

Guided Study

The text chapter should be studied one section at a time. Before you read, preview each section by skimming it, noting headings and boldface items. Then read the appropriate section objectives from the following outline. Keep these objectives in mind and, as you read the chapter section, search for the information that will enable you to meet each objective. Once you have finished a section, write out answers for its objectives.

What is Psychology? (pp. 2–6)

1. Define psychology and trace its historical development.

2. Describe the different perspectives from which psychologists examine behavior and mental processes.

3. Identify the major subfields of psychology.

Scientific Attitudes and Approaches (pp. 6–8)

4. Discuss the attitudes that have characterized scientific inquiry and describe the scientific method which psychologists use to describe, predict, and explain behavior.

Psychology's Methods and Aims (pp. 8–13)

5. Describe three methods psychologists use to systematically observe and describe behavior.

6. Discuss why correlations yield prediction but not explanation.

7. Describe the nature and advantages of experimentation.

Commonly Asked Questions About Psychology (pp. 13–17)

8. Discuss questions regarding the artificiality of experimentation and explain why psychologists study animals.

9. Discuss the ethics of experimentation and how psychologists' values influence their work.

10. Discuss the relevance of the "I-knew-it-all-along" phenomenon and whether application of psychological principles is potentially dangerous.

How to Study This Book (pp. 17–18)

11. Briefly explain the SQ3R study technique.

Chapter Review

When you have finished reading the chapter, use the material that follows to review it. Complete the sentences and answer the questions. As you proceed, evaluate your performance for each chapter section by consulting the answer key at the end of this chapter. Do not continue with the next section until you've understood each answer. If you need to, review or reread the appropriate chapter section in the textbook before continuing.

What Is Psychology? (pp. 2–6)

1. The historical roots of psychology include the fields of _____ and

_____.

2. The first psychological laboratory was founded in 1879 by Wilhelm _____.

3. Some early psychologists included Ivan Pavlov, who pioneered the study of _conditioning_; the personality theorist _____

_____; Jean Piaget, who studied _Cognitive_ ; and _____

_____, the author of one of the first psychology textbooks.

4. In its earliest years, psychology was defined as the science of _____ life. From about 1920 until 1960, under the influence of

_____ _____,

psychology in America was redefined as the science of _____. The author of your textbook defines psychology as the science of _*behaviour*_ and _*mental*_ processes.

5. Psychologists who study hereditary influences on behavior, how messages are transmitted within the brain, and similar phenomena are working within the _*biological*_ perspective on behavior.

6. The _*psychoanalytic*_ perspective assumes that behavior is the product of unconscious drives. This perspective builds on the ideas of _*S*_ _*Freud*_.

7. Psychologists who study the mechanisms by which observable responses are acquired in particular environments are working within the _*behavioural*_ perspective.

8. The emphasis on our capacity to choose our own life patterns and to grow to higher levels of maturity is characteristic of the _*humanistic*_ perspective.

9. The _*cognitive*_ perspective explores how our minds process and use information.

10. Among professional psychologists, approximately _____ work in the mental health fields. Most of the remaining psychologists are involved in conducting

    _____ _____,
    which builds up psychology's base of knowledge,
    or _____ _____,
    which seeks solutions to practical problems.

11. Psychologists who explore the links between biology and behavior are known as _*biological*_ psychologists.

12. Psychologists who study physical, mental, and social changes during the life cycle are called _*developmental*_ psychologists.

13. Psychologists who use experiments to study areas like sensation, learning, and motivation are called _*general*_ _*experimental*_ psychologists.

14. Psychologists who study how individuals are influenced by enduring inner factors are called _*personality*_ psychologists.

15. Psychologists who study how people influence and are influenced by other people are called _*social*_ psychologists.

16. Psychologists who assess and treat people with psychological difficulties are called _*clinical*_ psychologists. Mental health clinicians who have earned a medical degree are called _*psychiatrists*_.

17. Psychologists who provide guidance to students are called _*counseling*_ psychologists. Those who evaluate children and work with teachers and parents are called _*school*_ psychologists.

18. Psychologists who study human behavior in the workplace are called _*industrial*_/ _*organizational*_ psychologists.

Explain the difference between basic and applied research and give an example of each.

Scientific Attitudes and Approaches (pp. 6–8)

19. The scientific ideal is characterized by the attitudes of _*skepticism*_ and _*humility*_. Because of these attitudes, scientists try to _*replicate*_ their research findings, rather than assuming these are correct.

20. An integrated set of principles that organizes and predicts facts is a _*theory*_. Testable propositions that allow a scientist to evaluate a theory are called _*hypotheses*_.

Psychology's Methods and Aims (pp. 8–13)

21. The three research methods in psychology are _*observation*_, _*correlation*_, and _*experimentation*_; they help

psychologists describe, predict, and explain behavior.

22. The research method in which one individual is studied in depth in order to reveal general principles of behavior is the _____ case _____ _____ study _____ method.

23. The method in which a group of people is questioned about their attitudes or behavior is the _____ survey _____ method.

24. Surveys try to obtain a _____ random _____ sample, one that will be representative of the population being studied. In such a sample, every person _____ (does)/does not) have a chance of being included.

25. The method in which people or animals are directly observed in their natural environments is called _____ naturalistic _____ observation.

26. The case study, survey, and naturalistic observation methods do not explain behavior; they simply _____ describe _____ it.

27. When changes in one factor are accompanied by changes in another, the two factors are said to be _____ correlated _____. If the factors increase or decrease together, they are _____ positively, corr'd _____. If, however, one decreases as the other increases, they are _____ negatively _____ _____ corr'd _____.

28. A common error is to assume that a correlation between two factors means that one _____ causes _____ the other. To study cause-and-effect relationships, psychologists conduct _____ experiments _____.

If your level of test anxiety goes down as your time spent studying for an exam goes up, would you say these events are positively or negatively correlated? Explain your reasoning.

29. An experiment must involve at least two conditions: the _____ control _____ condition, in which the experimental treatment is absent, and the _____ experimental _____ condition, in which it is present.

30. The factor that is being manipulated in an experiment is called the _____ variable. The factor that may change as a result of these manipulations is called the _____ variable.

31. In an experiment, subjects are assigned to different groups by chance in order to minimize preexisting group differences. This procedure is known as _____ random _____ _____ assignment _____.

Explain at least one advantage of the experiment as a research method.

Commonly Asked Questions About Psychology (pp. 13–17)

32. Laboratory experiments in psychology are sometimes criticized as being _____. However, psychologists' concern is not with the specific behaviors that occur in the experiments, but with the underlying theoretical _____.

33. The tendency to perceive an outcome that has occurred as being obvious and predictable is called the _____-_____-_____ phenomenon.

FOCUS ON PSYCHOLOGY:
A Career in Psychology

Preparing for a career in psychology usually requires a graduate degree. To earn a doctorate in psychology (Ph.D. or Psy.D.), students complete a four- to six-year program, at the end of which they must design and conduct an original research project. Although a doctorate is required for many jobs in psychology—indeed, more than 60 percent of all psychologists hold this degree—the degree of Master of Arts (M.A.) is sufficient for others, such as teaching at some community colleges or being a school psychologist. The M.A. degree program typically requires one or two years of training beyond the undergraduate curriculum. A bachelor's degree does not prepare students to work as psychologists any more than it prepares them to work as physicians or attorneys.

The figures on this page indicate the percentages of psychologists working in various settings and fields of specialization. Traditionally, most psychologists ac-

cepted teaching or research positions at universities and four-year colleges. Because of declining college enrollments and general economic trends, however, college faculty positions and jobs in areas dependent upon government funding (such as many research positions) are expected to decline. Many of the employment opportunities for doctorates in psychology will derive from society's increased emphasis on health maintenance and meeting the needs of particular groups, such as the elderly. Business, industry, and private clinical practice are also expected to be good sources of employment.

During the late 1980s approximately 97,000 psychologists were in the work force with a median annual salary of $40,000 for all those with doctoral degrees. Since the 1970s, however, the rate at which new doctorates have been conferred has increased faster in psychology than in any other field, creating a tremendous need for alternative sources of employment for psychologists, particularly those with only a master's degree.

Training in psychology can, of course, provide benefits other than employment. Many of the findings of psychologists have obvious practical applications, such as improving how you study, helping you to understand the ways that groups influence a person's behavior, or helping you to eliminate undesirable habits. As a student of psychology, you may also develop the objective and skeptical eye of the behavioral scientist. This will help you evaluate information reported by the media. Developing this perspective will make you a more objective and better-informed citizen and consumer.

Sources: Hopke, W. E. (1987). *The Encyclopedia of Careers and Vocational Guidance* (7th ed.). Chicago: J. G. Ferguson Publishing Company.

Stapp, J., Tucker, A. M., and VandenBos, G. R. (1985). Census of Psychological Personnel: 1983. *American Psychologist, 40* (No. 12), 1317–1351.

American Psychological Association. (1986). *Careers In Psychology*. Washington, DC: American Psychological Association.

If you want information about how to prepare for a career in psychology and opportunities for employment, write to the American Psychological Association, 1200 Seventeenth St. N.W., Washington, D.C. 20036, and request this free pamphlet.

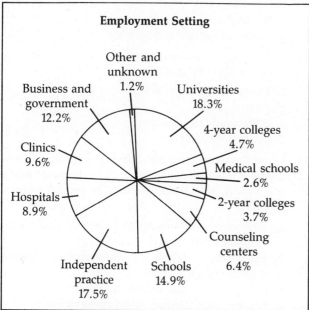

Employment Setting

Other and unknown 1.2%
Business and government 12.2%
Universities 18.3%
4-year colleges 4.7%
Clinics 9.6%
Medical schools 2.6%
2-year colleges 3.7%
Hospitals 8.9%
Counseling centers 6.4%
Independent practice 17.5%
Schools 14.9%

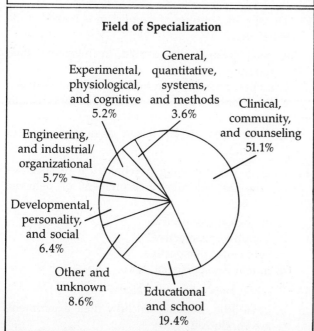

Field of Specialization

Experimental, physiological, and cognitive 5.2%
General, quantitative, systems, and methods 3.6%
Clinical, community, and counseling 51.1%
Engineering, and industrial/organizational 5.7%
Developmental, personality, and social 6.4%
Other and unknown 8.6%
Educational and school 19.4%

Progress Test 1

Multiple-Choice Questions

Circle your answers to the following questions and check them with the answer key at the end of this chapter. If your answer is incorrect, read the answer key explanation for why it is incorrect and then consult the appropriate pages of the text to understand the correct answer.

1. Psychology is defined as the:
   a. study of mental phenomena.
   b. study of conscious and unconscious activity.
   c. study of behavior.
   d. science of behavior and mental processes.

2. After detailed study of a gunshot wound victim, a psychologist concludes that the brain region destroyed is likely to be important for memory functions. Which research method did the psychologist use to deduce this?
   a. case study   c. correlational
   b. survey   d. experimental

3. In an experiment to determine the effects of exercise on motivation, exercise is the:
   a. control condition.
   b. intervening variable.
   c. independent variable.
   d. dependent variable.

4. In order to determine the effects of a new drug on memory, one group of subjects is given a pill that contains the drug. A second group is given a sugar pill that does not contain the drug. This second group constitutes the:
   a. random sample.   c. control group.
   b. experimental group. d. test group.

5. Theories are defined as:
   a. testable propositions.
   b. factors that may change in response to manipulation.
   c. statistical indexes.
   d. principles that help to organize, predict, and explain facts.

6. A psychologist studies the play behavior of third-grade children by watching groups during recess at school. Which research method is being used?
   a. correlational
   b. case study
   c. experimental
   d. naturalistic observation

7. Which psychological perspective emphasizes the interaction of the brain and body in behavior?
   a. biological perspective
   b. cognitive perspective
   c. behavioral perspective
   d. psychoanalytic perspective

8. A professor constructs a questionnaire to determine how students at the university feel about nuclear disarmament. Which of the following techniques should be used in order to survey a random sample of the student body?
   a. Every student should be sent the questionnaire.
   b. Only students majoring in psychology should be asked to complete the questionnaire.

   c. Only students living on campus should be asked to complete the questionnaire.
   d. From an alphabetical listing of all students, every tenth person should be asked to complete the questionnaire.

9. Which of the following psychologists would be most likely to study the effects of fraternity membership on an individual member's behavior?
   a. a clinical psychologist
   b. a developmental psychologist
   c. a personality psychologist
   d. a social psychologist

10. Psychologists use experimental research in order to reveal or to understand:
   a. correlational relationships.
   b. hypotheses.
   c. theories.
   d. cause-and-effect relationships.

11. Over half the psychologists in the United States work in fields related to:
   a. life-span development.
   b. mental health.
   c. undergraduate teaching.
   d. applied research.

12. Experimentation, which seeks to explain events, involves _____ factors, while correlation, which serves only to predict events, involves _____ factors.
   a. determining relationships between; direct manipulation of
   b. direct manipulation of; determining relationships between
   c. direct observation of; random selection of
   d. random selection of; direct observation of

13. The specific attitude of skepticism is based on the belief that:
   a. people are rarely candid in revealing their thoughts.
   b. mental processes cannot be studied objectively.
   c. the scientist's intuition about behavior is usually correct.
   d. ideas need to be tested against observable evidence.

14. Each of the following psychological perspectives emphasizes objective measurement of behavior *except* the:
   a. biological perspective.
   b. cognitive perspective.
   c. behavioral perspective.
   d. humanistic perspective.

15. Psychologists' personal values:
   a. have little influence on how their experiments are conducted.

b. do not influence the interpretation of experimental results because of the use of statistical techniques that guard against subjective bias.

c. can bias both scientific observation and interpretation of data.

d. have little influence on the methods of investigation but a significant effect on interpretation.

16. If shoe size and IQ are negatively correlated, which of the following is true?

   a. People with large feet tend to have high IQs.
   b. People with small feet tend to have high IQs.
   c. People with small feet tend to have low IQs.
   d. IQ is unpredictable based on a person's shoe size.

Matching Items

Match each subfield and psychological perspective with its defining feature.

Terms

_____g_____   **1.** biological psychology
_____   **2.** developmental psychology
_____c_____   **3.** general experimental psychology
_____   **4.** personality psychology
_____   **5.** social psychology
_____   **6.** clinical psychology
_____l_____   **7.** industrial/organizational psychology
_____   **8.** psychoanalytic perspective
_____f_____   **9.** behavioral perspective
_____b_____ **10.** humanistic perspective
_____ **11.** cognitive perspective
_____ **12.** basic research
_____i_____ **13.** applied research

17. Which of the following research methods would be the best way to determine whether alcohol impairs memory?

   a. case study research
   b. naturalistic observation
   c. survey research
   d. experimental research

18. Hypotheses are:

   a. integrated sets of principles that help organize observations.
   b. testable predictions, often derived from theories.
   c. hunches about mental processes.
   d. measures of relationships between two factors.

Definitions

   a. concerned with the study of behavior throughout the life cycle
   b. emphasizes a person's capacity to grow to higher levels of fulfillment
   c. concerned with studying, by means of experiments, principles underlying sensation, learning, motivation, and other behaviors
   d. concerned with the study of practical problems
   e. concerned with the role of unconscious drives and conflicts in determining human behavior
   f. concerned with the mechanisms by which observable responses are acquired
   g. concerned with the exploration of the links between biology and behavior
   h. concerned with how the mind processes, retains, and retrieves information
   i. concerned with adding to psychology's knowledge base
   j. concerned with how enduring, inner factors influence behavior
   k. concerned with the assessment and treatment of people with psychological difficulties
   l. concerned with the exploration of human behavior in the workplace
   m. concerned with how people influence others.

Progress Test 2

Progress Test 2 should be completed during a final chapter review. Answer the following questions after you thoroughly understand the correct answers for the Chapter Review and Progress Test 1.

Multiple-Choice Questions

1. The first psychology laboratory was established by

_____ in the year _____.

   a. Wundt; 1879   **c.** Freud; 1899
   b. James; 1890   **d.** Watson; 1913

2. If eating saturated fat and the likelihood of cancer are positively correlated, which of the following is true?

   a. Saturated fat causes cancer.

b. People who are prone to develop cancer prefer foods containing saturated fat.

c. A separate factor links the consumption of saturated fat to cancer.

d. None of the above is necessarily true.

3. In an experiment to determine the effects of attention on memory, memory is the:

a. control condition.
c. independent variable.
b. intervening variable.
d. dependent variable.

4. The group that receives the treatment of interest in an experiment is the:

a. test group.
c. experimental group.
b. random sample.
d. control group.

5. Which of the following best describes the I-knew-it-all-along phenomenon?

a. Events seem more predictable before they have occurred.
b. Events seem more predictable after they have occurred.
c. A person's intuition is usually correct.
d. A person's intuition is usually not correct.

6. The procedure designed to ensure that the experimental and control groups do not differ in any way that might affect the experiment's results is called:

a. variable controlling.
b. random assignment.
c. representative sampling.
d. stratification.

7. Two historical roots of psychology are the disciplines of:

a. philosophy and chemistry.
b. physiology and chemistry.
c. philosophy and physiology.
d. philosophy and physics.

8. Which of the following individuals is also a physician?

a. clinical psychologist
b. experimental psychologist
c. psychiatrist
d. biological psychologist

9. Why are animals frequently used in psychology experiments?

a. The processes that underline behavior in animals and humans are often similar.
b. Animal behavior is generally simpler to understand.
c. Animals are worthy of study for their own sake.
d. For all the above reasons.

10. Which psychological perspective is primarily concerned with the ways in which the mind processes and retains information?

a. the biological perspective

b. the psychoanalytic perspective
c. the behavioral perspective
d. the cognitive perspective

11. According to your textbook:

a. because laboratory experiments are artificial, any principles discovered cannot be applied to everyday behaviors.
b. no psychological theory can be considered true until tested.
c. psychology's theories simply reflect common sense.
d. psychology has few ties to other disciplines.

12. Dr. Jones's research centers on the relationship between changes in our thinking over the life span and changes in moral reasoning. Dr. Jones is most likely a:

a. clinical psychologist.
b. personality psychologist.
c. social psychologist.
d. developmental psychologist.

13. Which subfield is most directly concerned with studying human behavior in the workplace?

a. clinical psychology
b. personality psychology
c. industrial/organizational psychology
d. social psychology

14. Dr. Ernst, who follows the ideas of Freud, explains behavior in terms of unconscious drives. Dr. Ernst is working within the:

a. behavioral perspective.
b. humanistic perspective.
c. psychoanalytic perspective.
d. cognitive perspective.

15. Which perspective emphasizes the importance of environmental influences upon behavior?

a. behavioral
c. psychoanalytic
b. humanistic
d. cognitive

16. Which type of research would allow you to determine whether students' college grades accurately predict later income?

a. case study research
b. naturalistic observation
c. experimental research
d. correlational research

17. In a test of the effects of air pollution, groups of students performed a reaction-time task in either a polluted or unpolluted room. To what condition were students in the unpolluted room exposed?

a. experimental
c. randomly assigned
b. control
d. dependent

18. In order to study the effects of lighting on mood, Dr. Cooper had students fill out questionnaires in

brightly lit or dimly lit rooms. In this study, the independent variable consisted of:

a. the number of subjects assigned to each group.
b. the students' responses to the questionnaire.
c. the room lighting.
d. the subject matter of the questions asked.

19. A psychologist who studies how worker productivity might be increased by changing office layout is engaged in _____ research.

a. applied
b. basic
c. clinical
d. developmental

Matching Items

Match each term with its definition.

Terms

e	1. hypothesis
h	2. theory
b	3. independent variable
c	4. dependent variable
j	5. experimental condition
d	6. control condition
a	7. case study
k	8. survey
f	9. replication
g	10. random assignment
i	11. experiment

Definitions

a. an in-depth observational study of one person
b. the variable being manipulated in an experiment
c. the variable being measured in an experiment
d. the "treatment-absent" condition in an experiment
e. testable proposition
f. repeating an experiment to see whether the same results are obtained
g. the process in which subjects are selected by chance for different groups in an experiment
h. an integrated set of principles that organizes observations
i. the research method in which the effects of one or more variables on behavior are tested
j. the "treatment-present" condition in an experiment
k. the research method in which a representative sample of individuals is questioned.

Key Terms

Using your own words, write a brief definition or explanation of each of the following.

1. psychology

2. biological perspective

3. psychoanalytic perspective

4. behavioral perspective

5. humanistic perspective

6. cognitive perspective

7. biological psychology

8. developmental psychology

9. general experimental psychology

10. personality psychology

11. social psychology

12. clinical psychology

13. psychiatry

14. industrial/organizational psychology

15. replication

16. theory

17. hypothesis

18. case study

19. survey

20. random sample

21. naturalistic observation

22. correlation

23. experiment

24. control condition

25. experimental condition

26. independent variable

27. dependent variable

28. random assignment

29. I-knew-it-all-along phenomenon

30. SQ3R

Answers

CHAPTER REVIEW

1. physiology; philosophy
2. Wundt
3. learning; Sigmund Freud; children; William James
4. mental; John Watson; behavior; behavior; mental
5. biological
6. psychoanalytic; Sigmund Freud
7. behavioral
8. humanistic
9. cognitive
10. 60 percent; basic research; applied research
11. biological
12. developmental
13. general experimental
14. personality
15. social

16. clinical; psychiatrists
17. counseling; school
18. industrial/organizational

Psychologists who are engaged in basic research attempt to build up the field's general knowledge base, with little concern for specific practical applications. An example of basic research would be the study of how human memory is structured. In contrast, psychologists who are engaged in applied research focus on specific practical problems, such as how a person might improve his or her memory through the use of better study techniques.

19. skepticism; humility; replicate
20. theory; hypotheses
21. observation; correlation; experimentation
22. case study
23. survey
24. random; does
25. naturalistic observation
26. describe
27. correlated; positively correlated; negatively correlated
28. causes; experiments

This is an example of a negative correlation. As one factor (time spent studying) increases, the other factor (anxiety level) decreases.

29. control; experimental
30. independent; dependent
31. random assignment

Experimentation has the advantage of increasing the investigator's control of both relevant and irrelevant variables that might influence behavior. Experiments also permit the investigator to go beyond observation and description to uncover cause-and-effect relationships in behavior.

32. artificial; principles
33. I-knew-it-all-along

PROGRESS TEST 1

Multiple-Choice Questions

1. **d.** is the answer. (p. 2)

   a. In its earliest days psychology was defined as the science of mental phenomena.

   b. Psychology has never been defined in terms of conscious and unconscious activity.

   c. From about 1920 to 1960, under the influence of John B. Watson, psychology was defined as the science of behavior.

2. **a.** is the answer. In a case study one subject is studied in depth. (p. 8)

   b. In survey research a group of people are interviewed.

   c. In correlational research an experimenter attempts to determine whether two factors are related.

   d. In experimental research an investigator manipulates one variable to observe its effect on another.

3. **c.** is the answer. Exercise is the variable being manipulated by the experiment. (p. 12)

   a. A control condition for this experiment would be a group of people not permitted to exercise.

   b. An intervening variable is a variable other than those being manipulated that may influence behavior.

   d. The dependent variable is the behavior measured by the experimenter — in this case, the *effects* of exercise.

4. **c.** is the answer. The control group is that for which the experimental treatment (the new drug) is absent. (p. 11)

   a. A random sample is a subset of a population in which every person has an equal chance of being selected.

   b. The experimental condition is the group for which the experimental treatment (the new drug) is present.

   d. "Test group" is an ambiguous term; both the experimental and control group are tested.

5. **d.** is the answer. (p. 7)

   a. Hypotheses are testable propositions.

   b. Dependent variables are factors that may change in response to manipulated independent variables.

   c. Statistical indexes, including correlations, may be used to test specific hypotheses (and therefore as indirect tests of theories), but they are merely mathematical tools, not general principles, as are theories.

6. **d.** is the answer. In this case the children are being observed in their normal environment, rather than in a laboratory. (p. 9)

   a. The correlational method measures relationships between two factors. The psychologist may later want to determine whether there are correlations between the variables that are studied using the method of naturalistic observation.

   b. In a case study *one* subject is studied in depth.

   c. This is not an experiment because the psychologist is not directly controlling the variables being studied.

7. **a.** is the answer. (p. 2.)

   b. The cognitive perspective is concerned with how we process and use information.

   c. The behavioral perspective studies the mechanisms by which observable responses are acquired.

   d. The psychoanalytic perspective emphasizes the influence of unconscious drives on personality and behavior.

8. **d.** is the answer. Selecting every tenth person would probably result in a representative sample of the entire population of students at the university. (p. 9)

   a. It would be difficult, if not impossible, to survey every student on campus.

   b. Psychology students are not representative of the entire student population.

   c. This answer is incorrect for the same reason as b. This would constitute a biased sample.

9. **d.** is the answer. Social psychologists are interested in the ways in which groups influence the behavior of individuals. (p. 5)

   a. Clinical psychologists study and treat psychologically troubled people.

   b. Developmental psychologists study the psychological, physical, and social changes that occur over the life span.

   c. Personality psychologists study how people are influenced by enduring inner factors.

10. **d.** is the answer. (p. 10)

    a. Correlational relationships can be revealed by statistical analysis of data; experimentation is not involved.

    b. & c. Hypotheses and theories give *direction* to experimental research.

11. **b.** is the answer. (p. 5)

12. **b.** is the answer. (p. 10)

    a. Correlational research does not involve direct manipulation of factors.

    c. & d. Both experimentation and correlational research involve hypotheses, which are testable predictions of relationships between specific, rather than random, factors.

13. **d.** is the answer. (p. 7)

    a. & b. These may be true, but neither is the basis of scientific skepticism.

    c. The skeptical attitude of scientists is based on the belief that intuition often is *incorrect*.

14. **d.** is the answer. Humanistic psychology's concern with the individual's *subjective* experiences does not lend itself to the use of objective assessment. (p. 4)

15. **c.** is the answer (pp. 15–16)

   a. & d. Psychologists' personal values can influence both how experiments are conducted and how experimental findings are interpreted.

   b. Although statistical techniques assist in the interpretation of experimental outcomes, they do not eliminate the possibility that psychologists' personal values will bias the results.

16. **b.** is the answer. (p. 10)

   a. & c. These answers would have been correct had the question stated that there is a *positive* correlation between shoe size and IQ.

   d. This answer would have been correct had the question stated that there is *no* correlation between shoe size and IQ, which is probably the case!

17. **d.** is the answer. In an experiment it would be possible to manipulate alcohol consumption and observe the effects, if any, on memory. (p. 10)

18. **b.** is the answer. (p. 7)

   a. This answer describes theories, not hypotheses.

   c. Hypotheses are formal, testable propositions; they are not simply hunches.

   d. This answer describes correlations between two events.

Matching Items

1. g (p. 5)	6. k (p. 5)	10. b (p. 4)
2. a (p. 5)	7. l (p. 6)	11. h (p. 4)
3. c (p. 5)	8. e (p. 3)	12. i (p. 5)
4. j (p. 5)	9. f (p. 3)	13. d (p. 5)
5. m (p. 5)		

PROGRESS TEST 2

Multiple-Choice Questions

1. **a.** is the answer. (p. 2)

2. **d.** is the answer. (p. 10)

   a. Correlation does not imply causality.

   b. Again, a positive correlation simply means that two factors tend to increase or decrease together; further relationships are not implied.

   c. A separate factor may or may not be involved. That the two factors are correlated does not imply a separate factor, however. There may, for example, be a direct causal relationship between the two factors themselves.

3. **d.** is the answer. (p. 12)

   a. The control condition is the comparison group, in which the experimental treatment is absent.

   b. Memory is a directly observed and measured dependent variable in this experiment.

   c. Attention is the dependent variable, which is being manipulated.

4. **c.** is the answer. (p. 11)

   a. Both the experimental and control groups are test groups.

   b. A random sample is a representative sample from the group under study. If one were to use a random sample in an experiment, one would use it for both the control and the experimental groups.

   d. The control condition is the condition in which the treatment is absent.

5. **b.** is the answer. (p. 16)

   a. The phenomenon is related to hindsight rather than foresight.

   c. & d. The phenomenon doesn't involve the correctness or incorrectness of intuitions but rather people's attitude that they had the correct intuition.

6. **b.** is the answer. If enough subjects are used in an experiment and they are randomly assigned to the two groups, any differences that emerge between the groups should stem from the experiment itself. (p. 12)

7. **c.** is the answer. Psychology emerged from these disciplines in particular. (p. 2)

   a., b., & d. Chemistry and physics were not roots of psychology.

8. **c.** is the answer. After earning their M.D. degrees, psychiatrists specialize in the diagnosis and treatment of mental health disorders. (p. 5)

   a., b., & d. These psychologists generally earn a Ph.D. rather than an M.D.

9. **d.** is the answer. All of these are reasons that psychologists study animal behavior. (pp. 14–15)

10. **d.** is the answer. (p. 4)

   a. The biological perspective studies the biological bases for a range of psychological phenomena.

   b. The psychoanalytic perspective is concerned with how unconscious drives and conflicts may shape behavior.

   c. The behavioral perspective studies the mechanisms by which observable responses are acquired and modified in particular environments.

11. **b.** is the answer. (p. 7)

   a. In fact, the artificiality of experiments is part of an intentional attempt to create a controlled environment in which to test theoretical principles that are applicable to *all* behaviors.

c. Some psychological theories go against what we consider common sense; furthermore, on many issues that psychology addresses, it's far from clear what the "commonsense" position is.

d. Psychology has always had ties to other disciplines, and in recent times, these ties have been increasing.

12. **d.** is the answer. The emphasis on change during the life span indicates that Dr. Jones is most likely a developmental psychologist. (p. 5)

a. Clinical psychologists study and treat people who are psychologically troubled.

b. Personality psychologists study the ways in which enduring traits influence behavior.

c. Social psychologists are concerned with the ways in which a person's behavior is influenced by others.

13. **c.** is the answer. (p. 6)

a. Clinical psychologists study and treat people with psychological disorders.

b. & d. Personality and social psychologists do not usually study people in work situations.

14. **c.** is the answer. (p. 3)

a. Psychologists who follow the behavioral perspective emphasize observable, external influences on behavior.

b. The humanistic perspective reacted *against* the explanation of behavior in terms of unconscious drives.

d. The cognitive perspective places emphasis on conscious, rather than unconscious, processes.

15. **a.** is the answer. (p. 3)

b. The humanistic perspective emphasizes people's capacities to make choices and rejects the idea that specific environmental factors determine behavior.

c. & d. The psychoanalytic and cognitive perspectives each emphasize internal, rather than external, factors: unconscious drives in one case and cognitive processes in the other.

16. **d.** is the answer. Correlations show how well one factor can be predicted from another. (p. 10)

a. Since case study research focuses in great detail on the behavior of individuals, it's unlikely to be useful in showing whether predictions are possible.

b. Naturalistic observation is a method of describing, rather than predicting, behavior.

c. In experimental research the effects of manipulated independent variables on dependent variables are measured. It is not clear how an experiment could help determine whether IQ tests predict academic success.

17. **b.** is the answer. The control condition is the one in which the treatment—in this case, pollution—is absent. (p. 11)

a. Students in the polluted room would be in the experimental condition.

c. Presumably, all students in both the experimental and control conditions were randomly assigned to their groups. Random assignment is a method for establishing groups, rather than a condition.

d. The word *dependent* refers to a kind of variable in experiments; conditions are either experimental or control.

18. **c.** is the answer. The lighting is the factor being manipulated. (p. 12)

a. & d. These answers are incorrect because they involve aspects of the experiment other than the variables.

b. This answer is the dependent, not the independent, variable.

19. **a.** is the answer. The research is addressing a practical issue. (p. 5)

b. Basic research is aimed at contributing to the base of knowledge in a given field, not at resolving particular practical problems.

c. & d. Clinical and developmental research would focus on issues relating to psychological disorders and life-span changes, respectively.

Matching Items

1. e (p. 7)	**5.** j (p. 11)	**9.** f (p. 7)
2. h (p. 7)	**6.** d (p. 11)	**10.** g (p. 12)
3. b (p. 12)	**7.** a (pp. 8)	**11.** i (p. 11)
4. c (p. 12)	**8.** k (pp. 8)	

KEY TERMS

1. **Psychology** is the science of behavior and mental processes. (p. 2)

2. Psychologists who adopt the **biological perspective** emphasize the influences of heredity and physiology upon behavior. (p. 2)

3. The **psychoanalytic perspective** maintains that behavior is determined by unconscious drives and impulses. (p. 3)

4. The **behavioral perspective** emphasizes environmental influences on behavior. (p. 3)

5. The **humanistic perspective** emphasizes the individual's capacity for growth and studies people's subjective experiences. (p. 4)

6. The **cognitive perspective** emphasizes how peo-

ple process information and use it to reason and solve problems. (p. 4)

Example: A **cognitive psychologist** might be interested in, among other things, studying how experience affects the mental strategies people use to solve problems.

7. **Biological psychology** is a branch of psychology concerned with the links between biology and behavior. (p. 5)

8. **Developmental psychology** studies the physical, cognitive, and social changes that occur throughout the life cycle. (p. 5)

Example: **Developmental psychologists** study the ways in which behaviors change, or *develop*, throughout the lifespan.

9. **General experimental psychology** studies aspects of behavior (perception, learning, motivation, etc.) using the experimental method. (p. 5)

10. **Personality psychology** studies how behavior is influenced by enduring inner factors, or traits. (p. 5)

11. **Social psychology** studies interpersonal behavior —the ways in which people influence and are influenced by other people. (p. 5)

12. **Clinical psychology** studies psychological disorders; clinical psychologists also assess and treat people with such disorders. (p. 5)

13. **Psychiatry** is the branch of medicine concerned with the physical diagnosis and treatment of psychological disorders. (p. 6)

14. **Industrial/organizational psychology** is the branch of psychology concerned with human behavior in the workplace. (p. 6)

Example: **Industrial/organizational psychologists** might advise employers on how to improve worker morale and productivity.

15. **Replication** is the process of repeating an experiment, often with different subjects and in different situations, in order to test the reliability of experimental findings. (p. 7)

16. A **theory** is an integrated set of principles that organizes a set of observations and makes testable predictions. (p. 7)

17. A **hypothesis** is a testable prediction derived from a theory; testing the hypothesis helps scientists to test the theory. (p. 7)

Example: In order to test his theory of why people conform, Solomon Asch formulated the testable **hypothesis** that an individual would be more likely to go along with the majority opinion of a large group than with that of a smaller group.

18. The **case study** is a method of observation in which one person is studied in great depth, often with the intention of discovering general principles. (p. 8)

Example: When a psychologist studies the effects of a stroke on an individual's mental capacities, he or she is doing a **case study**.

19. The **survey** is a method of observation in which a sample of people are questioned about their attitudes or behavior. (p. 8)

20. A **random sample** is one that is representative because every member of the population has an equal chance of being included. (p. 9)

21. **Naturalistic observation** involves observing and recording behavior in naturally occurring situations, without trying to influence the situation. (p. 9)

Example: Jane Goodall's studies of ape behavior in the wild are a classic example of **naturalistic observation**.

22. The **correlation** is a statistical measure that indicates the extent to which two factors vary together and thus how well one factor can be predicted from the other; correlations can be positive or negative. (pp. 10)

Example: If there is a **positive correlation** between air temperature and ice cream sales, the warmer (higher) it is, the more ice cream is sold. If there is a **negative correlation** between air temperature and sales of cocoa, the cooler (lower) it is, the more cocoa is sold.

23. The **experiment** is the research method in which an investigator directly manipulates one or more factors in order to observe their effect on another factor; experiments therefore make it possible to establish cause-and-effect relationships. (p. 11)

24. The **control condition** of an experiment is one in which the treatment of interest, or independent variable, is withheld so that comparison to the experimental group can be made. (p. 11)

Example: The **control condition** for an experiment testing the effects of a new drug on reaction time would be a group of subjects given a placebo (inactive drug or sugar pill) instead of the drug being tested.

25. The **experimental condition** of an experiment is one in which subjects are exposed to the independent variable being studied. (p. 11)

Example: In the study of the effects of a new drug on reaction time, subjects in the **experimental condition** would actually receive the drug being tested.

26. The **independent variable** of an experiment is the

factor being manipulated and tested by the investigator. (p. 12)

Example: In the study of the effects of a new drug on reaction time, the drug is the **independent variable**.

27. The **dependent variable** of an experiment is the factor being measured by the investigator. (p. 12)

Example: In the study of the effects of a new drug on reaction time, the subjects' reaction time is the **dependent variable**.

28. **Random assignment** is the procedure of assigning subjects to the experimental and control groups by chance, in order to minimize preexisting differences between the groups. (p. 12)

29. The **I-knew-it-all-along phenomenon** refers to the human tendency to exaggerate the obviousness of an outcome—including a psychological research finding—after one has heard about it. (p. 16)

30. **SQ3R** is an acronym for Survey, Question, Read, Recite, Review, a method of studying primarily intended to improve reading comprehension. (p. 17)

Example: This study guide is designed so that students can use the **SQ3R** technique of active study.

Chapter 2 | Biological Roots of Behavior

Chapter Overview

Chapter 2 is concerned with the functions of the nervous system and the brain, which together are the basis for all human behavior. Under the direction of the brain, the nervous system coordinates a variety of voluntary and involuntary behaviors and serves as the body's mechanism for communication with the external environment.

The brain consists of three regions: the brainstem, the limbic system, and the cerebral cortex. Knowledge of the workings of the brain has increased with recent advances in neuropsychological methods. Studies of split-brain patients have also given researchers a great deal of information about the specialized functions of the brain's right and left hemispheres.

Many students find the technical material in this chapter difficult to master. Not only are there many terms for you to remember, but you must also know the organization and function of the various divisions of the nervous system. Learning this material will require a great deal of rehearsal. Working the chapter review several times, drawing and labeling brain diagrams, and mentally reciting terms are all useful techniques for rehearsing this type of material.

Guided Study

The text chapter should be studied one section at a time. Before you read, preview each section by skimming it, noting headings and boldface items. Then read the appropriate section objectives from the following outline. Keep these objectives in mind and, as you read the chapter section, search for the information that will complete each one. Once you have finished a section, write out answers for its objective.

The Nervous System (pp. 21–27)

1. Explain why psychologists are concerned with human biology.

2. Identify the major divisions of the nervous system.

    CNS   Peripheral
    Somatic
    Vol   Invol

3. Describe the structure of neurons and identify three types.

4. Describe how nerve cells communicate and discuss the importance of neurotransmitters for human behavior.

17

The Brain (pp. 27–44)

5. Describe the overall organization of the brain, and the functions served by various structures within the brainstem.

6. Identify the methods used in studying the brain.

7. Describe the structure and functions of the limbic system and explain its relationship to the endocrine system.

8. Describe the structure and functions of the cerebral cortex and discuss how damage to several different cortical areas can impair language functioning.

9. Describe research on the split brain and discuss what it reveals regarding normal brain functioning.

10. Discuss the capacity of the brain to reorganize following injury or illness.

Chapter Review

When you have finished reading the chapter, use the material that follows to review it. Complete the sentences and answer the questions. As you proceed, evaluate your performance for each chapter section by consulting the answer key at the end of this chapter. Do not continue with the next section until you understand why each term is the correct answer. If you need to, review or reread the appropriate chapter section in the text before continuing.

1. The theory that linked the brain's functions to various bumps on the skull was

   _____.

2. In the most basic sense, every idea, mood, memory, and behavior that an individual has ever experienced is a _____ phenomenon.

The Nervous System (pp. 21–27)

3. The circuitry of the body consists of billions of nerve cells, or _____.

4. The brain and spinal cord comprise the _____ nervous system.

5. The neurons that link the brain and spinal cord to the rest of the body form the _____ nervous system.

6. The division of the PNS that transmits sensory input to the CNS and directs the movements of the skeletal muscles is the _____ nervous system. These movements are usually under _____ control.

7. Involuntary, self-regulating responses—those of the glands and the muscles of internal organs— are controlled by the _____ nervous system.

8. The body is made ready for action by the

_____ division of the
autonomic nervous system.

9. The _____ division of the
autonomic nervous system produces relaxation.

Describe and explain the sequence of physical reactions that occur in the body as an emergency is confronted and then passes.

10. Information arriving in the central nervous system from the body travels in afferent, or _____, neurons.

11. The neurons involved in processing this information in the central nervous system are the _____.

12. The central nervous system sends instructions to the body's muscles by means of efferent, or _____, neurons.

13. Automatic, inborn responses to stimuli are called _____.

14. The extensions of a neuron that receive impulses from other neurons are the _____ .

15. The extensions of a neuron that transmit information to other neurons are the _____.

16. Identify the major parts of the neuron diagrammed below:

    a. _____   c. _____

    b. _____

17. In order to trigger a nerve impulse, a stimulus must be greater in intensity than the neuron's _____. Increasing a stimulus above this level _____ (will/will not) increase the nerve impulse's speed and intensity. This phenomenon is called an

    _____–_____–

    _____ response.

18. The gap between two neurons is called a

    _____.

19. The chemical messengers that convey information across the gaps between neurons are called _____. These chemicals unlock "gates" on receptor sites, allowing electrically charged _____ to enter the neuron.

20. Neurotransmitters that increase the likelihood of a neuron firing are called _____; those that decrease the likelihood of a neuron firing are called _____.

21. A neurotransmitter that is important in motor control and muscle contraction is

    _____.

22. Naturally occurring morphinelike neurotransmitters that are present in the brain are called _____.

Outline the sequence of reactions that occurs when a nerve impulse is generated and transmitted from one neuron to another.

The Brain (pp. 27–44)

23. (Box) The oldest technique for studying the brain involves _____

    _____ of patients with brain injuries or diseases.

24. (Box) Researchers have also studied brain function by producing _____, or selectively destroyed areas of brain tissue.

25. (Box) The _____ is a recording of the electrical activity of the whole brain.

26. (Box) A computer-generated image of a "slice" of the brain based on a series of x-rays taken from different positions is called a _____.

27. (Box) The technique depicting the level of activity of brain areas by measuring the brain's consumption of glucose is called the _____ _____.

28. (Box) A technique that produces clearer images of the brain by using magnetic fields and radio waves is known as _____.

29. The brain can be divided into regions corresponding to three stages of brain evolution; in order of increasing complexity of function, these regions are the _____, the _____ _____, and the _____ _____.

30. At the base of the brainstem, where the spinal cord enters the skull, lies the _____, which controls _____ and _____.

31. At the rear of the brainstem lies the _____. Its major function is coordination of movement and _____ control.

32. At the top of the brainstem sits the _____, which serves as the brain's sensory switchboard.

33. The _____ _____ system is contained inside the brainstem and is designed to control _____ and _____.

34. Between the brainstem and cerebral hemispheres is the _____ system. This system is important in memory and the regulation of _____ and basic _____.

35. Rage or terror will result from stimulation of different regions of the _____.

36. Below the thalamus is the _____, which regulates body maintenance behaviors by secreting _____ and by triggering activity in the _____ nervous system. Olds and Milner discovered that this region also contains _____ centers, which animals will work hard to have stimulated.

List several behaviors regulated by the hypothalamus.

37. In addition to the nervous system, the body has another communication network called the _____ system.

38. During an emergency, the _____ glands become active, releasing the hormones _____ and _____, which prepare the body for danger.

39. The most influential gland, the _____, produces hormones that regulate other glands, as well as body growth. The secretions of this gland are regulated by the _____.

40. The most complex functions of human behavior are linked to the most developed part of the brain, the _____ _____, which is divided into two _____, each of which consists of four lobes.

41. Label these four lobes in the sketch on page 21.

    a. _____   c. _____

    b. _____   d. _____

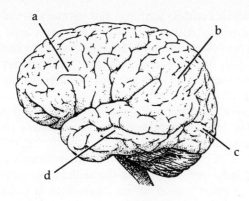

42. Electrical stimulation of one side of the
_____ cortex, an arch-shaped
region at the back of the _____
lobe, will produce movement on the opposite
side of the body.

43. At the front of the parietal lobe lies the
_____ cortex, which, when
stimulated, elicits a sensation of
_____.

44. Visual information is received in the
_____ lobes, whereas auditory
information is received in the _____
lobes.

45. Areas of the brain that don't receive sensory
information or direct movement but, rather,
integrate and interpret information received by
other regions are known as _____
_____. Such areas in the
_____ lobe are involved in
making judgments, carrying out plans, and some
aspects of personality.

46. Brain injuries may produce an impairment in
language use called _____.
Studies of people with such impairments have
shown that _____
_____ is involved in producing
speech, _____ _____
is involved in understanding speech, and the
_____ _____
is involved in recording printed words into
auditory form.

47. Because damage to it will impair language and

reasoning, the _____
hemisphere came to be known as the
_____ hemisphere. Some
biological psychologists, however, do not believe
that this hemispheric distinction is valid.

Beginning with the sensory receptors in the skin, trace
the course of the spinal reflex as a person reflexively
jerks his or her hand away from an unexpectedly hot
burner on a stove.

Outline the brain pathways and endocrine response to
the above situation.

48. In an attempt to control the severity of epileptic
seizures, surgeons sometimes separate the two
hemispheres of the brain by cutting the
_____ _____.
People who have had this surgery are referred to
as _____ – _____
patients.

49. In such a patient, only the _____
hemisphere will be aware of an unseen object
held in the left hand. In this case, the person
will not be able to _____ the
object. When different words are shown in the
left and right visual fields, if the patient fixates
on a point on the center line between the fields,
the patient will be able to say only the word
shown on the _____.

Explain why a split-brain patient would be able to read aloud the word *pencil* flashed to his or her right visual field, but would be unable to identify a pencil by touch using only the left hand.

50. Identify the hemisphere to which each of the following adjectives best applies:

    a. logical, ————————————————;

    b. intuitive, ————————————————;

    c. rational, ————————————————;

    d. nonverbal, ————————————————;

    e. sequential, ————————————————.

51. Neurons in the CNS ———————————— (will/will not) regenerate.

52. The quality of the brain that makes it possible for undamaged brain areas to reorganize and take over the functions of damaged regions is known as ————————————.

FOCUS ON PSYCHOLOGY:
Magnetic Resonance Imaging Reveals Possible Cause of Autism

Autism, a devastating psychological disorder that occurs in 2 to 4 children out of every 10,000 under age 15, was first described in 1943 by Leo Kanner, a child psychiatrist. Since then, psychologists have been looking without success for its cause(s). Symptoms of autistic behavior include social withdrawal, language disturbance, and emotional detachment. One of the most striking characteristics of the disorder is the autistic child's noticeable lack of interest in other people. For this reason, one theory held that autism is a psychosocial disorder caused in part by an abnormal parent-child relationship. Recent findings, however, suggest that autism may be a disorder of the brain rather than a response to the environment.

A key piece to the puzzle of autism was found as a result of technological advances in brain study. Using MRI (magnetic resonance imaging), a computer-generated brain image based on magnetic fields and radio waves, neuroscientists at Children's Hospital in San Diego studied the brains of 18 autistic children. The MRI scans consistently showed that a particular region of the cerebellum — the "little brain" that is important

in muscular control, learning, and memory — was unusually small. Although researchers have long suspected that some form of brain pathology was likely in those with autism — many autistic children develop epileptic seizures as they get older — this was the first specific abnormality ever found.

Several interpretations of these findings are possible. One is that because of the cerebellum's role in high-level mental functioning, damage during its critical period of prenatal development may directly cause autistic behavior. Another is that autism is controlled by some other region of the brain that is damaged along with the cerebellum.

Whatever the final conclusion regarding the link between the brain and autism, these findings illustrate the importance of biology to psychology and underscore an important theme in the history of the neurosciences: Our understanding of the brain and behavior is often paced by advances in the technologies scientists base their observations on.

Sources: Rosenhan, D. L., & Seligman, M. E. P. (1989). *Abnormal Psychology* (2nd ed.). New York: W. W. Norton.

Wray, Herbert. (1989, June). New evidence: Autism is a brain disorder. *Psychology Today.*

Progress Test 1

Circle your answer to the following questions and check them with the answer key at the end of this chapter. If your answer is incorrect, read the answer key explanation for why it is so and then consult the appropriate pages in the text to understand the correct answer.

Multiple-Choice Questions

1. Afferent is to efferent as ———————————— is to ————————————.
   a. central; peripheral
   b. sensory; motor
   c. motor; sensory
   d. peripheral; central

2. Heartbeat, digestion, glandular, and other self-regulating body functions are governed by the:
   a. voluntary nervous system.
   b. parasympathetic division of the autonomic nervous system.
   c. sympathetic division of the autonomic nervous system.
   d. somatic nervous system.

3. A strong stimulus can increase:
   a. the speed of the impulse the neuron fires.

b. the intensity of the impulse the neuron fires.

c. the number of times the neuron fires.

d. the threshold that must be reached before the neuron fires.

4. The pain of heroin withdrawal may be attributable to the fact that:

a. under the influence of heroin, the brain ceases production of endorphins.

b. under the influence of heroin, the brain ceases production of all neurotransmitters.

c. during withdrawal, the brain's production of all neurotransmitters is greatly increased.

d. heroin destroys endorphin receptors in the brain.

5. (Box) The brain research technique that involves monitoring the brain's usage of glucose is called the:

a. PET scan.   **c.** EEG.

b. CAT scan.   **d.** MRI.

6. A split-brain patient has a picture of a knife flashed to her left hemisphere and that of a fork to her right hemisphere. She will be able to:

a. identify the fork using her left hand.

b. identify the knife using her left hand.

c. identify the knife using either hand.

d. identify the fork using either hand.

7. Though there is no single "control center" for emotions and drives, their regulation is primarily attributed to the brain region known as the:

a. limbic system.   **c.** brainstem.

b. reticular system.   **d.** cerebral cortex.

8. A stroke leaves a patient paralyzed on the left side of the body. Which region of the brain has been damaged?

a. the reticular system   **c.** the left hemisphere

b. the limbic system   **d.** the right hemisphere

9. Generally speaking, the brains of
_____ exhibit greater plasticity than those of _____.

a. adults; children   **c.** males; females

b. children; adults   **d.** females; males

10. The type of aphasia in which a person loses the ability to comprehend language results from injury to:

a. the angular gyrus.

b. Broca's area.

c. Wernicke's area.

d. frontal lobe association areas.

11. The characteristic of the human brain most related to our intelligence is:

a. its large size.

b. the high ratio of brain to body weight.

c. the size of the frontal lobes.

d. the amount of association area.

12. Voluntary movements, such as writing with a pencil, are directed by:

a. the sympathetic nervous system.

b. the somatic nervous system.

c. the parasympathetic nervous system.

d. the autonomic nervous system.

13. You are able to pull your hand quickly away from hot water before a sensation of pain is felt because:

a. movement of the hand is a reflex that involves intervention of the spinal cord only.

b. movement of the hand does not require intervention by the central nervous system.

c. the brain reacts quickly to prevent severe injury.

d. the autonomic nervous system intervenes to speed contraction of the muscles of the hand.

14. Which is the correct sequence in the transmission of a neural impulse?

a. axon $\rightarrow$ dendrite $\rightarrow$ cell body $\rightarrow$ synapse

b. dendrite $\rightarrow$ axon $\rightarrow$ cell body $\rightarrow$ synapse

c. dendrite $\rightarrow$ cell body $\rightarrow$ axon $\rightarrow$ synapse

d. axon $\rightarrow$ synapse $\rightarrow$ cell body $\rightarrow$ dendrite

15. Communication between the endocrine system and target tissues is based on chemicals called:

a. chromosomes.   **c.** hormones.

b. neutrotransmitters.   **d.** enzymes.

16. Following a head injury, a person has ongoing difficulties staying awake and focusing attention. Most likely, the damage occurred to the:

a. thalamus.

b. corpus callosum.

c. reticular activating system.

d. cerebellum.

17. Based on the current research, which of the following seems true about the specialized functions of the right and left hemispheres?

a. The specialization of the hemispheres is greater in men than in women.

b. The specialization of the hemispheres is greater in women than in men.

c. Most complex tasks emerge from the activity of one *or* the other hemisphere.

d. Most complex activities emerge from the integrated activity of both hemispheres.

18. Cortical areas that are not primarily concerned with sensory, motor, or language functions are:

a. called projection areas.

b. called association areas.

c. located mostly in the parietal lobe.

d. located mostly in the temporal lobe.

Matching Items

Match each structure with its corresponding description or function.

Structures

_____ 1. hypothalamus
_____ 2. frontal lobe
_____ 3. parietal lobe
_____ 4. temporal lobe
_____ 5. reticular activating system
_____ 6. occipital lobe
_____ 7. thalamus
_____ 8. corpus callosum
_____ 9. cerebellum
_____ 10. amygdala
_____ 11. medulla

Functions

a. includes auditory areas
b. includes visual areas
c. serves as sensory switchboard
d. contains pleasure centers
e. includes sensory cortex
f. includes motor cortex
g. controls arousal
h. links cerebral hemispheres
i. elicits rage and terror
j. regulates breathing and heartbeat
k. enables coordinated movement

Progress Test 2

Progress Test 2 should be completed during a final chapter review. Do this test after you thoroughly understand the correct answers for the Chapter Review and Progress Test 1.

Multiple-Choice Questions

1. Following an injury, undamaged brain areas may take over the functions of damaged areas. This phenomenon results from the _____ of brain tissue.

   a. recombination
   b. regeneration
   c. enrichment
   d. plasticity

2. The visual cortex is located in the:

   a. occipital lobe.
   b. temporal lobe.
   c. frontal lobe.
   d. parietal lobe.

3. When Sandy scalded her toe in a hot tub of water, the pain message was carried to her spinal cord by the _____ nervous system.

   a. somatic
   b. sympathetic
   c. parasympathetic
   d. central

4. Which of the following are governed by the simplest neural pathways?

   a. emotions
   b. physiological drives, such as hunger
   c. reflexes
   d. movements, such as walking

5. Melissa is so elated after running a marathon that she feels little fatigue or discomfort. Her lack of pain is probably the result of the release of:

   a. ACh.
   b. endorphins.
   c. epinephrine.
   d. norepinephrine.

6. Dr. Johnson briefly flashed a picture of a key in the right visual field of a split-brain patient. The patient could probably:

   a. verbally report that a key was seen.
   b. write the word *key* using the left hand.
   c. draw a picture of a key using the left hand.
   d. do none of the above.

7. In order to pinpoint the location of a tumor, a neurosurgeon electrically stimulated parts of the patient's sensory cortex. If the patient was conscious during the procedure, which of the following was probably experienced?

   a. "hearing" faint sounds
   b. "seeing" random visual patterns
   c. movement of the arms or legs
   d. a sense of having the skin touched

8. Nerve impulses communicate across a gap called a(n):

   a. synapse.
   b. dendrite.
   c. axon.
   d. neurotransmitter.

9. The neurotransmitter acetylcholine (ACh) is most likely to be found:

   a. at the junction between sensory neurons and muscle fibers.
   b. at the junction between motor neurons and muscle fibers.
   c. at junctions between interneurons.
   d. in all the above locations.

10. The gland that regulates body growth is the:

    a. adrenal.
    b. thyroid.
    c. hypothalamus.
    d. pituitary.

11. Epinephrine and norepinephrine are _____ that are released by the _____ gland.

    a. neurotransmitters; pituitary
    b. hormones; pituitary

c. neurotransmitters; adrenal
d. hormones; adrenal

12. Jessica experienced difficulty keeping her balance after receiving a blow to the back of her head. It is likely that she injured her:

a. medulla.　　　　　b. hypothalamus.
b. thalamus.　　　　　d. cerebellum.

13. Moruzzi and Magoun caused a cat to lapse into a coma by severing neural connections between the cortex and the:

a. reticular activating system.
b. hypothalamus.
c. thalamus.
d. cerebellum.

14. In order of increasing complexity, the three stages of brain evolution are:

a. cerebral cortex; brainstem; limbic system
b. brainstem; limbic system; cerebral cortex
c. limbic system; brainstem; cerebral cortex
d. limbic system; cerebral cortex; brainstem

15. If Dr. Rogers wishes to conduct an experiment on the effects of stimulating the "pleasure center" of a rat's brain, Dr. Rogers should insert an electrode into the:

a. thalamus.　　　　　c. hypothalamus.
b. sensory cortex.　　　d. corpus callosum.

16. The nerve fibers that have been severed in split-brain patients form a structure called the

_____   _____ .

a. reticular formation　　c. corpus callosum
b. association areas　　　d. parietal lobes

17. Beginning at the front of the brain and working backward then down and around, which of the following is the correct order of cortical regions?

a. occipital lobe; temporal lobe; parietal lobe; frontal lobe
b. temporal lobe; frontal lobe; parietal lobe; occipital lobe
c. frontal lobe; occipital lobe; temporal lobe; parietal lobe
d. frontal lobe; parietal lobe; occipital lobe; temporal lobe

18. Following a gunshot wound to his head, Jack became more uninhibited, irritable, and profane. It is likely that his personality change was the result of injury to his:

a. parietal lobe.　　　　c. occipital lobe.
b. temporal lobe.　　　　d. frontal lobe.

Matching Items

Match each structure or term with its corresponding function or definition.

Structures or Terms

_____ 1. right hemisphere
_____ 2. brainstem
_____ 3. pituitary
_____ 4. aphasia
_____ 5. adrenal glands
_____ 6. Broca's area
_____ 7. Wernicke's area
_____ 8. limbic system
_____ 9. association areas
_____ 10. left hemisphere
_____ 11. angular gyrus

Functions

a. controls speech production
b. sequential reasoning
c. translates writing into speech
d. intuitive reasoning
e. regulates body growth
f. language disorder
g. oldest part of the brain
h. regulates emotions
i. helps us to respond to emergencies
j. language comprehension
k. "silent" brain area

In the diagrams to the right, the numbers refer to brain locations that have been damaged. Match each location with its probable effect on behavior.

Location	Behavioral Effect
1. _____	**a.** vision disorder
2. _____	**b.** insensitivity to touch
3. _____	**c.** motor paralysis
4. _____	**d.** hearing problem
5. _____	**e.** lack of coordination
6. _____	**f.** abnormal hunger
7. _____	**g.** split brain
8. _____	**h.** sleep/arousal disorder
9. _____	**i.** loss of smell
	j. loss of taste
	k. altered personality

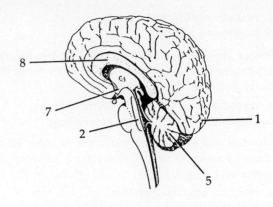

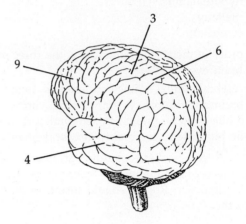

Key Terms

Using your own words, write a brief description or explanation of each of the following terms.

1. phrenology

2. nervous system

3. central nervous system (CNS)

4. peripheral nervous system (PNS)

5. somatic nervous system

6. autonomic nervous system

7. sympathetic nervous system

8. parasympathetic nervous system

9. neuron

10. sensory neurons

11. motor neurons

12. interneurons

13. reflex

14. dendrites

15. axon

16. threshold

17. all-or-none response

18. synapse

19. neurotransmitters

20. acetylcholine (ACh)

21. endorphins

22. lesion (Box)

23. electroencephalogram (EEG) (Box)

24. CAT (computerized axial tomograph) scan (Box)

25. PET (positron emission tomograph) scan (Box)

26. MRI (magnetic resonance imaging) (Box)

27. brainstem

28. medulla

29. cerebellum

30. thalamus

31. reticular activating system

32. limbic system

33. amygdala

34. hypothalamus

35. hormones

36. endocrine system

37. adrenal glands

38. pituitary

39. cerebral cortex

40. frontal lobes

41. parietal lobes

42. occipital lobes

43. temporal lobes

44. motor cortex

45. sensory cortex

46. association areas

47. aphasia

48. Broca's area

49. Wernicke's area

50. corpus callosum

51. split brain

52. plasticity

Answers
CHAPTER REVIEW

1. phrenology
2. biological

3. neurons
4. central
5. peripheral
6. somatic; voluntary
7. automomic
8. sympathetic
9. parasympathetic

In response to an emergency, the sympathetic division of the autonomic nervous system becomes aroused. The physiological changes that occur include accelerated heart rate, elevated blood sugar, dilation of arteries, slowing of digestion, and increased perspiration to cool the body. When the emergency is over, the parasympathetic nervous system produces the opposite physical reactions.

10. sensory
11. interneurons
12. motor
13. reflexes
14. dendrites
15. axons
16. a. dendrites
    b. cell body
    c. axon
17. threshold; will not; all-or-none
18. synapse
19. neurotransmitters; ions (atoms)
20. excitatory; inhibitory
21. acetylcholine (ACh)
22. endorphins

A nerve impulse is generated by an appropriate stimulus that exceeds the neuron's threshold. The stimulus is received through the dendrites, combined in the cell body, and electrically transmitted in an all-or-none fashion down the length of the axon. When the signal reaches the end of the axon, chemical messengers called neurotransmitters are released into the synaptic gap between two neurons. Neurotransmitter molecules bind to receptor sites on the dendrites of neighboring neurons and have either an excitatory or inhibitory influence on that neuron's tendency to generate its own nerve impulse.

23. clinical observation
24. lesions
25. electroencephalogram (EEG)
26. CAT scan
27. PET scan
28. MRI (magnetic resonance imaging)
29. brainstem; limbic system; cerebral cortex

30. medulla; breathing; heartbeat

31. cerebellum; balance

32. thalamus

33. reticular activating; attention; arousal

34. limbic; emotions; drives

35. amygdala

36. hypothalamus; hormones; autonomic; pleasure

Behaviors regulated by the hypothalamus include hunger, thirst, body temperature, and sexual behavior.

37. endocrine

38. adrenal; epinephrine; norepinephrine

39. pituitary; hypothalamus

40. cerebral cortex; hemispheres

41. a. frontal lobe
    b. parietal lobe
    c. occipital lobe
    d. temporal lobe

42. motor; frontal

43. sensory; touch

44. occipital; temporal

45. association areas; frontal

46. aphasia; Broca's area; Wernicke's area; angular gyrus

47. left; dominant (major)

From sensory receptors in the skin the message travels via sensory neurons to an interneuron in the spinal cord, which in turn activates a motor neuron. This motor neuron causes the muscles in the hand to contract, and the person jerks his or her hand away from the heat.

At the same time that the spinal reflex is initiated, other interneurons carry the message up the spinal cord to the brain, where the pain message will be processed. It reaches the thalamus, which routes it to the sensory cortex. Along the way to the thalamus, the sensory input would also reach the reticular activating system, which would arouse the cerebral cortex, the hypothalamus, and the sympathetic division of the autonomic nervous system. Activation of these systems would cause the release of adrenal hormones that accelerate the heartbeat, dilate arteries, and produce other responses that mobilize the body's resources to meet this threat.

48. corpus callosum; split brain

49. right; name; right

The word *pencil* when flashed to a split-brain patient's right visual field would project only to the opposite, or left, hemisphere of the patient's brain. Because the left hemisphere contains the language control centers of the brain, the patient would be able to read the word aloud. The left hand is controlled by the right hemisphere of the brain. Because the right hemisphere would not be aware of the word, it would not be able to guide the left hand in identifying a pencil by touch.

50. a. left
    b. right
    c. left
    d. right
    e. left

51. will not

52. plasticity

PROGRESS TEST 1

Multiple-Choice Questions

1. **b.** is the answer. Afferent means inward, and sensory neurons transmit information inward from the body's tissues to the CNS; efferent means outward, and efferent neurons transmit information outward from the CNS to the body's tissues. (p. 23)

   a. & d. Afferent and efferent neurons are found in both the central and peripheral divisions of the nervous system.

   c. If the question had read "Efferent is to afferent," this answer would have been correct.

2. **b.** is the answer. The autonomic nervous system controls internal functioning, including heartbeat, digestion, and glandular activity. (p. 22)

   a. The functions mentioned are all automatic, rather than voluntary, so this answer cannot be correct.

   c. This answer is incorrect since most organs are affected by both divisions of the autonomic nervous system.

   d. The somatic nervous system transmits sensory input to the CNS and directs the movements of skeletal muscles.

3. **c.** is the answer. Stimulus strength can affect only the number of times a neuron fires or the number of neurons that fire. (p. 24)

   a., b., & d. These answers are incorrect because firing is an all-or-none response, so intensity remains the same regardless of stimulus strength. Nor can stimulus strength change the neuronal threshold or the impulse speed.

4. **a.** is the answer. Endorphins are neurotransmitters that function as natural painkillers. When the body has a supply of artificial painkillers like heroin, endorphin production stops. (p. 27)

   b. The production of neurotransmitters other than endorphins does not cease.

c. Neurotransmitter production does not increase during withdrawal.

d. Heroin makes use of the same receptor sites as endorphins.

5. **a.** is the answer. The PET scan measures glucose consumption in different areas of the brain to determine their levels of activity. (p. 31)

b. The CAT scan is a series of brain x-rays taken from different positions and then analyzed by a computer to create an image representing a slice through the brain.

c. The EEG is a measure of electrical activity in the brain.

d. MRI uses magnetic fields and radio waves to produce computer-generated images of soft tissues of the body.

6. **a.** is the answer. The left hand, controlled by the right hemisphere, would be able to identify the fork, the picture of which is flashed to the right hemisphere. (pp. 40–41)

b. Because the corpus callosum is severed, the right hemisphere, which controls the left hand, would not be aware of the picture of the knife, which was flashed to the left hemisphere.

c. The patient would be able to identify the knife only with her right hand, which is controlled by the hemisphere to which the picture was flashed.

d. The patient would be able to identify the fork only with her left hand, which is controlled by the hemisphere to which the picture was flashed.

7. **a.** is the answer. (p. 32)

b. The reticular activating system is linked to arousal and attention.

c. The brainstem governs the mechanisms of basic survival—heartbeat and breathing—and has many other roles.

d. The cerebral cortex governs the "higher" functions of the brain.

8. **d.** is the answer. The motor cortex in each hemisphere controls movement on the opposite side of the body. If the left side is paralyzed, the damage occurred in the right hemisphere. (p. 40)

a. The reticular system is involved in arousal, not the control of movement.

b. The limbic system regulates emotional and motivational states; it does not control movement.

c. A stroke in the left hemisphere would result in paralysis on the right side of the body.

9. **b.** is the answer. The plasticity of the brain decreases with age. (p. 44)

c. & d. There is no difference in the plasticity of male and female brains.

10. **c.** is the answer. Wernicke's area is involved in comprehension, and aphasics with damage to Wernicke's area are unable to understand what is said to them. (p. 39)

a. The angular gyrus translates printed words into speech sounds; damage would result in the inability to read.

b. Broca's area is involved in the physical production of speech; damage would result in the inability to speak fluently.

d. The association areas of the cortex are involved, among other things, in processing language; damage to these areas wouldn't specifically affect comprehension.

11. **d.** is the answer. As animals increase in complexity, there is an increase in the amount of association areas. (p. 38)

a. & b. Body and brain weight are poor predictors of intelligence.

c. The frontal lobe is concerned with personality, planning, and other mental functions, but its size is unrelated to intelligence.

12. **b.** is the answer. (p. 22)

a., c., & d. The autonomic nervous system, which is divided into the sympathetic and parasympathetic divisions, is concerned with regulating basic bodily maintenance functions.

13. **a.** is the answer. Since this reflex is an automatic response and involves only the spinal cord, the hand is jerked away before the brain has even received the information that causes the sensation of pain. (p. 23)

b. The spinal cord *is* part of the central nervous system.

c. The brain is not involved in directing spinal reflexes.

d. The autonomic nervous system controls the glands and muscles of the internal organs, not the skeletal muscles.

14. **c.** is the answer. A neuron receives incoming stimuli on its dendrites. From there these electrochemical signals travel to the cell body, where they are summed, generating an impulse that travels down the length of the axon, causing the release of neurotransmitter substances into the synaptic gap. (pp. 24–25)

15. **c.** is the answer. (p. 33–34)

a. Chromosomes are structures within the cell's nucleus, containing genetic material.

b. Neurotransmitters, including endorphins, are the chemicals involved in synaptic transmission in the nervous system.

d. Enzymes are chemicals that facilitate various chemical reactions throughout the body but are not involved in communication between the endocrine system and its target tissues.

16. **c.** is the answer. The reticular activating system plays an important role in the functions of arousal and attention. (pp. 29–30)

    a. The thalamus relays sensory input.

    b. The corpus callosum links the two cerebral hemispheres.

    d. The cerebellum is involved in coordination of movement.

17. **d.** is the answer. (p. 42)

18. **b.** is the answer. Association areas are located throughout the cortex. (p. 38)

Matching Items

1. d (p. 32)
2. f (p. 36)
3. e (p. 36)
4. a (p. 36)
5. g (p. 29)
6. b (p 36)
7. c (p. 29)
8. h (p. 40)
9. k (p. 29)
10. i (p. 32)
11. j (p. 29)

PROGRESS TEST 2

Multiple-Choice Questions

1. **d.** is the answer. Plasticity refers to the ability of other regions of the brain to assume the function of damaged areas. (p. 43)

    a. Recombination is an unrelated process involved in the mechanisms of heredity.

    b. Regeneration is the ability of damaged tissue to repair itself or to regrow. Regeneration of neural tissue does not occur.

    c. Enrichment is a general description of growth-promoting experiences in the environment.

2. **a.** is the answer. The visual cortex is located at the very back of the brain. (p. 37)

3. **a.** is the answer. Sensory neurons in the somatic nervous system relay such messages. (p. 23)

    b. & c. These divisions of the autonomic nervous system are concerned with the regulation of body maintenance functions such as heartbeat, digestion, and glandular activity.

    d. The spinal cord itself is part of the central nervous system, but the message is carried to the spinal cord by the somatic division of the peripheral nervous system.

4. **c.** is the answer. As automatic responses to stimuli, reflexes are the simplest complete units of behavior and require only simple neural pathways. (p. 23)

a., b., & d. Emotions, drives, and voluntary movements are all behaviors that are much more complex than reflexes and therefore involve much more complicated neural pathways.

5. **b.** is the answer. Endorphins are neurotransmitters that function as natural painkillers and are evidently involved in the "runner's high" and other situations in which discomfort or fatigue would be expected but are not experienced. (p. 26)

    a. ACh is a neurotransmitter involved in muscular control.

    c. & d. Epinephrine and norepinephrine are adrenal hormones released to help us respond in moments of danger.

6. **a.** is the answer. The right visual field projects directly to the left hemisphere, which is verbal. (pp. 40–41)

    b. & c. The left hand is controlled by the right hemisphere, which, in this situation, would be unaware of the word since the picture has been flashed to the left hemisphere.

7. **d.** is the answer. Stimulation of the sensory cortex elicits a sense of touch, as the experiments of Penfield demonstrated. (p. 37)

    a., b., & c. Hearing, seeing, or movement might be expected if the temporal, occipital, and motor regions of the cortex, respectively, were stimulated.

8. **a.** is the answer. (p. 25)

    b. Dendrites are the neuron extensions that receive incoming signals from other neurons.

    c. Axons are the neuron extensions that transmit signals to other neurons.

    d. Neurotransmitters are chemical messengers that cross the synaptic gap between neurons.

9. **b.** is the answer. ACh is a neurotransmitter that causes the contraction of muscle fibers when stimulated by motor neurons. This function explains its location. (p. 26)

    a. & c. Sensory neurons and interneurons do not directly stimulate muscle fibers.

10. **d.** is the answer. The pituitary regulates body growth, and some of its secretions regulate the release of hormones from other glands. (p. 34)

    a. The adrenal glands are stimulated by the autonomic nervous system to release epinephrine and norepinephrine.

    b. The thyroid gland produces a hormone that controls the rates of various chemical reactions in the body.

    c. The hypothalamus regulates the pituitary but does not itself directly regulate growth.

11. d. is the answer. Also known as adrenaline and noradrenaline, epinephrine and norepinephrine are hormones released by the adrenal glands. (p. 34)

12. d. is the answer. The cerebellum is involved in the coordination of voluntary muscular movements. (p. 29)

a. The medulla regulates breathing and heartbeat.

b. The thalamus relays sensory inputs to the appropriate higher centers of the brain.

c. The hypothalamus is concerned with the regulation of basic drives and emotions.

13. a. is the answer. The reticular activating system controls arousal via its connections to the cortex. Thus, separating the two produces a coma. (pp. 29–30)

b., c., & d. None of these structures controls arousal. The hypothalamus regulates hunger, thirst, sexual behavior, and other basic drives. The thalamus is a relay station that routes sensory information to the appropriate cortical areas. The cerebellum is involved in coordination of voluntary movement.

14. b. is the answer. The oldest region, the brainstem, is present even in lower vertebrates; the limbic system is found in all mammals; and the most recently evolved structure, the cortex, is found only in higher mammals. (p. 28)

15. c. is the answer. As Olds and Milner discovered, electrical stimulation of the hypothalamus is a highly reinforcing event, precisely because it is there that the animal's pleasure centers are located. The other organs mentioned are not associated with pleasure centers. (p. 33)

16. c. is the answer. The corpus callosum is a thick band of neural fibers linking the right and left cerebral hemispheres. To sever the corpus callosum is in effect to split the brain. (p. 40)

17. d. is the answer. The frontal lobe is in the front of the brain. Just behind it is the parietal lobe. The occipital lobe is located at the very back of the head and just below the parietal lobe. Next to the occipital lobe and toward the front of the head is the temporal lobe. (p. 36)

18. d. is the answer. As demonstrated in the case of Phineas Gage, injury to the frontal lobe may produce such changes in personality. (p. 38)

a. Damage to the parietal lobe might disrupt functions involving the sensory cortex.

b. Damage to the temporal lobe might impair hearing.

c. Occipital damage might impair vision.

Matching Items

1. d (p. 42)	**5.** i (p. 34)	**9.** k (p. 38)
2. g (p. 29)	**6.** a (p. 39)	**10.** b (p. 42)
3. e (p. 34)	**7.** j (p. 39)	**11.** c (p. 39)
4. f (p. 39)	**8.** h (p. 32)	

Brain Damage Diagram (pp. 32–43)

1. a (occipital lobe)	**5.** e (cerebellum)
2. h (reticular activating system)	**6.** b (sensory cortex)
3. c (motor cortex)	**7.** f (hypothalamus)
4. d (temporal lobe)	**8.** g (corpus callosum)
	9. k (frontal lobe)

KEY TERMS

1. The theory of **phrenology**, which has been discarded, maintained that the shape of a person's skull was related to their personality. (p. 21)

2. The **nervous system** is the electrochemical system that underlies all thought, feeling, and behavior. (p. 21)

3. The **central nervous system (CNS)** consists of the brain and spinal cord; it is located at the *center*, or internal core, of the body. (p. 22)

4. The **peripheral nervous system (PNS)** connects the central nervous system to the rest of the body; it is at the *periphery* of the body relative to the brain and spinal cord. (p. 22)

5. The **somatic nervous system** is the division of the PNS that transmits sensory information to the CNS and directs voluntary movements of the skeletal muscles. (p. 22)

6. The **autonomic nervous system** is the division of the PNS that controls the glands and the muscles of internal organs and thereby controls internal functioning; it regulates the *automatic* behaviors necessary for survival. (p. 22)

7. The **sympathetic nervous system** is the division of the autonomic nervous system that arouses the body and mobilizes its resources in stressful situations. (p. 23)

8. The **parasympathetic nervous system** is the division of the autonomic nervous system that often calms the body. (p. 23)

9. The **neuron**, or nerve cell, is the basic building block of the nervous system. (p. 21)

10. Sensory neurons transmit information about internal and external stimuli to the central nervous system for processing. (p. 23)

11. Motor neurons carry information and instructions for action from the central nervous system to muscles and glands. (p. 23)

12. **Interneurons** are the neurons of the central nervous system that link the sensory and motor neurons in the transmission of sensory input and motor output. (p. 23)

13. A **reflex** is an automatic response to a stimulus; it is governed by a very simple neural pathway. (p. 23)

14. The **dendrites** of a neuron are the extensions that receive incoming signals from other nerve cells and transmit them to the cell body. (p. 24)

15. The **axons** of a neuron are the extensions that transmit impulses away from the cell body and to other nerve cells. (p. 24)

16. A neuron's **threshold** is the level of stimulation that must be exceeded in order for the neuron to fire, or generate an electrical impulse. (p. 24)

17. The neuron has an **all-or-none response**. If its threshold is not exceeded, it will not generate an electrical impulse. If its threshold is exceeded, it will generate *all* the electrical responses it is capable of. (p. 24)

18. A **synapse** is the gap between the axon of one neuron and the dendrite or cell body of another neuron. (p. 25)

19. **Neurotransmitters** are chemicals that, when released into synaptic gaps, *transmit neural messages* from neuron to neuron. (p. 25)

20. **Acetylcholine (ACh)** is a neurotransmitter that triggers muscle contractions. (p. 26)

21. **Endorphins** are naturally occurring neurotransmitters linked to pain control and pleasure. (p. 26)
    Memory aid: <u>End</u>orphins *end* pain.

22. A **lesion** is a destruction of tissue; studying the consequences of lesions—both surgically produced in animals and naturally occurring—in different regions of the brain helps researchers to determine the normal functions of these regions. (p. 30)

23. An **electroencephalogram (EEG)** is an amplified recording of the waves of electrical activity of the brain. *Encephalo* comes from a Greek word meaning "related to the brain." (p. 31)
    Example: While a person is solving a complicated mathematical problem, scalp electrodes recording brain waves reveal increased activity in the left hemisphere.

24. The **CAT (computerized axial tomograph) scan** is a series of x-rays of the brain taken from different positions and analyzed by computer, creating an image that represents a slice through the brain. (p. 31)

25. The **PET (positron emission tomograph) scan** measures the levels of activity of different areas of the brain by tracing their consumption of glucose, the brain's fuel. (p. 31)

26. **MRI (magnetic resonance imaging)** uses magnetic fields and radio waves to produce computer-generated images that show brain structures more clearly. (p. 31)

27. The **brainstem**, the oldest major subdivision of the brain, is an extension of the spinal cord and is the central core of the brain; its structures direct automatic survival functions. (p. 29)
    Memory aid: As a flower sits on top of its stem, the brain rests on its **brainstem**.

28. Located in the brainstem, the **medulla** is involved in the regulation of breathing and heart rate. (p. 29)

29. The **cerebellum**, also part of the brainstem, assists in balance and the coordination of movement (p. 29)

30. Located on top of the brainstem, the **thalamus** routes incoming messages to the appropriate cortical centers and transmits replies to the medulla and cerebellum. (p. 29)

31. Also a part of the brainstem, the **reticular activating system** plays an important role in arousing the higher centers of the brain and also in controlling attention. (p. 29)

32. The second oldest subdivision of the brain, the **limbic system** plays an important role in the regulation of emotions and basic physiological drives. Its name comes from the Latin word *limbus*, meaning "border"; the limbic system is at the border of the brainstem and cerebral hemispheres. (p. 32)

33. The **amygdala** is part of the limbic system and is involved in regulation of the emotions of fear and rage. (p. 32)

34. Also part of the limbic system, the **hypothalamus** regulates hunger, thirst, body temperature, and the secretion of hormones, and contains the so-called pleasure centers of the brain. (p. 32)

35. **Hormones** are the chemical messengers of the endocrine system; they are secreted by endocrine glands and circulate via the bloodstream to their target tissues, on which they have specific effects. (p. 33)

36. The **endocrine system**, the body's "slower" communication system, consists of glands that secrete hormones into the bloodstream. (p. 34)

37. The **adrenal glands** produce epinephrine and norepinephrine, hormones that prepare the body to deal with emergencies or stress. (p. 34)

38. The **pituitary** regulates growth and directs the secretion of hormones by many other endocrine glands. (p. 34)

39. The **cerebral cortex** is the outer covering of the cerebral hemispheres. The cortex is the seat of information processing; it is responsible for those complex functions that make us distinctively human. (p. 35)

    Memory aid: *Cortex* in Latin means "bark." As bark covers a tree, the **cerebral cortex** is the "bark of the brain."

40. Located at the front of the brain, just behind the forehead, the **frontal lobes** contain the motor cortex and are involved in making plans and judgments. (p. 36)

41. Situated between the frontal and occipital lobes, the **parietal lobes** contain the sensory cortex. (p. 36)

42. Located at the back and base of the brain, the **occipital lobes** contain the visual cortex, which receives information from the eyes. (p. 36)

    Example: The "stars" that one sees when hit in the back of the head result from activation of the cells in the visual cortex in the **occipital lobe**.

43. Located on the sides of the brain, the **temporal lobes** contain the auditory areas, which receive information from the ears. (p. 36)

    Memory aid: The **temporal lobes** are located near the *temples*.

44. Located at the back of the frontal lobe, the **motor cortex** controls voluntary movement. (p. 36)

    Example: When you have decided to hit a backhand in tennis, the **motor cortex** is alerted to initiate the sequence of motor neuron activity that results in the execution of the shot.

45. The **sensory cortex** is located at the front of the parietal lobe, bordering the motor cortex. It receives information from the skin senses. (p. 37)

46. Located throughout the cortex, **association areas** of the brain are involved in higher mental functions, such as learning, memory, and abstract thinking. (p. 38)

    Memory aid: Among their other functions, **association areas** of the cortex are involved in integrating, or associating, information from different areas of the brain.

47. **Aphasia** is an impairment of language as a result of damage to any of several cortical areas, including Broca's area and Wernicke's area. (p. 39)

48. **Broca's area** is located on the left frontal lobe and is involved in controlling the motor ability to produce speech. (p. 39)

49. **Wernicke's area** is located on the left temporal lobe and is involved in language comprehension. (p. 39)

50. The **corpus callosum** is a thick band of nerve fibers that links the right and left cerebral hemispheres. Without this band of nerve fibers, the two hemispheres could not interact. (p. 40)

51. The **split-brain** patient has had the major connections between the two cerebral hemispheres (the corpus callosum) severed, literally resulting in a split brain. (p. 40)

52. **Plasticity** refers to the ability of the brain to reorganize itself to compensate for destruction of brain tissue. The plasticity of the brain diminishes with age. (p. 43)

Chapter 3 | The Developing Person Through the Life Span

Developmental psychologists study the life cycle, from conception to death, examining how we develop physically, cognitively, and socially. This chapter describes the human journey through life, focusing on (1) the relative impact of genes and experience on behavior, (2) whether development is best described as gradual and continuous or as a sequence of predetermined stages, and (3) whether the individual's personality remains stable or changes over the life span. The chapter concludes with a review of current thinking on these issues.

Chapter 3 also examines several important stage theories of development, including Piaget's theory of cognitive development, Kohlberg's theory of moral development, Erikson's theory of psychosocial development, and Levinson's proposed stages of adulthood.

Although there are not too many terms to learn in this chapter, there are quite a number of important research findings to remember. Pay particular attention to the sections concerned with the origins and effects of secure attachment, Piaget's theory, evidence for intellectual stability or decline during adulthood, and studies of personality development in twins.

Guided Study

The text chapter should be studied one section at a time. Before you read, preview each section by skimming it, noting headings and boldface items. Then read the appropriate section objectives from the following outline. Keep these objectives in mind and, as you read the chapter section, search for the information that will enable you to meet each objective. Once you have finished a section, write out answers for its objectives.

Prenatal Development and the Newborn (pp. 50–52)

1. Discuss the course of prenatal development.

2. Describe the capacities of the newborn.

Infancy and Childhood (pp. 52–66)

3. Describe brain and motor development from infancy through childhood.

4. Describe Piaget's view of how the mind develops and describe his cognitive stages.

5. Discuss the origins of attachment and the effects of early attachment patterns with parents and child-care workers on later life.

6. Explain how children's behavior can provide evidence of an emerging self-concept and identify some of the ways males and females differ, and the extent of such differences over the life span.

7. Discuss possible effects of different parenting styles on the child.

Adolescence (pp. 66–73)

8. Identify the major physical changes that occur in adolescence.

9. Describe Piaget's final stage of cognitive development and Kohlberg's theory of moral development.

10. Discuss the search for identity and the nature of social relationships during the adolescent years.

Adulthood and Aging (pp. 73–82)

11. Identify the major physical changes that occur in middle and late adulthood.

12. Describe the major cognitive changes that occur in adulthood and old age.

13. Explain why stage theories of adult social development are controversial.

14. Discuss the importance of family and career commitments in adult development.

15. Discuss the psychological reactions of the dying and of those who have lost a loved one.

Reflections on the Major Developmental Issues (pp. 82–86)

16. Summarize the results and implications of research on the nature-nurture issue.

17. State current views of psychologists on the issues of continuity versus stages and stability versus change in lifelong development.

Chapter Review

When you have finished reading the chapter, use the material that follows to review it. Complete the sentences and answer the questions. As you proceed, evaluate your performance for each chapter section by consulting the answer key at the end of this chapter. Do not continue with the next section until you've understood each answer. If you need to, review or reread the appropriate chapter section in the textbook before continuing.

Prenatal Development and the Newborn (pp. 50–52)

1. The reproductive cycle begins when an egg, or _____ovum_____, is released by the female's ovary.

2. The body's genetic plans are stored within the _____. In number, each person inherits _____ of these structures, _____ from each parent. Each is composed of long threads of _____DNA_____.

3. The twenty-third pair of chromosomes are the sex chromosomes. The mother invariably contributes a(n) _____X_____ chromosome. When the father contributes a(n) _____X_____ chromosome, the individual will be female; when the father contributes a(n) _____Y_____ chromosome, the individual will be male.

4. The presence of the Y chromosome triggers production of _____testosterone_____, the principal male hormone.

Write several sentences describing the moment of conception and the beginning of prenatal development.

5. Fertilized human eggs are called _____zygote_____. From about 2 until 8 weeks of age the developing human is called a(n) _____embryo_____. During the final stage of prenatal development, the developing human is called a(n) _____fetus_____.

6. Since the fetus gets its nutrients from the mother, premature births or stillbirths may occur if the mother is severely _____malnourished_____ during the later stages of pregnancy. Along with nutrients, a range of harmful substances, together known as _____toxic_____, can also pass through the placenta.

7. At birth, infants possess a number of simple responses called _____reflexes_____. When an infant's cheek is touched, it will vigorously search for a nipple, a response known as the _____.

Give some evidence supporting the claim that a newborn's sensory equipment is biologically prewired to facilitate social responsiveness.

Infancy and Childhood (pp. 52–66)

8. At birth the human nervous system _____ (is/is not) fully mature. This may explain why most people have no memory of events before age __2__ 3 or 4 .

9. Infants pass the milestones of motor development at different rates, but the basic sequence of biological growth processes, called _maturation_, is fixed. As an example, maturation creates a readiness to walk in children at about age __1__ . Until the necessary muscular and neural maturation is complete, experience has a _____ (large/small) effect on behavior.

10. The first researcher to show that the cognitive processes of adults and children are very different was _Piaget_.

11. To organize his or her experiences, the developing child constructs cognitive concepts called _Schemas_.

12. The interpretation of new experiences in terms of existing ideas is called _____. The adaptation of existing ideas to fit new experiences is called _____.

13. The term for all the mental activities associated with thinking, knowing, and remembering is _____.

14. In Piaget's first stage of development, that of _____ intelligence, children experience the world through their motor activities and sensory impressions. This stage occurs between infancy and age _____.

15. The development of an awareness that things continue to exist even when they are removed from view is called _____ _____. This awareness begins to develop at about _____ months of age. At about this same time, a new fear, called _____ _____, emerges.

16. Preschoolers are often unable to perceive things from another person's point of view. This inability is called _____ and it is characteristic of Piaget's _____ stage, which lasts until age _____ .

17. The principle that the quantity of a substance remains the same even when the appearance of its container changes is called _____. Preschoolers _____ (have/have not) developed this concept. Children become able to understand this concept at about _____ years of age, when they enter the _____ _____ stage.

Write a sentence explaining how contemporary researchers have modified some of Piaget's ideas.

18. The development of a strong social bond between infant and parent is called _____.

19. Harlow's studies of monkeys have shown that mother-infant attachment does not depend on the mother providing nourishment so much as it does on her providing the comfort of _____ _____.

20. Lorenz discovered that young birds would follow almost any object if it were the first moving thing they observed. This phenomenon is called _____. In some animals

attachment will occur only during a restricted time called a _____

_____.

21. Placed in a strange play situation, children show one of two patterns of attachment: _____ attachment or _____ attachment.

22. Differences in the emotional reactivity, or _____, of newborns _____ (are/are not) likely to persist. Such differences _____ (are/are not) likely to be innate.

23. According to Erikson, infants develop a sense of either _____ or _____, depending on the nature of their attachment experiences.

24. Harlow found that monkeys reared in social isolation reacted with either fear or _____ when placed with other monkeys.

25. A child's self-image generally becomes stable by the age of _____ or _____.

26. For most psychological traits, variation _____ (between/within) the sexes is greater than variation _____ (between/within) the sexes.

Write a sentence describing several characteristics of children who have formed a positive self-image.

27. Parents who make few demands of their children and tend to submit to their children's desires are identified as _____ parents.

28. Parents who impose rules and expect blind obedience are exhibiting a _____ style of parenting.

29. Setting and enforcing standards after discussion with their children is the approach taken by _____ parents.

30. Studies have shown that there tends to be a correlation between high self-esteem on the part of the child and the _____ style of parenting.

Adolescence (pp. 66–73)

31. Adolescence begins with the time of developing sexual maturity known as _____. A two-year growth spurt begins in girls at about the age of _____ and in boys at about age _____. This growth spurt is marked by the development of the reproductive organs, or _____ _____ characteristics, as well as by the development of traits such as pubic hair and enlarged breasts in females and facial hair in males. These nonreproductive traits are known as _____ _____ characteristics.

32. The first menstrual period, called _____, occurs by about age _____. In boys the first ejaculation occurs by about age _____.

33. Piaget's final stage of cognitive development is the stage of _____ _____. The adolescent in this stage is capable of thinking logically about _____ as well as concrete propositions.

34. The theorist who proposed that moral thought progresses through six stages is _____. These stages are divided into three basic levels: _____, _____, and _____.

35. In the preconventional stages of morality, characteristic of children, the emphasis is on obeying rules in order to avoid _____ or gain _____.

36. Conventional morality usually emerges by early _____. The emphasis is on

gaining social _____ or upholding the social _____.

37. Individuals who base moral judgments on their own perceptions of universal ethical principles are said by Kohlberg to employ _____ morality.

Summarize the criticisms of Kohlberg's theory of moral development.

38. According to Erikson, the task of adolescence is to develop a clear sense of self, or _____. Erikson sees this development as a prerequisite for the development of _____ in young adulthood. According to Carol Gilligan, this sequence of developmental tasks is more typical of _____ (males/ females) than it is of the opposite sex.

39. Adolescence is typically a time of increasing influence from one's _____ and decreasing influence from _____.

Adulthood and Aging (pp. 73–82)

40. Early adulthood extends from about age _____ to age _____. During adulthood, age _____ (is/is not) a very good predictor of a person's traits.

41. The cessation of the menstrual cycle, known as _____, occurs at about age _____. This biological change results from lowered levels of the hormone _____. A woman's experience during this time depends largely on her _____.

42. Although men experience no equivalent to menopause, they do experience a gradual decline in _____ count and in the hormone _____ during later life.

43. Older adults suffer from short-term ailments such as flu _____ (more/less) often than younger adults.

44. The disease that causes progressive senility is _____ disease. This disease has been linked to an insufficient supply of the neurotransmitter _____.

45. Studies of developmental changes in learning and memory show that during adulthood there is a decline in the ability to _____ new information but not in the ability to _____ such information.

46. A research study in which people of various ages are tested at the same time is called a _____-_____ study. A research study in which the same people are retested several times over a period of years is called a _____ study. This first kind of study found evidence of intellectual _____ during adulthood, whereas the second found evidence of intellectual _____.

47. The accumulation of stored information that comes with education and experience is called _____ intelligence, which tends to _____ with age.

48. The ability to reason abstractly is referred to as _____ intelligence, which tends to _____ with age.

49. Levinson has proposed a stage theory of adulthood in which there are early, midlife, and late adult _____, each stressful but followed by a period of stability.

50. Contrary to popular opinion, job and marital dissatisfaction do not surge during the forties, thus suggesting that a midlife _____ need not occur.

51. The term used to refer to the culturally preferred timing for leaving home, getting a job, marrying, and so on is the _____. Today the timing of such life events is becoming _____ (more/less) predictable.

52. In Erikson's theory, the conflict between intimacy and __isolation__ refers to the challenge of becoming less self-absorbed and more caring and productive during adulthood.

53. According to Freud, the healthy adult is one who can _____ and _____.

54. The "traditional family" of father, mother, and children represents a _____ (minority/majority) of American households.

55. For most couples, the children's leaving home produces a feeling of greater freedom and marital satisfaction. Some, however, become distressed and feel a loss of purpose. This is called the _____ _____ syndrome.

56. The theorist who proposed that dying patients experience an adjustment sequence of five stages is __K Ross__.

Write a sentence naming and describing each of these five stages.

Explain why identical twins are of particular interest to psychologists.

59. Through research on identical twins raised apart, psychologists are able to study the influence of the _____.

60. Studies of adoptive families show that people who grow up together _____ (do/do not) tend to have similar personalities.

61. The effect of genes and experience on personality is best described as an _____ between the two factors.

62. Stage theories that have been considered in this chapter include the theory of cognitive development proposed by _____, the theory of moral development proposed by _____, and the theory of psychosocial development proposed by _____.

Briefly summarize the textbook's conclusions on the three major issues: nature versus nurture, continuity versus stages, and stability versus change in development.

Reflections on the Major Developmental Issues (pp. 82–86)

57. One of the oldest debates in developmental psychology concerns the relative importance of genes and experiences in determining behavior; this debate is called the _____-_____ question.

58. Research on the influence of heredity includes studies of twins. Twins who developed from a single egg are genetically _____. Twins who developed from different fertilized eggs are no more genetically alike than siblings and are called _____ twins.

FOCUS ON PSYCHOLOGY:
The Changing Meanings of Age and Aging

In most societies, including our own, age is an important dimension of social organization, a determinant of how people relate to one another, and a major index by which individuals evaluate their lives. In an illuminating article, Bernice and Dail Neugarten discuss the historical development of life periods in Western societies and the blurring of these periods in contemporary society. With the emergence of the "young-old" and "hurried child" concepts and with changes in the pattern and timing of marriage, education, and career, age has become a poor predictor of life events. In the authors' words, today "we have conflicting images rather than stereotypes of age: the 70-year-old in a wheelchair, but also the 70-year old on the tennis court; the 18-year-old who is married and supporting a family, but also the 18-year-old college student who brings his laundry home to his mother each week."

Research on aging has not helped clarify the situation very much, tending to emphasize age-related losses in function while neglecting the substantial variation in functional ability among older adults. Reviewing the literature on the relationship of aging to physical and mental health, researchers John Rowe and Robert Kahn argue that the effects of aging have been exaggerated, and that many age-related declines can be explained in terms of lifestyle, nutrition, exercise, and such psychosocial factors as individual autonomy and the presence or absence of social support. They suggest that researchers should refocus their efforts. By first distinguishing *usual aging,* or that which is statistically average, from *successful aging,* in which older people experience minimal physiological loss, researchers might help elucidate how the proportion of the elderly engaged in successful aging can be increased.

One thing is clear: The proportion of aged people is increasing and will continue to do so. As a result of declining birth rates and improved health habits and medical care, the fastest growing age group today is over 65; between 1950 and 1988, this group increased from about 7 to 12 percent of the population of the United States. During the same time period, the percentage of the population under age 14 decreased from 30 to 20 percent.

In the past, the shape of the population distribution was a pyramid, with the youngest (and largest) age groups at the bottom and the smallest (and oldest) at the top. If present trends continue, by the year 2030 the pyramid will become a rectangle and the population of the United States will be divided roughly into thirds—one-third aged 30 and younger, one-third aged 30 to 59, and one-third aged 60 and older.

Some experts warn that this "squaring" of the demographic pyramid will create many new social problems, including runaway health care costs for the elderly and a lessening concern for the education of children. In order to successfully face the challenges created by an aging population, policymakers, voters, and all members of society must be able to separate the true meanings of age and aging from ageist stereotypes. For this reason, research in developmental psychology is of increasing importance to everyone's well-being.

The changing population of the United States (in millions)

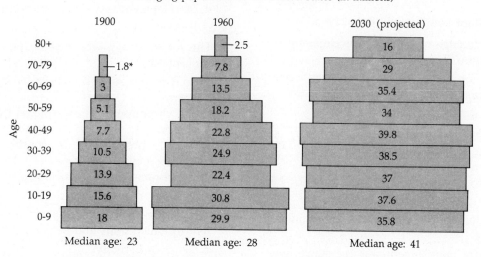

*Those older than 79 are included in the figure for those aged 70-79

Sources: Berger, K. S. (1988). *The Developing Person Through the Life Span* (2nd ed.), New York: Worth, p. 528.

Neugarten, B. L., & Neugarten, D. A. (1987, May). The changing meanings of age. *Psychology Today,* 29–33.

Rowe, J. W., & Kahn, R. L. (1987, July 10). Human Aging: Usual and successful. *Science, 237,* 143–149.

Progress Test 1

Circle your answers to the following questions and check them with the answer key at the end of this chapter. If your answer is incorrect, read the answer key explanation for why it is incorrect and then consult the appropriate pages of the text to understand the correct answer.

1. Piaget's theory is primarily concerned with:
   a. motor development.
   b. social development.
   c. biological development.
   d. cognitive development.

2. Piaget held that egocentrism is characteristic of the:
   a. sensorimotor stage.
   b. preoperational stage.
   c. concrete operational stage.
   d. formal operational stage.

3. Which parenting style usually produces children with the greatest confidence and self-esteem?
   a. permissive
   b. authoritarian
   c. authoritative
   d. There is no evidence of a relationship between parental style and self-esteem.

4. If a mother is severely malnourished during the last third of her pregnancy:
   a. the placenta will replace any missing nutrients.
   b. the effects will not be as damaging as those resulting from malnutrition earlier in the pregnancy.
   c. the risk of a premature birth or a stillbirth is increased.
   d. mother-infant bonding will be delayed.

5. During which stage of cognitive development do children acquire object permanence?
   a. sensorimotor   c. concrete operational
   b. preoperational   d. formal operational

6. The rooting reflex occurs when:
   a. a newborn's foot is tickled.
   b. a newborn's cheek is touched.
   c. a newborn hears a loud noise.
   d. a newborn makes eye contact with his or her caregiver.

7. Harlow's studies of attachment in monkeys showed that:
   a. provision of nourishment was the single most important factor motivating attachment.
   b. a cloth mother produced the greatest attachment response.
   c. whether a cloth or wire mother was present mattered less than the presence or absence of other infants.
   d. attachment in monkeys is based on imprinting.

8. If a toddler's father points out the lion at the zoo and calls it "kittie," he is trying to help his son modify his schema for cat through the process of

_____ in order to incorporate the new experience.
   a. accommodation   c. cognition
   b. assimilation   d. conservation

9. When psychologists discuss maturation they are referring to stages of growth that are *not* influenced by:
   a. conservation.   c. nurture.
   b. nature.   d. continuity.

10. The phenomenon in which young birds follow the first moving object they observe is:
    a. imprinting.   c. assimilation.
    b. bonding.   d. accommodation.

11. The developmental theorist who suggests that children develop an attitude of basic trust or mistrust is:
    a. Piaget.   c. Harlow.
    b. Erikson.   d. Freud.

12. Which of the following best describes the view of development taken by theorists who emphasize the role of learning and experience?
    a. Development is a sequence of stages that do not necessarily occur in any particular order.
    b. Development is a sequence of stages that occur in a specific order.
    c. Development is a slow, continuous shaping process.
    d. Development is a slow, discontinuous shaping process.

13. The fertilized egg will develop into a boy if, at conception:
    a. an X chromosome is contributed by the father's sperm.
    b. a Y chromosome is contributed by the father's sperm.
    c. an X chromosome is contributed by the mother's egg.
    d. a Y chromosome is contributed by the mother's egg.

14. The nature-nurture controversy considers the extent to which traits and behaviors reflect:
    a. genes or heredity.
    b. genes or experience.
    c. continuity or stages.
    d. life-span stability or change.

15. One of the best ways to distinguish how much genetic and environmental factors affect behavior is to compare children who have:
    a. the same genes and environments.
    b. different genes and environments.
    c. similar genes and similar families.
    d. the same genes but different environments.

16. Fraternal twins result when:
    a. a single egg is fertilized by a sperm and then splits.
    b. a single egg is fertilized by two sperm.
    c. two eggs are fertilized by different sperm.
    d. either a single egg is fertilized by one sperm or two eggs are fertilized by different sperm.

17. Several studies of long-separated identical twins have found that these twins:
    a. have little in common, due to the different environments in which they were raised.
    b. have many similarities, in everything from medical histories to personality.
    c. have similar personalities, but very different likes, dislikes, and lifestyles.
    d. are no more similar than are fraternal twins reared apart.

18. Which of the following stage theorists is associated with the idea that adult development proceeds through cycles of stability and change?
    a. Erikson   c. Kohlberg
    b. Levinson   d. Kübler-Ross

19. In Kübler-Ross's theory, which of the following is the correct sequence of stages?
    a. denial; anger; bargaining; depression; acceptance
    b. anger; denial; bargaining; depression; acceptance
    c. depression; anger; denial; bargaining; acceptance
    d. bargaining; anger; depression; denial; acceptance

20. In preconventional morality:
    a. one obeys out of a sense of social duty.
    b. one conforms to gain social approval.
    c. one obeys to avoid punishment or to gain concrete rewards.
    d. one follows the dictates of one's conscience.

21. Which of the following is correct?
    a. Early maturation places both boys and girls at a distinct social advantage.
    b. Early-maturing girls are more popular and self-assured than girls who mature late.
    c. Early maturation places both boys and girls at a distinct social disadvantage.
    d. Early-maturing boys are more popular and self-assured than boys who mature late.

22. A person's general ability to think abstractly is called _____ intelligence. This ability generally _____ with age.
    a. fluid; does not decrease
    b. fluid; decreases

    c. crystallized; decreases
    d. crystallized; does not decrease

23. Adolescence is marked by the onset of:
    a. an identity crisis.
    b. parent-child conflict.
    c. the concrete operational stage.
    d. puberty.

24. Which of the following cognitive abilities has been shown to decline during adulthood?
    a. ability to recall new information
    b. ability to recognize new information
    c. ability to learn meaningful new material
    d. ability to use judgment in dealing with daily life problems

25. Which of the following statements concerning the effects of aging is true?
    a. Aging almost inevitably leads to senility if the individual lives long enough.
    b. Aging increases susceptibility to short-term ailments such as the flu.
    c. Significant increases in life satisfaction are associated with aging.
    d. The aging process can be significantly affected by the individual's activity patterns.

26. Longitudinal tests:
    a. study people of different ages at the same time.
    b. study the same people at different times.
    c. usually involve a larger sample size than do cross-sectional tests.
    d. usually involve a smaller sample size than do cross-sectional tests.

27. The cessation of menstruation is called:
    a. menarche.   c. the midlife crisis.
    b. menopause.   d. early adulthood.

28. Most contemporary developmental psychologists believe that:
    a. personality is essentially formed during infancy.
    b. personality continues to be formed until adolescence.
    c. the shaping of personality continues during adolescence and well beyond.
    d. adolescent development has very little impact on adult personality.

29. Among the landmark events of growing up are a boy's first ejaculation and a girl's first menstrual period, which is also called:
    a. puberty.   c. menarche.
    b. menopause.   d. generativity.

30. Based on the text's discussion of rate of maturation and popularity, who among the following is probably the most popular sixth grader?

a. Jessica, the most physically mature girl in the class

b. Roger, the most intellectually mature boy in the class

c. Rob, the tallest, most physically mature boy in the class

d. Cindy, who is average in physical development and is on the school debating team

31. "Hospice" refers to:

a. a group of terminally ill patients involved in educating the general public as to the needs of the dying.

b. a group of physicians who believe that terminally ill patients should be allowed to die whenever they wish to.

c. a research institution studying the causes of Alzheimer's disease.

d. an organization that supports dying people and their families.

32. In considering the research on gender differences, it is important to keep in mind that:

a. as yet, none of the proposed gender differences have been supported by solid evidence.

b. there usually is greater diversity between the sexes than there is within the sexes.

c. in many ways males and females are very similar.

d. researchers have typically studied age groups in which gender differences are smaller than average.

Progress Test 2

Progress Test 2 should be completed during a final chapter review. Do this test after you thoroughly understand the correct answers for the Chapter Review and Progress Test 1.

1. Assimilation refers to:

a. the application of existing schemas to new experiences.

b. the modification of schemas to fit new experiences.

c. the progression of a child through the various stages of cognitive development.

d. the bonding of mother and infant.

2. Which of the following statements about child abuse is correct?

a. Abused children generally come from high-income families.

b. Most children are abused between 10 and 15 years of age.

c. Abused children are more likely than others to become abusive parents.

d. Most abused children have authoritative parents.

3. Each cell of the human body has a total of:

a. twenty-three chromosomes.

b. twenty-three genes.

c. forty-six chromosomes.

d. forty-six genes.

4. Stranger anxiety develops at the same time as:

a. the concept of conservation.

b. egocentrism.

c. the ability to pretend.

d. the concept of object permanence.

5. The primary social achievement of infancy is the development of:

a. a self-concept.   **c.** attachment.

b. gender identity.   **d.** initiative.

6. Developmental theorists who emphasize the importance of maturation see development as a:

a. sequence of predictable stages.

b. slow, continuous shaping process.

c. completely unpredictable process.

d. sequence of stages, not necessarily in a particular order.

7. An authoritarian child-rearing style involves:

a. discipline through give-and-take discussion.

b. love without discipline.

c. neither love nor discipline.

d. discipline that demands unquestioning obedience.

8. Which is the correct sequence of stages in Piaget's theory of cognitive development?

a. sensorimotor, preoperational, concrete operational, formal operational

b. sensorimotor, preoperational, formal operational, concrete operational

c. preoperational, sensorimotor, concrete operational, formal operational

d. preoperational, sensorimotor, formal operational, concrete operational

9. As a child observes, liquid is transferred from a tall, thin tube into a short, wide jar. The child is asked if there is now less liquid, in order to determine if she has mastered:

a. the processes of accommodation and assimilation.

b. the concept of object permanence.

c. the concept of conservation.

d. the ability to reason abstractly.

10. Which is the correct order of stages of prenatal development?

a. zygote, fetus, embryo

b. zygote, embryo, fetus

c. embryo, zygote, fetus
d. embryo, fetus, zygote

11. The term *critical period* refers to:
a. prenatal development.
b. the initial 2 hours after a child's birth.
c. the preoperational stage.
d. a restricted time for learning.

12. Children who in infancy formed secure attachments to their parents are more likely than other children to:
a. prefer the company of adults to that of other children.
b. become permissive parents.
c. show a great deal of competence in social situations.
d. be less achievement oriented.

13. The term that refers to the rudiments of an individual's personality, especially emotional excitability, is:
a. ego.
c. temperament.
b. self-concept.
d. autonomy.

14. The cross-sectional method:
a. studies people of different ages at the same time.
b. studies the same group of people at different times.
c. tends to paint too favorable a picture of the effects of aging on intelligence.
d. is a more appropriate method for studying intellectual change over the life span than the longitudinal method.

15. The "social clock" refers to:
a. an individual or society's distribution of work and leisure time.
b. adulthood responsibilities.
c. typical ages for starting a career, marrying, etc.
d. age-related changes in one's circle of friends.

16. Which of the following is a true statement regarding the stage of formal operations?
a. It must be attained before moral reasoning of any sort is possible.
b. It is attained by everyone sooner or later.
c. It is followed by the stage of concrete operations.
d. It involves an ability to think abstractly.

17. To which of Kohlberg's levels would moral reasoning based on the existence of fundamental human rights pertain?
a. preconventional morality
b. conventional morality
c. postconventional morality
d. generative morality

18. In Erikson's theory, individuals generally focus on developing _____ during adolescence and then _____ during young adulthood.
a. identity; intimacy
c. basic trust; identity
b. intimacy; identity
d. identity; basic trust

19. Which of the following changes does *not* involve a secondary sex characteristic?
a. breast development
b. growth of pubic hair
c. voice change in males
d. onset of menstruation

20. After menopause, most women:
a. experience anxiety and a sense of worthlessness.
b. lose their sexual interest.
c. secrete unusually high levels of estrogen.
d. feel a new sense of freedom.

21. Notable achievements in fields such as _____ are often made by younger adults in their late twenties or early thirties, when _____ intelligence is at its peak.
a. mathematics; fluid
b. science; crystallized
b. philosophy; fluid
d. literature; crystallized

22. The mid-twenties are usually the peak years for all but which of the following?
a. physical strength
b. reaction time
c. recall memory
d. professional achievements

23. Moral development is associated most closely with _____ development.
a. perceptual
c. emotional
b. physical
d. cognitive

24. Underlying Alzheimer's disease is a deterioration in neurons that produce:
a. epinephrine.
c. serotonin.
b. norepinephrine.
d. acetylcholine.

25. A person's accumulation of stored information, called _____ intelligence, generally _____ with age.
a. fluid; declines
c. crystallized; declines
b. fluid; increases
d. crystallized; increases

26. Sam, a junior in high school, regularly attends church because his family and friends think he should. Which state of moral reasoning is Sam in?
a. preconventional
b. conventional
c. postconventional
d. Too little information to tell.

27. One criticism of stage theories is that they fail to consider that development may be significantly affected by:
    a. variations in the social clock.
    b. each individual's experiences.
    c. each individual's historical and cultural setting.
    d. all of the above.

Key Terms

Using your own words, wrote a brief definition or explanation of each of the following.

1. ovum

2. chromosomes

3. DNA (deoxyribonucleic acid)

4. genes

5. X chromosome

6. Y chromosome

7. testosterone

8. zygote

9. embryo

10. fetus

11. teratogens

12. rooting reflex

13. maturation

14. schemas

15. assimilation

16. accommodation

17. cognition

18. sensorimotor stage

19. object permanence

20. stranger anxiety

21. preoperational stage

22. egocentrism

23. conservation

24. concrete operational stage

25. attachment

26. critical period

27. imprinting

28. temperament

29. basic trust

30. gender

31. adolescence

32. puberty

33. primary sex characteristics

34. secondary sex characteristics

35. menarche

36. formal operational stage

37. identity

38. intimacy

39. menopause

40. Alzheimer's disease

41. cross-sectional study

42. longitudinal study

43. crystallized intelligence

44. fluid intelligence

45. social clock

46. generativity

47. hospice

48. nature-nurture issue

49. identical twins

50. fraternal twins

51. interaction

Answers

CHAPTER REVIEW

1. ovum
2. chromosomes; forty-six; twenty-three; DNA
3. X; X; Y
4. testosterone

An egg has been released by the ovary; during intercourse, millions of sperm are deposited in the vagina and travel toward the egg. At the moment of conception, those few sperm that reach the egg release digestive enzymes that eat away at the egg's protective coating, allowing one sperm to penetrate. An electrical charge then blocks the other sperm from entering. The fertilizing sperm is drawn into the egg, where the egg nucleus and sperm nucleus fuse and the chromosomes are paired. The process of cell division and differentiation begins.

5. zygotes; embryo; fetus

6. malnourished; teratogens

7. reflexes; rooting reflex

Newborns reflexively turn their heads in the direction of human voices, but not toward artificial sounds. They gaze longer at a drawing of a human face than at a geometric pattern. They focus best on objects about 9 inches away, which is about the distance between a nursing infant's eyes and the mother's.

8. is not; 3 or 4

9. maturation; 1; small

10. Piaget

11. schemas

12. assimilation; accommodation

13. cognition

14. sensorimotor; 2

15. object permanence; 8; stranger anxiety

16. egocentrism; preoperational; 6

17. conservation; have not; 7; concrete operational

Contemporary researchers contend that Piaget underestimated the competence of young children. When tests of egocentrism and conservation are simplified, 5- and 6-year-olds will exhibit some understanding of conservation and an emerging ability to take another's perspective.

18. attachment

19. body contact

20. imprinting; critical period

21. secure; insecure

22. temperament; are; are

23. basic trust; mistrust

24. aggression

25. 8; 10

26. within; between

Children who have formed a positive self-concept tend to be more confident, independent, optimistic, assertive, and sociable.

27. permissive

28. authoritarian

29. authoritative

30. authoritative

31. puberty; 11; 13; primary sex; secondary sex

32. menarche; 13; 14

33. formal operations; abstract

34. Kohlberg; preconventional; conventional; postconventional

35. punishment; rewards

36. adolescence; approval; order

37. postconventional

Critics of Kohlberg's theory point out that morality also lies in a person's actions, which are influenced by factors besides moral reasoning. They also argue that the perception of postconventional moral reasoning as the highest level of moral development reflects a Western cultural bias.

38. identity; intimacy; males

39. peers; parents

40. 20; 40; is not

41. menopause; 50; estrogen; attitude

42. sperm; testosterone

43. less

44. Alzheimer's; acetylcholine

45. recall; recognize

46. cross-sectional; longitudinal; decline; stability

47. crystallized; increase

48. fluid; decrease

49. transitions

50. transition or crisis

51. social clock; less

52. generativity

53. love; work

54. minority

55. empty nest

56. Kübler-Ross

In her interviews with dying patients, Kübler-Ross identified five stages the dying move through: *denial* of the terminal condition, *anger* at the seeming unfairness of their situation, *bargaining* for more time, *depression* stemming from the impending loss, and finally, *acceptance* of their fate.

57. nature-nurture

58. identical; fraternal

Since identical twins are genetic replicas of each other, the findings that identical twins are highly similar in a trait—significantly more so than fraternal twins or other siblings—suggest that there is a substantial genetic influence on that trait. In this way, identical twins can give psychologists a greater understanding of the role of heredity.

59. environment

60. do not

61. interaction

62. Piaget; Kohlberg; Erikson

The nature-nurture issue represents a false dichotomy in the sense that both biological and social factors interact in directing behavior. Although stage theories have been harshly criticized for failing to recognize the underlying continuity in human development, they have led to the realization that people think and act differently at every age. And, although the first two years of life provide a poor basis for predicting later behavior, some traits, such as temperament, are fairly consistent over the life span.

PROGRESS TEST 1

1. **d.** is the answer. Piaget's theory is concerned with the qualitatively different stages of thinking, or cognition, that occur in children. (p. 56)

2. **b.** is the answer. The preoperational child sees the world from his or her own vantage point. (p. 57)

   a. As immature as egocentrism is, it represents a significant cognitive advance over the sensorimotor child, who knows the world only through senses and actions. Even simple self-awareness takes a while to develop.

   c. & d. As children attain the operational stages, they become more able to see the world through the eyes of others.

3. **c.** is the answer. Children of authoritative parents tend to develop self-reliance and a positive self-image. (p. 64)

   a. & b. Children seem to fare best when they have been raised by parents who are neither permissive nor authoritarian, but authoritative—exerting control without depriving their children of a sense of control over their own lives.

   d. The relationship between style of parenting and self-esteem in children is well established.

4. **c.** is the answer. (p. 51)

   a. The placenta is a filter through which nutrients in the mother's blood pass; it does not contribute nutrients on its own.

   b. The effects of malnourishment are greatest late in the pregnancy, when the demand for nutrients peaks.

   d. There is not an established relationship between bonding, which occurs after birth, and prenatal nutrition.

5. **a.** is the answer. Before object permanence is attained, "out of sight" is truly "out of mind." (p. 56)

   b., c., & d. Developments associated with the preoperational, concrete operational, and formal operational stages include the ability to pretend, conservation, and abstract reasoning, respectively.

6. **b.** is the answer. The infant turns its head and begins sucking when its cheek is stroked. (p. 52)

   a., c., & d. These stimuli produce other reflexes in the newborn.

7. **b.** is the answer. (p. 60)

   a. When given the choice between a wire surrogate with a bottle and a cloth surrogate without, the monkeys preferred the cloth surrogate.

   c. The presence of other infants made no difference.

   d. Imprinting plays no role in the attachment of higher primates.

8. **a.** is the answer. (p. 55)

   b. Assimilation is the process by which new experiences are incorporated into existing schemas.

   c. Cognition is a general term, referring to all mental activities associated with thinking, knowing, and remembering.

   d. Conservation is the ability to recognize that objects do not change whenever their appearance changes.

9. **c.** is the answer. Through maturation—an orderly sequence of biological growth processes that are relatively unaffected by experience—all humans develop. (p. 53)

   a. Conservation is the cognitive awareness that objects do not change with changes in appearance.

   b. The forces of nature *are* those that direct maturation.

   d. The continuity-discontinuity debate concerns whether development is a gradual and continuous process or a discontinuous, stagelike process. In fact, those who emphasize maturation see development as occurring in stages rather than continuously.

10. **a.** is the answer. (p. 61)

    b. Bonding refers to the more general process, seen in a number of species, of immediate mutual attachment between infant and parent, formed on the basis of physical contact.

    c. & d. Assimilation and accommodation refer to Piagetian processes by which cognitive schemas develop.

11. **b.** is the answer. Erikson proposed that psychosocial development occurs in a series of stages, in the

first of which the child develops an attitude of either basic trust or mistrust. (p. 63)

a. Piaget's theory is concerned with cognitive development.

c. Harlow conducted research on attachment and deprivation.

d. Freud's theory is concerned with personality development.

12. **c.** is the answer. Theorists who emphasize the role of learning and experience see these as shaping experience in a gradual but continuous way. (p. 85)

a. & d. These answers do not correspond to any of the commonly held views of development.

b. The view of development as a series of fixed stages is generally associated with theorists who emphasize maturation.

13. **b.** is the answer. (p. 50)

a. If the father's sperm contributes an X chromosome, a female will be produced.

c. The mother's egg always contributes an X chromosome.

d. This statement is factually incorrect. The mother's egg always contributes an X chromosome; a Y chromosome can be contributed only by the sperm.

14. **b.** is the answer. Nature = genes; nurture = experience. (p. 82)

a. Genes and heredity both refer to the nature side of the nature-nurture controversy.

c. & d. Whether development is continuous or occurs in stages and whether it is characterized by stability or change over the life span are two other developmental issues.

15. **d.** is the answer. To separate the influences of heredity and experience on behavior, one of the two must be held constant. (p. 83)

a., b., & c. These situations would not allow one to separate the contribution of heredity and environment.

16. **c.** is the answer. (p. 83)

a. This situation would produce identical twins.

b. Only one sperm can fertilize an egg.

d. This answer is incorrect because a single fertilized egg would not produce fraternal twins.

17. **b.** is the answer. (pp. 83–84)

a., c., & d. Despite being raised in different environments, long-separated identical twins often have much in common, including likes, dislikes, and lifestyles. This indicates the significant heritability of many traits.

18. **b.** is the answer. (p. 85)

a. Erikson is best known for his theory of psychosocial development over the life span.

c. Kohlberg is known for his work on the development of moral reasoning.

d. Kübler-Ross is known for her work on the emotional stages through which the terminally ill pass.

19. **a.** is the answer. (p. 81)

20. **c.** is the answer. At the preconventional level, moral reasoning centers on one's self-interest, whether this means obtaining rewards or avoiding punishment. (pp. 69–70)

a. & b. Moral reasoning based on a sense of social duty or a desire to gain social approval is associated with the conventional level of moral development.

d. Reasoning based on one's own ethical principles is characteristic of the postconventional level of moral development.

21. **d.** is the answer. Boys who show early physical maturation are generally stronger and more athletic than boys who mature late; these qualities may lead to greater popularity and self-assurance. (p. 68)

a. & c. Early maturation tends to be socially advantageous for boys but not for girls.

b. Early-maturing girls often suffer embarrassment and are objects of teasing.

22. **b.** is the answer. (p. 77)

a. Fluid intelligence tends to decrease with age.

c. & d. Crystallized intelligence refers to the accumulation of facts and general knowledge that takes place during a person's life. Crystallized intelligence generally does not decrease with age.

23. **d.** is the answer. The physical changes of puberty mark the onset of adolescence. (p. 66)

a. & b. An identity crisis or parent-child conflict may or may not occur during adolescence; neither of these formally marks its onset.

c. Formal operational thought, rather than concrete reasoning, typically develops in adolescence.

24. **a.** is the answer. (p. 77)

b., c., & d. These cognitive abilities remain essentially unchanged as the person ages.

25. **d.** is the answer. "Use it or lose it" seems to be the rule: Often, changes in activity patterns contribute significantly to problems regarded as being part of usual aging. (p. 78)

a. Most elderly people do *not* become senile; even among the very old, senility is relatively uncommon.

b. Although the elderly are more subject to long-term ailments than younger adults, they actually suffer fewer short-term ailments.

c. There is no tendency for people of any particular age to report greater happiness or satisfaction with life.

26. **b.** is the answer. (p. 76)

a. This answer describes cross-sectional research.

c. & d. Sample size does not distinguish cross-sectional from longitudinal research.

27. **b.** is the answer. (p. 74)

a. Menarche refers to the onset of menstruation.

c. When it does occur, the midlife crisis is a psychological, rather than biological, phenomenon.

d. Menopause occurs during middle adulthood.

28. **c.** is the answer. Contemporary psychologists believe that, despite considerable stability, personality can continue to be shaped throughout the life span. (p. 66)

29. **c.** is the answer. (p. 67)

a. Puberty refers to the early adolescent period during which accelerated growth and sexual maturation occur, not to the first menstrual period.

b. Menopause is the cessation of menstruation, which typically occurs in the early fifties.

d. In Erikson's theory, generativity, or the sense of contributing and being productive, is the task of middle adulthood.

30. **c.** is the answer. Early-maturing boys tend to be more popular. (p. 68)

a. Early-maturing girls may temporarily suffer embarrassment and be the objects of teasing.

b. & d. The social benefits of early or late maturation are based on physical development, not cognitive skills.

31. **d.** is the answer. Hospice staff and volunteers work in special facilities and in people's homes to support the terminally ill. (p. 81)

32. **c.** is the answer. Although certain gender differences in behavior and abilities have been found, by and large the sexes are similar. (p. 64)

a. There has been ample evidence of, for example, differences in aggressiveness.

b. Within-sex diversity is generally greater than that between the sexes.

d. In fact, researchers have most often studied young adults, the age group in which gender differences are greatest.

PROGRESS TEST 2

1. **a.** is the answer. When new experiences are interpreted in terms of existing schemas, assimilation occurs. (p. 55)

b. This answer describes accommodation.

c. & d. These answers have no relationship to the cognitive process of assimilation.

2. **c.** is the answer. About 30 percent of abused children become abusive parents; this rate of child abuse is about six times the national figure. (p. 63)

a. Abusive parents are found in every socioeconomic group.

b. Abuse occurs to children of all ages.

d. There is no established relationship between authoritative parenting and abuse.

3. **c.** is the answer. (p. 50)

b. & d. Each cell of the human body contains hundreds of genes.

4. **d.** is the answer. With object permanence, a child develops schemas for familiar objects, including faces, and may become upset when with a stranger who does not fit any of these schemas. (p. 56)

a. The concept of conservation develops during the concrete operational stage, whereas stranger anxiety develops during the earlier sensorimotor stage.

b. & c. Egocentrism and the ability to pretend both develop during the preoperational stage. This follows the sensorimotor stage, during which stranger anxiety develops.

5. **c.** is the answer. Attachment develops in infancy and has profound repercussions for the individual's subsequent psychosocial growth. (p. 60)

a. & b. Self-concept and gender identity, which is part of self-concept, emerge during the preschool years.

d. In Erikson's stages of psychosocial development, the emergence of initiative is associated with the preschool years.

6. **a.** is the answer. (p. 85)

b. This answer reflects the viewpoint of those who emphasize learning in development.

c. All researchers see behavior and development as somewhat predictable.

d. This answer is incorrect for the same reason that **a.** *is* correct.

7. **d.** is the answer. Authoritarian parents impose rules that children are expected to follow in an unquestioning manner. (p. 64)

a. This is a description of authoritative parents.

b. Discipline is very much a part of the authoritarian style of child-rearing.

c. By definition, authoritarian parents discipline their children, but love or its absence is not correlated with any particular parenting style.

8. **a.** is the answer. (p. 57)

9. **c.** is the answer. This test is to determine if the child understands that the quantity of liquid is conserved, despite the shift to a container that is different in shape. (p. 58)

a. These are general processes related to concept building.

b. Object permanence is the concept that an object continues to exist even when not perceived; in this case, the water is perceived throughout the experiment.

d. This experiment does not require abstract reasoning, only the ability to reason logically about the concrete.

10. **b.** is the answer. (pp. 50–51)

11. **d.** is the answer. A critical period is a restricted time during which an organism must be exposed to certain influences or experiences for a particular kind of learning to occur. (p. 61)

a. Critical periods refer to developmental periods after birth.

b. Critical periods vary from behavior to behavior, but they are not confined to the hours following birth.

c. Critical periods are not specifically associated with the preoperational period.

12. **c.** is the answer. Thus, for example, Sroufe found that children who were securely attached at 12 months of age were, as 2- to 3-year-olds, more outgoing than other children and more enthusiastic when working on challenging tasks. (pp. 62–63)

a., c., & d. There is no indication that securely attached children prefer to be with adults, become permissive parents, or are less achievement oriented.

13. **c.** is the answer. (p. 61)

a. *Ego* is a Freudian term that has come to refer to an individual's sense of self.

b. Self-concept refers to how individuals perceive themselves, rather than to their personality.

d. Autonomy is only one factor of personality—specifically, that relating to an individual's independence, or self-determination.

14. **a.** is the answer. (p. 76)

b. This answer describes the longitudinal research method.

c. & d. Cross-sectional studies have tended to exaggerate the effects of aging on intellectual functioning; for this reason they may not be the most appropriate method for studying life span development.

15. **c.** is the answer. Different societies have somewhat different ideas about the age at which major life events should ideally occur. (p. 78)

16. **d.** is the answer. (p. 59)

a. Formal operational thought is required only for postconventional stages of morality; the other stages of moral reasoning may develop before formal operational thought.

b. Not everyone reaches the stage of formal operations.

c. Concrete operational thought *precedes* formal operational thought.

17. **c.** is the answer. (p. 70)

a. Preconventional morality is based on avoiding punishment and obtaining rewards.

b. Conventional morality is based on gaining the approval of others and/or on following the law and social convention.

d. There is no such thing as generative morality.

18. **a.** is the answer. (pp. 71–72)

b. According to Erikson, identity develops before intimacy.

c. & d. The formation of basic trust is the task of infancy.

19. **d.** is the answer. Menstruation directly involves the reproductive organs, which are primary sex characteristics. That is, the onset of menstruation reflects the development of body structures that enable reproduction. (p. 67)

a., b., & c. These answers are incorrect because each is a secondary sex characteristic.

20. **d.** is the answer. (p. 74)

a. Most women do not experience anxiety and distress following menopause; moreover, the woman's experience will depend largely on her attitude.

b. Sexual interest does not decline in postmenopausal women.

c. Menopause is caused by a *reduction* in estrogen.

21. **a.** is the answer. A mathematician's skills are likely to reflect abstract reasoning, or fluid intelligence, which declines with age. (p. 77)

b. & d. Philosophy and literature are fields in which individuals often do their most notable work later in life, after more experiential knowledge (crystallized intelligence) has accumulated.

c. Scientific achievements generally reflect fluid, rather than crystallized, intelligence.

22. **d.** is the answer. In most fields, especially those in which crystallized intelligence is important, the greatest professional achievements occur later in life. (p. 77)

a., b., & c. Physical strength, reaction time, and recall memory all decline with age.

23. **d.** is the answer. Following Piaget's lead, Kohlberg

proposed that moral reasoning develops in stages, paced by cognitive development. (p. 69)

a., b., & c. Kohlberg's theory does not claim that perceptual, physical, or emotional development play a role in the development of moral reasoning.

24. **d.** is the answer. Significantly, drugs that block the activity of the neurotransmitter acetylcholine produce Alzheimer-like symptoms. (p. 75)

a. & b. Epinephrine and norepinephrine are *hormones* produced by glands of the endocrine system.

c. Serotonin is a neurotransmitter, and hence produced by neurons, but it has not been implicated in Alzheimer's disease.

25. **d.** is the answer. (p. 77)

a. & b. Fluid intelligence, which decreases with age, refers to the ability to reason abstractly.

c. Crystallized intelligence increases with age.

26. **b.** is the answer. Conventional morality is partially based on a desire to gain others' approval. (p. 70)

a. Preconventional reasoning is based on external incentives such as gaining a reward or avoiding punishment.

c. Postconventional morality reflects an affirmation of agreed-upon rights or universal ethical principles.

d. Fear of others' disapproval is one of the bases of conventional moral reasoning.

27. **d.** is the answer. (p. 78)

KEY TERMS

1. **Ovum** (the Latin word for "egg") refers to the female reproductive cell, which, if united with a sperm, develops into a new individual. (p. 50)

2. **Chromosomes** are made up of DNA molecules, which contain the genes. In conception, the twenty-three chromosomes in the egg are paired with the twenty-three chromosomes in the sperm. (p. 50)

3. **DNA (deoxyribonucleic acid)** is the chemical substance of which chromosomes are composed. (p. 50)

4. **Genes** are the biochemical units of heredity; they are segments of the DNA molecules of which the chromosomes are composed. (p. 50)

   Example: Biologists have suggested that aging, and the moment of death itself, are genetically programmed. Each of the trillions of cells in our bodies may have its own timing mechanism with specific **genes** that turn off cell division and provoke cell death.

5. An **X chromosome** is found in both males and females. At conception, the egg always contributes an X chromosome; if the sperm also contributes an X chromosome, the child will be a girl. (p. 50)

6. A **Y sex chromosome** is found only in males. If, in addition to the X chromosome contributed by the egg, the sperm contributes a Y chromosome, the child will be a boy. (p. 50)

7. **Testosterone** is the principal male sex hormone. (p. 50)

8. The **zygote** (a term derived from the Greek word for "joined") is the fertilized egg—that is, the cluster of cells formed during conception by the union of sperm and egg. (p. 50)

9. The **embryo** is the developing prenatal organism from about 2 weeks until 2 months after conception. (p. 51)

10. The **fetus** is the developing prenatal human from about 8 weeks after conception to birth. (p. 51)

11. **Teratogens** (literally, poisons) are any medications, drugs, viruses, or other substances that cross the mother's placenta and can harm the developing embryo or fetus. (p. 51)

12. The **rooting reflex** is the newborn's tendency, when his or her cheek is stroked, to orient toward the stimulus and begin sucking. (p. 52)

13. **Maturation** is a biological growth process that is relatively uninfluenced by experience or other environmental factors. (p. 53)

    Example: The ability to walk depends on a certain level of neural and muscular **maturation**. For this reason, until the toddler's body is physically ready to walk, practice "walking" has little effect.

14. In Piaget's theory of cognitive development, **schemas** are mental concepts that help organize existing and new information. (p. 55)

15. **Assimilation** refers to the interpretation of new information in light of existing cognitive schemas. (p. 55)

    Example: When a young child points to buses, tractors, and other four-wheeled vehicles in a picture book and calls them "car," the child is **assimilating** new information to an existing schema.

16. **Accommodation** refers to the modification of existing schemas in order to incorporate new information. (p. 55)

    Example: **Accommodation** of the schema "car" will occur as the child gains information about vehicles: This schema will be narrowed, and new schemas ("buses," "tractors," etc.) will develop.

17. **Cognition** refers to the mental processes by which knowledge is acquired and thinking occurs. (p. 56)

18. In Piaget's theory of cognitive stages, the **sensori-motor stage** lasts from birth to about age 2. During this stage, infants gain knowledge of the world through their senses and their motor activities. (p. 56)

19. **Object permanence**, which develops during the sensorimotor stage, is the awareness that things do not cease to exist when they are out of sight. (p. 56)

20. **Stranger anxiety** is the fear of strangers that infants begin to display at about 8 months of age. (p. 56)

21. In Piaget's theory, the **preoperational stage** lasts from about 2 to 7 years of age. During this stage language development is rapid, but the child is unable to think logically or symbolically. (pp. 57)

22. **Egocentrism** refers to the difficulty that preoperational children have in considering another's viewpoint. "Ego" means "self," and "centrism" indicates "in the center"; the preoperational child is "self-centered." (p. 57)

23. **Conservation** is the principle that properties such as number, volume, and mass remain constant despite changes in the appearance of objects; it is acquired during the concrete operational stage. (p. 58)

24. During the **concrete operational stage**, lasting from about ages 7 to 12, children can think logically about events and objects but are not able to reason abstractly. (p. 58)

25. **Attachment** refers to the process by which young children develop closeness to a caregiver. (p. 60)

26. A **critical period** is a limited time during which an organism must be exposed to certain experiences or influences if it is to develop properly. (p. 61)

27. **Imprinting** is the process by which certain animals form attachments early in life, usually during a limited critical period. (p. 61)

28. **Temperament** refers to the rudiments of personality and a child's characteristic emotional excitability. Temperament is a trait that is strongly linked to heredity. (p. 61)

29. According to Erikson, **basic trust** is a sense that the world is predictable and trustworthy—a concept that infants form if their needs are met by responsive caregiving. (p. 63)

30. **Gender** is the social category of male or female. (p. 64)

31. **Adolescence** refers to the life stage from puberty to young adulthood, denoted physically by a growth spurt and maturation of primary and secondary sex characteristics, cognitively by the onset of formal operational thought, and socially by the formation of identity. (p. 66)

32. **Puberty** is the early adolescent period marked by accelerated growth and by sexual maturation. (p. 67)

33. The **primary sex characteristics** are the body organs that enable reproduction. (p. 67)

34. The **secondary sex characteristics** are the nonreproductive sexual characteristics—for example, female breasts, male voice change, and body hair. (p. 67)

35. **Menarche** is the first menstrual period. (p. 67)

36. In Piaget's theory the **formal operational stage** begins at about age 12 and is the period during which logical reasoning about abstract concepts becomes possible. (p. 68)

37. In Erikson's theory, **identity**, or establishing a sense of self, is the primary task of adolescence. (p. 71)

38. In Erikson's theory, **intimacy**, or the ability to establish close relationships, is the primary task of early adulthood. (p. 72)

39. **Menopause** is the cessation of menstruation and typically occurs in the early fifties. (p. 74)

40. **Alzheimer's disease** is an irreversible brain disorder caused by deterioration in neurons that produce acetylcholine. It is characterized by a progressive loss of memory and general cognitive function. (p. 75)

41. In a **cross-sectional study**, people of different ages are tested at the same time. (p. 76)

42. In a **longitudinal study** the same people are tested and retested over a period of years. (p. 76)

    Memory aid: A **longitudinal study** takes a *long* time to complete because the same people are followed for many years.

43. **Crystallized intelligence** refers to those aspects of intellectual ability, such as vocabulary and general information, that reflect accumulated learning. Crystallized intelligence tends to increase with age. (p. 77)

44. **Fluid intelligence** refers to a person's ability to reason abstractly. Fluid intelligence tends to decline with age. (p. 77)

45. The **social clock** refers to the culturally preferred timing of life events, such as leaving home, marrying, having children, and retiring. (p. 78)

46. In Erikson's theory, **generativity**, or the sense of contributing and being productive through work or child rearing, is the task of middle adulthood. (p. 79)

Memory aid: To "generate" is to create or produce. Parents and workers achieve generativity through their children and their jobs.

47. A **hospice** is an organization that provides support for the terminally ill and for their families. (p. 81)

48. The **nature-nurture issue** is the long-standing debate over the relative importance of heredity (nature) and experience (nurture) in determining psychological traits. (p. 82)

49. **Identical twins** develop from a single fertilized egg that splits in two and are therefore genetically identical. (p. 83)

50. **Fraternal twins** develop from two separate eggs fertilized by different sperm and therefore are no more genetically similar than ordinary siblings. (p. 83)

51. An **interaction** occurs when two factors work together to produce an effect that neither factor would produce by itself. (p. 85)

Chapter 4 | Sensation and Perception

Chapter Overview

Sensation refers to the process by which stimuli are detected and encoded. This chapter describes the senses of vision, hearing, taste, touch, smell, kinesthesis, and equilibrium. It also explores the ways in which we organize and interpret our sensations into meaningful perceptions.

There are many terms and theories to learn in this chapter. Many of the terms are related to the structure of the eye, ear, and other sensory receptors. Doing the chapter review several times, labeling the diagrams, and rehearsing what you have learned frequently will help you to memorize the structures of these receptors and their functions.

The last two sections of the chapter deal with important issues. The first is the relative roles of experience and heredity in perception. Make sure you understand the results of studies of recovery from blindness, early sensory restriction, adaptation to distorted environments, and perceptual set. The second issue concerns ESP, or perception without sensation. You should be able to discuss both the claims made for ESP and the criticisms of those claims.

Guided Study

The textbook chapter should be studied one section at a time. Before you read, preview each section by skimming it, noting headings and boldface items. Then read the appropriate section objectives from the following outline. Keep these objectives in mind and, as you read the chapter section, search for the information that will enable you to meet each objective. Once you have finished a section, write out answers for its objectives.

1. Contrast the processes of sensation and perception.

Sensing the World: Some Basic Principles
(pp. 92–96)

2. Distinguish between absolute and difference thresholds and discuss research findings on subliminal stimulation.

3. Describe the phenomenon of sensory adaptation and show how it focuses our attention on changing stimulation.

Vision (pp. 97–103)

4. Explain the visual process, including the stimulus input, the structure of the eye, and how the eye transforms light energy into neural activity.

5. Discuss the different levels of visual information processing.

6. Discuss how both the Young-Helmholtz theory and the opponent-process theory contribute to our understanding of color vision.

The Other Senses (pp. 104–111)

7. Explain the auditory process, including the stimulus input, the structure of the ear, and the way sounds are located.

8. Describe the sense of touch and explain the basis of pain.

9. Describe the senses of taste, smell, kinesthesis, and equilibrium. Comment on the nature of sensory interaction.

Perceptual Organization (pp. 111–120)

10. Discuss Gestalt psychology's contribution to our understanding of perception.

11. Explain the figure-ground relationship and identify principles of perceptual grouping in form perception.

12. Discuss research on depth perception involving the use of the visual cliff and describe some of the binocular and monocular cues involved in depth perception.

13. Describe the perceptual constancies and show how they operate in visual illusions.

Interpretation (pp. 120–124)

14. Describe the nativism-empiricism debate on the nature of perception.

15. Discuss research findings on sensory restriction and restored vision.

16. Explain what the use of distorting goggles indicates regarding the adaptability of perception.

17. Discuss the effects of perceptual set and context on our perceptions.

Is There Perception Without Sensation?
(pp. 124–128)

18. State the claims of ESP and explain why most research psychologists remain skeptical.

Chapter Review

When you have finished reading the chapter, use the material that follows to review it. Complete the sentences and answer the questions. As you proceed, evaluate your performance for each chapter section by consulting the answer key at the end of this chapter. Do not continue with the next section until you've understood each answer. If you need to, go back and review or reread the appropriate chapter section in the textbook before continuing.

1. The process by which a stimulus is detected and encoded is _____. The active mental process by which sensations are organized and interpreted is _____.

Sensing the World: Some Basic Principles
(pp. 92–96)

2. The _____ _____ refers to the minimum amount of stimulation necessary for a stimulus to be detected _____ percent of the time.

3. Some people claim to have learned material as a result of exposure to "below threshold," or _____, stimuli, but their claims are probably unwarranted.

4. Some weak stimuli may trigger in our sense receptors a response that is processed by the brain even though the response doesn't cross the threshold into _____ awareness.

5. The minimum difference required to distinguish two stimuli 50 percent of the time is called the

_____ _____.

Another term for this value is the

_____ _____

_____.

6. The principle that the difference threshold is not a constant amount, but a constant percentage, is known as _____ _____.

7. After constant exposure to a stimulus, the receptor cells of our senses begin to fire less vigorously; this phenomenon is called

_____ _____.

Explain why sensory adaptation is beneficial.

Vision (pp. 97–103)

8. Our sensory system converts light energy into
_____ activity.

9. The visible spectrum of light is a small portion
of the larger spectrum of _____
waves.

10. The distance from one light wave peak to the
next is called _____. This
value determines the wave's color, or
_____.

11. The amount of energy, or _____,
determines the _____ of a light.

Label each part of the eye numbered in the diagram
below.

12. _____
13. _____
14. _____
15. _____
16. _____
17. _____

18. Light enters the eye through a small opening
called the _____; the size of
this opening is controlled by the colored
_____.

19. By changing its curvature, the _____
can focus the image of an object onto the
_____, which lines the back of
the eyeball.

20. The process by which the lens changes shape to
focus light is called _____.

21. The retina's receptor cells are the
_____ and _____.

22. From the rods and cones the neural signals pass
to the neighboring _____ cells,
then to a network of _____
cells. The ganglion cells converge to form the
_____ _____,
which carries the visual information to the
_____.

23. Where this nerve leaves the eye, there are no
receptors; thus the area is called the
_____ _____.

24. Unlike cones, in dim light the rods are
_____ (sensitive/insensitive).
Adapting to a darkened room will take the retina
approximately _____ minutes.

25. Hubel and Wiesel discovered that certain neurons
in the _____ _____ of
the brain respond only to specific features of
what is viewed. They called these neurons
_____ _____.

Summarize the steps involved in visual information
processing.

26. That color deficiency is genetically sex-linked is
indicated by the fact that it occurs most often in
_____ (males/females).

27. According to the Young-Helmholtz trichromatic
theory, the eyes have three color receptors: one
reacts most strongly to _____,
one to _____, and one to
_____.

Explain how, according to the trichromatic (three-color) theory, we perceive a color such as yellow, for which the retina has no "yellow cone."

28. After staring at a green square for a while, you will see the color _____, its _____ color.

29. Hering's theory of color vision is called the

   _____-_____

   theory. According to this theory, after visual information leaves the receptors it is analyzed in terms of pairs of opposing colors:

   _____ versus _____,

   and _____ versus

   _____.

Summarize the two stages of color processing.

The Other Senses (pp. 104–111)

30. The tendency of vision to dominate the other senses is referred to as _____

   _____.

31. The stimulus for hearing, or _____, is sound waves, created by changes in

   _____ _____.

32. The height, or _____, of a sound wave determines the sound's

   _____.

33. The pitch of a sound is derived from the length, and therefore the _____, of its wave.

34. The ear is divided into three main parts: the

   _____ ear, the _____

   ear, and the _____ ear.

35. The outer ear channels sound waves toward the

_____, a membrane that then vibrates.

36. The middle ear amplifies the sound via the vibrations of three small bones: the

   _____, _____,

   and _____.

37. In the inner ear a coiled tube called the

   _____ contains the receptor cells for hearing.

38. We detect the location of sounds on the basis of slight differences in _____ experienced by our two ears.

39. The sense of touch is a mixture of at least four senses: _____, _____,

   _____, and _____.

40. A sensation of pain in an amputated leg is referred to as a _____

   _____ sensation.

41. The pain system _____ (is/is not) triggered by one specific type of physical energy. The body _____ (does/does not) have specialized receptor cells for pain.

42. Melzack and Wall have proposed a theory of pain called the _____-

   _____ theory. This theory proposes that there is a neurological

   _____ in the _____

   _____ that blocks pain signals or lets them through. It may be opened by activation of _____ (small/large) nerve fibers and closed by activation of _____ (small/large) nerve fibers.

43. Pain can also stimulate the release of painkilling substances called _____.

List some pain control techniques used in the Lamaze method of prepared childbirth.

44. The four basic taste sensations are

    _____, _____,

    _____, and _____.

45. The _____ of the tongue tends
    to be especially sensitive to sweet and salty
    sensations, the _____ of the
    tongue to bitter sensations.

46. When the sense of smell is blocked, as when we
    have a cold, foods do not taste the same; this
    illustrates the principle of _____

    _____.

47. Like taste, smell is a _____
    sense. Unlike light, an odor _____
    (can/cannot) be separated into more elemental
    odors.

48. The system for sensing the position and
    movement of body parts is called
    _____. The receptors for this
    sense are located in the _____,

    _____, and _____

    of the body.

49. The sense that monitors the movement of the
    whole body is _____. The
    receptors for this sense are located in the
    _____ canals and

    _____ _____

    of the ear.

Perceptual Organization (pp. 111–120)

50. According to the _____ school
    of psychology, we tend to organize separate
    sensations into a meaningful form. This tendency
    can be illustrated using a figure called a
    _____ cube.

51. When we view a scene, we see the central
    object, or _____, as distinct
    from surrounding stimuli, or the

    _____.

Identify the major contributions of Gestalt psychology
to our understanding of perception.

52. Proximity, similarity, closure, and continuity are
    examples of Gestalt rules of _____.

53. The principle that we organize stimuli into
    smooth, continuous patterns is called
    _____. The principle that we
    fill in gaps to create a complete, whole object is
    _____. The grouping of items
    that are close to each other is the principle of
    _____; the grouping of items
    that look alike is the principle of

    _____.

54. The ability to see objects in three dimensions
    despite their two-dimensional representations on
    our retinas is called _____

    _____.

55. Gibson and Walk developed the

    _____ _____

    to test depth perception in infants.

Summarize the results of Gibson and Walk's studies of
depth perception.

For questions 56–64, identify the depth perception cue
that is defined.

56. Any cue that requires both eyes:

    _____

57. Any cue that requires only one eye:

    _____

58. The greater the difference between the images
    received by the two eyes, the nearer the object:

    _____ _____

59. The more our eyes focus inward when we view

an object, the nearer the object:

_____

60. If two objects are presumed to be the same size, the one that casts a smaller retinal image is perceived as farther away: _____

_____

61. An object partially covered by another is seen as farther away: _____

62. Objects lower in the visual field are seen as nearer: _____ _____

63. Parallel lines appear to converge in the distance:

_____ _____

64. Dimmer objects seem farther away:

_____ _____

65. Our tendency to see objects as unchanging in size, shape, and brightness is called

_____ _____.

66. Several illusions, including the moon and Müller-Lyer illusions, are explained by the interplay between perceived _____ and perceived _____. When distance cues are removed, these illusions are _____ (diminished/ strengthened).

Explain how the size-distance relationship accounts for the moon illusion.

67. When your view is restricted to only part of a familiar object, the object's color may seem to vary with the light that shines upon it. This shows that _____ constancy depends on the _____ in which an object is viewed.

Interpretation (pp. 120–124)

68. The idea that knowledge comes from innate ways of organizing sensory experiences was proposed by the philosophical school called

_____. One philosopher of this school was _____.

69. On the other side were philosophers who maintained that we learn to perceive the world by experiencing it. These philosophers were the _____. One philosopher of this school was _____.

70. Studies of cases in which vision has been restored to a person who was blind from birth show that, upon *seeing* tactilely familiar objects for the first time, the person _____ (can/cannot) recognize them.

71. Studies of sensory restriction demonstrate that visual experiences during _____ are crucial for perceptual development. Such experiences suggest that there is a

_____ _____

for normal perceptual development.

72. Humans given glasses that shift or invert the visual field _____ (will/will not) adapt to the distorted perception.

73. A mental predisposition that influences perception is called a _____

_____.

74. Another factor that influences the perceptual response to a given stimulus is its immediate

_____.

Is There Perception Without Sensation?
(pp. 124–128)

75. Perception outside the range of normal sensation is called _____ _____.

76. Psychologists who study ESP are called

_____.

77. The form of ESP in which people claim to be capable of reading others' minds is called _____. A person who "senses" that a friend is in danger might claim to have the ESP ability of _____. An ability to "see" into the future is called

_____.

78. A person who claims to be able to levitate and move objects is claiming the power of

_____.

79. When the clairvoyance experiment conducted by Layton and Turnbull was repeated, the results of both experiments were nearly identical to what one would expect on the basis of

_____.

Explain why scientists are skeptical about ESP.

FOCUS ON PSYCHOLOGY:
Psychological Factors in Perception

As the Gestalt psychologists were fond of saying, "The whole is greater than the sum of its parts." Applying this statement to perception we can say that there is much more to perception than the stimulus information to which our senses are exposed. Perception is highly individualistic and influenced by experience, attitudes, and many other psychological factors.

One such factor, according to psychologist Paul Chance, is motivation. Several studies have shown that people are more likely to perceive ambiguous drawings as food when they are hungry than when they have recently eaten. This comes as no surprise to dieters, who "see" calorie-laden foods around every corner and in nearly every object.

Chance offers a convincing demonstration of how learnnig also influences what we see. In reading the previous sentence you probably were a victim of the "proofreader's illusion" and did not notice the misspelled word. Your retinas cannot be blamed for your insensitivity to this typographical error; rather, your knowledge of grammar caused you to see the word spelled correctly.

Our beliefs and biases also affect our perception. In another famous experiment, researchers showed pictures to groups of police officers, police cadets, and college students. One half of each picture depicted an act of violence, such as a person holding a smoldering gun standing over an apparent victim lying on the ground. The other half was a nonviolent scene, such as a landscape or a person from a college yearbook. After each picture was flashed on a screen for a very brief period, the subjects were asked to describe what they saw. Although college students were about equally likely to report seeing the violent and nonviolent scenes, the police cadets—and even more so, the vet-

eran police officers—were much more likely to report seeing the violent scenes.

Chance also offers a chilling, real-life example of the apparent operation of psychological factors in perception. On July 3, 1988, a United States naval warship shot down a civilian aircraft, resulting in the deaths of 290 people. Although the radar screen, which later functioned perfectly, showed that the aircraft was climbing as if it were taking off, the sailors apparently "saw" the plane descending, as if it were attacking their ship. As Chance notes, "What we see . . . also depends upon what we know, or think we know, about people. . . . Seeing is believing."

Source: Chance, Paul (1989, January-February). Seeing is believing. *Psychology Today*, p. 26.

Progress Test 1
Multiple-Choice Questions

Circle your answers to the following questions and check them with the answer key at the end of this chapter. If your answer is incorrect, read the answer key explanation for why it is incorrect and then consult the appropriate pages of the text to understand the correct answer.

1. The absolute threshold for a stimulus is the minimum amount of stimulation necessary for the stimulus to:
   a. trigger a receptor response.
   b. be detected 50 percent of the time.
   c. be detected 75 percent of the time.
   d. be detected 60 percent of the time.

2. Stimuli that are too weak to cross the threshold for conscious awareness:
   a. cannot be processed at all.
   b. will not be processed by the brain.
   c. may trigger a small response in the sense receptors.
   d. may disrupt our concentration on stimuli of which we *are* aware.

3. If you can just notice the difference between 10- and 11-pound weights, which of the following weights could you differentiate from a 100-pound weight?
   a. 101-pound weight.
   b. 105-pound weight.
   c. 110-pound weight.
   d. There is no basis for prediction.

4. The size of the pupil is controlled by the:
   a. lens.   c. cornea.
   b. retina.   d. iris.

5. The process by which the lens changes its curvature is:
   a. accommodation.   c. focusing.
   b. sensory adaptation. d. transduction.

6. The receptor of the eye that functions best in dim light is the:
   a. ganglion cell.   c. cone.
   b. rod.   d. bipolar cell.

7. The Young-Helmholtz theory proposes that:
   a. there are three different types of color-sensitive cones.
   b. retinal cells are excited by one color and inhibited by its complementary color.
   c. there are four different types of cones.
   d. rods, not cones, account for the best vision in daylight.

8. The receptors for hearing are located:
   a. in the outer ear.
   b. in the middle ear.
   c. in the inner ear.
   d. throughout the ear.

9. According to the gate-control theory, a way to alleviate pain would be to stimulate the _____ nerve fibers that _____ the spinal gate.
   a. small; open   c. large; open
   b. small; close   d. large; close

10. The conversion of light energy into nerve impulses takes place in the:
    a. iris.   c. lens.
    b. retina.   d. optic nerve.

11. You are shopping for a new stereo and discover that you cannot hear any difference between models A and C. The difference between A and C is below your:
    a. absolute threshold.   c. receptor threshold.
    b. subliminal threshold. d. difference threshold.

12. Kinesthesis involves:
    a. the bones of the middle ear.
    b. information from the muscles, tendons, and joints.
    c. membranes within the cochlea.
    d. the body's sense of balance.

13. If one light appears reddish and another greenish, the reason is that they differ in:
    a. wavelength.   c. frequency.
    b. intensity.   d. opponent processes.

14. Which of the following is an example of sensory adaptation?
    a. finding the cold water of a swimming pool warmer after you have been in it for a while

b. developing an increased sensitivity to salt the more you use it on foods
    c. becoming very irritated at the continuing sound of a dripping faucet
    d. all of the above

15. A person who is color deficient will probably:
    a. be male.
    b. be unable to tell any colors apart.
    c. also suffer from poor vision.
    d. have sharper vision to compensate for the deficit.

16. Which theory of perception holds that knowledge comes from innate ways of organizing our sensory experiences?
    a. behaviorist   c. empiricist
    b. nativist   d. Gestalt

17. The historical movement associated with the statement "The whole is different from the sum of its parts" is:
    a. parapsychology.
    b. behavioral psychology.
    c. functional psychology.
    d. Gestalt psychology.

18. Figures tend to be perceived as whole, complete objects, even if spaces or gaps exist in their representation, thus demonstrating the principle of:
    a. closure.   c. continuity.
    b. similarity.   d. proximity.

19. The figure-ground relationship demonstrates that:
    a. perception is largely innate.
    b. perception is simply a point-for-point representation of sensation.
    c. the same stimulus can trigger more than one perception.
    d. different people see different things when viewing a scene.

20. When we stare at an object, each of our eyes receives a slightly different image, providing a depth cue known as:
    a. convergence.   c. overlap.
    b. linear perspective. d. retinal disparity.

21. As we move, viewed objects cast changing shapes on our retinas, although we do not perceive the objects as changing. This is part of the phenomenon of:
    a. perceptual constancy. c. linear perspective.
    b. sensory interaction. d. continuity.

22. Which of the following illustrates the principle of visual capture?
    a. We tend to form first impressions of other people on the basis of appearance.

b. Because visual processing is automatic, we can pay attention to a visual image and any other sensation at the same time.

c. We cannot simultaneously attend to a visual image and another sensation.

d. When there is a conflict between visual information and that from another sense, vision tends to dominate.

23. A person claiming to be able to read another's mind is claiming to have the ESP ability of:

a. psychokinesis.   c. clairvoyance.
b. precognition.   d. telepathy.

24. Congenitally blind adults who have had their vision restored:

a. are almost immediately able to recognize familiar objects.

b. typically fail to recognize familiar objects.

c. are unable to follow moving objects with their eyes.

d. have excellent eye-hand coordination.

25. Studies with the visual cliff have provided evidence that much of depth perception is:

a. innate.
b. learned.
c. innate in lower animals but learned in humans.
d. innate in humans but learned in lower animals.

26. Which of the following is *not* a monocular depth cue?

a. relative size   c. retinal disparity
b. relative height   d. linear perspective

27. The moon illusion occurs in part because distance cues at the horizon make the moon seem:

a. farther away and therefore larger.
b. closer and therefore larger.
c. farther away and therefore smaller.
d. closer and therefore smaller.

28. Figure is to ground as _____ is to _____ .

a. night; day   c. cloud; sky
b. top; bottom   d. sensation; perception

29. The fact that newly hatched chicks, day-old kittens, and the young of other animals are able to perceive depth serves to support the _____ school of thought.

a. empiricist   c. Gestalt
b. nativist   d. behaviorist

30. Although carpenter Smith perceived a briefly viewed object as a screwdriver, police officer Wesson perceived the same object as a knife. This illustrates that perception is guided by:

a. linear perspective.   c. retinal disparity.
b. shape constancy.   d. perceptual set.

31. Jack claims that he often has dreams that predict future events. He claims to have the power of:

a. telepathy.   c. precognition.
b. clairvoyance.   d. psychokinesis.

32. In their experiment on _____ , Layton and Turnbull asked students to guess the contents of a sealed envelope.

a. telepathy   c. precognition
b. clairvoyance   d. psychokinesis

Matching Items

Match each of the structures with its function.

Structures

_____ 1. lens
_____ 2. iris
_____ 3. pupil
_____ 4. rods
_____ 5. cones
_____ 6. middle ear
_____ 7. inner ear
_____ 8. tip of tongue
_____ 9. back of tongue
_____ 10. semicircular canals
_____ 11. sensors in joints

Functions

a. amplifies sound
b. sweet receptors
c. equilibrium sense
d. controls pupil
e. accommodation
f. kinesthetic sense
g. sour receptors
h. admits light
i. color vision
j. vision in dim light
k. transformation of sound

Progress Test 2

Progress Test 2 should be completed during a final chapter review. Do this test after you thoroughly understand the correct answers for the Chapter Review and Progress Test 1.

Multiple-Choice Questions

1. Of the four distinct skin senses, the only one that has definable receptors is:
   a. warmth.   c. pressure.
   b. cold.   d. pain.

2. The inner ear contains receptors for:
   a. audition and kinesthesis.
   b. kinesthesis and equilibrium.
   c. audition and equilibrium.
   d. audition, kinesthesis, and equilibrium.

3. According to the opponent-process theory:
   a. there are three types of color-sensitive cones.
   b. the process of color vision begins in the cortex.
   c. neurons involved in color vision are stimulated by one color's wavelengths and inhibited by another.
   d. all of the above are true.

4. What enables you to feel yourself wiggling your toes even with your eyes closed?
   a. sense of equilibrium
   b. sense of kinesthesis
   c. the skin senses
   d. sensory interaction

5. Hubel and Wiesel discovered feature detectors in the _____ of a monkey's visual system.
   a. retina   c. iris
   b. optic nerve   d. cortex

6. Weber's law states that:
   a. the absolute threshold for any stimulus is a constant.
   b. the jnd for any stimulus is a constant.
   c. the absolute threshold for any stimulus is a constant percentage.
   d. the jnd for any stimulus is a constant percentage.

7. In the opponent-process theory, the three pairs of processes are:
   a. red-green, blue-yellow, black-white.
   b. red-blue, green-yellow, black-white.
   c. red-yellow, blue-green, black-white.
   d. dependent on the individual's past experience.

8. Concerning the evidence for subliminal stimulation, which of the following is the best answer?

   a. The brain processes some information without our awareness.
   b. Stimuli too weak to cross our thresholds for awareness may trigger a response in our sense receptors.
   c. Because the "absolute" threshold is a statistical average, we are able to detect weaker stimuli some of the time.
   d. All of the above are true.

9. Which of the following is the most accurate description of how we process color?
   a. Throughout the visual system, color processing is divided into separate red, green, and blue systems.
   b. Throughout the visual system, red-green, blue-yellow, and black-white opponent processes operate.
   c. Color processing occurs in two stages: (1) a three-color system in the retina and (2) opponent-process cells en route to the visual cortex.
   d. Color processing occurs in two stages: (1) an opponent-process system in the retina and (2) a three-color system en route to the visual cortex.

10. While competing in the Olympic trials, marathoner Kirsten O'Brien suffered a stress fracture in her left leg. That she did not experience significant pain until the race was over is probably attributable to the fact that during the race:
    a. the pain gate in her spinal cord was closed by information coming from her brain.
    b. her body's production of endorphins decreased.
    c. an increase in the activity of small-diameter pain fibers closed the pain gate.
    d. a decrease in the activity of large-diameter pain fibers closed the pain gate.

11. According to the _____ view, we learn to perceive the world.
    a. behaviorist   c. empiricist
    b. nativist   d. Gestalt

12. The tendency to organize stimuli into smooth, uninterrupted patterns is called:
    a. closure.   c. similarity.
    b. continuity.   d. proximity.

13. Which of the following is a monocular depth cue?
    a. relative size
    b. convergence
    c. retinal disparity
    d. All of the above are monocular depth cues.

14. Experiments with distorted visual environments demonstrate that:
    a. adaptation rarely takes place.
    b. animals adapt readily, but humans do not.

c. humans adapt readily, while lower animals typically do not.

d. adaptation is possible during a critical period in infancy but not thereafter.

15. The phenomenon that refers to the ways in which an individual's expectations influence perception is called:

a. perceptual set.   c. convergence.

b. binocular disparity.   d. visual capture.

16. The phenomenon of size constancy is based upon the close connection between an object's perceived _____ and its perceived _____.

a. size; shape   c. size; brightness

b. size; distance   d. shape; distance

17. Which of the following statements best describes the effects of sensory restriction?

a. It produces functional blindness when experienced for any length of time at any age.

b. It has greater effects on humans than on animals.

c. It has more damaging effects when experienced during infancy.

d. It has greater effects on adults than on children.

18. Psychologists who study ESP are called:

a. clairvoyants.   c. parapsychologists.

b. telepaths.   d. levitators.

19. Which of the following statements concerning ESP is true?

a. Most ESP researchers are quacks.

b. There have been a large number of reliable demonstrations of ESP.

c. Most research psychologists are skeptical of the claims of defenders of ESP.

d. There have been reliable laboratory demonstrations of ESP, but the results are no different from those that would occur by chance.

20. Each time you see your car, it projects a different image on the retinas of your eyes, yet you do not perceive it as changing. This is because of:

a. perceptual set.   c. perceptual constancy.

b. retinal disparity.   d. convergence.

21. The term *gestalt* means:

a. grouping.   c. perception.

b. sensation.   d. whole.

22. The fact that a white object under dim illumination appears lighter than a gray object under bright illumination is called:

a. relative luminance.

b. perceptual adaptation.

c. color contrast.

d. brightness constancy.

23. When two familiar objects of equal size cast unequal retinal images, the object that casts the smaller retinal image will be perceived as being:

a. closer than the other object.

b. more distant than the other object.

c. larger than the other object.

d. smaller than the other object.

Labeling

Label the parts of the eye numbered in the diagram at right.

1. _____

2. _____

3. _____

4. _____

5. _____

6. _____

7. _____

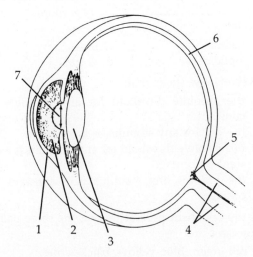

Label the parts of the ear numbered in the diagram at right.

1. _____
2. _____
3. _____
4. _____
5. _____
6. _____
7. _____
8. _____

Key Terms

Using your own words, write a brief definition or explanation of each of the following terms.

1. sensation

2. perception

3. absolute threshold

4. subliminal

5. difference threshold (jnd)

6. Weber's law

7. sensory adaptation

8. wavelength (hue)

9. intensity (brightness)

10. pupil

11. iris

12. lens

13. accommodation

14. retina

15. rods and cones

16. optic nerve

17. blind spot

18. feature detectors

19. Young-Helmholtz trichromatic (three-color) theory

20. opponent-process theory

21. visual capture

22. audition

23. amplitude (loudness)

24. frequency (pitch)

25. middle ear

26. inner ear

27. cochlea

28. gate-control theory

29. sensory interaction

30. kinesthesis

31. equilibrium

32. gestalt

33. figure-ground relationship

34. grouping

35. proximity

36. similarity

37. continuity

38. closure

39. depth perception

40. visual cliff

41. binocular cue

42. monocular cue

43. retinal disparity

44. convergence

45. relative size

46. overlap

47. relative height

48. linear perspective

49. relative brightness

50. shape constancy

51. size constancy

52. brightness constancy

53. color constancy

54. nativism

55. empiricism

56. perceptual adaptation

57. perceptual set

58. extrasensory perception (ESP)

59. parapsychology

Answers

CHAPTER REVIEW

1. sensation; perception
2. absolute threshold; 50
3. subliminal
4. conscious
5. difference threshold; just noticeable difference
6. Weber's law
7. sensory adaptation

Although sensory adaptation reduces our sensitivity, it enables us to focus our attention on informative changes in the environment without being distracted by the uninformative, constant stimulation that bombards our senses.

8. neural
9. electromagnetic
10. wavelength; hue
11. intensity; brightness
12. pupil
13. iris
14. lens
15. retina
16. blind spot
17. optic nerve
18. pupil; iris
19. lens; retina
20. accommodation
21. rods; cones
22. bipolar; ganglion; optic nerve; brain
23. blind spot
24. sensitive; 20
25. visual cortex; feature detectors

Visual information processing begins when light reaches the retina. As we view a scene, the rods and cones of the retina transform the reflected light into neural impulses that are sent to the brain via the optic nerve. In the brain, feature detectors break the image into bars, edges, gradients of light, and other elementary features. Higher-level brain cells reassemble the features into the perceived image.

26. males

27. red; green; blue

The Young-Helmholtz theory suggests that although the retina has only receptors that are sensitive to red, green, and blue, when combinations of these receptors are stimulated, other colors are perceived. In the case of yellow, red- and green-sensitive receptors are stimulated.

28. red; opponent

29. opponent-process; red; green; yellow; blue

If the first stage of color processing, the retina's red, green, and blue cones respond in varying degrees to different color stimuli, as suggested by the three-color theory. The resulting signals are then processed by red-green, blue-yellow, and black-white opponent-process cells, which are stimulated by one wavelength and inhibited by its complement.

30. visual capture

31. audition; air pressure

32. amplitude; loudness

33. frequency

34. outer; middle; inner

35. eardrum

36. hammer; anvil; stirrup

37. cochlea

38. intensity (or loudness)

39. pressure; warmth; cold; pain

40. phantom limb

41. is not; does not

42. gate-control; gate; spinal cord; small; large

43. endorphins

The Lamaze method of prepared childbirth combines several pain control techniques, including distraction, deep breathing and muscle relaxation, and counter-stimulation through gentle massage.

44. sweet; sour; salty; bitter

45. tip; back

46. sensory interaction

47. chemical; cannot

48. kinesthesis; muscles; tendons; joints

49. equilibrium; semicircular; vestibular sacs

50. Gestalt; Necker

51. figure; ground

The Gestalt psychologists described some key principles of perceptual organization and, in so doing, demonstrated that perception is far more than a simple, sensory process. The reversible figure-ground relationship, for example, demonstrates that a single stimulus can trigger more than one perception. As Gestalt psychologists showed, we continually filter sensory information and construct our perceptions in ways that make sense to us.

52. grouping or perceptual organization

53. continuity; closure; proximity; similarity

54. depth perception

55. visual cliff

Research on the visual cliff suggests that in many species the ability to perceive depth is present at, or very shortly after, birth.

56. binocular

57. monocular

58. retinal disparity

59. convergence

60. relative size

61. overlap

62. relative height

63. linear perspective

64. relative brightness

65. perceptual constancy

66. size; distance; diminished

A partial reason for the illusion that the moon at the horizon appears up to 50 percent larger than the moon directly overhead is that cues to the distance of objects at the horizon make the moon, behind them, seem farther away and therefore larger. When we see the moon overhead in the sky, these misleading cues are lacking.

67. color; context

68. nativism; Kant

69. empiricists; Locke

70. cannot

71. infancy; critical period

72. will

73. perceptual set

74. context

75. extrasensory perception

76. parapsychologists

77. telepathy; clairvoyance; precognition

78. psychokinesis

79. chance

Skeptics of ESP point out that gullible audiences are easily duped into believing that stage tricks and illusions are examples of psychic powers. Scientists are especially skeptical of the existence of ESP because of the lack of a reliable, reproducible ESP effect.

PROGRESS TEST 1

Multiple-Choice Questions

1. **b.** is the answer. (p. 93)

    a. The absolute threshold is a threshold of *awareness*. Stimuli too weak to cross this threshold may nevertheless trigger a response in our sensory receptors.

    c. & d. The absolute threshold is defined as the minimum stimulus that is detected *50 percent* of the time.

2. **c.** is the answer. It appears that stimuli too weak to cross the threshold for conscious awareness may trigger a small response in sense receptors and even, in this way, be processed by the brain. But as shown by researchers' skepticism of subliminal persuasion, there is no evidence that such stimuli overpower stimuli of which we *are* consciously aware. (pp. 93–94)

3. **c.** is the answer. According to Weber's law, the difference threshold is a constant proportion of the stimulus. There is a 10 percent difference threshold between 10 and 11 pounds; since the difference threshold is a constant proportion, the weight closest to 100 pounds that can nonetheless be differentiated from it is 110 pounds (or 100 pounds plus 10 percent). (pp. 94–95)

4. **d.** is the answer. (p. 98)

    a. The lens lies behind the pupil and focuses light on the retina.

    b. The retina lies at the back of the eyeball and contains the rods and cones.

    c. The cornea lies in front of the pupil and is the first structure that light passes through as it enters the eye.

5. **a.** is the answer. (p. 98)

    b. Sensory adaptation is our diminishing sensitivity to an unchanging stimulus

    c. Focusing is the process through which light converges onto the retina as a sharp image. The image is focused *because* the lens accommodates its shape.

    d. Transduction refers to the conversion of an environmental stimulus, such as light, into a nerve impulse by a receptor—a rod or a cone.

6. **b.** is the answer. (p. 99)

    a. The ganglion cells are not receptors; they converge into the optic nerve.

    c. Cones have a higher threshold for brightness than rods and therefore do not function as well in dim light.

    d. Bipolar cells are not receptors; they are neurons in the retina that link rods and cones with ganglion cells, which make up the optic nerve.

7. **a.** is the answer. The Young-Helmholtz theory proposes that there are red-, green-, and blue-sensitive cones. (p. 102)

    b. This answer describes Hering's opponent-process theory.

    c. The Young-Helmholtz theory proposes that there are *three* types of cones, not four.

    d. The Young-Helmholtz theory concerns only color vision, not sharpness of vision.

8. **c.** is the answer. The receptors for hearing—those cells that transform sound energy into neural impulses—are the hair cells lining the basilar membrane of the inner ear. (p. 105)

9. **d.** is the answer. The small fibers conduct most pain signals; the large fibers conduct most other sensory signals from the skin. The gate either allows pain signals to pass on to the brain or blocks them from passing. When the large fibers are stimulated, the pain gate is closed and other sensations are felt in place of pain. (p. 107)

10. **b.** is the answer. (p. 99)

    a. The iris controls the diameter of the pupil.

    c. The lens accommodates its shape to focus images on the retina.

    d. The optic nerve carries nerve impulses from the retina to the visual cortex.

11. **d.** is the answer. (p. 94)

    a. The absolute threshold refers to whether a single stimulus can be detected, not to whether two stimuli can be differentiated.

    b. If a stimulus is subliminal, it is by definition below the threshold of awareness. "Subliminal threshold" is therefore a meaningless term.

    c. A receptor threshold is the minimum amount of energy that will elicit a nerve impulse in a receptor cell.

12. **b.** is the answer. Kinesthesis, or the sense of the position and movement of body parts, is based on information from the muscles, tendons, and joints. (p. 110)

    a. & c. The ear and its parts play no role in kinesthesis.

    d. Equilibrium, or the sense of balance, is not involved in kinesthesis but is, rather, a companion sense.

13. **a.** is the answer. Wavelength determines hue, or color. (p. 97)

    b. The intensity of light determines the brightness of the color.

c. Frequency helps characterize the stimulus for hearing, not for vision.

d. Opponent processes are neural systems involved in color vision, not properties of light.

14. **a.** is the answer. Sensory adaptation means a diminishing sensitivity to an unchanging stimulus. Only the adjustment to cold water involves a decrease in sensitivity; the other examples involve an *increase*. (p. 95)

15. **a.** is the answer. Color deficiency is genetically sex-linked. (p. 101)

b. Those who are color deficient are usually not "color blind" in a literal sense. Instead, they lack functioning red or green cones and have difficulty discriminating between these two colors.

c. & d. Color deficiency does not enhance or impair visual sharpness. A deficit in one sense often is compensated for by overdevelopment of another sense, for example, hearing in blind people.

16. **b.** is the answer. (p. 120)

a. & c. Behaviorists and empiricists both hold that knowledge is not innate but comes through learning.

d. Gestalt psychology made no claims about the source of knowledge.

17. **d.** is the answer. Gestalt psychology, which developed in Germany at the turn of the century, was interested in how clusters of sensations are organized into "whole" perceptions. (p. 111)

a. Parapsychology is the study of ESP and other paranormal phenomena.

b. & c. Behavioral and functional psychology were schools that developed later in the United States.

18. **a.** is the answer. (p. 112)

b. Similarity refers to the tendency to group similar items.

c. Continuity refers to the tendency to group stimuli into smooth, continuous patterns.

d. Proximity refers to the tendency to group items that are close to each other.

19. **c.** is the answer. Although we always differentiate a stimulus into figure and ground, which elements of the stimulus we perceive as figure and which as ground may change. In this way, the same stimulus can trigger more than one perception. (p. 112)

a. The figure-ground relationship has no bearing on the issue of whether perception is innate.

b. Perception cannot be simply a point-for-point representation of sensation, since, in figure-ground relationships, a single stimulus can trigger more than one perception.

d. Figure-ground relationships demonstrate the existence of general, rather than individual, principles of perceptual organization. Significantly, even the same person can see different figure-ground relationships when viewing a scene.

20. **d.** is the answer. The more the retinal disparity, or difference between the images, the less the distance. (p. 114)

a. Convergence is the extent to which the eyes move inward when looking at an object.

b. Linear perspective is the monocular distance cue in which parallel lines appear to converge in the distance.

c. Overlap is the partial blocking of a distant object by one nearer to the viewer.

21. **a.** is the answer. Perception of constant shape, like perception of constant size, is part of the phenomenon of perceptual constancy. (p. 116)

b. Sensory interaction is the principle that one sense may be influenced by another.

c. Linear perspective is a monocular distance cue in which lines we know to be parallel appear to converge in the distance, thus indicating depth.

d. Continuity is the perceptual tendency to group items into continuous patterns.

22. **d.** is the answer. (p. 104)

a., b., & c. Visual capture has nothing to do with forming impressions of people or whether we can attend to more than one stimulus at a time.

23. **d.** is the answer. (p. 125)

a. Psychokinesis refers to the claimed ability to perform acts of "mind over matter."

b. Precognition refers to the claimed ability to perceive future events.

c. Clairvoyance refers to the claimed ability to perceive remote events.

24. **b.** is the answer. Because they have not had early visual experiences, these adults typically have great difficulty learning to perceive objects. (p. 121)

a. Such patients typically could not visually recognize objects with which they were familiar by touch, and in some cases this inability persisted.

c. Being able to perceive figure-ground relationships, patients *are* able to follow moving objects with their eyes.

d. This answer is incorrect because eye-hand coordination is an acquired skill and requires much practice.

25. **a.** is the answer. Human infants and the newborn of other species alike refuse to go over a "visual cliff," which suggests that depth perception is innate. (p. 113)

b. If depth perception were learned, newborn animals would be willing to go over an apparent cliff, but as the studies show, they are not.

c. & d. The studies indicate that depth perception is at least partially innate in *both* humans and lower animals.

26. **c.** is the answer. Retinal disparity is a *binocular* cue; all the other cues mentioned are monocular. (pp. 114–115)

27. **a.** is the answer. The moon appears larger at the horizon than overhead in the sky because objects at the horizon provide distance cues that make the moon seem farther away and therefore larger. In the open sky, of course, there are no such cues. (p. 117)

28. **c.** is the answer. We see a cloud as a figure against the background of sky. (p. 112)

    a., b., & d. The figure-ground relationship refers to the organization of the visual field into objects (figures) that stand out from their surroundings (ground).

29. **b.** is the answer. The nativists stressed the innateness of aspects of perception. (p. 120)

    a. The empiricist position, that knowledge comes from experience in interacting with the environment, is not consistent with the ability of newborn animals to perceive depth.

    c. & d. The Gestalt and behaviorist schools of thought have no positions regarding the origins of depth perception.

30. **d.** is the answer. The two people interpreted a briefly perceived object in terms of their perceptual sets, or mental predispositions, in this case conditioned by their work experiences. (pp. 122–123)

    a. Since both Smith and Wesson had the same sensory experience of the object, linear perspective cues would not distinguish their perceptions.

    b. Shape constancy refers to the perception that objects remain constant in shape even when their retinal image changes with viewing angle.

    c. Retinal disparity refers to the fact that each of a person's eyes views the world from a slightly different angle; it has nothing to do with individual differences in perception.

31. **c.** is the answer. (p. 125)

    a. This answer would be correct had Jack claimed to be able to read someone else's mind.

    b. This answer would be correct had Jack claimed to be able to sense remote events, such as a friend in distress.

    d. This answer would be correct had Jack claimed to be able to levitate objects or bend spoons without applying any physical force.

32. **b.** is the answer. As the contents of the envelope were not presented to the senses, the experiment involved clairvoyance. (p. 125)

    a. The experiment involved written numerals, not thoughts.

    c. The experiment did not require students to "see the future."

    d. The experiment had nothing to do with the mental manipulation of matter.

Matching Items

1. e (p. 98)
2. d (p. 98)
3. h (p. 98)
4. j (pp. 99–100)
5. i (pp. 99–100)
6. a (p. 105)
7. k (p. 105)
8. b (p. 108)
9. g (p. 108)
10. c (p. 110)
11. f (p. 110)

PROGRESS TEST 2

Multiple-Choice Questions

1. **c.** is the answer. Researchers have identified receptors for pressure but have been unable to do so for the other skin senses. (p. 106)

2. **c.** is the answer. The inner ear contains the receptors for audition (hearing) and equilibrium; those for kinesthesis are located in the muscles, tendons, and joints. (pp. 105–110)

3. **c.** is the answer. After leaving the receptor cells, visual information is analyzed in terms of pairs of opponent colors; neurons stimulated by one member of a pair are inhibited by the other. (p. 103)

    a. The idea that there are three types of color-sensitive cones is the basis of the Young-Helmholtz three-color theory.

    b. According to the opponent-process theory, and all other theories of color vision, the process of color vision begins in the retina.

4. **b.** is the answer. Kinesthesis, the sense of movement of body parts, would enable you to feel your toes wiggling. (p. 110)

    a. Equilibrium is concerned with movement and position, or balance, of the whole body, not of its parts.

    c. The skin, or tactile, senses are pressure, pain, warmth, and cold; they have nothing to do with movement of body parts.

    d. Sensory interaction, the principle that the senses influence each other, does not play a role in this example, which involves only the sense of kinesthesis.

5. **d.** is the answer. Feature detectors are cortical neurons and hence are located in the visual cortex. (p. 101)

a. The retina contains the rods and cones.

b. The optic nerve contains neurons that relay nerve impulses from the retina to higher centers in the visual system.

c. The iris is simply a ring of muscle tissue, which controls the diameter of the pupil.

6. **d.** is the answer. Weber's law concerns difference thresholds (jnd), not absolute thresholds, and states that these are constant proportions of the stimuli, not that they remain constant. (p. 95)

7. **a.** is the answer. The three pairs of processes, which are biologically determined and the same in all people, are red-green, blue-yellow, and black-white. (p. 103)

8. **d.** is the answer. (pp. 93–94)

9. **c.** is the answer. (pp. 102–103)

a. This answer is incorrect because separate red, green, and blue systems operate only in the retina.

b. This answer is incorrect because opponent-process systems operate en route to the brain, after visual processing in the receptors is completed.

d. This answer is incorrect because it reverses the correct order of the two stages of processing.

10. **a.** is the answer. (p. 107)

b. Since endorphins relieve pain, had their production decreased during the race, the marathoner would have been more likely to experience pain. Moreover, as they are released in response to pain, their production would probably have *increased*.

c. Neural activity in small-diameter fibers tends to *open* the pain gate.

d. An *increase* in large-fiber activity would tend to close the pain gate.

11. **c.** is the answer. (p. 120)

a. & d. The behaviorist and Gestalt views make no claims about the origins of perception.

b. Nativists claim that knowledge is innate.

12. **b.** is the answer. (p. 112)

a. Closure refers to the tendency to perceptually fill in gaps in recognizable objects in the visual field.

c. Similarity refers to the tendency to group items that are similar.

d. Proximity refers to the tendency to group items that are near one another.

13. **a.** is the answer. (p. 114)

b., c., & d. Convergence and retinal disparity are both binocular cues that depend on information from both eyes.

14. **c.** is the answer. Humans and certain animals, such as monkeys, are able to adjust to upside-down worlds and other visual distortions, figuring out the relationship between the perceived and the actual reality; lower animals, such as chickens and fish, are typically unable to adapt. (pp. 121–122)

a. Humans and certain animals are able to adapt quite well to distorted visual environments (and then to readapt).

b. This answer is incorrect because humans are the *most* adaptable of creatures.

d. Humans are able to adapt at any age to distorted visual environments.

15. **a.** is the answer. (pp. 122–123)

b. Binocular, or retinal, disparity is a depth cue, based on the fact that each eye receives a slightly different view of the world.

c. Convergence is the binocular depth cue based on the fact that the eyes swing inward to focus on nearby objects.

d. Visual capture refers to the tendency of vision to dominate the other senses.

16. **b.** is the answer. (p. 116)

17. **c.** is the answer. There appears to be a critical period for perceptual development, in that sensory restriction has severe, even permanently, disruptive effects when it occurs in infancy but not when it occurs later in life. (p. 121)

a. & d. Sensory restriction does not have the same effects at all ages, and it is more damaging to children than to adults. This is because there is a critical period for perceptual development, and whether functional blindness will result depends in part on the nature of the sensory restriction.

b. Research studies have not indicated that sensory restriction is more damaging to humans than to animals.

18. **c.** is the answer. (p. 124)

a., b., & d. These are different kinds of psychics, who claim to exhibit the phenomena studied by parapsychologists.

19. **c.** is the answer. (pp. 124–125)

a. Many ESP researchers are sincere, reputable researchers.

b. & d. There have been no reliable demonstrations of ESP.

20. **c.** is the answer. Because of perceptual constancy, we see the car's shape and size as always the same. (p. 116)

a. Perceptual set is a mental predisposition to perceive one thing and not another.

b. Retinal disparity refers to the fact that our right and left eyes each receive slightly different images.

d. Convergence is a form of muscular feedback in which the eyes swing in, or out, as we view objects at different distances.

21. **d.** is the answer. *Gestalt* means "form" or "organized whole." (p. 111)

22. **d.** is the answer. Although the amount of light reflected from a white object is less in dim light than in bright light—and may be less than the amount of light reflected from a brightly lit gray object—the brightness of the white object is perceived as remaining constant. Because a white object reflects a higher percentage of the light falling on it than does a gray object, and the brightness of objects is perceived as constant despite variations in illumination, white is perceived as brighter than gray even under dim illumination. (p. 118)

a. Relative illuminance refers to the relative intensity of light falling on surfaces that are in close proximity. Brightness constancy is perceived despite variations in illumination.

b. Perceptual adaptation refers to the ability to adjust to an artificially modified perceptual environment, such as an inverted visual field.

c. Color contrast has not been discussed in this text.

23. **b.** is the answer. The phenomenon described is the basis for the monocular cue of relative size. (p. 114)

a. The object casting the *larger* retinal image would be perceived as closer.

c. & d. Because of size constancy, familiar objects remain constant in perceived size, despite changes in their retinal image size.

Labeling

Eye Diagram (pp. 98)

1. cornea
2. iris
3. lens
4. optic nerve
5. blind spot
6. retina
7. pupil

Ear Diagram (p. 105)

1. outer ear
2. middle ear
3. inner ear
4. auditory nerve
5. cochlea
6. semicircular canal
7. eardrum
8. auditory canal

KEY TERMS

1. **Sensation** is the process by which stimulus energies such as light, sound, taste, touch, and smell are detected and encoded. (p. 91)

2. **Perception** is the process by which the brain organizes and interprets sensory information. (p. 91)

3. The **absolute threshold** is the minimum-intensity stimulus that can be detected 50 percent of the time. (p. 93)

4. A stimulus that is **subliminal** is one that is below the threshold of awareness. (p. 93)

Memory aid: *Limen* is the Latin word for "threshold." A stimulus that is **subliminal** is one that is *sub-* ("below") the *limen*, or threshold.

5. The **difference threshold**, or **just noticeable difference (jnd)**, is the minimum difference in two stimuli that a subject can detect 50 percent of the time. (p. 94)

Example: Because trained musicians can hear very small differences in tones, they have lower **difference thresholds** for tones than do nonmusicians.

6. **Weber's law** states that the just noticeable difference between two stimuli is a constant minimum percentage. (p. 94)

Example: If a difference of 10 percent in weight is noticeable, **Weber's law** predicts that a person could discriminate 10- and 11-pound weights or 50- and 55-pound weights.

7. **Sensory adaptation** refers to the decreased sensitivity that occurs with continued exposure to an unchanging stimulus. (pp. 94–95)

Example: When she left the steamy parking lot and first entered the air-conditioned shopping mall, Janice felt unbearably cold. After a few minutes she felt comfortable—**sensory adaptation** had taken place.

8. **Wavelength**, which refers to the length of light waves, gives rise to the perceptual experience of **hue**, or color. (p. 97)

Example: The visible spectrum consists of electromagnetic energy ranging between **wavelengths** of about 350 and 750 nanometers.

9. The **intensity** of light is determined by the amplitude of the waves and is experienced as **brightness**. (p. 97)

10. The **pupil** is the adjustable opening in the eye through which light enters. (p. 98)

11. The **iris** is the colored part of the eye that controls the diameter of the pupil. (p. 98)

Example: Persons with light-colored eyes have **irises** that are less effective than those of darker-colored eyes in preventing light from entering the eye. As a result, they often find bright light more painful.

12. The **lens** is the structure of the eye behind the pupil that changes shape to focus images on the retina. (p. 98)

13. **Accommodation** is the process by which the lens

of the eye changes shape to focus near or distant objects on the retina. (p. 98)

Memory aid: To **accommodate** is to change in order to adapt to a new experience. The lens of the eye accommodates its shape in order to focus objects at varying distances.

14. The **retina** is the multilayered inner surface of the eye that contains the rods and cones, as well as neurons that form the beginning of the optic nerve. (p. 98)

15. The **rods and cones** are visual receptors that transform light into nerve impulses. The rods detect black and white and function well in dim light. The cones enable color vision and function best in daylight or bright light. (p. 99)

Example: Further evidence of the function of **rods and cones** comes from the study of nocturnal animals, which possess only rods, and diurnal animals, which possess only cones.

16. Comprised of the axons of retinal ganglion cells, the **optic nerve** carries neural impulses from the eye to the brain. (p. 99)

Example: At the optic chiasma, half the **optic nerve** fibers from each eye cross over to the opposite side, so information from the left and right visual fields projects directly to the right and left sides of the brain, respectively.

17. The **blind spot** is the region of the retina where the optic nerve leaves the eye. Because there are no rods or cones in this area, this is a spot where the eye is visually insensitive. (p. 99)

Example: The fact that we are unaware of our **blind spots** indicates that the brain must perceptually "fill in" the missing visual detail.

18. **Feature detectors**, located in the visual cortex of the brain, are nerve cells that selectively respond to specific visual features, such as movement, shape, or angle. Feature detectors are evidently the basis of visual information processing. (p. 101)

19. The **Young-Helmholtz trichromatic (three-color) theory** maintains that the retina contains red-, green-, and blue-sensitive color receptors that in combination can produce the perception of any color. This theory explains the first stage of color processing. (p. 102)

20. The **opponent-process theory** maintains that color vision depends on pairs of opposing retinal processes (red-green, yellow-blue, and white-black). This theory explains the second stage of color processing. (p. 103)

21. **Visual capture** is the tendency for vision to dominate other senses. (p. 104)

22. **Audition** refers to the sense of hearing. (p. 104)

Memory aid: An **audition** is a trial *hearing* of an actress, musician, or some other performer.

23. **Amplitude** is the maximum height of a wave; it determines the loudness of a sound wave and the brightness of a light wave. (p. 104)

24. The **pitch** of a sound is determined by its **frequency**, that is, the number of complete wavelengths that can pass a point in a given time. Frequency, in turn, is directly related to wavelength: Longer waves produce lower pitch; shorter waves produce higher pitch. (p. 104)

25. The **middle ear** is the air-filled chamber between the eardrum and cochlea containing the three bones (hammer, anvil, and stirrup) that direct the eardrum's vibrations into the inner ear. (p. 105)

Example: The "pop" that you feel in your ears when ascending or descending in an airplane occurs when the air pressure in the **middle ear** becomes equalized to the external pressure on your eardrums.

26. The **inner ear** contains the cochlea, the semicircular canals, and the receptors that transform sound energy into nerve impulses. Because it also contains the vestibular sacs, the inner ear plays an important role in balance, as well as in audition. (p. 105)

27. The **cochlea** is the coiled, fluid-filled tube of the inner ear where the transformation of sound waves into nerve impulses occurs. (p. 105)

28. The **gate-control theory** maintains that a "gate" in the spinal cord determines whether pain signals are permitted to reach the brain. When the neural activity in large nerve fibers exceeds that in smaller fibers, or when the brain so dictates, the gate is closed. (p. 107)

Example: The **gate-control theory** gained support with the discovery of endorphins. Production of these morphine-like chemicals may be the brain's mechanism for closing the spinal gate.

29. **Sensory interaction** is the principle that one sense may influence another. (p. 109)

Example: There is considerable **sensory interaction** between taste and smell. Food tastes bland when you have a cold and cannot savor aromas.

30. **Kinesthesis** is the sense of the position and movement of the parts of the body. (p. 110)

Example: In performing their intricate exercises, gymnasts rely extensively on **kinesthetic** feedback from sensory receptors in their muscles, tendons, and joints.

31. The sense of body movement, position, and balance is called **equilibrium**. (p. 110)

32. **Gestalt** means "organized whole." The Gestalt

psychologists emphasized our tendency to integrate sensory impressions into meaningful perceptions. (p. 111)

33. The **figure-ground relationship** refers to the organization of the visual field into two parts: the figure, which stands out from its surroundings, and the surroundings, or back*ground*. (p. 112)

    Example: Sometimes **figure-ground relationships** are ambiguous, so that what is first perceived as figure is then perceived as ground, and vice versa.

34. **Grouping** is the process by which we associate stimuli together in order to arrive at meaningful forms. Gestalt psychologists identified various principles of grouping. (p. 112)

35. **Proximity** is the Gestalt principle that we tend to group together sensory stimuli that are near one another. (p. 112)

    Example: The **proximity** of individual notes in a piece of music leads to the perception of measures and other musical groupings based on intervals of time.

36. **Similarity** is the Gestalt principle that we tend to group together sensory stimuli that are similar. The basis for the similarity may be appearance, size, color, or any of many other dimensions. (p. 112)

37. The Gestalt principle of **continuity** is the perceptual tendency to group stimuli into smooth, continuous patterns. (p. 112)

38. **Closure** is the perceptual tendency to fill in incomplete figures to create the perception of a whole object, as identified by the Gestalt psychologists. (p. 112)

39. **Depth perception** is the ability to create three-dimensional perceptions from the two-dimensional images that strike the retina. (p. 113)

40. The **visual cliff** is a laboratory device for testing depth perception, especially in infants and animals. In their experiments with the visual cliff, Gibson and Walk found strong evidence that depth perception is at least in part innate. (p. 113)

41. **Binocular cues** are depth cues that depend on information from both eyes. (p. 114)

    Memory aid: Bi- indicates "two"; *ocular* means something pertaining to the eye. **Binocular cues** are cues for the "two eyes."

42. **Monocular cues** are depth cues that depend on information from only one eye. (p. 114)

    Memory aid: Mono- means one; a monocle is an eyeglass for one eye. A **monocular cue** is one that is available to either the left or the right eye.

43. **Retinal disparity** refers to the differences between the images received by the left eye and the right as a result of viewing the world from slightly different angles. It is a binocular depth cue, since the greater the difference between the two images, the nearer the object. (p. 114)

    Example: A forerunner of the 3-D movie, the stereoscope is an optical instrument that presents slightly different images of the same scene to the two eyes. The **retinal disparity** that results imparts a three-dimensional effect.

44. **Convergence** is a binocular depth cue based on the extent to which the eyes *converge*, or turn inward, when looking at near or distant objects. The more the eyes converge, the nearer the objects. (p. 114)

45. **Relative size** is a monocular depth cue; when two objects are presumed to be the same size, the one producing the smaller retinal image is judged more distant. (p. 114)

    Example: As you stare at a person walking away from you, the **relative size** of the image their body projects onto your retinas decreases.

46. **Overlap** is a monocular depth cue; nearby objects often partially obscure more distant objects. (p. 114)

47. A monocular cue for depth, **relative height** refers to our tendency to perceive higher objects as more distant. (p. 115)

    Example: Before the development of perspective in art, artisans indicated distance by the **relative height** of an object in the visual plane.

48. A monocular depth cue, **linear perspective** refers to our tendency to perceive the apparent convergence of parallel lines as indicating increasing distance. (p. 115)

49. A monocular depth cue, **relative brightness** refers to our tendency to perceive brighter objects as closer and dimmer objects as more distant. (p. 115)

50. **Shape constancy** is the tendency to perceive objects as remaining constant in shape despite changes in the shapes of their retinal images. (p. 116)

51. **Size constancy** is the tendency to perceive an object as remaining the same size despite changes in the size of its retinal image. (p. 116)

    Example: Because of **size constancy**, when the retinal image of an airplane grows smaller, we perceive the size of the object as remaining the same and its distance as increasing.

52. **Brightness constancy** is our tendency to perceive the brightness of an object as constant despite variations in its illumination. (p. 118)

    Example: As the sun passed from behind a cloud, the hood of Brenda's car suddenly glowed brightly; if not for **brightness constancy**, she would have feared the engine was about to explode!

53. **Color constancy** is the perceptual tendency to perceive the color of an object as constant despite variations in illumination. (p. 119)

54. **Nativism** is the theory that practically all functions of the organism, including mental and perceptual ones, are inherited. (p. 120)

    Memory aid: <u>Nativ</u>ist philosophers, such as Immanuel Kant, maintain that knowledge comes from our *in<u>nate</u>* ways of interpreting sensory experiences.

55. **Empiricism** is the theory that all knowledge originates in experience. In contrast to the nativist view, empiricists maintain that perceptions are learned through experience. (p. 120)

56. **Perceptual adaptation** refers to our ability to adapt to visual distortions. Given distorting lenses, we perceive things accordingly, but soon adjust by learning the relationship between our distorted perceptions and the reality. (p. 121)

57. **Perceptual set** is a mental predisposition to perceive the environment in a particular way. (p. 122)

    Example: When police officers and college students were shown ambiguous scenes, their different **perceptual sets** were indicated by the greater tendency of the officers to perceive violence in the images.

58. **Extrasensory perception (ESP)** refers to perception that occurs without sensory input. Supposed ESP powers include telepathy, clairvoyance, and precognition. (p. 124)

    Memory aid: *Extra-* means "beyond" or "in addition to"; **extrasensory perception** is perception outside or beyond the normal senses.

59. **Parapsychology** is the study of ESP, psychokinesis, and other paranormal forms of interaction between the individual and the environment. (p. 124)

    Memory aid: *Para-*, like *extra-*, indicates "beyond"; thus, *paranormal* is beyond the normal and **parapsychology** is the study of phenomena beyond the realm of psychology and known natural laws.

Chapter 5 | States of Consciousness

Chapter Overview

Consciousness—a focused awareness of perceptions, thoughts, and feelings—can be experienced in various states. Chapter 5 examines not only waking consciousness, but also covers daydreaming, sleep and dreaming, hypnosis, and drug-altered states.

Most of the terminology in this chapter is introduced in the sections on Sleep and Dreams and on Drugs and Consciousness. Among the issues discussed in the chapter are why we sleep and dream, whether hypnosis is a unique state of consciousness, and possible psychological and social roots of drug use.

Guided Study

The textbook chapter should be studied one section at a time. Before you read, preview each section by skimming it, noting headings and boldface items. Then read the appropriate section objectives from the following outline. Keep these objectives in mind and, as you read the chapter section, search for the information that will enable you to meet each objective. Once you have finished a section, write out answers for its objectives.

Studying Consciousness (pp. 133–134)

1. Discuss the nature of consciousness and its significance in the history of psychology.

Daydreams and Fantasies (pp. 135–136)

2. Discuss the content and potential functions of daydreams, fantasies, and meditation.

Sleep and Dreams (pp. 136–144)

3. Describe the cyclical nature and possible functions of sleep.

4. Identify major sleep disorders.

5. Discuss the possible functions of dreams.

Hypnosis (pp. 144–150)

6. Discuss hypnosis and describe the behavior of hypnotized people.

7. Discuss the controversy over whether hypnosis is an altered state of consciousness.

Drugs and Consciousness (pp. 150–157)

8. Describe the physiological and psychological effects of specific drugs and discuss the factors that contribute to their use.

Chapter Review

When you have finished reading the chapter, use the material that follows to review it. Complete the sentences and answer the questions. As you proceed, evaluate your performance for each chapter section by consulting the answer key at the end of this chapter. Do not continue with the next section until you've understood each answer. If you need to, go back and review or reread the appropriate chapter section in the textbook before continuing.

Studying Consciousness (pp. 133–134)

1. The study of _____ was central in the early years of psychology and in recent decades, but for quite some time it was displaced by the study of observable _____.

Define consciousness in a sentence.

2. At any moment our conscious attention is focused on only a very limited aspect of all the sensory stimuli present; this indicates that our attention is _____.

3. The ability to attend selectively to one voice among many is referred to as the

_____ _____

effect. We _____ (can/cannot) react to stimuli that have not been consciously perceived.

4. In comparison with unconscious processing, conscious processing has a(n)

_____ (limited/unlimited)

capacity, is relatively _____ (fast/slow), and processes information

_____ (simultaneously/in

sequence).

Daydreams and Fantasies (pp. 135–136)

5. Most people _____ (do/do not) daydream every day. Compared to older adults, young adults spend _____ (more/less) time daydreaming. About 4 percent of the population has such vivid fantasies and daydreams that they are referred to as

_____-_____

personalities.

Explain why some psychologists consider daydreaming to be adaptive.

6. A relaxed state of awareness that is more focused than daydreaming is _____.

Sleep and Dreams (pp. 136–144)

7. The sleep-waking cycle follows a 24-hour clock called the _____ _____.

8. The rhythm of sleep cycles was discovered when Aserinksy noticed that, at periodic intervals during the night, the _____ of a sleeping child moved rapidly.

9. The relatively slow brain waves of the awake but relaxed state are known as _____ waves.

Describe Stage 1 sleep.

10. Rhythmic bursts of brain-wave activity that occur during Stage 2 sleep are termed

_____ _____.

In Stage 2, a person clearly _____ (is/is not) asleep.

11. Large, slow brain waves are called _____ waves. These predominate during Stage _____ sleep. A person in this stage of sleep generally will be _____ (easy/difficult) to awaken. It is during this stage that people may engage in sleep _____ and sleep _____.

Describe the bodily changes that accompany REM sleep.

12. During REM sleep, the motor cortex is _____ (active/relaxed), while the muscles are _____ (active/relaxed). For this reason, REM is often referred to as _____ sleep.

13. The rapid eye movements generally signal the beginning of _____.

14. The sleep cycle repeats itself about every _____ minutes. As the night progresses, Stage 4 sleep becomes _____ (longer/briefer) and REM periods become _____ (longer/briefer). Approximately _____ percent of a night's sleep is spent in REM sleep.

Describe the effects of sleep deprivation.

15. Studies have indicated that, after strenuous exercise, we tend to sleep for longer periods and to increase our Stage _____ sleep.

16. During sleep a growth hormone is released by the _____ gland. Adults sleep _____ (more/less) than children and so release _____ (more/less) growth hormone.

17. Newborns spend about _____ of their time asleep; elderly people, only about _____.

18. Webb and Campbell found that the sleep patterns of identical twins were similar, suggesting a possible _____ basis for individual differences in sleep habits.

19. A recurring difficulty in falling asleep is characteristic of _____. Sleeping pills and alcohol may make the problem worse since they tend to _____ (increase/reduce) REM sleep.

20. The sleep disorder in which a person experiences uncontrollable sleep attacks is _____.

21. Individuals suffering from _____ stop breathing while sleeping.

22. The sleep disorder characterized by extreme fright and rapid heartbeat and breathing is called

    _____ _____.

    Unlike nightmares, these episodes usually happen early in the night, during Stage _____ sleep.

23. The genital arousal that typically occurs during REM sleep usually _____ (does/does not) reflect a sexual dream.

24. Freud referred to the actual content of a dream as its _____ content. Freud believed that this is a censored version of the true meaning, or _____ _____, of the dream.

    According to Freud, most of the dreams of adults reflect _____ wishes.

25. A second theory of dreams is that they serve a(n) _____-processing function. Support for this theory is provided by the fact that, after intense learning experiences, _____ (REM/Stage 4) sleep tends to increase.

26. Other theories propose that dreaming serves some _____ function, for example, that REM sleep provides the brain with needed _____. Such an explanation is supported by the fact that _____ (infants/adults) spend the most time in REM sleep.

27. Yet other theories propose that dreams are elicited by _____ activity originating in lower regions of the brain, such as the _____.

28. REM sleep _____ (does/does not) occur in other mammals.

29. After being deprived of REM sleep, a person spends more time in REM sleep; this is the

    _____ _____ effect.

Hypnosis (pp. 144–150)

30. The suggestion that a person forget things that occurred while he or she was under hypnosis may produce _____

    _____.

31. Most people are _____ (somewhat/not at all) hypnotically suggestible.

32. The hypnotic demonstration in which a subject supposedly relives earlier experiences is referred to as _____ _____. Research studies show that the subjects in such demonstrations have memories that are _____ (more/no more) accurate than the memories of fully conscious persons.

33. Hypnotherapists have helped some people diet and quit smoking through the use of _____ suggestions.

34. One theory of hypnotic pain relief is that hypnosis separates, or _____, the sensory and emotional aspects of pain. Another is that hypnotic pain relief is due to selective _____, that is, to the person's focusing on stimuli other than pain.

Summarize the argument that hypnosis is not an altered state of consciousness.

35. Hilgard has advanced the idea that during hypnosis there is a _____, or split, between different levels of consciousness.

Drugs and Consciousness (pp. 150–157)

36. Drugs that alter moods and perceptions are called _____ drugs.

37. Drug users who require increasing doses to experience a drug's effects have developed _____ for the drug.

38. If a person begins experiencing withdrawal symptoms after ceasing to use a drug, the person has developed a physical _____. Regular use of a drug to relieve stress is an

example of a _____
dependence.

39. The three broad categories of drugs discussed in the textbook include _____, which tend to slow body functions; _____, which speed body functions; and _____, which alter perception. These drugs all work by mimicking or affecting the activity of the brain's _____.

40. Low doses of alcohol, which is classified as a _____, slow the activity of the _____ nervous system. Alcohol also affects memory by interfering with the process of transferring experiences into _____-_____ memory.

Describe how a person's expectations can influence the behavioral effects of alcohol.

41. Tranquilizers, or _____ drugs, tend to _____ (excite/depress) activity in the sympathetic nervous system.

42. Opium, morphine, and heroin all _____ (excite/depress) neural functioning. Together, these drugs are called the _____. When they are present, the brain eventually stops producing _____.

43. The most widely used stimulants are _____, _____, _____, and _____. Stimulants _____ (are/are not) habit forming.

44. The importance of a user's expectations on the effect of a drug is indicated by the fact that users often cannot distinguish actual drugs from chemically inert drugs called _____.

45. Hallucinogens are also referred to as _____. Two common synthetic hallucinogens are _____ and _____.

46. The reports of people who have had near-death experiences are very similar to the _____ reported by drug users. These experiences may be the result of a deficient supply of _____ or other traumas to the brain.

47. The active ingredient in marijuana is abbreviated _____. Marijuana has been used therapeutically with those who suffer from _____ and cancer.

Describe some of the physical and psychological effects of marijuana.

48. Tolerance and withdrawal may be explained in part by the principle that emotions trigger _____ _____.

Identify some of the psychological and social roots of drug use.

FOCUS ON PSYCHOLOGY:
Cycles of Craving in Drug Abuse

Drug experts are generally cautious in identifying historical trends in the use of specific drugs. Harvard psychiatrist Norman Zinberg, after studying drug-abuse patterns in the United States for the past quarter century, contends, however, that society's drug of choice has shifted four times: LSD and other hallucinogens dominated the early 1960s, marijuana took over through the late 1960s, heroin was the most popular drug during the early 1970s, and today cocaine leads the way. Zinberg believes that drugs become popular when they do because they fit the public mood. "Cocaine became the drug of the '80s because it's a stimulant. People were looking for action," says the psychiatrist.

Experts are less reluctant to specify patterns of drug use. For example, they all agree that drug use typically begins with more affluent individuals looking for a new thrill, filters down into the middle classes, and finally reaches the lower socioeconomic groups. Cocaine use in the 1980s provides a good example of this pattern. Researchers noted the social class of all callers to 1-800-COCAINE, a national hot line for abusers of the powerful stimulant. In 1983, more than half the calls came from college-educated individuals with incomes of at least $25,000; by 1987, fewer than 20 percent of the calls were from this group.

Experts also agree that certain categories of drugs tend to be abused simultaneously. Cocaine abusers, for example, often use an opiate such as heroin to counteract the stimulating effects of cocaine. Officials at the United States Drug Enforcement Agency were not surprised to find that both cocaine- and heroin-related deaths increased dramatically between 1984 and 1988. This pattern of drug use may best be explained in terms of the opposing physiological effects of certain psychoactive drugs on the nervous system.

David Musto, a medical historian at Yale University, has observed another, more positive trend over the past decade: a growing public intolerance toward illegal drugs that has led to decreased drug use by the middle class. Musto attributes this trend largely to society's outrage at the epidemic abuse of "crack," a smokable, relatively inexpensive yet highly addictive form of cocaine, which "created a consensus in society against drugs and ended the ambivalence that had been prevalent for decades."

And what does the future hold? Historian Musto is concerned that drug abuse is being swept under the historical carpet in the American educational system. For example, the California school system recently revised its syllabus for teaching American history. In the revised syllabus the history of drug abuse is not mentioned. Musto fears that "a society that forgets its history of abuse is doomed to repeat it." If children are made to read the devastating effects of the widespread abuse of cocaine during the 1920s and the 1980s, they might avoid the mistakes of earlier generations.

One thing is clear: the problem of drug abuse has many biological, social, and psychological roots, each of which must be understood before the problem can be solved. As Zinberg and Musto make clear, social and historical trends in drug abuse offer important insights into these roots. Failing to understand and remember our history may bring us into yet another orbit within the vicious cycle of drug abuse.

Source: Hurley, D. (1989, August). Cycles of craving. *Psychology Today*, 54–60.

Progress Test 1

Multiple-Choice Questions

Circle your answers to the following questions and check them with the answer key at the end of this chapter. If your answer is incorrect, read the answer key explanation for why it is incorrect and then consult the appropriate pages of the text to understand the correct answer.

1. As defined by the text, consciousness includes which of the following?
   a. daydreaming
   b. sleeping
   c. hypnosis
   d. all of the above

2. Which of the following groups tends to daydream the most?
   a. elderly men
   b. elderly women
   c. middle-aged adults
   d. young adults

3. Sleep spindles predominate during which stage of sleep?
   a. Stage 2
   b. Stage 3
   c. Stage 4
   d. REM sleep

4. During which stage of sleep does the body experience increased heart rate, rapid breathing, and genital arousal?
   a. Stage 2
   b. Stage 3
   c. Stage 4
   d. REM sleep

5. The duration of the sleep cycle is approximately _____ minutes.
   a. 30
   b. 50
   c. 75
   d. 90

6. Sleep deprivation typically leads to:
   a. disruption of muscular coordination.
   b. hallucinations and other abnormal conditions.
   c. moments of inattention on monotonous tasks.
   d. all of the above.

7. One effect of sleeping pills is to:
   a. depress REM sleep.
   b. increase REM sleep.
   c. depress Stage 2 sleep.
   d. increase Stage 2 sleep.

8. A person who falls asleep in the midst of a heated argument probably suffers from:
   a. sleep apnea.
   b. narcolepsy.
   c. night terrors.
   d. insomnia.

9. Which of the following is classified as a depressant?
   a. amphetamines
   b. LSD
   c. marijuana
   d. alcohol

10. Which of the following statements concerning hypnosis is true?
    a. People will do anything under hypnosis.
    b. Hypnosis is the same as sleeping.
    c. Hypnosis is not associated with a distinct physiological state.
    d. Hypnosis has very little effect on pain.

11. The cocktail party effect refers to:
    a. the effects of random noise on a person's perception of low pitches.
    b. the effects of random noise on a person's mood.
    c. the ability to attend selectively to one stimulus.
    d. the cumulative effect of multiple uses of a depressant drug.

12. According to Freud, dreams are:
    a. a symbolic fulfillment of erotic wishes.
    b. the result of random neural activity in the brain stem.
    c. the brain's mechanism for self-stimulation.
    d. transparent representations of the individual's conflicts.

13. Psychoactive drugs affect behavior and perception through:
    a. the power of suggestion.
    b. the placebo effect.
    c. alteration of neural activity in the brain.
    d. psychological, rather than physiological, influences.

14. When students closely attended to a prose passage presented to one ear:
    a. they failed to notice, and were unaffected by, simple tunes played to the other ear.
    b. they were able to divide their attention and comprehend both the prose passage and a simple message presented to the other ear.
    c. they were able to divide their attention and comprehend both the prose passage and a message presented to the other ear, but only if the two messages were spoken by different people.
    d. they later were unable to recognize simple tunes played to the other ear, but preferred them to tunes they had not heard before.

15. As a child, Jane enjoyed intense make-believe play with dolls, stuffed animals, and imaginary companions. As an adult she spends an unusually large amount of time fantasizing. Sometimes she's uncertain whether something occurred in her life or just in her fantasies. A psychologist would most likely describe Jane as:
    a. highly suggestible.
    b. fantasy prone.
    c. a daydreamer.
    d. a dissociator.

16. REM sleep is referred to as "paradoxical sleep" because:
    a. studies of people deprived of REM sleep indicate that REM sleep is unnecessary.
    b. the body's muscles remain relaxed while the brain and eyes are active.
    c. it is very easy to awaken a person from REM sleep.
    d. the body's muscles are very tense while the brain is in a nearly meditative state.

17. An attorney wants to know if the details and accuracy of an eyewitness's memory for a crime would be improved under hypnosis. Based on the results of relevant research, what should you tell the attorney?
    a. Most hypnotically retrieved memories are combinations of fact and fiction.
    b. Hypnotically retrieved memories are usually more accurate than conscious memories.
    c. Hypnotically retrieved memories are purely the product of the subject's imagination.
    d. Hypnosis only improves memory of anxiety-provoking childhood events.

18. Dan has recently begun using an addictive euphoria-producing drug. Which of the following will probably occur if he repeatedly uses this drug?
    a. As tolerance to the drug develops, Dan will experience increasingly pleasurable "highs."
    b. The dosage needed to produce the desired effect will decrease.
    c. The depression he feels during withdrawal from the drug will get stronger.
    d. All of the above will probably occur.

Matching Items

Match each term with its appropriate definition or description.

Definitions

———— 1. surface meaning of dreams
———— 2. deeper meaning of dreams
———— 3. stage of sleep associated with delta waves
———— 4. stage of sleep associated with muscular relaxation
———— 5. relaxed state in which attention may be focused on a particular word or phrase
———— 6. sleep disorder occurring in Stage 4 sleep
———— 7. depressant
———— 8. hallucinogen
———— 9. stimulant
———— 10. twilight stage of sleep associated with imagery resembling hallucinations
———— 11. inert substance
———— 12. sleep disorder in which breathing stops

Terms

a. marijuana
b. alcohol
c. Stage 1 sleep
d. night terrors
e. manifest content
f. cocaine
g. placebo
h. sleep apnea
i. Stages 3 and 4 sleep
j. REM sleep
k. latent content
l. meditation

Progress Test 2

Progress Test 2 should be completed during a final chapter review. Do this test after you thoroughly understand the correct answers for the Chapter Review and Progress Test 1.

Multiple-Choice Questions

1. Which of the following statements regarding REM sleep is true?
   a. Adults spend more time than infants in REM sleep.
   b. REM sleep deprivation results in a REM rebound.
   c. People deprived of REM sleep adapt easily.
   d. After a stressful experience, a person's REM sleep decreases.

2. Alcohol has the most profound effect on:
   a. the transfer of experiences to long-term memory.
   b. immediate memory.
   c. previously established long-term memories.
   d. all of the above.

3. A person's EEG shows a high proportion of alpha waves. This person is most likely:
   a. dreaming.   c. in Stage 4 sleep.
   b. in Stage 2 sleep. d. awake and relaxed.

4. Circadian rhythms are the:
   a. brain waves that occur during Stage 4 sleep.
   b. muscular tremors that occur during opiate withdrawal.
   c. regular body cycles that occur on a 24-hour schedule.
   d. brain waves that are indicative of Stage 2 sleep.

5. A person who requires increasing amounts of a drug in order to feel its effect has developed:
   a. tolerance.
   b. physical dependency.
   c. psychological dependency.
   d. resistance.

6. Which of the following statements concerning near-death experiences are true?
   a. Fewer than 1 percent of patients who come close to dying report having them.
   b. They may be caused by a deficiency of oxygen to the brain.
   c. They are more commonly experienced by females than by males.
   d. They are more commonly experienced by males than by females.

7. Which of the following is characteristic of REM sleep?
   a. genital arousal
   b. increased muscular tension
   c. night terrors
   d. slow, regular breathing

8. Which of the following is not a stimulant?
   a. amphetamines   c. nicotine
   c. caffeine   d. alcohol

9. Bruce has just completed his first day of military basic training. Physically exhausted from the strenuous exercise, he will probably spend an increased amount of time in which stage of sleep?
   a. REM   c. Stage 2
   b. Stage 1   d. Stage 4

10. According to Hilgard, hypnosis is:
    a. no different from a state of heightened motivation.
    b. a hoax perpetrated by frauds.
    c. the same as dreaming.
    d. a dissociation between different levels of consciousness.

11. Which of the following is a psychoactive drug?
    a. LSD   c. caffeine
    b. sleeping pills   d. all of the above

12. Being engrossed in her new novel, Kathy isn't easily distracted by the usual dormitory noise. Her behavior is best explained in terms of:
    a. fantasy-prone behavior.
    b. selective attention.
    c. dissociation.
    d. divided consciousness.

13. Which of the following is usually the most powerful determinant of whether teenagers begin using drugs?
    a. family strength   c. school adjustment
    b. religiousness   d. peer influence

14. Robert is moderately intoxicated by alcohol. Which of the following changes in his behavior is likely to occur?
    a. If angered, he is more likely to become aggressive than when he is sober.
    b. He will be less self-conscious about his behavior.
    c. If sexually aroused, he will be less inhibited about engaging in sexual activity.
    d. All of the above are likely.

15. Jill remembered a dream in which her boyfriend pushed her into the path of an oncoming car. Her psychoanalyst suggested that the dream might symbolize her fear that her boyfriend was rushing her into sexual activity she was not yet ready for. The analyst was evidently attempting to interpret the _____ of Jill's dream.
    a. manifest content   c. dissociated content
    b. latent content   d. erotic content

16. Barry has just served for four nights as a subject in a sleep study in which he was awakened each time he entered REM sleep. Now that the experiment is over, which of the following can be expected to occur?
    a. Barry will be extremely irritable until his body has made up the lost REM sleep.
    b. Barry will sleep so deeply for several nights that dreaming will be minimal.
    c. There will be an increase in sleep stages 1–4.
    d. There will be an increase in Barry's REM sleep.

17. Which of the following is true?
    a. REM sleep tends to increase following intense learning periods.
    b. Non-REM sleep tends to increase following intense learning periods.
    c. REM-deprived people remember less presleep material than people deprived of Stage 1–4 sleep.
    d. Sleep control centers are located in the higher, association areas of the cortex, where memories are stored.

18. Which of the following is not true of meditation?
    a. It is a more focused state of awareness than daydreaming.
    b. It is associated with changes in blood pressure, heart rate, and metabolism that are typical of people who are very alert and highly aroused.
    c. It is sometimes used in the control of pain and stress.
    d. It often involves the recitation of a word or phrase.

19. Of the following individuals, who is likely to be the most hypnotically suggestible?
    a. Bill, a reality-oriented stockbroker
    b. Janice, a fantasy-prone actress
    c. Megan, a sixth-grader who has trouble focusing her attention on a task
    d. Darren, who never has been able to really "get involved" in movies or novels

Matching Items

Match each term with its appropriate definition or description.

Definitions

_____ 1. brain-wave activity during Stage 1 sleep
_____ 2. disorder in which sleep attacks occur
_____ 3. brain wave of awake, relaxed person
_____ 4. brain-wave activity during Stage 2 sleep
_____ 5. sleep stage associated with dreaming
_____ 6. drugs that reduce anxiety and depress central nervous system activity
_____ 7. recurring difficulty in falling or staying asleep
_____ 8. neurotransmitter that LSD resembles
_____ 9. ongoing perceptions, thoughts, and feelings
_____ 10. theory that dreaming reflects erotic drives
_____ 11. theory that hypnosis is a split in consciousness.

Terms

a. Freud's theory
b. serotonin
c. theta wave
d. alpha wave
e. dissociation
f. narcolepsy
g. consciousness
h. sleep spindle
i. insomnia
j. REM
k. barbiturates

Key Terms

Using your own words, write a brief definition or explanation of each of the following terms.

1. consciousness

2. selective attention

3. cocktail party effect

4. fantasy-prone personality

5. meditation

6. circadian rhythm

7. REM sleep

8. alpha waves

9. hallucinations

10. sleep spindles

11. delta waves

12. insomnia

13. narcolepsy

14. sleep apnea

15. night terrors

16. manifest and latent content

17. REM rebound effect

18. hypnosis

19. posthypnotic amnesia

20. age regression

21. posthypnotic suggestion

22. dissociation

23. psychoactive drugs

24. tolerance

25. withdrawal

26. addiction

27. psychological dependence

28. depressants

29. stimulants

30. hallucinogens

31. barbiturates

32. opiates

33. amphetamines

34. placebo

35. LSD (lysergic acid diethylamide)

36. near-death experience

37. THC

Answers
CHAPTER REVIEW

1. consciousness; behavior

Consciousness can be defined as selective attention to ongoing perceptions, thoughts, and feelings.

2. selective

3. cocktail party; can

4. limited; slow; in sequence

5. do; more; fantasy-prone

Daydreams help us prepare for future events by serving as mental rehearsals. For children, daydreaming in the form of imaginative play is important to social and cognitive development. Daydreams may also substitute for impulsive behavior (delinquents and drug users tend to have fewer vivid fantasies).

6. meditation

7. circadian rhythm

8. eyes

9. alpha

During Stage 1 sleep, breathing rate slows and brain waves become light and irregular. Theta waves are common. Stage 1 is a twilight state in which people often have sensory experiences very similar to hallucinations. During this stage of sleep the person is easily awakened.

10. sleep spindles; is

11. delta; 4; difficult; walking; talking

During REM sleep, brain waves become as rapid as those of Stage 1 sleep, heart rate and breathing become more rapid, genital arousal occurs, and rapid eye movements occur.

12. active; relaxed; paradoxical

13. dreams

14. 90; briefer; longer; 20 to 25

The major effect of sleep deprivation is sleepiness. Other effects include diminished immunity to disease, irritability, and occasional inattention on monotonous tasks.

15. 4

16. pituitary; less; less

17. two-thirds: one-fourth

18. genetic or hereditary

19. insomnia; reduce

20. narcolepsy

21. sleep apnea

22. night terrors; 4

23. does not

24. manifest; latent content; erotic

25. information; REM

26. physiological; stimulation; infants

27. neural; brainstem

28. does

29. REM rebound

30. posthypnotic amnesia

31. somewhat

32. age regression; no more

33. posthypnotic

34. dissociates; attention

Although the issue is still unsettled, most studies have found that hypnosis does not produce any unique changes in physiological processes—and we would expect such changes if hypnosis is an altered state of consciousness. Nor is the behavior of hypnotized subjects fundamentally different from that of other people. Therefore, hypnosis may be mainly a social phenomenon, with hypnotized subjects acting out the role of a "good hypnotic subject."

35. dissociation

36. psychoactive

37. tolerance

38. dependence or addiction; psychological

39. depressants; stimulants; hallucinogens; neurotransmitters

40. depressant; sympathetic; long-term

Studies have found that if people believe that alcohol affects social behavior in certain ways, then, when they drink alcohol (or even mistakenly think that they have been drinking alcohol), they will behave according to their expectations. For example, if people believe alcohol promotes sexual feeling, on drinking they will be likely to behave in a sexually aroused way.

41. barbiturate; depress

42. depress; opiates; endorphins

43. caffeine; nicotine; amphetamines; cocaine; are

44. placebos

45. psychedelics; LSD; PCP

46. hallucinations; oxygen

47. THC; glaucoma

Like alcohol, marijuana relaxes, disinhibits, and may produce a euphoric feeling. Also like alcohol, marijuana impairs perceptual and motor skills. Marijuana is a mild hallucinogen; it can slow the perceived passage of time and amplify sensitivity to colors, sounds, tastes, and smells.

48. opposing emotions

A psychological factor in drug use is the feeling that one's life is meaningless and lacks direction. Regular users of psychoactive drugs often have experienced stress or failure and are somewhat depressed. Drug use often begins as a temporary way to relieve depression, anger, anxiety, or insomnia. A powerful social factor in drug use, especially among adolescents, is peer influence. Peers influence attitudes about drugs, provide drugs, and establish the social context for their use.

PROGRESS TEST 1

Multiple-Choice Questions

1. **d.** is the answer. (p. 133)

2. **d.** is the answer. (p. 135)

3. **a.** is the answer. (p. 138)

   b. & c. Delta waves predominate during Stages 3 and 4. Stage 3 is the transition between Stages 2 and 4 and is associated with a pattern that has elements of both these stages.

   d. Faster, nearly waking brain waves occur during REM sleep.

4. **d.** is the answer. (p. 137)

   a., b., & c. During non-REM Stages 1–4 heart rate and breathing are slow and regular and the genitals are not aroused.

5. **d.** is the answer. (p. 139)

6. **c.** is the answer. Sleep deprivation can have serious consequences for monotonous tasks like long-distance driving, although short, highly motivated tasks are evidently unaffected. No significant physical, emotional, or cognitive effects have been found. (p. 139)

7. **a.** is the answer. Like alcohol, sleeping pills carry the undesirable consequence of reducing REM sleep and may make insomnia worse in the long run. (p. 140)

b., c., & d. Sleeping pills do not produce these effects.

8. **b.** is the answer. Narcolepsy is the sleep disorder characterized by uncontrollable sleep attacks. (p. 140)

a. Sleep apnea is characterized by the temporary cessation of breathing while asleep.

c. Night terrors are characterized by high arousal and terrified behavior, occurring during Stage 4 sleep.

d. Insomnia refers to chronic difficulty in falling or staying asleep.

9. **d.** is the answer. Alcohol, which slows body functions and neural activity, is a depressant. (p. 151)

a. Amphetamines are stimulants.

b. & c. LSD and marijuana are hallucinogens.

10. **c.** is the answer. (p. 145)

a. Hypnotized subjects usually perform only acts they might perform normally.

b. The brain waves of hypnotized subjects are like those seen in relaxed, awake states, not like those associated with sleeping.

d. Hypnotized subjects often experience significant relief of pain.

11. **c.** is the answer. An example of selective attention, the cocktail party effect is the ability to attend to one voice among many. (p. 134)

12. **a.** is the answer. Freud saw dreams as a psychic escape valve that discharges unacceptable feelings that are often related to erotic wishes. (p. 142)

b. & c. These physiological theories of dreaming are not associated with Freud.

d. According to Freud, dreams represent the individual's conflicts and wishes but in disguised, rather than transparent, form.

13. **c.** is the answer. Such drugs work primarily at synapses, altering neural transmission. (p. 150)

a. What people believe will happen after taking a drug will be likely to have some effect on their individual reaction, but psychoactive drugs actually work by altering neural transmission.

b. Since a placebo is a substance without active properties, this answer is incorrect.

d. This answer is incorrect since the effects of psychoactive drugs on behavior, perception, and so forth have a physiological basis.

14. **d.** is the answer. The results of this study demonstrate that although attention is selective, even unattended-to stimuli can affect our behavior, in this case by increasing the subjects' fondness for previously played tunes. (p. 134)

15. **b.** is the answer. Although all people daydream, people with fantasy-prone personalities daydream far more and far more vividly. (p. 135)

a. Jane may very well also be suggestible to hypnosis; fantasy-prone personalities tend to be. The stated characteristics, however, do not necessarily indicate that she is.

c. The description indicates that Jane goes well beyond what is usually thought of as daydreaming.

d. There is no such personality as a "dissociator." Dissociation refers to a split in consciousness that allows some thoughts and behaviors to occur simultaneously with others.

16. **b.** is the answer. Although the body is aroused internally, the messages of the activated motor cortex do not reach the muscles. (p. 139)

a. Studies of REM-deprived subjects indicate just the opposite.

c. It is difficult to awaken a person from REM sleep.

d. Just the opposite occurs in REM sleep: the muscles are relaxed, yet the brain is aroused.

17. **a.** is the answer. Although people recall more under hypnosis, they "recall" a lot of fiction along with fact and appear unable to distinguish between the two. (p. 145)

b. Hypnotically retrieved memories are usually no more accurate than conscious memories.

c. Although the hypnotized subject's imagination may influence the memories retrieved, there is some actual memory retrieval occurring as well.

d. Hypnotically retrieved memories don't normally focus on anxiety-provoking events.

18. **c.** is the answer. Continued use of a drug produces a tolerance, so, to experience the same "high," Dan will have to use larger and larger doses. As the doses become larger, the negative aftereffects, or withdrawal symptoms, become worse. (pp. 150–151)

Matching Items

1. e (p. 142)	**5.** l (p. 135)	**9.** f (p. 153)
2. k (p. 142)	**6.** d (p. 141)	**10.** c (p. 138)
3. i (p. 138)	**7** b (p. 151)	**11.** g (p. 154)
4. j (p. 137)	**8.** a (p. 155)	**12.** h (p. 141)

PROGRESS TEST 2

Multiple-Choice Questions

1. **b.** is the answer. Following REM deprivation, people temporarily increase their amount of REM

sleep, in a phenomenon known as REM rebound. (p. 143)

a. Just the opposite is true: the amount of REM sleep is greatest in infancy.

c. Deprived of REM sleep by repeated awakenings, people return more and more quickly to the REM stages after falling back to sleep. They by no means adapt easily to the deprivation.

d. Just the opposite occurs: following stressful experiences, REM sleep tends to increase.

2. **a.** is the answer. Alcohol disrupts the processing of experiences into long-term memory but has little effect on either immediate or previously established memories. (p. 153)

3. **d.** is the answer. (p. 138)

a. The brain waves of REM sleep (dream sleep) are more like those of nearly awake, Stage 1 sleepers.

b. Stage 2 is characterized by sleep spindles.

c. Stage 4 is characterized by slow, rolling delta waves.

4. **c.** is the answer. Since circadian rhythms occur regularly over a 24-hour period, the other answers cannot be correct. (p. 137)

5. **a.** is the answer. (p. 150)

b. Physical dependence may occur in the absence of tolerance. The hallmark of physical dependence is the presence of withdrawal symptoms when off the drug.

c. Psychological dependence refers to a felt, or psychological, need to use a drug, for example, a drug that relieves stress.

d. There is no such thing as drug "resistance."

6. **b.** is the answer. (p. 155)

a. Approximately one-third of all such patients interviewed report having had near-death experiences.

c. & d. Similar proportions of males and females report having had such experiences.

7. **a.** is the answer. (p. 138)

b. During REM sleep, muscular tension is low.

c. Night terrors are associated with Stage 4 sleep.

d. During REM sleep, respiration is rapid and irregular.

8. **d.** is the answer. Alcohol is a depressant. (p. 151)

9. **d.** is the answer. The amount of time a person spends in Stage 4 sleep often increases following strenuous exercise. This indicates that sleep helps to restore exhausted body tissues. (p. 138)

a. REM sleep tends to increase following stressful experiences or intense learning periods.

b. & c. The amount of time a person spends in Stage 1 or 2 sleep does not increase following strenuous exercise.

10. **d.** is the answer. Hilgard believes that hypnosis reflects a dissociation, or split, in consciousness, as occurs normally, only to a much greater extent. (pp. 149–150)

11. **d.** is the answer. All of these are psychoactive drugs. (pp. 150–156)

12. **b.** is the answer. Selective attention means focusing on a particular stimulus—the novel in Kathy's case. (pp. 133–134)

a. Becoming engrossed in a novel is characteristic of a fantasy-prone person but is not, in itself, enough to indicate this personality characteristic.

c. & d. Dissociation and divided consciousness refer to splits in consciousness, which allow different mental activities to go on simultaneously. In the example, Kathy is engaged in one activity.

13. **d.** is the answer. If adolescents' friends use drugs, the odds are that they will, too. (p. 157)

a., b., & c. These are also predictors of drug use but seem to operate mainly through their effects on peer associations.

14. **d.** is the answer. Alcohol reduces self-consciousness and it loosens inhibitions, making people more likely to act on their feelings of anger or sexual arousal. (pp. 151–153)

15. **b.** is the answer. The analyst was evidently trying to go beyond the events in the dream and understand the hidden meaning they symbolized, or the dream's latent content. (p. 142)

a. The manifest content of a dream is its actual story line.

c. Dissociation refers to a split in levels of consciousness.

d. The latent content might be an erotic wish, as Freud suggested, but the analyst would be looking for the latent content, whether or not it was erotic.

16. **d.** is the answer. Because of the phenomenon known as REM rebound, Barry, having been deprived of REM sleep, will now increase his REM sleep. (p. 143)

a. Increased irritability is an effect of sleep deprivation in general and not of REM deprivation specifically.

b. Because of the REM rebound, Barry will dream *more* than normal.

c. The increase in REM is necessarily accompanied by decreases in Stages 1–4.

17. **a.** is true. The fact that REM sleep tends to increase following intense learning periods has led to

the theory that dreams may help sift, sort, and fix in memory the day's experiences. (p. 142)

b. Non-REM Stage 4 sleep tends to increase following strenuous physical exertion, but non-REM sleep usually does not increase following intense learning periods.

c. There is no evidence that REM-deprived people have poorer recall of presleep experiences than non-REM-deprived people.

d. Sleep control centers are actually located in the lower centers of the brainstem, not in the association areas of the cortex.

18. **b.** is the answer. In fact, just the opposite is true. Experienced meditators exhibit physiological changes that are like those of people who are deeply relaxed. (p. 135)

19. **b.** is the answer. Fantasy-prone people have essentially the characteristics associated with hypnotic suggestibility: rich fantasy lives, the ability to become imaginatively absorbed, etc. The fact that Janice is an actress also suggests she possesses such traits. (pp. 135–145)

a. Bill's reality orientation makes him an unlikely candidate for hypnosis.

c. The hypnotically suggestible are generally able to focus on tasks or on imaginative activities.

d. People who are hypnotically suggestible tend to become deeply engrossed in novels and movies.

Matching Items

1. c (p. 138)   5. j (p. 137)   9. g (p. 133)
2. f (p. 140)   6. k (p. 153)   10. a (p. 142)
3. d (p. 138)   7. i (p. 140)   11. e (p. 148)
4. h (p. 138)   8. b (p. 154)

KEY TERMS

1. The textbook defines **consciousness** as selective attention to ongoing perceptions, thoughts, and feelings. (p. 133)

   Example: The study of **consciousness** includes not only alert wakefulness, but also altered states, such as sleep and dreaming, daydreams, and states induced by hypnosis and drugs.

2. **Selective attention** refers to the fact that at any given moment our conscious awareness is focused on only a small amount of what we could be experiencing. (pp. 133–134)

3. The **cocktail party effect**, an example of selective attention, is our ability to focus on only one voice or conversation and block out others. (p. 134)

4. The **fantasy-prone personality** is one who has a vivid imagination and spends an unusual amount of time fantasizing. (p. 135)

5. **Meditation** is a relaxed state of awareness in which the individual remains fully conscious and focuses attention on a particular word or phrase. (p. 135)

6. A **circadian rhythm** is any regular biological rhythm, such as body temperature and sleep-wakefulness, that follows a 24-hour cycle. (p. 137)

   Memory aid: In Latin, *circa* means "about" and *dies* means "day." A **circadian rhythm** is one with a cycle of about a day, or 24 hours, in duration.

7. **REM sleep** is the sleep stage in which the brain and eyes are active, the muscles are relaxed, and dreaming occurs. (p. 137)

   Memory aid: **REM** is an acronym for *rapid eye movement*, the distinguishing feature of this sleep stage that led to its discovery.

8. **Alpha waves** are the relatively slow brain waves characteristic of an awake, relaxed state. (p. 138)

9. **Hallucinations** are illusions, or false sensory experiences; they occur without a sensory stimulus. (p. 138)

   Example: The fantastic imagery of the near-death experience and that of drug-induced **hallucinations** are often quite similar.

10. **Sleep spindles** are periodic bursts of brain activity that distinguish Stage 2 sleep. (p. 138)

11. **Delta waves** are the larger, slow brain waves associated with deep, Stage 4 sleep. (p. 138)

12. **Insomnia** is a sleep disorder in which the person regularly has difficulty in falling or staying asleep. (p. 140)

    Example: Taking sleeping pills to cure **insomnia** is usually counterproductive because they suppress REM sleep.

13. **Narcolepsy** is a sleep disorder in which the victim suffers sudden, uncontrollable sleep attacks, characterized by entry directly into REM. (p. 140)

14. **Sleep apnea** is a sleep disorder in which the person ceases breathing while asleep, briefly arouses to gasp for air, falls back asleep, and repeats this cycle throughout the night. (p. 141)

    Example: One theory of the Sudden Infant Death Syndrome is that it is caused by **sleep apnea**.

15. A person suffering from **night terrors** experiences episodes of high arousal with apparent terror. Night terrors usually occur during Stage 4 sleep. (p. 141)

16. In Freud's theory of dreaming, the **manifest content** is the remembered story line, the **latent con-**

tent the underlying meaning of a dream. (p. 142)

Memory aid: Manifest means "clearly apparent, obvious"; *latent* means "hidden, concealed." A dream's **manifest content** is that which is obvious; its **latent content** remains hidden until its symbolism is interpreted.

17. The **REM rebound** is the tendency for REM sleep to increase following deprivation because of an experiment or the use of sleeping pills. (p. 143)

18. **Hypnosis** is the state of heightened suggestibility in some people that enables a hypnotist's directions to trigger specific behaviors, perceptions, and possibly memories. (p. 144)

19. **Posthypnotic amnesia** is the condition in which, in response to the hypnotist's suggestion, subjects are unable to recall what happened while they were under hypnosis. (p. 145)

20. In hypnosis, **age regression** is the supposed retrieval of earlier memories and experiences. (p. 146)

21. A **posthypnotic suggestion** is a suggestion made by a hypnotist that is to be carried out when the subject is no longer hypnotized. (p. 148)

Example: To help patients curb their desire for nicotine, the hypnotist gave them the **posthypnotic suggestion** that when awake, the mere thought of smoking a cigarette would make them nauseated.

22. **Dissociation** is a split between different levels of consciousness, allowing a person to divide attention between two or more thoughts. (p. 148)

23. **Psychoactive drugs**—stimulants, depressants, hallucinogens—alter mood and perception. They work by affecting or mimicking the activity of neurotransmitters. (pp. 150–151)

24. **Tolerance** is the diminishing of a psychoactive drug's effect that occurs with repeated use and the need for progressively large doses in order to produce the same effect. (p. 150)

25. **Withdrawal** refers to the unpleasant physical and psychological symptoms that accompany the discontinued use of some drugs. (p. 151)

Example: The painful symptoms of opiate **withdrawal** may occur because while the opiate was available, the drug user's body stopped its production of pain-reducing endorphins.

26. **Addiction** is defined as physical dependence on a drug and is indicated by the presence of withdrawal symptoms when the drug is not taken. (p. 151)

27. The psychological need to use a drug is referred to as **psychological dependence**. (p. 151)

28. **Depressants** are psychoactive drugs, such as alcohol, opiates, and barbiturates, that reduce neural activity and slow down body functions. (pp. 151–153)

29. **Stimulants** are psychoactive drugs, such as caffeine, nicotine, amphetamines, and cocaine, that speed up body functions. (pp. 153–154)

30. **Hallucinogens** are psychoactive drugs, such as LSD and marijuana, that distort perception and evoke sensory imagery in the absence of sensory input. (pp. 154–156)

31. **Barbiturates** are depressants, sometimes used to induce sleep or reduce anxiety. (p. 153)

32. **Opiates** are depressants derived from the opium poppy, such as opium, morphine, and heroin; they reduce neural activity and relieve pain. Opiates are among the most strongly addictive of all psychoactive drugs. (p. 153)

33. **Amphetamines** are a type of stimulant and, as such, speed up body functions and neural activity. (p. 153)

33. A **placebo** is a chemically inactive substance sometimes administered to research subjects, who are told they are taking an actual drug, so that researchers can distinguish between the effects of the drug and the effects of people's beliefs about the drug. (p. 154)

Example: The "**placebo** effect" refers to the influence of a person's beliefs or expectancy on the effectiveness of a drug.

35. **LSD (lysergic acid diethylamide)** is a powerful hallucinogen capable of producing vivid false perceptions and disorganization of thought processes. LSD produces its unpredictable effects partially because it blocks the action of the neurotransmitter serotonin. (p. 154)

36. The **near-death experience** is an altered state of consciousness that has been reported by some people who have had a close brush with death. (p. 155)

37. The active ingredient in marijuana, **THC** is classified as a mild hallucinogen. (p. 155)

Chapter 6 | Learning

Chapter Overview

No topic is closer to the heart of psychology than learning, a relatively permanent change in an organism's behavior due to experience. Chapter 6 covers the basic principles of three forms of learning: classical conditioning, in which we learn associations between events; operant conditioning, in which we learn to engage in behaviors that are rewarded and to avoid behaviors that are punished; and observational learning, in which we learn by observing and imitating others.

The chapter also covers several important issues, including the generality of principles of learning, the role of cognitive processes in learning, and the ways in which learning is constrained by the biological predispositions of different species.

Guided Study

The textbook chapter should be studied one section at a time. Before you read, preview each section by skimming it, noting headings and boldface items. Then read the appropriate section objectives from the following outline. Keep these objectives in mind and, as you read the chapter section, search for the information that will enable you to meet each objective. Once you have finished a section, write out answers for its objectives.

Classical Conditioning (pp. 162–169)

1. Describe the nature of classical conditioning and show how it demonstrates learning by association.

2. Explain the processes of acquisition, extinction, spontaneous recovery, generalization, and discrimination.

3. Explain the behaviorist position and show how it was strengthened by Pavlov's work in classical conditioning.

4. Discuss cognitive and biological constraints on classical conditioning.

Operant Conditioning (pp. 170–179)

5. Describe the process of operant conditioning, including the procedure of shaping.

6. Identify the different types of reinforcers and describe the major schedules of partial reinforcement.

7. Discuss the effects of punishment on behavior.

8. Describe some major applications of operant conditioning.

9. Discuss the importance of cognitive and biological processes in operant conditioning.

Learning by Observation (pp. 179–182)

10. Describe the process of observational learning.

Chapter Review

When you have finished reading the chapter, use the material that follows to review it. Complete the sentences and answer the questions. As you proceed, evaluate your performance for each chapter section by consulting the answer key at the end of this chapter. Do not continue with the next section until you've understood each answer. If you need to, review or reread the appropriate chapter section in the textbook before continuing.

1. A relatively permanent change in an organism's behavior due to experience is called _learning_.

2. The type of learning in which the organism learns to anticipate significant events is called _classical_ conditioning.

3. The tendency of organisms to repeat acts that produce favorable outcomes forms the basis of _operant_ conditioning, also called _instrumental_ conditioning.

4. Learning by watching others is called _observational_ _learning_.

Classical Conditioning (pp. 162–169)

5. During the seventeenth century, philosophers such as John Locke argued that an important factor in learning is our tendency to _associate_ events that occur in a sequence.

6. Classical conditioning was first explored by the Russian physiologist _Ivan_ _Pavlov_.

7. An animal will salivate when food is placed in its mouth. Pavlov called this salivation the _unconditioned_ _response_.

8. In Pavlov's classic experiment, a bell, or _neutral cond_ _stimulus_, is sounded just before food, the _uncond_ _stimulus_, is placed in the animal's mouth.

9. Eventually, the dogs in Pavlov's experiment would salivate on hearing the tone. This salivation is called the _conditioned_ _response_.

10. The initial learning, or _acquisition_, of a conditioned response is facilitated when the interval between the neutral stimulus and the unconditioned stimulus is approximately _1/2 sec_.

Explain why learning theorists consider classically conditioned behaviors to be biologically adaptive.

11. When the UCS is presented prior to the CS, conditioning _CR_ (does/does not) occur.

12. If a CS is repeatedly presented without the UCS, _extinction_ soon occurs; that is, the CR diminishes.

13. Following a rest, however, the CR reappears in response to the CS; this phenomenon is called _spontaneous recovery_.

14. Subjects often respond to a similar stimulus as they would to the original CS. This phenomenon is called _generalization_. Subjects can, however, also be trained not to respond to these similar stimuli. This learned ability is called _discrimination_.

List several ways that the study of classical conditioning has been important.

15. Pavlov's work, by showing how phenomena could be studied without relying upon subjective techniques, gave momentum to the emerging American school of _____.

16. One of the founders of this school was the American psychologist _____.

17. In their famous experiment, Watson and Rayner used _classical_ conditioning to train an infant to fear a rat.

Explain in more detail the Watson and Rayner experiment.

18. Experiments by Rescorla and Wagner found that the _____ (more/less) predictable the association between the CS and US, the stronger the CR. This demonstrates the importance of _____ processes in conditioning.

Describe two issues that have led to the recent reconsideration of behaviorism.

19. The importance of cognitive processes in human conditioning is demonstrated by the failure of classical conditioning as a treatment for _____.

20. Garcia discovered that rats would develop aversions to _____, but not to other stimuli. Results such as these demonstrate that the principles of learning are constrained by the _____ predispositions of each animal species and that they help each species _____ to its environment.

Operant Conditioning (pp. 170–179)

21. Classical conditioning involves _invi_ (voluntary/involuntary) responses. For _____ (voluntary/involuntary) responses, _____ conditioning is more relevant.

22. Skinner has referred to the automatic responses of classical conditioning as _____ behavior. In contrast, he labels behavior that is more spontaneous and that is influenced by its consequences as _____ behavior.

23. Skinner designed an apparatus, called the _____ _____, to investigate learning in animals.

24. The procedure in which a person teaches an animal to perform an intricate behavior by building up to it in small steps is called behavior _____. This method involves reinforcing successive _____ of the desired behavior.

25. A stimulus that strengthens behavior that leads to its presentation is a _____ _____.

26. A stimulus that reinforces the behavior that leads to its termination is a _____ _____.

27. Reinforcers, such as food and shock, that are related to basic needs and therefore do not rely on learning are called _____ _____. Reinforcers that must be conditioned and therefore derive their power through association are called _____ _____.

28. Immediate reinforcement _____ (is/is not) more effective than its alternative, namely, _____ reinforcement.

29. The procedure involving reinforcement of each and every response is called _____ _____. Under these conditions, learning is _____ (rapid/slow). When this type of reinforcement is discontinued, extinction is _____ (rapid/slow).

30. The procedure in which responses are only intermittently reinforced is called _____ reinforcement. Under these conditions, learning is generally _____ (faster/slower) than it is

with continuous reinforcement. Behavior reinforced in this manner is _____ (very/not very) resistant to extinction.

31. Reinforcement of the first response after a set interval of time defines the _____-_____ schedule.

32. Unpredictable pop quizzes are an example of a _____-_____ schedule of reinforcement.

33. When behavior is reinforced after a set number of responses, a _____-_____ schedule is in effect.

34. Three-year-old Yusef knows that if he cries when he wants a treat, his mother will sometimes give in. When, as in this case, reinforcement occurs after an unpredictable number of responses, a _____-_____ schedule is being used.

Describe the typical patterns of response under fixed-interval, fixed-ratio, variable-interval, and variable-ratio schedules of reinforcement.

35. An aversive consequence that decreases the likelihood of the behavior that preceded it is called _____.

Describe some drawbacks to the use of punishment.

36. The use of teaching machines and programmed textbooks was an early application of the operant conditioning procedure of _____ to education.

List some of the advantages of computer-assisted instruction.

37. In boosting productivity in the workplace, positive reinforcement is _____ (more/less) effective when applied to specific behaviors than when given to reward general merit. For such behaviors, immediate reinforcement is _____ (more/ no more) effective than delayed reinforcement.

38. When a well-learned route in a maze is blocked, rats sometimes choose an alternative route, acting as if they were consulting a

_____   _____.

39. Animals may learn from experience even when reinforcement is not available. When learning is not apparent until reinforcement has been provided, _____ _____ is said to have occurred.

Learning by Observation (pp. 179–182)

40. Learning by imitation is called modeling, or

_____   _____.

The psychologist best known for research in this area is _____.

41. In one experiment, the child who viewed an adult punch an inflatable doll played _____ (more/less) aggressively than the child who had not observed aggressive behavior.

42. Children will also model positive, or _____, behaviors.

FOCUS ON PSYCHOLOGY:
The Prenatal University

Rene Van de Carr is a California obstetrician who became interested in "prenatal psychology" after a patient reported that when she poked her baby through her abdomen it poked back. This observation, as well as extensive research, led him to establish a course for prospective parents who want to "teach" their unborn children.

Van de Carr claims that his course, which involves a complex program of words, sounds, and tactile stimulation, teaches the developing child to attend to specific stimuli, a skill that supposedly facilitates the later acquisition of a variety of intellectual abilities. The training begins during the fifth month of pregnancy when parents are urged to respond to the baby's natural kicking by gently pushing back and verbally reinforcing the movement by saying, "Good baby, kick again!" The first evidence of learning occurs within several weeks when kicking, like any voluntary response subjected to positive reinforcement, becomes more frequent.

In the seventh month of prenatal development parents begin to teach their babies to associate spoken words with touch. Twice a day, in five-minute sessions, parents say, "Rub, rub, rub, rub," as they rub the mother's abdomen, or "Shake, shake, shake, shake," as the mother (and baby) gently wiggle.

Some of Van de Carr's prenatal students continue on for "postgraduate education" as their parents attempt to teach more difficult words, such as "hot," "cold," and "wet," and give their children an early advantage in auditioning for the school orchestra by playing various instruments and saying the note names aloud.

Does Van de Carr's program work? In a recent longitudinal study, he compared the development of children who were graduates of his program with that of children who had some exposure to the training techniques and children who had not participated in the program. The findings indicated that graduates spoke their first words earlier, advanced to the two-word stage of language at a younger age, and demonstrated object constancy (the awareness that objects continue to exist even when out of sight) earlier than did the partially trained babies. Babies who had not participated in the prenatal program developed each of these abilities even later.

Although Van de Carr contends that more than 1,500 babies have been helped by his program, other psychologists are skeptical of its effectiveness. For one thing, parents who stimulate their babies before birth are more likely to provide above-average intellectual stimulation after birth as well. It may be this later stimulation, rather than the prenatal program, that leads to the developmental advantage.

Clinical psychologist Amy Altenhaus also notes that "It is often difficult to predict behavior from developmental milestones before the age of 3. A 6-month-old who achieves exceptional development may not necessarily be exceptional down the road." The meaning of early attainment of these abilities is therefore not clear.

The opposing views on the prenatal program reflect the controversy over the value of early learning. On one side are those who believe that children have a much greater capacity to learn at an early age than was previously thought. Parents who take this position are flocking to enroll in programs that help them teach their infants to swim, read, do math, learn a foreign language, play chess, and master musical instruments.

Taking the opposite viewpoint are those parents, psychologists, and educators who believe—as David Elkind, the author of *The Hurried Child*, does—that many parents are pushing their children too hard. These people maintain that while there is little evidence of early instruction having lasting benefits, evidence of its potential for lasting harm is considerable.

What then are prospective parents to believe? As with many other issues, the truth probably lies somewhere between the two extremes. Intellectually, "too much, too soon" may very well be unhealthy for the child. Yet, some aspects of the programs may be beneficial. As psychologist Altenhaus says, "Such things as music and massage, if they calm the mother down, can only be positive for the fetus."

Sources: Prentice, K. (1988, March 2). Toddling onto the fast track? *Detroit Free Press*, 1B, 3B.

Weintraub, P. (1989, August). Preschool? *Omni*, 34–38, 42–47.

Progress Test 1

Multiple-Choice Questions

Circle your answers to the following questions and check them with the answer key at the end of this chapter. If your answer is incorrect, read the answer key explanation for why it is incorrect and then consult the appropriate pages of the text in order to understand the correct answer.

1. Learning is best defined as:
   a. any behavior emitted by an organism without being elicited.
   b. a change in the behavior of an organism.
   c. a relatively permanent change in the behavior of an organism due to experience.
   d. behavior based on operant rather than respondent conditioning.

2. The type of learning associated with B. F. Skinner is:
   a. classical conditioning.
   b. operant conditioning.
   c. respondent conditioning.
   d. observational learning.

3. In Pavlov's original experiment with dogs, the meat served as a(n):
   a. conditioned stimulus.
   b. conditioned response.
   c. unconditioned stimulus.
   d. unconditioned response.

4. You always rattle the box of dog biscuits before giving your dog a treat. As you do so, your dog salivates. Rattling the box is a(n) _____; your dog's salivation is a(n) _____.
   a. conditioned stimulus; conditioned response
   b. conditioned stimulus; unconditioned response
   c. unconditioned stimulus; conditioned response
   d. unconditioned stimulus; unconditioned response

5. In order to obtain a reward a monkey learns to press a lever when a 1000-Hz tone is on but not when a 1200-Hz tone is on. What kind of training is this?
   a. extinction   c. discrimination
   b. generalization   d. classical conditioning

6. Which of the following statements concerning reinforcement is correct?
   a. Learning is most rapid with partial reinforcement, but continuous reinforcement produces the greatest resistance to extinction.
   b. Learning is most rapid with continuous reinforcement, but partial reinforcement produces the greatest resistance to extinction.
   c. Learning is fastest and resistance to extinction is greatest following continuous reinforcement.
   d. Learning is fastest and resistance to extinction is greatest following partial reinforcement.

7. You are expecting an important letter in the mail. As the regular delivery time approaches you glance more and more frequently out the window, searching for the letter carrier. Your behavior in this situation typifies that associated with which schedule of reinforcement?
   a. fixed-ratio   c. fixed-interval
   b. variable-ratio   d. variable-interval

8. Which of the following schedules of reinforcement produces the highest and most consistent rate of response?
   a. fixed-ratio   c. fixed-interval
   b. variable-ratio   d. variable-interval

9. Jack finally takes out the garbage in order to get his father to stop pestering him. Jack's behavior is being influenced by:
   a. a positive reinforcer.   c. a primary reinforcer.
   b. a negative reinforcer.   d. punishment.

10. When a conditioned stimulus is presented without an accompanying unconditioned stimulus, _____ will soon take place.

a. generalization   c. extinction
b. discrimination   d. aversion

11. One difference between classical and operant conditioning is that:
    a. in classical conditioning the responses are voluntary.
    b. in operant conditioning the responses are triggered by preceding stimuli.
    c. in classical conditioning the responses are involuntary.
    d. in operant conditioning the responses are involuntary.

12. In Garcia's studies of taste aversion learning, rats learned to associate:
    a. taste with electric shock.
    b. sights and sounds with sickness.
    c. taste with sickness.
    d. taste and sounds with electric shock.

13. Mrs. Ramirez often tells her children that it is important to buckle their seat belts while riding in the car, but she rarely does so herself. Her children will probably learn to:
    a. use their seat belts and tell others it is important to do so.
    b. use their seat belts but not tell others it is important to do so.
    c. tell others it is important to use seat belts but rarely use them themselves.
    d. neither tell others that seat belts are important nor use them.

14. The researcher best known for studying observational learning is:
    a. Bandura.   c. Pavlov.
    b. Skinner.   d. Watson.

15. Punishment is a controversial way to control behavior because:
    a. behavior is not forgotten and may return.

b. punishing stimuli often create fear.
c. punishment often increases aggressiveness.
d. of all of the above reasons.

16. It is easy to teach a pigeon to flap its wings to avoid shock but not to do so for food reinforcement. According to the textbook, what is the most likely reason that this is so?
    a. Pigeons are biologically predisposed to flap their wings in order to escape aversive events and to use their beaks to obtain food.
    b. Shock is a more motivating stimulus for birds than food is.
    c. Hungry animals have difficulty delaying their eating long enough to learn *any* new skill.
    d. All of the above are likely reasons for this phenomenon.

17. From the viewpoint of an owner of a slot machine, which of the following jackpot-payout schedules would be the most desirable for reinforcing customer use of the machine?
    a. variable-ratio   c. variable-interval
    b. fixed-ratio   d. fixed- interval

18. After finding that her usual route home was closed due to road repairs, Sharetta was able to find an alternative route based on her knowledge of the city and sense of direction. Her behavior is an example of using:
    a. latent learning.
    b. observational learning.
    c. shaping.
    d. a cognitive map.

19. For the most rapid conditioning, a CS should be presented:
    a. about 1 second after the UCS.
    b. about one-half second before the UCS.
    c. about 15 seconds before the UCS.
    d. at the same time as the UCS.

Matching Items

Match each definition or description with the appropriate term.

Definitions

_____ 1. learned ability to distinguish a CS from other stimuli

_____ 2. tendency for similar stimuli to evoke a CR

_____ 3. terminating an aversive stimulus

_____ 4. an innately reinforcing stimulus

_____ 5. an acquired reinforcer

_____ 6. responses are reinforced after an unpredictable amount of time

_____ 7. each and every response is reinforced

_____ 8. reinforcing closer and closer approximations of a behavior

_____ 9. the reappearance of an extinguished CR

_____ 10. presenting an aversive stimulus

_____ 11. learning that becomes apparent only after reinforcement is provided

Terms

a. shaping
b. punishment
c. spontaneous recovery
d. latent learning
e. discrimination
f. negative reinforcement
g. primary reinforcement
h. generalization
i. secondary reinforcement
j. continuous reinforcement
k. variable-interval schedule

Progress Test 2

Progress Test 2 should be completed during a final chapter review. Do this test after you thoroughly understand the correct answers for the Chapter Review and Progress Test 1.

Multiple-Choice Questions

For questions 1 to 4, use the following information.

As a child you were playing in the yard one day when a neighbor's cat wandered over. Your mother (who has a terrible fear of animals) screamed and snatched you into her arms. Her behavior caused you to cry. You now have a fear of cats.

1. Identify the CS.
   a. your mother's behavior
   b. your crying
   c. the cat
   d. your fear today

2. Identify the UCS.
   a. your mother's behavior
   b. your crying
   c. the cat
   d. your fear today

3. Identify the CR.
   a. your mother's behavior
   b. your crying
   c. the cat
   d. your fear today

4. Identify the UCR.
   a. your mother's behavior
   b. your crying
   c. the cat
   d. your fear today

5. In Pavlov's studies of classical conditioning of a dog's salivary responses, spontaneous recovery occurred:
   a. during acquisition, when the CS was first paired with the UCS.
   b. during extinction, when the CS was first presented by itself.
   c. when the CS was reintroduced following extinction of the CR and a rest period.
   d. during discrimination training, when several conditioned stimuli were introduced.

6. The manager of a manufacturing plant wishes to use positive reinforcement to increase the productivity of her workers. Which of the following procedures would probably be the most effective?
   a. Deserving employees are given a general merit bonus at the end of each fiscal year.
   b. A productivity goal that seems attainable, yet actually is unrealistic, is set for each employee.
   c. Employees are given immediate bonuses for specific behaviors related to productivity.
   d. Employees who fail to meet standards of productivity receive pay cuts.

7. In distinguishing between negative reinforcers and punishment, we note that:
   a. punishment, but not negative reinforcement, involves use of an aversive stimulus.
   b. in contrast to punishment, with negative reinforcement the likelihood of a response is decreased by the presentation of an aversive stimulus.
   c. in contrast to punishment, with negative reinforcement the likelihood of a response is increased by the presentation of an aversive stimulus.
   d. in contrast to punishment, with negative reinforcement the likelihood of a response is increased by the termination of an aversive stimulus.

8. The "piecework," or commission, method of payment is an example of which reinforcement schedule?
   a. fixed-interval   c. fixed-ratio
   b. variable-interval d. variable-ratio

9. You teach your dog to fetch the paper by giving him a cookie each time he does so. This is an example of:
   a. operant conditioning.
   b. classical conditioning.
   c. secondary reinforcement.
   d. partial reinforcement.

10. Bill once had a blue car that was in the shop more than it was out. He now will not even consider owning blue- or green-colored cars. His aversion to green cars is an example of:
    a. discrimination.
    b. generalization.
    c. latent learning.
    d. spontaneous recovery.

11. After watching coverage of the Olympics on television recently, Lynn and Susan have been staging their own "summer games." Which of the following best accounts for their behavior?
    a. classical conditioning
    b. observational learning
    c. latent learning
    d. shaping

12. After exploring a complicated maze for several days, a rat subsequently ran the maze with very few errors when food was placed in the goal box for the first time. This performance illustrates:
    a. classical conditioning.
    b. discrimination learning.
    c. observational learning.
    d. latent learning.

13. Leon's psychology instructor has scheduled an exam every third week of the term. Leon will probably study the most just before an exam and the least just after an exam. This is because the schedule of exams is reinforcing studying according to which schedule?
    a. fixed-ratio   c. fixed-interval
    b. variable-ratio   d. variable-interval

14. Operant conditioning is to _____ as respondent conditioning is to _____.
    a. Pavlov; Watson
    b. Skinner; Bandura
    c. involuntary behavior; voluntary behavior
    d. voluntary behavior; involuntary behavior

15. Computer-assisted instruction (CAI) is an application of the operant conditioning principles of:
    a. shaping and immediate reinforcement.
    b. immediate reinforcement and punishment.
    c. shaping and primary reinforcement.
    d. continuous reinforcement and punishment.

16. Fishing is reinforced according to which schedule?
    a. fixed-interval   c. variable-interval
    b. fixed-ratio   d. variable-ratio

17. Which of the following is the best example of a secondary reinforcer?
    a. putting on a coat on a cold day
    b. relief from pain after the dentist stops drilling your teeth
    c. receiving a cool drink after washing your mother's car on a hot day
    d. receiving an approving nod from the boss for a job well done

18. Two groups of rats receive classical conditioning trials in which a tone and electric shock are presented. For Group 1 the electric shock always follows the tone. For Group 2 the tone and shock occur randomly. Which of the following is likely to result?
    a. The tone will become a CS for Group 1 but not Group 2.
    b. The tone will become a CS for Group 2 but not Group 1.
    c. The tone will become a CS for both groups.
    d. The tone will not become a CS for either group.

True-False Items

Indicate whether each statement is true or false by placing *T* or *F* in the blank next to the item.

_____ 1. Operant conditioning involves behavior that is primarily involuntary.

_____ 2. The optimal interval between CS and UCS is about 15 seconds.

_____ 3. Negative reinforcement decreases the likelihood that a response will recur.

_____ 4. The learning of a new behavior proceeds most rapidly with continuous reinforcement.

_____ 5. As a rule, variable schedules of reinforcement produce more consistent rates of responding than fixed schedules.

_____ 6. Cognitive processes are of relatively little importance in learning.

_____ 7. Although punishment may be effective in suppressing behavior, it can have several undesirable side effects.

_____ 8. All animals, including rats and birds, are biologically predisposed to associate taste cues with sickness.

_____ 9. Whether the CS or UCS is presented first seems not to matter in terms of the ease of classical conditioning.

_____ 10. Spontaneous recovery refers to the tendency of extinguished behaviors to reappear suddenly.

Key Terms

Using your own words, write a brief definition or explanation of each of the following terms.

1. learning

2. classical (or Pavlovian) conditioning

3. unconditioned response (UCR)

4. unconditioned stimulus (UCS)

5. conditioned response (CR)

6. conditioned stimulus (CS)

7. acquisition

8. extinction

9. spontaneous recovery

10. generalization

11. discrimination

12. behaviorism

13. operant, or instrumental, conditioning

14. respondent behavior

15. operant behavior

16. Skinner box

17. shaping (successive approximations)

18. reinforcer

19. positive reinforcement

20. negative reinforcement

21. primary reinforcers

22. secondary reinforcers

23. continuous reinforcement

24. partial (intermittent) reinforcement

25. fixed-interval schedule

26. variable-interval schedule

27. fixed-ratio schedule

28. variable-ratio schedule

29. punishment

30. cognitive map

31. latent learning

32. observational learning

33. modeling

34. prosocial behavior

Answers

CHAPTER REVIEW

1. learning

2. classical

3. operant; instrumental

4. observational learning

5. associate

6. Ivan Pavlov

7. unconditioned response

8. conditioned stimulus; unconditioned stimulus

9. conditioned response

10. acquisition; one-half second

Learning theorists consider classical conditioning to be adaptive because conditioned responses help organisms to prepare for good or bad events (unconditioned stimuli) that are about to occur.

11. does not

12. extinction

13. spontaneous recovery

14. generalization; discrimination

Classical conditioning has led to the discovery of general principles of learning that are the same for all species tested, including people. Classical conditioning has proven to have many helpful applications to human health and well-being. Classical conditioning also provided an example to the young field of psychology of how complex behaviors could be studied objectively.

15. behaviorism

16. John B. Watson

17. classical

In Watson and Rayner's experiment, classical conditioning was used to condition a fear of a rat in Albert, an 11-month-old infant. When Albert touched the white rat (neutral stimulus), a loud noise (unconditioned stimulus) was sounded. After several pairings of the rat with the noise, Albert began crying at the mere sight of the rat. The rat had become a conditioned stimulus, eliciting a conditioned response of fear.

18. more; cognitive

The early behaviorists believed that all learned behavior could be reduced to stimulus-response mechanisms. This discounting of mental (cognitive) processes has been strongly challenged by experiments suggesting that even in animals cognition is important for learning. Second, the behaviorists' belief that learning principles would generalize from one response to another and from one species to another has been questioned by research indicating that conditioning principles are constrained by each organism's biological predispositions.

19. alcoholism

20. taste; biological; adapt

21. involuntary; voluntary; operant

22. respondent; operant

23. Skinner box

24. shaping; approximations

25. positive reinforcer

26. negative reinforcer

27. primary reinforcers; secondary reinforcers

28. is; delayed

29. continuous reinforcement; rapid; rapid

30. partial; slower; very

31. fixed-interval

32. variable-interval

33. fixed-ratio

34. variable-ratio

Following reinforcement on a fixed-interval schedule, there is a pause in responding and then an increasing rate of response as time for the next reinforcement draws near. On a fixed-ratio schedule there also is a post-reinforcement pause, followed, however, by a return to a consistent, high rate of response. Both kinds of variable schedules produce steadier rates of response, without the pauses associated with fixed schedules.

35. punishment

Because punished behavior is merely suppressed, it may reappear. Punishment can lead to fear and a sense of helplessness, as well as to the association of the aversive event with the person who administers it.

Punishment also often increases aggressiveness. Finally, punishment alone does not guide the organism toward more desirable behavior.

36. shaping

For some types of educational tasks, such as teaching reading, math, and other skills based on "drill and practice" techniques, CAI is very effective. The computer engages students actively, paces material individually, provides immediate feedback, and keeps detailed records of achievement.

37. more; more

38. cognitive map

39. latent learning

40. observational learning; Bandura

41. more

42. prosocial

PROGRESS TEST 1

Multiple-Choice Questions

1. c. is the answer. (p. 161)

a. This answer is incorrect because it simply describes any behavior that is voluntary rather than being triggered, or elicited, by a specific stimulus.

b. This answer is too general, since behaviors can change for reasons other than learning.

d. Respondently conditioned behavior also satisfies the criteria of our definition of learning.

2. b. is the answer. (pp. 170–171)

a. & c. Classical conditioning is associated with Pavlov; respondent conditioning is the same thing as classical conditioning.

d. Observational learning is most closely associated with Bandura.

3. c. is the answer. Meat automatically triggers the response of salivation and is therefore an unconditioned stimulus. (p. 163)

a. A conditioned stimulus acquires its response-eliciting powers through learning. A dog does not *learn* to salivate at meat.

b. & d. Responses are behaviors elicited in the organism, in this case the dog's salivation. The meat is a stimulus.

4. a. is the answer. Your dog had to *learn* to associate the rattling sound with the food. Rattling is therefore a conditioned, or learned, stimulus, and salivation in response to this rattling is a learned, or conditioned, response. (p. 163)

5. c. is the answer. In learning to distinguish between the conditioned stimulus and another, simi-

lar stimulus, the monkey has received training in discrimination. (p. 165)

a. In extinction training, a stimulus and/or response is allowed to go unreinforced.

b. Generalization training involves responding to stimuli similar to the conditioned stimulus; here the monkey is being trained *not* to respond to a similar stimulus.

d. This cannot be classical conditioning since the monkey is acting in order to obtain a reward. Thus, this is an example of operant conditioning.

6. b. is the answer. A continuous association will naturally be easier to learn than one that occurs on only some occasions, so learning is most rapid with continuous reinforcement. Yet once the continuous association is no longer there, as in extinction training, extinction will occur more rapidly than it would have, had the organism not always experienced reinforcement. (p. 173)

7. c. is the answer. Reinforcement (the letter) comes after a fixed interval, and as the likely end of the interval approaches, your behavior (glancing out the window) becomes more frequent. (p. 173)

a. & b. These answers are incorrect because with ratio schedules, reinforcement is contingent on the number of responses rather than on the passage of time.

d. Assuming that the mail is delivered at about the same time each day, the interval is fixed rather than variable. Your behavior reflects this, since you glance out the window more often as the delivery time approaches.

8. b. is the answer. (p. 174)

a. Response rate is high with fixed-ratio schedules, but there is a pause following each reinforcement.

c. & d. Because reinforcement is not contingent on the *rate* of response, interval schedules, especially fixed-interval schedules, produce lower response rates than ratio-schedules.

9. b. is the answer. By taking out the garbage, Jack terminates an aversive stimulus: his father's nagging. (p. 171)

a. Positive reinforcement would involve a desirable stimulus that increases the likelihood of the response that preceded it.

c. This answer would have been correct if Jack had taken the garbage out in order to receive a reward that satisfies basic needs, such as hunger.

d. Punishment suppresses behavior; Jack is emitting a behavior in order to obtain reinforcement.

10. c. is the answer. In this situation, the CR will decline, a phenomenon known as extinction. (p. 165)

a. Generalization occurs when the subject makes a CR to stimuli similar to the original CS.

b. Discrimination is when the subject does not make a CR to stimuli other than the original CS.

d. An aversion is a CR to a CS that has been associated with an unpleasant UCS, such as shock or a nausea-producing drug.

11. **c.** is the answer. (p. 170)

a. In *operant conditioning* the responses are voluntary.

b. In *classical conditioning* responses are triggered, or elicited, by preceding stimuli.

d. In *classical conditioning* responses are involuntary.

12. **c.** is the answer. (p. 168)

a. & d. Garcia's studies also indicated that rats are biologically predisposed to associate visual and auditory stimuli, but not taste, with shock.

b. Rats are biologically predisposed to associate taste with sickness.

13. **c.** is the answer. Studies indicate that when a model says one thing but does another, subjects do the same and learn not to practice what they preach. (p. 180)

14. **a.** is the answer. (p. 179)

b. Skinner is best known for studies of operant learning.

c. Pavlov is best known for classical conditioning.

d. Watson is best known as an early proponent of behaviorism.

15. **d.** is the answer. (pp. 174–175)

16. **a.** is the answer. As in this example, conditioning must be consistent with the particular organism's biological predispositions. (pp. 171–173)

b. Some behaviors, but certainly not all, are acquired more rapidly than others when shock is used as negative reinforcement.

c. Pigeons are able to acquire many new behaviors when food is used as reinforcement.

17. **a.** is the answer. Ratio schedules maintain higher rates of responding—gambling in this example—than do interval schedules. Variable schedules are not associated with the pause in responding following reinforcement that is typical of fixed schedules. The slot machine would therefore be used more often, and more consistently, if jackpots were scheduled according to a variable-ratio schedule. (pp. 173–174)

18. **d.** is the answer. Sharetta is guided by her mental representation of the city, or cognitive map. (p. 178)

a. Latent learning, or learning in the absence of reinforcement that is demonstrated when reinforcement becomes available, has no direct relevance to the example.

b. Observational learning refers to learning from watching others.

c. Shaping is the technique of reinforcing successive approximations of a desired behavior.

19. **b.** is the answer. (p. 164)

a. Backward conditioning, in which the UCS precedes the CS, is ineffective.

c. This interval is longer than is optimum for the most rapid acquisition of a CS-UCS association.

d. Simultaneous presentation of CS and UCS is ineffective because it does not permit the subject to anticipate the UCS.

Matching Items

1. e (p. 165)	5. i (p. 172)	9. c (p. 165)
2. h (p. 165)	6. k (p. 173)	10. b (p. 174)
3. f (p. 171)	7. j (p. 173)	11. d (p. 178)
4. g (p. 172)	8. a (p. 170)	

PROGRESS TEST 2

Multiple-Choice Questions

1. **c.** is the answer. The cat, the stimulus you learned to respond to with fear, is the CS. (p. 163)

2. **a.** is the answer. Your mother's scream and evident fear, which naturally *caused* you to cry, was the UCS. (p. 163)

3. **d.** is the answer. Your fear of cats is the CR. An acquired fear, or phobia, is always a *conditioned* response. (p. 163)

4. **b.** is the answer. Your crying, automatically *elicited* by your mother's scream and fear, was the UCR. (p. 163)

5. **c.** is the answer. (p. 165)

a., b., & d. Spontaneous recovery occurs after a CR has been extinguished, and in the absence of the UCS. The situations described in these answers all involve the continued presentation of the UCS and, therefore, the further strengthening of the CR.

6. **c.** is the answer. (p. 176)

a. Positive reinforcement is most effective in boosting productivity in the workplace when *specific* behavior, rather than vaguely defined general merit, is rewarded. Also, immediate reinforcement is much more effective than delayed reinforcement, as this example is based on.

b. Positive reinforcement is most effective in

boosting productivity when performance goals are achievable, rather than unrealistic.

d. The text does not specifically discuss the use of punishment in the workplace. Elsewhere it points out that although punishment may temporarily suppress unwanted behavior, it does not guide one toward more desirable behavior. Therefore, workers who receive pay cuts for poor performance may learn nothing about how to improve their productivity.

7. **d.** is the answer. (p. 171)

a. Both involve an aversive stimulus.

b. All reinforcers, including negative reinforcers, *increase* the likelihood of a response.

c. In negative reinforcement an aversive stimulus is withdrawn following a desirable response.

8. **c.** is the answer. Payment is given after a fixed number of pieces have been completed. (p. 173)

a. & b. Interval schedules reinforce according to the passage of time, not the amount of work accomplished.

d. Fortunately for those working on commission, the work ratio is fixed and therefore predictable.

9. **a.** is the answer. You are teaching your dog by rewarding him when he produces the desired behavior. (p. 170)

b. This is not classical conditioning because the cookie is a primary reinforcer presented after the *operant* behavior of the dog fetching the paper.

c. Food is a primary reinforcer; it satisfies an innate need.

d. Because you reward your dog each time he fetches the paper, this is continuous reinforcement.

10. **b.** is the answer. Bill is extending a learned aversion to blue cars to cars that are green. (p. 165)

a. Whereas discrimination involves responding only to a particular stimulus, Bill is extending his aversive response to other stimuli (green cars) as well.

c. Latent learning is learning that becomes apparent only after reinforcement becomes available.

d. Bill's aversion to blue cars was never extinguished, so there is no need for recovery.

11. **b.** is the answer. The girls are imitating behavior they have observed. (p. 179)

a. Because these behaviors are clearly voluntary rather than elicited, classical conditioning plays no role.

c. Latent learning plays no role in this example.

d. Shaping is a procedure for teaching the acquisi-

tion of a new response by reinforcing successive approximations of the behavior.

12. **d.** is the answer. The rat had learned the maze, and it displayed this learning once reinforcement became available. (p. 178)

a. Negotiating a maze is clearly voluntary, emitted, *operant* behavior.

b. This example does not involve learning to distinguish between stimuli.

c. This is not observational learning because the rat has no one to observe!

13. **c.** is the answer. Because reinforcement (earning a good grade on the exam) is available according to the passage of time, studying is reinforced according to an interval schedule. Because the interval between exams is constant, this is an example of a fixed-interval schedule. (p. 173)

14. **d.** is the answer. Operant conditioning works on voluntary behaviors, and respondent (classical) conditioning works on involuntary behaviors. (p. 170)

a. Pavlov and Watson are both associated with respondent conditioning.

b. Bandura is associated with observational learning.

15. **a.** is the answer. CAI applies operant principles such as reinforcement, immediate feedback, and shaping to the teaching of new skills. (pp. 170–173)

b. & d. CAI provides immediate, and continuous, reinforcement for correct responses, but does not make use of aversive control procedures such as punishment.

c. CAI is based on feedback for correct responses; this feedback constitutes secondary, rather than primary, reinforcement.

16. **c.** is the answer. In fishing, an unpredictable amount of time passes between catches. (p. 173)

a. This answer is incorrect because the interval between catching successive fish is unpredictable.

b. & d. There is no contingency between "fishing rate" and when the *next* fish reinforcement will occur.

17. **d.** is the answer. An approving nod from the boss is a secondary reinforcer, in that it doesn't satisfy an innate need but has become linked with desirable consequences. Cessation of cold, cessation of pain, and a drink are all primary reinforcers, which meet innate needs. (p. 172)

18. **a.** is the answer. Classical conditioning proceeds most effectively when the CS and UCS are reliably paired and therefore appear predictably asso-

ciated. Only for Group 1 is this likely to be true. (p. 163)

True-False Items

1. F (p. 170)
2. F (p. 164)
3. F (p. 171)
4. T (p. 173)
5. T (p. 173)

6. F (p. 178)
7. T (pp. 174–175)
8. F (p. 172)
9. F (p. 164)
10. T (p. 165)

KEY TERMS

1. **Learning** is defined as any relatively permanent change in an organism's behavior as the result of experience. (p. 161)

2. Also known as respondent conditioning, **classical (or Pavlovian) conditioning** is a type of learning in which a neutral stimulus becomes capable of eliciting a conditioned response after having become associated with an unconditioned stimulus. (p. 162)

3. In classical conditioning, the **unconditioned response (UCR)** is the unlearned, involuntary response to the unconditioned stimulus. (p. 163)

   Memory aid: A behavior that is unconditioned is one that did not require training, or conditioning. Examples of such reflexive and involuntary responses are shivering, changes in pupil size, and blinking.

4. In classical conditioning, the **unconditioned stimulus (UCS)** is the stimulus that naturally and automatically elicits the reflexive unconditioned response. (p. 163)

   Example: Cold temperatures, changes in light intensity, and puffs of air to the eye are the **unconditioned stimuli** that elicit the unconditioned responses of shivering, changes in pupil size, and blinking.

5. In classical conditioning, the **conditioned response (CR)** is the learned response to a conditioned stimulus, which results from the acquired association between the CS and UCS. (p. 163)

6. In classical conditioning, the **conditioned stimulus (CS)** is an originally neutral stimulus that comes to elicit a CR after being paired with an unconditioned stimulus. (p. 163)

7. In a learning experiment, **acquisition** refers to the initial stage of conditioning in which the new response is gradually strengthened. (p. 164)

   Example: The operant procedure of shaping is a technique for facilitating the **acquisition** of a new response.

8. **Extinction** refers to the weakening of a CR when the CS is no longer followed by the UCS; in operant conditioning extinction occurs when a response is no longer reinforced. (p. 165)

   Example: In order to **extinguish** the child's tantrum behavior, the teacher ignored it until it ceased.

9. **Spontaneous recovery** is the reappearance of an extinguished CR after a rest period. (p. 165)

   Example: Although Craig hadn't smoked in years, he still often found himself tempted to have a cigarette with his after-dinner coffee. This **spontaneous recovery** of his former habit seemed impossible to extinguish.

10. **Generalization** refers to the tendency for stimuli similar to the original CS to evoke a CR. (p. 165)

    Example: After little Albert had been conditioned to fear a rat, his fear **generalized** to rabbits, hamsters, and even fur pieces.

11. **Discrimination** in classical conditioning refers to the ability to distinguish the CS from other similar stimuli. (p. 165)

    Example: In an early experiment, Pavlov taught a dog to **discriminate** a circle from an ellipse.

12. **Behaviorism** is the school of thought maintaining that psychology should be an objective science, study only observable behaviors, and avoid references to mental processes. (p. 167)

    Example: Because he was an early advocate of the study of overt behavior, John Watson is often called the father of **behaviorism**.

13. **Operant, or instrumental, conditioning** is a type of learning in which voluntary behavior becomes more or less probable when followed by reinforcing or punishing stimuli. (p. 170)

    Example: Unlike classical conditioning, which works on involuntary behaviors, **operant conditioning** works on voluntary behaviors that are willfully emitted by an organism.

14. **Respondent behavior** is that which occurs as an automatic, involuntary response to some stimulus. (p. 170)

    Example: Conditioned and unconditioned responses, in classical conditioning, are examples of **respondent behavior** in that they are involuntary responses elicited by specific stimuli.

15. In Skinner's theory, **operant behavior** is voluntary behavior the organism emits that operates on the environment and produces consequences such as reinforcement and punishment. (p. 170)

16. A **Skinner box** is an experimental chamber for the operant conditioning of an animal such as a pigeon or rat. The controlled environment enables the investigator to present visual or auditory stimuli, de-

liver reinforcement or punishment, and precisely measure simple responses such as bar presses or key pecking. (p. 170)

17. **Shaping** is the operant conditioning procedure for establishing a new response by reinforcing **successive approximations** of the desired behavior. (p. 170)

18. A **reinforcer** is any event that increases the likelihood of the behavior it follows. (p. 171)

19. **Positive reinforcement** refers to the presentation of a rewarding stimulus following a response. The effect of positive reinforcement is to strengthen the response. (p. 171)

20. **Negative reinforcement** refers to the withdrawal of an unpleasant stimulus, the effect of which is to reinforce, or strengthen, the preceding response. (p. 171)

    Memory aid: In operant conditioning, "positive" and "negative" do *not* mean good and bad, but to present or withdraw a stimulus, respectively.

21. The powers of **primary reinforcers** are automatic, inborn, and do not depend on learning. (p. 172)

    Example: To a hungry organism, food is a **primary reinforcer**.

22. **Secondary reinforcers** are stimuli that acquire their reinforcing power through their association with an established reinforcer. (p. 172)

    Example: Because money can be exchanged for a variety of primary reinforcers, such as food or shelter, it is a powerful **secondary reinforcer**.

23. **Continuous reinforcement** is the operant procedure of reinforcing each and every response. In promoting the acquisition of a new response it is best to use continuous reinforcement. (p. 173)

25. **Partial (or intermittent) reinforcement** is the operant procedure of reinforcing a response intermittently. A response that has been partially reinforced is much more resistant to extinction than one that has been continuously reinforced. (p. 173)

25. In operant conditioning, a **fixed-interval schedule** is one in which a response is reinforced after a specified time has elapsed. (p. 173)

    Example: Weekly quizzes are an example of a **fixed-interval schedule**. Studying tends to be minimal just after the previous exam and to peak just before the next one.

26. In operant conditioning, a **variable-interval schedule** is one in which responses are reinforced after varying intervals of time. (p. 173)

    Example: Pop quizzes are an example of a **vari-able-interval schedule**. Because the exact time of reinforcement is unpredictable on such a schedule, studying will tend to take place much more consistently.

27. In operant conditioning, a **fixed-ratio schedule** is one in which reinforcement is presented after a set number of responses. (p. 173)

    Example: Continuous reinforcement is a special kind of **fixed-ratio schedule**: reinforcement is presented after *each* response, so the ratio of reinforcements to responses is one to one.

28. In operant conditioning, a **variable-ratio schedule** is one in which reinforcement is presented after a varying number of responses. (p. 174)

    Example: Because reinforcement is contingent on the rate of responding even though the ratio of responses to reinforcements is unpredictable, **variable-ratio schedules** of reinforcement produce the highest and most stable rates of response.

29. In operant conditioning, **punishment** is the presentation of an aversive stimulus, such as shock, which weakens the behavior it follows. (p. 174)

    Memory aid: Many people confuse negative reinforcement with **punishment**. The former strengthens behavior, while the latter weakens it.

30. A **cognitive map** is a mental picture of one's environment. (p. 178)

    Example: The discovery that rats in mazes often behave as though they were employing **cognitive maps** led to a renewed interest in animal cognition.

31. **Latent learning** is learning that occurs in the absence of reinforcement but only becomes apparent when there is an incentive to demonstrate it. (p. 178)

32. **Observational learning** is learning by watching and imitating others. (p. 179)

33. **Modeling** is the process of watching and then imitating a specific behavior and is thus an important means through which observational learning occurs. (p. 179)

34. The opposite of antisocial behavior, **prosocial behavior** is positive, helpful, and constructive, and is subject to the same principles of observational learning as is undesirable behavior, such as aggression. (p. 180)

    Example: In an effort to promote **prosocial behavior** among sports fans, professional clubs offer public service announcements describing courteous conduct in the stands. Their slogan: "Courtesy is contagious."

Chapter 7 | Memory

Chapter Overview

Chapter 7 explores human memory as a system that processes information in three steps. *Encoding* refers to the process of putting information into the memory system. *Storage* is the purely passive mechanism by which information is maintained in memory. *Retrieval* is the process by which information is accessed from memory through recall or recognition.

Chapter 7 also discusses the importance of meaning, imagery, and organization in encoding new memories, how memory is represented physically in the brain, and how forgetting may result from failure to encode or store information or to find appropriate retrieval cues. As you study this chapter, try applying some of the memory tips discussed in the text.

Guided Study

The textbook chapter should be studied one section at a time. Before you read, preview each section by skimming it, noting headings and boldface items. Then read the appropriate section objectives from the following outline. Keep these objectives in mind, and as you read the chapter section, search for the information that will enable you to meet each objective. Once you have finished a section, write out answers for its objectives.

Forming Memories (pp. 186–202)

1. Distinguish the processes of encoding, storage, and retrieval, and describe the role of the sensory registers in the memory system.

2. Distinguish between automatic and effortful processing and explain the importance of meaning, imagery, and organization in the encoding process.

3. Describe memory capacity and discuss research findings on the physical basis of memory.

4. Contrast recall, recognition, and relearning measures of memory and describe the importance of retrieval cues.

5. Explain what is meant by state-dependent memory and discuss the evidence for memory's being constructive.

Forgetting (pp. 202–208)

6. Explain why the capacity to forget can be beneficial and discuss the role of encoding failure, decay, and interference in the process of forgetting.

7. Describe motivated forgetting and explain the concept of repression.

Chapter Review

When you have finished reading the chapter, use the material that follows to review it. Complete the fill-in sentences and answer the essay items in complete sentences. As you proceed, evaluate your performance for each chapter section by consulting the answer key at the end of this chapter. Do not continue with the next section until you've understood each term. If you need to, review or reread the appropriate chapter section in the textbook before continuing.

1. Learning that persists over time indicates the existence of _____ for that learning.

2. Memories for emotional moments that are especially clear are called _____ memories.

Forming Memories (pp. 186–202)

3. Human memory can be viewed as an information-processing system that performs three tasks: _____, _____ and _____.

4. Experiments by George Sperling revealed that we have a fleeting photographic, or _____, memory.

5. Sensory memory for sounds is called _____ memory. This memory

fades _____ (more/less) rapidly than photographic memory.

6. Encoding the meaning of words is referred to as _____ encoding; encoding by sound is called _____ encoding; encoding the image of words is _____ encoding.

7. Asked to repeat letters immediately after seeing a list of them, people tend to make acoustic errors _____ (more/less) often than they do visual errors. One hour later, errors tend to be _____.

8. According to some psychologists, this error pattern reflects the operation of two types of memory: _____-_____ memory and _____-_____ memory.

9. A distinction is made between memory processing of incidental and well-learned information that is _____ and processing that requires attention and is therefore _____.

Give examples of material encoded by automatic processing and by effortful processing.

10. A pioneering researcher of verbal memory was _____. In one experiment he found that the longer he studied a list of nonsense syllables, the _____ (fewer/greater) the number of repetitions he required to relearn it later.

11. The tendency to remember the first and last items in a list best is called the _____ _____. Following a delay, first items are remembered _____ (more/less) than last items.

12. Memory that consists of mental pictures is based on the use of _____.

13. Your earliest memories are most likely of events that occurred when you were about _____ years old.

14. Concrete, high-imagery words tend to be remembered _____ (better/less well) than abstract, low-imagery words.

15. Memory aids are known as _____ devices. For example, the first letters of to-be-remembered words might be grouped to form a word, called a(n) _____.

16. Using a jingle, such as the one that begins "one is a bun," is an example of the _____-_____ system.

17. Memory may be aided by grouping information into meaningful units called _____.

18. In addition, material may be processed into _____, which are composed of a few broad concepts divided into lesser concepts, categories, and facts.

19. If you are able to retrieve something from memory, you must have engaged in the passive process of _____.

20. Our short-term memory capacity is approximately _____ items.

21. In contrast to short-term memory—and contrary to popular belief—the capacity of permanent memory is essentially _____.

22. Penfield's electrically stimulated patients _____ (do/do not) provide reliable evidence that our stored memories are precise and durable.

23. Lashley attempted to locate memory by cutting out pieces of rats' _____ after they had learned a maze. He found that no matter where he cut, the rats _____ (remembered/forgot) the maze.

24. Gerard found that a hamster's memory remained even after its body temperature was lowered to a point where the brain's _____ activity stopped.

25. Amnesic patients typically have suffered damage to the _____ or the _____ of their limbic systems. These brain structures are important in the processing and storage of _____ (facts/skills). More primitive regions of the brain are important in the processing of _____ (facts/skills).

26. Memories of facts are also known as _____ memories, while memories of skills are also known as _____ memories.

Explain what researchers have learned about memory from studying amnesic patients.

27. A blow or electrical shock to the brain will disrupt _____ (recent/old) memories.

28. Researchers believe that memory involves a structural change, which occurs at the _____ between neurons.

29. Researchers Kandel and Schwartz have found that when learning occurs in the sea snail *Aplysia*, the neurotransmitter _____ is released in greater amounts, making synapses more efficient.

30. Certain disorders, such as _____ disease, disrupt memory through the loss of brain tissues that secrete important neurotransmitters.

31. Alcohol and other drugs classified as _____ impede memory formation.

32. Hormones released under stress often _____ (facilitate/impair) learning and memory.

33. The ability to retrieve information that is not present in conscious awareness is called _____.

34. Bahrick found that, 25 years after graduation, people were not able to _____ the names of their classmates but were able to _____ both their names and their yearbook pictures.

35. If you have learned something and then forgotten it, you will probably be able to _____ it _____ (more/less) quickly than you did originally.

36. The process by which the activation of particular associations in memory can lead to retrieval is called _____.

37. Studies have shown that retention is best when learning and testing are done in _____ (the same/different) contexts.

Summarize the textbook's explanation of the déjà vu experience.

38. The type of memory in which moods or particular physiological states serve as retrieval cues is referred to as _____- _____ memory.

Describe the effects of mood on memory.

39. Research has shown that recall of an event is often influenced by past experiences, present assumptions, and so forth. The workings of these influences illustrate the process of memory _____.

Describe what Loftus's studies have shown about the effects of misleading post-event information on eye-witness reports.

Forgetting (pp. 202–208)

40. Most memory failures reflect a failure to properly _____ the material.

41. Studies by Ebbinghaus and by Bahrick indicate that most forgetting occurs _____ (soon/a long time) after material was learned.

42. When information that is stored in memory temporarily cannot be found, _____ failure has occurred.

43. Research suggests that memories are lost not only because they fade with time, but also as a result of _____, which is especially possible if we simultaneously learn similar, new material.

44. The disruptive effect of previous learning on current learning is called _____. The disruptive effect of learning new material on efforts to recall material previously learned is called _____ _____.

45. Jenkins and Dallenbach found that if subjects went to sleep after learning, their memory for a list of nonsense syllables was _____ (better/worse) than it was if they stayed awake.

46. Freud proposed that motivated forgetting, or _____, may protect a person from painful memories.

FOCUS ON PSYCHOLOGY:
How the Brain Records a Memory

Memories consist of patterns of individual pieces of information linked in such a way that awareness of one piece often triggers awareness of the entire pattern. A single feature on the face of a passerby, for example, may remind us of the face of a friend.

Recent studies of neural functioning are beginning to reveal how associative memories are formed. Daniel Alkon and his colleagues at the National Institute of Neurological and Communicative Disorders and Stroke have found that when the brain records a memory, a sequence of molecular changes occurs in certain neurons that permanently changes their electrical excitability.

Alkon and his co-workers studied the acquisition of conditioned responses in rabbits and the marine snail *Hermissenda crassicornis*. In the rabbit conditioning procedure, an audible tone was paired with a blink-triggering puff of air to the animal's eye. Learning was demonstrated when the rabbit consistently blinked its eye in response to the conditioned stimulus (the tone), which preceded the unconditioned stimulus (the puff of air). The memory formed in order to learn the conditioned response involved an association between the separate neural pathways underlying the responses to the tone and the puff of air.

Alkon's experiments demonstrated that these separate pathways converged on and stimulated increased electrical activity in specialized neurons in the hippocampus of the rabbit brain. This increased electrical activity lasted for many days, which suggests that a long-lasting increase in excitability within a neural network is well-suited for storing lasting associations, or memories.

These hippocampal neurons are exceedingly complex and may each possess as many as 200,000 dendritic inputs from other nerve cells. A few days of conditioning trials, however, may alter the structure of these neurons in such a way as to limit the number of inputs. This "neural streamlining," similar to that observed during early brain development when neurons compete for limited synaptic opportunities, presumably allows each neuron to store thousands of separate memories.

Although our understanding of the physical basis of memory is far from complete, the pioneering research of Daniel Alkon and his colleagues has led to many important findings, not the least of which is that neurons involved in memory are dynamic and capable of dramatic changes in structure and function in order to represent the range of phenomena that constitute memory.

Source: Alkon, Daniel L. (1989, July). Memory storage and neural systems. *Scientific American*, 42–50.

Progress Test 1

Multiple-Choice Questions

Circle your answers to the following questions and check them with the answer key at the end of this chapter. If your answer is incorrect, read the answer key explanation for why it is incorrect and then consult the appropriate pages of the text in order to understand the correct answer.

1. The three steps in memory information processing are:
   a. input, processing, output.
   b. input, storage, output.
   c. input, storage, retrieval.
   d. encoding, storage, retrieval.

2. Which of the following is *not* a *measure* of retention?
   a. recall.   c. relearning.
   b. recognition.   d. retrieval.

3. Our immediate memory span is approximately _____ items.
   a. 2   c. 7
   b. 5   d. 15

4. Memory techniques such as acronyms and the peg-word system are called:
   a. consolidation techniques.
   b. imagery techniques.
   c. encoding strategies.
   d. mnemonics.

5. One way to increase the amount of information in memory is to group it into larger, familiar units. This process is referred to as:
   a. consolidating.   c. memory construction.
   b. chunking.   d. encoding.

6. Kandel and Schwartz have found that when learning occurs, more of the neurotransmitter _____ is released into synapses.
   a. ACh   c. serotonin
   b. dopamine   d. noradrenaline

7. Research on memory construction reveals that:
   a. memories are stored as exact copies of experience.
   b. memories reflect a person's biases and assumptions.
   c. memories may be chemically transferred from one organism to another.
   d. long-term memories usually decay within about five years.

8. Context cues are important in memory. In one study, people learned words while on land or under water. In a later test of recall, those with the best retention had:
   a. learned the words on land, that is, in the more familiar context.
   b. learned the words under water, that is, in the more exotic context.
   c. learned the words and been tested on them in different contexts.

d. learned the words and been tested on them in the same context.

9. Most memory failure can be attributed to failure in:

   a. automatic processing. c. storage.
   b. encoding.   d. retrieval.

10. Complete this analogy: Fill-in-the-blank test questions are to multiple-choice questions as:

    a. encoding is to storage.
    b. storage is to encoding.
    c. recognition is to recall.
    d. recall is to recognition.

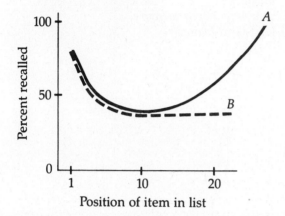

Position of item in list

11. The above figure depicts the recall of a list of words under two conditions. Which of the following best describes the difference between the conditions?

    a. In *A* the words were studied and retrieved in the same context; in *B* the contexts were different.
    b. In *B* the words were studied and retrieved in the same context; in *A* the contexts were different.
    c. The delay between presentation of the last word and the test of recall was longer for *A* than for *B*.
    d. The delay between presentation of the last word and the test of recall was longer for *B* than for *A*.

12. Darren was asked to memorize a list of letters that included *v*, *q*, *y*, and *j*. He later recalled these letters as *e*, *u*, *i*, and *k*, suggesting that the original letters had been encoded:

a. automatically.   c. semantically.
b. visually.   d. acoustically.

13. Janice keeps confusing the combination of her new school locker with that of her old one. She is experiencing:

    a. proactive interference.
    b. retroactive interference.
    c. encoding failure.
    d. storage failure.

14. The eerie feeling of having been somewhere before is an example of:

    a. state dependency.   c. priming.
    b. encoding failure.   d. déjà vu.

15. After suffering damage to the hippocampus, a person would probably:

    a. lose memory for skills such as bicycle riding.
    b. be incapable of being classically conditioned.
    c. lose the ability to store new facts.
    d. experience all of the above changes.

16. Which of the following has been proposed as a neurophysiological explanation of infantile amnesia?

    a. The slow maturation of the hippocampus leaves the infant's brain unable to store images and events.
    b. The deficient supply of serotonin until about age 3 makes encoding very limited.
    c. The limited availability of association areas of the cortex until about age 3 impairs encoding and storage.
    d. All of the above explanations have been proposed.

17. In Sperling's memory experiment, subjects were shown three rows of three letters, followed immediately by a low-, medium, or high-pitched tone. The subjects were able to report:

    a. all three rows with perfect accuracy.
    b. only the top row of letters.
    c. only the middle row of letters.
    d. any one of the three rows of letters.

Matching Items

Match each definition or description with the appropriate term.

Definition

_____ 1. a limitless and relatively permanent storage component of memory

_____ 2. the process by which information gets into the memory system

_____ 3. mental pictures that aid memory

_____ 4. the blocking of painful memories

_____ 5. the phenomenon in which one's mood can influence retrieval

_____ 6. memory for a list of words is affected by word order

_____ 7. "one is a bun, two is a shoe" mnemonic device

_____ 8. a limited-capacity, brief storage component of memory

_____ 9. new learning interferes with previous knowledge

_____ 10. a more sensitive test of memory than recall

_____ 11. old knowledge interferes with new learning

Term

a. repression
b. relearning
c. serial position effect
d. peg-word system
e. short-term memory
f. proactive interference
g. retroactive interference
h. encoding
i. imagery
j. state-dependent memory
k. long-term memory

Progress Test 2

Progress Test 2 should be completed during a final chapter review. Do this test after you thoroughly understand the correct answers for the Chapter Review and Progress Test 1.

Multiple-Choice Questions

1. Which of the following best describes the typical forgetting curve?
   a. a steady, slow decline in retention over time
   b. a steady, rapid decline in retention over time
   c. a rapid initial decline in retention becoming stable thereafter
   d. a slow initial decline in retention becoming rapid thereafter

2. In order to minimize interference-induced forgetting, what is the best sequence to follow if you want to improve your recall on your psychology midterm?
   a. study—eat—test
   b. study—exercise—test
   c. study—listen to music—test
   d. study—sleep—test

3. Which of the following measures of retention is the least sensitive in triggering retrieval?
   a. recall
   b. recognition
   c. relearning
   d. déjà vu

4. In order to remember the name of the classmate who sat behind her in fifth grade, Martina mentally recited the names of other classmates who sat near her. Martina's effort to refresh her memory by activating related associations is an example of:
   a. déjà vu.
   b. encoding.
   c. relearning.
   d. priming.

5. According to the serial position effect, when recalling a list of words you should have the greatest difficulty with those:
   a. at the beginning of the list.
   b. in the middle of the list.
   c. at the end of the list.
   d. at the end and in the middle of the list.

6. Lashley's studies, in which rats learned a maze and then had various parts of their brains surgically removed, showed that:
   a. the memory was lost when surgery took place within 1 hour of learning.
   b. the memory was lost when surgery took place within 24 hours of learning.
   c. the memory was lost when any region of the brain was removed.
   d. the memory remained no matter which area of the brain was tampered with.

7. The disruption of memory caused by Alzheimer's

disease or excessive consumption of alcohol provides evidence for the importance of:

a. neurotransmitters in the formation of new memories.

b. neurotransmitters in the retrieval of long-term memories.

c. nutrition in normal neural functioning.

d. all of the above.

8. Which type of substance tends to disrupt memory formation?

a. stimulants   **c.** depressants

b. stress hormones   **d.** opiates

9. Studies by Loftus and Palmer, in which subjects were quizzed about a film of an accident, indicate that:

a. when quizzed immediately, subjects can recall very little, due to the stress of witnessing an accident.

b. when questioned as little as one day later, their memory was very inaccurate.

c. most subjects had very accurate memories as much as 6 months later.

d. subjects' recall may easily be affected by misleading information.

10. Being in a bad mood after a hard day of work, Susan could think of nothing positive in her life. This is *best* explained as an example of:

a. priming.

b. memory construction.

c. retrieval failure.

d. state-dependent memory.

11. Walking through the halls of his high school ten years after graduating, Tom experienced a flood of old memories. Tom's experience showed the role of:

a. state-dependent memory.

b. context effects.

c. retroactive interference.

d. proactive interference.

12. Amnesic patients typically experience disruption of:

a. procedural memories.

b. declarative memories.

c. short-term memory.

d. long-term memory.

13. The first thing Karen did when she discovered that she had misplaced her keys was to recreate in her mind the sequence of the day's events. That she had little difficulty in doing so illustrates:

a. automatic processing.

b. effortful processing.

c. state-dependent memory.

d. priming.

14. Textbook chapters are often organized into _____ in order to facilitate information processing.

a. mnemonic devices   **c.** hierarchies

b. chunks   **d.** peg words

15. Which of the following is the best example of a flashbulb memory?

a. suddenly remembering to buy bread while standing in the checkout line at the grocery store

b. recalling the name of someone from high school while looking at his or her yearbook snapshot

c. remembering to make an important phone call

d. remembering what you were doing the day the space shuttle *Challenger* exploded

16. When Carlos got promoted, he moved into a new office and his phone extension changed. When asked for his new phone number, his old extension comes to mind first, illustrating the effects of:

a. proactive interference.

b. retroactive interference.

c. encoding failure.

d. storage failure.

True-False Items

Indicate whether each statement is true or false by placing *T* or *F* in the blank next to the item.

_____ 1. Studying that is distributed over time produces better retention than cramming.

_____ 2. Additional rehearsal of material that has already been learned usually interferes with retention.

_____ 3. Generally speaking, memory for pictures is better than memory for words.

_____ 4. Studies of hypnotic age regression indicate that memory is permanent, due to the reliability of such reports.

_____ 5. Most people do not have memories of events that occurred before the age of 3 or 4.

_____ 6. Studies by Ebbinghaus show that most forgetting occurs soon after learning.

_____ 7. There is no evidence that people repress memories as Freud suggested.

_____ 8. Recall of newly acquired knowledge is no better after sleeping than after being awake for the same period of time.

_____ 9. Time spent in developing imagery, chunking, and associating material with what you already know is more effective than time spent repeating information again and again.

_____ 10. Procedural memories are processed in more primitive parts of the brain than are declarative memories.

8. short-term memory

9. long-term memory

Key Terms

Using your own words, write a brief definition or explanation of each of the following terms.

1. memory

10. automatic processing

2. flashbulb memories

11. effortful processing

3. encoding (acoustic, visual, semantic)

12. rehearsal

4. storage

13. serial position effect

5. retrieval

14. imagery

6. iconic memory

15. mnemonics

7. echoic memory

16. chunking

17. hippocampus

18. declarative memories

19. procedural memories

20. recall

21. recognition

22. relearning

23. priming

24. déjà vu

25. state-dependent memory

26. proactive interference

27. retroactive interference

28. repression

Answers
CHAPTER REVIEW

1. memory
2. flashbulb
3. encoding; storage; retrieval
4. iconic
5. echoic; less
6. semantic; acoustic; visual
7. more; semantic
8. short-term; long-term
9. automatic; effortful

Automatic processing includes the encoding of information about space, time, and frequency—encoding that is evidently innate. Automatic processing also includes the encoding of word meaning, a type of encoding that appears to be learned. Effortful processing, or encoding that requires attention and effort, is used to encode material like telephone numbers, word lists, textbook chapters, etc.

10. Hermann Ebbinghaus; fewer
11. serial position effect; more
12. imagery
13. 3 or 4
14. better
15. mnemonic; acronym
16. peg-word
17. chunks; acronym
18. hierarchies
19. storage
20. 7
21. unlimited

22. do not

23. cortices; remembered

24. electrical

25. hippocampus; amygdala; facts; skills

26. declarative; procedural

Many amnesic patients are incapable of learning new facts or recalling anything they have recently done. They can, however, learn and remember new skills. Also, the old memories of amnesics are usually intact. Such patients typically have suffered damage to the hippocampus or amygdala, which are structures of the limbic system. That new skills can be remembered but new facts cannot indicates that the two are processed differently—facts through the (damaged) limbic system structures, skills in more primitive brain regions. That old facts are remembered suggests that the limbic system structures are "way stations" in the storage process, rather than areas where facts are ultimately stored.

27. recent

28. synapses

29. serotonin

30. Alzheimer's

31. depressants

32. facilitate

33. recall

34. recall; recognize

35. relearn; more

36. priming

37. the same

The *déjà vu* experience is most likely the result of being in a context similar to one that we *have* actually been in before. If we have previously been in a similar situation, though we cannot recall what it was, the current situation may present cues that unconsciously help us to retrieve the earlier experience.

38. state-dependent

The effect of state-dependent memory is that things learned in one state are most easily recalled when we are again in the same state. Moods also affect both our encoding of present experiences and our retrieval of past experiences. When happy, for example, we perceive things in a positive light and recall happy events; these perceptions and memories, in turn, prolong our good mood.

39. construction

When subjects viewed a film of a traffic accident and were quizzed a week later, misleading post-event information was found to influence recall of the event (although it did not affect people's ability to recognize what they had witnessed). Phrasing of questions af-

fected answers; the word "smashed," for instance, made subjects mistakenly think they had seen broken glass.

40. encode

41. soon

42. retrieval

43. interference

44. proactive interference; retroactive interference

45. better

46. repression

PROGRESS TEST 1

Multiple-Choice Questions

1. **d.** is the answer. Information must be encoded, or put into appropriate form; stored, or retained over time; and retrieved, or located and gotten out when needed. (p. 187)

2. **d.** is the answer. Retrieval refers to the *process* of remembering. (p. 187)

3. **c.** is the answer. (p. 195)

4. **d.** is the answer. (p. 192)

   a. There is no such term as "consolidation techniques."

   b. & c. Imagery and encoding strategies are important in storing new memories, but *mnemonics* is the general term for techniques that facilitate memory, such as acronyms and the peg-word system.

5. **b.** is the answer. (p. 193)

   a. There is no such process as "consolidating."

   c. Memory construction refers to the ways in which memories are altered by the individual's basic assumptions and experiences.

   d. Encoding refers to the processing of information into the memory system.

6. **c.** is the answer. Kandel and Schwartz found that when learning occurred in the sea snail *Aplysia*, serotonin was released at certain synapses, which then became more efficient at signal transmission. (p. 197)

   a., b., & d. These are all neurotransmitters, but none played a role in Kandel and Schwartz's studies.

7. **b.** is the answer. We in essence construct our memories, bringing them into line with our biases and assumptions, as well as with our subsequent experiences. (pp. 200–201)

   a. If this were true, it would mean that memory construction does not occur. Through memory construction, memories may deviate significantly from the original experiences.

c. There is no evidence that such chemical transfers occur.

d. Many long-term memories are apparently unlimited in duration.

8. **d.** is the answer. In general, being in a similar context to that where you experienced something will tend to help you recall the experience. (p. 198)

a. & b. The learning environment per se—and its familiarity or exoticness—had no effect on retention.

c. This answer is incorrect because d. is correct.

9. **b.** is the answer. In most cases, the information never made it into the memory system. (p. 203)

a. Automatic processing refers to the effortless encoding of incidental information, such as space, time, and frequency. The formation of memory does *not* require such processing; therefore, most memory failures cannot be attributed to the failure to process information automatically.

c. Storage is a passive process; moreover, most "memories-to-be" never make it this far.

d. Retrieval failure accounts for many memory failures, but for fewer than does encoding failure.

10. **d.** is the answer. (p. 198)

a. & b. In order to correctly answer either type of question, the knowledge must have been encoded and stored.

c. With fill-in-the-blank questions, the answer must be recalled with no retrieval cues other than the question. With multiple-choice questions, the correct answer merely has to be recognized from among several alternatives.

11. **d.** is the answer. (p. 198)

a. & b. These answers are incorrect because a serial position effect would presumably occur whether the study and retrieval contexts were the same or different.

c. As Craik and Watkins found, when recall is delayed, only the first items in a list are recalled more accurately than the others. With immediate recall both the first and the last items are recalled more accurately.

12. **d.** is the answer. That all four mistakes are based on a sound confusion suggests the letters were encoded acoustically. (p. 188)

a. Memorizing a letter list would involve effortful, rather than automatic, processing.

b. The mistakes do not involve letters that are similar in appearance.

c. Semantic encoding would have been suggested by errors based on similarities of meaning.

13. **a.** is the answer. Proactive interference occurs when old information makes it difficult to correctly remember new information. (p. 205)

b. Retroactive interference is the disruption of something you once learned by new information.

c. & d. Interference produces forgetting even when the forgotten material was effectively encoded and stored. Janice's problem is at the level of retrieval.

14. **d.** is the answer. (p. 199)

a. State-dependent memory is the phenomenon in which information is best retrieved when the person is in the same emotional or physiological state he or she was in when the material was learned.

b. Encoding failure occurs when a person has not processed information sufficiently for it to enter the memory system.

c. Priming is the process by which a memory is activated through retrieval of an associated memory.

15. **c.** is the answer. The hippocampus is involved in processing new facts for storage. (p. 196)

a., b., & d. Studies of amnesics with hippocampal damage show that neither classical conditioning nor skill memory are impaired, indicating that these aspects of memory are controlled by more primitive regions of the brain.

16. **a.** is the answer. We remember skills acquired in infancy, as such procedural memories are recorded in earlier developing brain regions, but declarative memories involve the hippocampus. (p. 197)

b., c., & d. There is no evidence that serotonin levels or association areas are deficient until age 3. Moreover, such proposals are unlikely, as they wouldn't explain why we remember skills learned in infancy while forgetting events experienced.

17. **d.** is the answer. Although when asked to recall all the letters, subjects could recall only about half, if immediately *after* the presentation they were signaled to recall a particular row, their recall was near perfect. This showed that they had a brief photographic memory—so brief that if faded in less time than it would have taken to say all nine letters. (p. 187)

Matching Items

1. k (p. 188)   5. j (p. 199)   9. g (p. 205)
2. h (p. 187)   6. c (p. 190)   10. b (p. 198)
3. i (p. 191)   7. d (p. 192)   11. f (p. 205)
4. a (p. 206)   8. e (p. 188)

PROGRESS TEST 2

Multiple-Choice Questions

1. **c.** is the answer. As Ebbinghaus and Bahrick both showed, most of the forgetting that is going to occur happens soon after learning. (p. 204)

2. **d.** is the answer. (pp. 204–205)

   a., b., & c. Being involved with other activities, even just eating or listening to music, is more disruptive than sleeping.

3. **a.** A test of recall presents the fewest retrieval cues and usually produces the most limited retrieval. (p. 198)

4. **d.** is the answer. Priming is the conscious or unconscious activation of particular associations in memory. (p. 198)

   a. Déjà vu is the false impression of having previously experienced a current situation.

   b. That Martina is able to retrieve her former classmates' names implies that they already have been encoded.

   c. Relearning is a measure of retention based on how long it takes to relearn something already mastered. Martina is recalling her former classmates' names, not relearning them.

5. **b.** is the answer. According to the serial position effect, items at the beginning and ends of a list tend to be remembered best. (p. 190)

6. **d.** is the answer. (p. 196)

   a. & b. Lashley's studies did not investigate the significance of the interval between learning and cortical lesioning.

   c. Surprisingly, Lashley found that no matter where he cut, the rats had at least a partial memory of how to solve the maze.

7. **a.** is the answer. Both alcohol and Alzheimer's disease disrupt memory by interfering with the neurotransmitter serotonin. (p. 197)

   b. The disruptive effects of alcohol and Alzheimer's disease are on the formation, rather than the retrieval, of memories.

   c. Although nutrition plays an important role in brain chemistry, the effects of Alzheimer's disease and alcohol are independent of nutrition.

8. **c.** is the answer. Alcohol is a prime example of the effect of depressants on memory formation. (p. 197)

   a. & b. These often facilitate encoding and retention.

   d. Opiates do not have a reliable influence, one way or the other, on memory.

9. **d.** is the answer. When misled by the phrasings of questions, subjects incorrectly recalled details of the film and even "remembered" objects that weren't there. (p. 201)

   a., b., & c. These were not findings of Loftus and Palmer.

10. **d.** is the answer. Susan's memories are affected by her state, in this case her bad mood. (p. 199)

    a. Priming refers to the conscious activation of particular associations in memory.

    b. Memory construction refers to changes in memory as new experiences occur.

    c. Although Susan's difficulty in recalling the good could be considered retrieval failure, it is caused by the state-dependent effect, which is therefore the *best* explanation.

11. **b.** is the answer. Being back in the context in which the original experiences occurred triggered memories of these experiences. (p. 199)

    a. The memories were triggered by similarity of place, not mood.

    c. Retroactive interference would involve difficulties in retrieving old memories.

    d. Proactive interference would involve difficulty in learning new material due to interference from earlier learning.

12. **b.** is the answer. Amnesics typically have suffered damage to the hippocampus, a brain structure involved in processing declarative memories for facts. (p. 196)

    a. Amnesics *do* retain procedural memories for how to do things; these are processed in the more ancient parts of the brain.

    c. & d. That amnesics are able to remember certain things (skills but not facts) indicates that their difficulty is not in short- or long-term memory *per se*, but with the processing of certain *types* of information.

13. **a.** is the answer. Time and space—and therefore sequences of events—are often automatically processed. (p. 188)

    b. That she had *little difficulty* indicates the processing was automatic, rather than effortful.

    c. & d. State-dependent memory and priming have nothing to do with the automatic processing of space and time.

14. **c.** is the answer. By breaking concepts down into subconcepts and yet smaller divisions and showing the relationships among these, hierarchies facilitate information processing. Use of main heads and subheads is an example of the organization of textbook chapters into hierarchies. (pp. 193–194)

    a. Mnemonic devices are rhymes, acronyms, and other memory *techniques* that facilitate retention.

b. Chunks are organizations of knowledge into familiar, manageable units.

d. Peg words are mnemonics in which to-be-remembered words are rhymed in a jingle.

15. **d.** is the answer. Flashbulb memories are unusually clear memories of emotionally significant moments in life. (p. 186)

16. **a.** is the answer. Proactive interference occurs when old information makes it difficult to recall new information. (p. 205)

b. If Carlos were having trouble remembering the *old* extension, this answer would be correct.

c. & d. Carlos has successfully encoded and stored the combination; he's just having problems retrieving it.

True-False Items

1. True (p. 190)
2. False (p. 189)
3. True (p. 191)
4. False (p. 195)
5. True (p. 197)
6. True (p. 203)
7. False (p. 195)
8. False (p. 205)
9. True (pp. 191–194)
10. True (p. 196)

KEY TERMS

1. **Memory** is simply any indication in an organism's behavior that learning has persisted over time. (p. 185)

2. **Flashbulb memories** are unusually vivid memories of emotionally important moments in our lives. (p. 186)

   Example: As if a photographer had snapped a picture of me at the moment I heard John Lennon had been killed, the **flashbulb memory** where I was and what I was doing is forever stored in my mind.

3. **Encoding** is the first step in memory; information is translated into some form that enables it to enter our memory system. Encoding may be **acoustic,** when sound is encoded, **visual,** when images are encoded, or **semantic,** when meaning is encoded. (pp. 187–188)

4. **Storage** refers to the passive process by which encoded information is maintained over time. (pp. 187 and 194)

5. **Retrieval** is the process of bringing to consciousness information from memory storage. (p. 187)

   Example: Oftentimes we think we have forgotten something when what actually has occurred is **retrieval failure**: at another time, in another place, the desired information may readily come to mind.

6. **Iconic memory** is the visual sensory register consisting of a perfect photographic memory, which lasts no more than a second or so. (p. 187)

Memory aid: *Icon* means "image," or "representation." **Iconic memory** consists of brief visual images.

7. **Echoic memory** is the momentary sensory memory of auditory stimuli, lasting about 3 or 4 seconds. (p. 187)

   Memory aid: An echo is the repetition of a sound; **echoic memory** is the persistence of sounds in our sensory register.

8. **Short-term memory** is conscious, working memory, which can hold about seven items for a short time and often represents information acoustically. (p. 188)

9. **Long-term memory** is the relatively permanent and unlimited capacity memory system into which information from short-term memory may pass. Long-term memory is typically based on semantic storage. (p. 188)

10. **Automatic processing** refers to our effortless encoding of incidental information such as space, time, and frequency. (p. 188)

    Example: Because of our dependence on language, the encoding of word meaning is an example of **automatic processing,** which does not require conscious control.

11. **Effortful processing** is encoding that requires conscious attention and some degree of effort. (p. 188)

    Example: Study techniques such as recitation, rehearsal, and chunking can often facilitate **effortful processing.**

12. **Rehearsal** is the conscious, effortful repetition of information that you are trying to encode for storage. (p. 189)

13. The **serial position effect** is the tendency for items at the beginning and end of a list to be more easily retained than those in the middle. (p. 190)

    Memory aid: An item's *position* within a *series* affects the ease with which it is retained.

14. **Imagery** refers to mental pictures and can be an important aid to memory. For example, concrete words, which can be associated to images, are better remembered than abstract words. (pp. 191–192)

15. **Mnemonics** are memory aids (acronyms, pegwords, etc.), which often use visual imagery. (p. 192)

    Example: The mnemonist, or professional memorizer, depends on a large repertoire of **mnemonics** in order to quickly encode to-be-remembered information.

16. **Chunking** is the memory technique of organizing material into familiar, meaningful units. (p. 193)

Example: In a classic experiment, the capacity of short-term memory was determined to be 7 ± 2 **chunks** of information. By regrouping, or **chunking**, single digits into groups of 3 and 4, subjects were able to increase the amount of information they could retain without rehearsal.

17. The **hippocampus** is a neural region within the limbic system that is important in the storage of names, images, events, and other facts in memory. (p. 196)

    Example: Many amnesic patients have suffered damage to the **hippocampus** and are unable to store new declarative memories.

18. **Declarative memories** are memories of facts, including names, images, and events. (p. 196)

19. **Procedural memories** are memories of skills, or procedures for how to do things. Procedural memories are evidently processed, not by the hippocampus, but by more primitive parts of the brain. (p. 196)

20. **Recall** is a measure of retention in which the person must remember, with few retrieval cues, information learned earlier. (p. 198)

    Example: Because fill-in-the-blank questions provide virtually no retrieval cues, they are tests of **recall**.

21. **Recognition** is a measure of retention in which one need only identify, rather than recall, previously learned information. (p. 198)

Example: Matching and multiple-choice test items require **recognition** of correct answers from among a set of alternatives.

22. **Relearning** is also a measure of retention in that the less time it takes to relearn information, the more that information has been retained. (p. 198)

23. **Priming** is the activation of a web of associations in memory in order to retrieve a specific memory. (p. 198)

    Example: In order to answer the trivia question about the 1968 Detroit Tigers, Denny **primed** his memory by mentally reciting the batting lineup.

24. **Déjà vu** is the false sense that you have already experienced a current situation. (p. 199)

25. **State-dependent memory** is the tendency to best recall information when in the same emotional or physiological state one was in at the time of learning. (p. 199)

26. **Proactive interference** is the disruptive effect of something you already have learned on your efforts to learn or recall new information. (p. 205)

27. **Retroactive interference** is the disruptive effect of something recently learned on old knowledge. (p. 205)

    Memory aid: *Retro* means "backward." **Retroactive interference** is "backward-acting" interference.

28. **Repression** is an example of motivated forgetting in that painful memories are prevented from entering consciousness. (p. 206)

Thinking, Language, and Intelligence

Chapter Overview

Perhaps more so than any other chapter in the text, Chapter 8 is concerned with what makes our species unique—thinking, language, and intelligence. The first part of the chapter deals with thinking, with emphasis on how people logically—or at times illogically—make decisions and solve problems. Also discussed are two common obstacles to problem solving: fixations that prevent us from taking a fresh perspective on a problem and our bias to seek information that confirms rather than challenges existing hypotheses.

The next part of the chapter is concerned with language, including its development in children and its relationship to thinking. Two theories of language acquisition are evaluated: Skinner's theory that language acquisition is based entirely on learning, and Chomsky's theory that humans have a biological predisposition to acquire language.

The last part of this chapter examines the enduring controversy in psychology of how best to define and measure intelligence. The historical origins of intelligence tests and several important issues concerning their use are discussed. These include the methods by which intelligence tests are constructed and whether such tests are valid and reliable. The chapter also discusses research attempts to assess whether intelligence is a single general ability or several specific ones, and the extent of genetic and environmental influences on intelligence.

Guided Study

The text chapter should be studied one section at a time. Before you read, preview each section by skimming it, noting headings and boldface items. Then read the appropriate section objectives from the following outline. Keep these objectives in mind, and as you read the chapter section, search for the information that will enable you to meet each objective. Once you have finished a section, write out the answers for its objectives.

Thinking (pp. 212–221)

1. Describe the nature, function, and formation of concepts.

2. Discuss the major problem-solving strategies and identify obstacles to problem solving.

3. Describe the heuristics that guide decision making and explain how overconfidence, framing, and belief perseverance can affect judgment.

Language (pp. 222–229)

4. Trace the course of language acquisition and discuss alternative theories of language development.

5. Describe the research on animal communication and discuss the controversy over whether animals have language.

6. Discuss the relationship between thought and language.

Intelligence (pp. 230–243)

7. Distinguish between aptitude and achievement tests and trace the origins of intelligence tests.

8. Identify the major principles of good test construction and illustrate their application to intelligence tests.

9. Describe the nature of intelligence and discuss whether it should be considered a general mental ability or many specific abilities.

10. Identify the factors associated with creativity.

11. Discuss evidence for both genetic and environmental influences on intelligence.

12. Discuss whether intelligence tests are biased.

Chapter Review

When you have finished reading the chapter, use the material that follows to review it. Complete the fill-in sentences and answer the essay items in complete sentences. As you proceed, evaluate your performance for each chapter section by consulting the answer key at the end of this chapter. Do not continue with the next section until you've understood each answer. If you need to, go back and review or reread the appropriate chapter section in the textbook before continuing.

Thinking (pp. 212–221)

1. People tend to organize specific items into general mental groupings called _____, and many such groupings often are further organized together into _____.

2. Concepts are typically formed through the development of a best example, or _____, of a category.

3. Although humans may not always think logically, we are especially capable of using our

reasoning powers for coping with new situations, or _____ _____.

Identify the steps involved in effective problem solving.

4. Logical, methodical, step-by-step procedures for solving problems are called _____.

5. Rule-of-thumb strategies that provide us with problem-solving shortcuts are referred to as

_____.

6. When you suddenly realize a problem's solution, _____ has occurred. Many psychologists believe that animals _____ (have/have not) been shown to possess this capability.

7. The tendency of people to look for information that verifies their preconceptions is called the

_____ _____.

8. Not being able to take a new perspective when attempting to solve a problem is referred to as _____. One example of this obstacle to problem solving is the inability to envision using an object in an atypical way. In such a situation _____ _____ is operating.

9. People judge how well something matches a particular prototype or concept; this is the

_____ _____.

10. When we judge the likelihood of something occurring in terms of how readily it comes to mind, we are using the _____

_____.

Explain how these two heuristics may lead us to make judgmental errors.

11. The tendency of people to overestimate the accuracy of their knowledge is called the _____ phenomenon.

12. Research has shown that, when subjects are given feedback on the accuracy of their judgments, such feedback generally _____ (does/does not) help them become more realistic about how much they know.

13. Decision making can be significantly affected by the phrasing, or _____, of an issue.

14. Research has shown that once we form a belief or a concept, it may take more convincing evidence for us to change the concept than it did to create it; this is called the _____ _____ phenomenon.

Language (pp. 222–229)

15. The first stage of language development, in which children spontaneously utter different sounds, is the _____ stage. This stage typically begins at about _____ months of age. The sounds children make during this stage _____ (are/are not) limited to the sounds of the language that they hear.

16. During the second stage, called the

_____-_____

stage, children convey complete thoughts using single words. This stage begins at about _____ year(s) of age.

17. During the two-word stage children speak in sentences containing mostly nouns and verbs. This type of speech is called _____ speech.

18. Skinner believes that language development follows the general principles of

_____.

19. Other theorists believe that humans are biologically predisposed to learn language. One such theorist is _____.

20. The Gardners attempted to communicate with the chimpanzee Washoe by teaching her

_____ _____ .

Summarize some of the arguments of skeptics of the "talking apes" research.

21. According to the _____ _____ hypothesis, language shapes our thinking. One linguist who proposed this hypothesis is _____ .

22. In several studies researchers have found that using the pronoun "he" (instead of "he or she") _____ (does/does not) influence people's thoughts concerning gender.

23. It appears that thinking _____ (can/cannot) occur without the use of language.

Summarize the probable relationship between thinking and language.

Intelligence (pp. 230–243)

24. Tests designed to predict one's ability to learn something new are called _____ tests. Tests designed to measure what you already have learned are called _____ tests.

25. The French psychologist who devised a test to predict the success of children in school was _____ . Predictions were made by comparing children's chronological ages with their _____ ages, which were determined by the test.

26. Lewis Terman's revision of Binet's test is referred to as the _____-_____ . This test enables one to derive an

_____ _____

for an individual.

Give the original and current formula for computing IQ and explain any terms used in the formula.

27. The most commonly used intelligence test is the

_____ _____

_____ _____ .

Consisting of eleven subtests, it provides not only a general IQ score but also separate _____ and _____ IQ scores.

28. Three requirements of a good test are

_____ , _____ ,

and _____ .

29. The administering of a test to a representative comparison group is called _____ .

30. When scores on a test are compiled, they generally result in a bell-shaped, or _____ , distribution.

Describe the normal curve and explain its significance in the standardization process.

31. If a test yields consistent results, it is said to be

_____ .

32. The Stanford-Binet, the WAIS, and the WISC have reliabilities of about _____ .

33. The degree to which a test measures or predicts what it is supposed to is referred to as the test's

_____ .

34. Generally speaking, the predictive validity of general aptitude tests _____ (is/is not) as high as their reliability. The predictive validity of these tests _____ (increases/diminishes) as individuals move up the educational ladder.

35. According to the textbook, intelligence can be defined as _____ _____

36. A controversy regarding the nature of intelligence centers on whether intelligence is one _____ ability or several _____ abilities.

37. The statistical procedure used to identify groups of items that appear to measure a common ability is called _____ _____.

38. Individuals who are mentally retarded yet possess one extraordinary skill are referred to as _____.

39. Howard Gardner proposes that there are _____ _____, each independent of the others.

40. Sternberg and Wagner distinguish three types of intelligence: _____ intelligence, _____ intelligence, and _____ intelligence.

41. Charles Spearman believed that a factor called g, or _____ _____, runs through the more specific aspects of intelligence.

42. The ability to produce novel ideas is called _____. A professional who is exceptionally creative will generally score _____ (higher/lower) on intelligence tests than less creative peers. The relationship between intelligence and creativity holds only up to a certain point—an IQ score of about _____.

Describe three other components of creativity.

43. The position that both heredity and environment exert some influence on intelligence is _____ (controversial/generally accepted) among psychologists.

44. The IQ scores of identical twins are _____ (more/no more) similar than those of fraternal twins.

45. The amount of variation in a trait that is attributable to genetic factors is called its _____. For intelligence, this has been estimated at roughly _____ percent.

46. Studies indicate that neglected children _____ (do/do not) show signs of recovery in IQ and behavior when placed in more nurturing environments.

Explain why it is possible for aptitude tests to be biased in one sense and not in another.

FOCUS ON PSYCHOLOGY:
Becoming a Mental Calculator

Steven Smith (1983) refers to individuals who can perform complex calculations in their heads as *mental calculators*. For example, Shyam Marathe determined that the twenty-third root of 24,242,900, 770,553, 981,941,874,678,268,486,966,725,193 was 57—and he performed the calculation mentally, in only 50 seconds.

Although people once believed that the ability to perform complex mental calculations was a sign of superior intelligence, we now know that almost anyone willing to learn a few systematic steps can do such calculations. As an illustration, consider the digits 0 through 9 and their cubes.

Digit (root)	Cube
0	0
1	1
2	8
3	27
4	64
5	125
6	216
7	343
8	512
9	729

Except in the cases of 2, 3, 7, and 8, the last digit of each cube is the same as its root. For these four numbers, the last digit of the cube is equal to the root subtracted from 10. For example, the last digit of the cube of 8 is 2 (10 − 8). Once you have committed the above ten cubes to memory, you can easily find the root of any perfect cube less than 1,000,000. In every case, the root will have only 1 or 2 digits. The last digit of the cube is either the root itself or the root subtracted from 10. Suppose you want to find the cube root of 274,625. The last digit is 5, which is also the second digit of its root. To find the first digit you need to remember the table and one additional rule. Determine which two cubes the digits to the left of the comma fall between. These digits, 274, fall between the cubes of 6 and 7 in the table. The first digit of the cube root you seek is simply the smaller of the two. Therefore, the cube root of 274,625 is 65. Try using this technique to determine the cube roots of 10,648 and 132,651. (For answers, see page 150)

Source: Smith, S. B. (1983). *The great mental calculators: The psychology, methods, and lives of calculating prodigies, past and present.* New York: Columbia University Press.

Progress Test 1

Multiple-Choice Questions

Circle your answers to the following questions and check them with the answer key at the end of this chapter. If your answer is incorrect, read the answer key explanation for why it is incorrect and then consult the appropriate pages of the text to understand the correct answer.

1. When forming a concept, people often develop a best example, or _____, of a category.
   a. denoter
   b. heuristic
   c. prototype
   d. algorithm

2. Confirmation bias refers to the tendency to:
   a. cling to a particular belief.
   b. overestimate the accuracy of one's beliefs.
   c. estimate the probability of an event in terms of how readily it comes to mind.
   d. look for information that is consistent with one's beliefs.

3. Which of the following is *not* true of babbling?
   a. It is imitation of adult speech.
   b. It is the same in all cultures.
   c. It typically occurs from about age 4 months to 1 year.
   d. Babbling increasingly comes to resemble a particular language.

4. Critics of ape language research argue that:
   a. ape language is merely imitation of the trainer's behavior.
   b. there is little evidence that apes can equal even a 3-year-old's ability to order words with proper syntax.
   c. by seeing what they wish to see, trainers attri-

bute greater linguistic ability to apes than actually exists.
   d. All of the above have been argued.

5. Whorf's linguistic relativity hypothesis states that:
   a. language is primarily a learned ability.
   b. language is partially an innate ability.
   c. the size of a person's vocabulary reflects his or her intelligence.
   d. our language shapes our thinking.

6. Which of the following best describes Chomsky's view of language development?
   a. Language is an entirely learned ability.
   b. Language is an innate ability.
   c. Humans have a biological predisposition to acquire language.
   d. There are no cultural influences on the development of language.

7. Failing to solve a problem that requires using an object in an unusual way illustrates the phenomenon of:
   a. confirmation bias.
   b. functional fixedness.
   c. framing.
   d. belief perseverance.

8. Which of the following is an example of the use of heuristics?
   a. trying every possible letter ordering when unscrambling a word
   b. considering each possible move when playing chess
   c. using the formula "Area = length × width" to find the area of a rectangle
   d. playing chess using a defensive strategy that has often been successful for you

9. The chimpanzee Sultan used a short stick to pull a longer stick that was out of reach into his cage. He then used the longer stick to reach a piece of fruit. Researchers hypothesized that Sultan's discovery of the solution to his problem was the result of:
   a. insight.
   b. trial and error.
   c. functional fixedness.
   d. an algorithm.

10. You hear that one of the Smith children is an outstanding Little League player and immediately conclude it's their one son rather than any of their four daughters. You reached your quite possibly erroneous conclusion as the result of:
   a. the confirmation bias.
   b. the availability heuristic.
   c. the representativeness heuristic.
   d. belief perseverance.

11. According to the textbook, language acquisition is best described as:
   a. the result of conditioning and reinforcement.
   b. a biological process of maturation.

c. an interaction between biology and experience.

d. a mystery researchers have no understanding of.

12. The linguistic relativity hypothesis is challenged by the finding that:

a. chimps can learn to communicate with one another spontaneously by using sign language.

b. people with no word for a certain color can still perceive that color accurately.

c. the Eskimo language contains a number of words for snow, whereas English has only one.

d. infants' babbling contains many sounds that do not occur in their own language and that they therefore cannot have heard.

13. Several studies have indicated that the generic pronoun "he":

a. tends for children and adults alike to trigger images of both males and females.

b. tends for adults to trigger images of both males and females, but for children to trigger images of males.

c. tends for both children and adults to trigger images of males but not females.

d. for both children and adults triggers images of females about one fourth of the time it is used.

14. A 6-year-old child has a mental age of 9. The child's IQ is:

a. 100.   b. 125.   c. 150.   d. 166.

15. Standardization refers to the process of:

a. determining the accuracy with which a test measures what it is supposed to.

b. defining meaningful scores relative to a representative pretested group.

c. determining the consistency of test scores obtained by retesting people.

d. measuring the success with which a test predicts the behavior it is designed to predict.

16. To say that the heritability of a trait is approximately 50 percent means that:

a. genes are responsible for 50 percent of the trait in an individual, and the environment is responsible for the rest.

b. the trait's appearance in a person will reflect approximately equal genetic contributions from both parents.

c. of the variation in the trait within a group of people, 50 percent can be attributed to heredity.

d. all of the above are true.

17. Which of the following best describes the relationship between creativity and intelligence?

a. Creativity appears to depend on the ability to think imaginatively and has little if any relationship to intelligence.

b. Creativity is best understood as a certain kind of intelligence.

c. The more intelligent a person is, the greater his or her creativity.

d. A certain level of intelligence is necessary but not sufficient for creativity.

18. Before becoming attorneys, law students must pass a licensing exam, which is a

_____ _____

test.

a. general achievement   c. general aptitude

b. specific achievement   d. specific aptitude

19. The existence of _____

_____ reinforces the generally accepted notion that intelligence is a multidimensional quality.

a. adaptive skills   c. general intelligence

b. mental retardation   d. savant syndrome

20. Which of the following provides the strongest evidence of the role of heredity in determining intelligence?

a. The IQ scores of identical twins raised separately are more similar than those of fraternal twins raised together.

b. The IQ scores of fraternal twins are more similar than those of ordinary siblings.

c. The IQ scores of identical twins raised together are more similar than those of identical twins raised apart.

d. The IQ scores of children who have been adopted show relatively weak correlations with scores of adoptive as well as biological parents.

21. Current estimates are that

_____ percent of the total variation among IQ scores can be attributed to genetic factors.

a. less than 10   c. between 50 and 60

b. approximately 25   d. over 75

22. If you compare the same trait in people of similar heredity who live in very different environments, heritability will be _____;

heritability is most likely to be

_____ among people of very different heredities who live in similar environments.

a. low; high

b. high; low

c. environmental; genetic

d. genetic; environmental

23. The bell-shaped distribution of IQ scores in the general population forms what is called a:

a. g curve.   c. bimodal curve.

b. standardization curve.   d. normal curve.

Matching Items

Match each item with its definition or description.

Terms

_____ **1.** IQ score
_____ **2.** g
_____ **3.** availability heuristic
_____ **4.** savant
_____ **5.** WAIS
_____ **6.** aptitude test
_____ **7.** achievement test
_____ **8.** Stanford-Binet
_____ **9.** validity
_____ **10.** overconfidence phenomenon
_____ **11.** reliability
_____ **12.** fixation

Definitions

a. a test designed to predict a person's ability to learn something new
b. a test designed to measure current knowledge
c. the consistency with which a test measures performance
d. the degree to which a test measures what it is designed to measure
e. Terman's revision of Binet's original intelligence test
f. presuming that something is likely if it comes readily to mind
g. an underlying, general intelligence factor
h. a person's score on an intelligence test based on performance relative to the average performance of people the same age
i. a mentally retarded individual who is extremely gifted in one ability
j. the tendency to overestimate the accuracy of one's judgments
k. most widely used intelligence test
l. being unable to see a new angle to a problem

Progress Test 2

Progress Test 2 should be completed during a final chapter review. Do this test after you thoroughly understand the correct answers for the Chapter Review and Progress Test 1.

Multiple-Choice Questions

1. Skinner and other behaviorists argue that language development is the result of:

  a. imitation.　　**c.** association.
  b. reinforcement.　　**d.** all of the above.

2. Many psychologists are skeptical of claims that chimpanzees can acquire language because the chimps have not shown the ability to:

  a. use symbols meaningfully.
  b. acquire speech.
  c. acquire even a limited vocabulary.
  d. use syntax in communicating.

3. Representatives and availability are examples of:

  a. confirmation bias.　　**c.** algorithms.
  b. heuristics.　　**d.** fixation.

4. Assume that Congress is considering revising its approach to welfare and to this end is hearing a range of testimony. A member of Congress who uses the availability heuristic would be most likely to:

  a. want to experiment with numerous possible approaches to see which of these seems to work best.
  b. want to cling to approaches to welfare that seem to have had some success in the past.
  c. refuse to be budged from his or her beliefs despite persuasive testimony to the contrary.
  d. base his or her ideas on the most vivid, memorable testimony, even though many statistics presented run counter to this testimony.

5. Which of the following illustrates the belief perseverance phenomenon?

  a. Your belief remains intact even in the face of evidence to the contrary.
  b. You refuse even to listen to arguments counter to your beliefs.
  c. You tend to become flustered and angered when your beliefs are refuted.
  d. You tend to search for information that supports your beliefs.

6. Which of the following is *not* cited by Chomsky as evidence that language acquisition cannot be explained by learning alone?

  a. Children master the complicated rules of grammar with ease.
  b. Children create sentences they have never heard.
  c. Children make the kinds of mistakes that suggest they are attempting to apply rules of grammar.
  d. Children raised in isolation from language spontaneously begin speaking words.

7. Your stand for or against an issue such as nuclear power involves personal judgment. In such a case, one memorable occurrence can weigh more heavily than a bookful of data, thus illustrating:

   a. belief perseverance.
   b. confirmation bias.
   c. the representativeness heuristic.
   d. the availability heuristic.

8. A dessert recipe that gives you the ingredients, their amounts, and the steps to follow is an example of:

   a. a prototype.
   b. an algorithm.
   c. an availability heuristic.
   d. a representativeness heuristic.

9. Which of the following is true regarding the relationship between thinking and language?

   a. "Real" thinking requires the use of language.
   b. People sometimes think in images rather than in words.
   c. A thought that cannot be expressed in a particular language cannot occur to speakers of that language.
   d. All of the above are true.

10. The test designed by Alfred Binet was designed specifically to:

    a. measure inborn intelligence in adults.
    b. measure inborn intelligence in children.
    c. predict school performance in children.
    d. identify mentally retarded children so that they could be institutionalized.

11. The formula for the intelligence quotient was devised by:

    a. Wechsler.   c. Binet.
    b. Stern.   d. Terman.

12. Current intelligence tests compute an individual's IQ score as:

    a. the ratio of mental age to chronological age multiplied by 100.
    b. the ratio of chronological age to mental age multiplied by 100.
    c. the amount by which the test-taker's performance deviates from the average performance of others the same age.
    d. the ratio of the test-taker's verbal intelligence score to his or her nonverbal intelligence score.

13. J. McVicker Hunt found that institutionalized children given "tutored human enrichment":

    a. showed no change in intelligence test performance compared with institutionalized children who did not receive such enrichment.
    b. responded so negatively as a result of their im-

poverished early experiences that he felt it necessary to disband the program.
    c. thrived intellectually and socially on the benefits of positive caregiving.
    d. actually developed higher IQs than control subjects who had lived in foster homes since birth.

14. If you want to develop a test of musical aptitude in North American children, which would be the appropriate standardization group?

    a. children all over the world
    b. North American children
    c. children of musical parents
    d. children with known musical ability

15. Although Don's IQ scores were only average, he has been enormously successful as a corporate manager. Psychologists Sternberg and Wagner would probably suggest that Don's _____ intelligence exceeds his _____ intelligence.

    a. verbal; performance   c. academic; practical
    b. performance; verbal   d. practical; academic

16. Most experts view intelligence as a person's:

    a. ability to perform well on IQ tests.
    b. innate mental capacity.
    c. capacity for goal–directed adaptive behavior.
    d. diverse skills acquired throughout life.

17. Originally, IQ was defined as:

    a. mental age divided by chronological age and multiplied by 100.
    b. chronological age divided by mental age and multiplied by 100.
    c. mental age subtracted from chronological age and multiplied by 100.
    d. chronological age subtracted from mental age and multiplied by 100.

18. Tests of _____ measure what an individual can do now; tests of _____ predict what an individual will be able to do later.

    a. aptitude; achievement
    b. achievement; aptitude
    c. reliability; validity
    d. validity; reliability

19. Which of the following statements most accurately reflects the textbook's position regarding the relative contribution of genes and environment in determining intelligence?

    a. Except in cases of a neglectful early environment, each individual's basic intelligence is largely the product of heredity.
    b. With the exception of those with genetic disorders like Down syndrome, intelligence is primarily the product of environmental experiences.

c. Both genes and life experiences significantly influence performance on intelligence tests.

d. Because IQ tests have such low predictive validity, the question cannot be addressed until psychologists agree on a more valid test of intelligence.

True-False Items

Indicate whether each statement is true or false by placing a *T* or *F* in the blank next to the item.

_____ 1. According to the confirmation bias, people often interpret ambiguous evidence as support for their beliefs.

_____ 2. Most human problem solving involves the use of heuristics rather than reasoning that systematically considers every possible solution.

_____ 3. When asked, most people underestimate the accuracy of their judgments.

_____ 4. Studies have shown that, in certain instances, even animals may have insight reactions.

_____ 5. Thinking without using language is not possible.

_____ 6. In the current version of the Stanford-Binet intelligence test, one's performance is compared only with the performance of others of the same age.

_____ 7. Most of the major aptitude tests have higher validity than reliability.

_____ 8. The IQ scores of adopted children are more similar to those of their adoptive parents than their biological parents.

_____ 9. The consensus among psychologists is that most intelligence tests are extremely biased.

_____ 10. Most psychologists agree that intelligence is primarily determined by heredity.

Key Terms

Using your own words, write a brief definition or explanation of each of the following terms.

1. concept

2. prototype

3. algorithm

4. heuristic

5. insight

6. confirmation bias

7. fixation

8. functional fixedness

9. representativeness heuristic

10. availability heuristic

11. overconfidence phenomenon

12. framing

13. belief perseverance

14. language

15. babbling stage

16. one-word stage

17. two-word stage

18. telegraphic speech

19. linguistic relativity hypothesis

20. aptitude tests

21. achievement tests

22. mental age

23. Stanford-Binet

24. intelligence quotient (IQ)

25. Wechsler Adult Intelligence Scale (WAIS)

26. standardization

27. normal curve

28. reliability

29. validity

30. mental retardation

31. Down syndrome

32. intelligence

33. savant syndrome

34. general intelligence (g)

35. creativity

36. heritability

Answers

CHAPTER REVIEW

1. concepts; hierarchies
2. prototype
3. problem solving

In order to solve problems effectively, one must: (1) define the problem, (2) develop a strategy for solving it, (3) carry out the strategy, and (4) determine if the strategy is working.

4. algorithms
5. heuristics
6. insight; have
7. confirmation bias
8. fixation; functional fixedness
9. representativeness heuristic
10. availability heuristic

Using these heuristics often prevents us from processing other relevant information, and because we overlook this information, we make judgmental errors. Thus, in the text example, the representativeness heuristic leads people to overlook the fact that there are many more truck drivers than Ivy League classics professors and so to wrongly conclude that the poetry reader is more likely to be an Ivy League classics professor.

11. overconfidence
12. does
13. framing
14. belief perseverance
15. babbling; 4; are not
16. one-word; 1
17. telegraphic
18. learning
19. Chomsky
20. sign language

Chimps have acquired only limited vocabularies and —in contrast to children—have acquired these vocabularies only with great difficulty. Also in contrast to children, it's unclear that chimps can use syntax to express meaning. Even simpler animals, such as birds, are capable of learning behavioral sequences that some chimp researchers consider language. Much of the signing of chimps is nothing more than imitation of the trainer's actions. People tend to interpret such ambiguous behavior in terms of what they want to see.

21. linguistic relativity; Whorf
22. does
23. can

The relationship is probably a two-way one: The linguistic relativity hypothesis suggests that language helps shape thought; that words come into the language to express new ideas indicates that thought also shapes language.

24. aptitude; achievement

25. Binet; mental

26. Stanford-Binet; intelligence quotient

In the original IQ formula, measured mental age was divided by chronological age and the result was multiplied by 100. "Mental age" refers to the chronological age that most typically corresponds to a given level of performance. Today, the IQ score reflects the test-taker's performance as compared with the average performance of people the same age.

27. Wechsler Adult Intelligence Scale (WAIS); verbal; performance

28. standardization; reliability; validity

29. standardization

30. normal

The normal curve describes the distribution of many physical phenomena and psychological attributes (including IQ scores), with most scores falling near the average and fewer and fewer near the extremes. When a test is standardized on a normal curve, individual scores are assigned according to how much they deviate above or below the distribution's average.

31. reliable

32. +.90

33. validity

34. is not; diminishes

35. the capacity for "goal-directed adaptive behavior"

36. general; specific

37. factor analysis

38. savants

39. multiple intelligences

40. academic; practical; creative

41. general intelligence

42. creativity; higher; 120

Creative people tend to have *expertise*, or a solid base of knowledge, *imaginative thinking skills*, which allow them to see things in new ways and make connections, and *intrinsic motivation*, or the tendency to focus on the pleasure and challenge of their work.

43. generally accepted

44. more

45. heritability; 50 to 60

46. do

An Aptitude test might be a perfectly valid and unbiased *predictor of performance* because it measures what it purports to measure and accurately differentiates successful and unsuccessful performance in all groups of individuals. At the same time, however, the test may reflect a particular cultural bias that discriminates against people from other cultural backgrounds.

PROGRESS TEST 1

Multiple-Choice Questions

1. c. is the answer. (p. 212)

    a. There is no such thing as a "denoter."

    b. & d. Heuristics and algorithms are problem-solving strategies.

2. d. is the answer. A major obstacle to problem solving, the confirmation bias refers to the common tendency to search for evidence that confirms one's beliefs and not for evidence that would disconfirm them. (p. 215)

    a. This is belief perseverance.

    b. This is the overconfidence phenomenon.

    c. This is the availability heuristic.

3. a. is the answer. Babbling is not an imitation of adult speech since babbling infants produce sounds from languages they have not heard and could not be imitating. (p. 223)

    b., c., & d. These are all true of babbling.

4. d. is the answer. Each of these arguments has been made by skeptics of ape language research. (pp. 225–226)

5. d. is the answer. (p. 227)

    a. This is Skinner's position.

    b. This is Chomsky's position.

    c. The linguistic relativity hypothesis is concerned with the content of thought, not intelligence.

6. c. is the answer. (pp. 224–225)

    a. This is the position of a behaviorist, such as Skinner.

    b. According to Chomsky, although the *ability* to acquire language is innate, the child must acquire his or her language.

    d. Cultural influences are an important example of the influence of learning on language development, an influence Chomsky fully accepts.

7. b. is the answer. Functional fixedness is the tendency to think of things only in terms of their usual functions. (p. 215)

    a. Confirmation bias is our tendency to search for information that confirms our ideas.

    c. Framing refers to the way an issue is posed; this often influences our judgment.

    d. Belief perseverance is the tendency to cling to one's beliefs even after they have been refuted.

8. d. is the answer. Heuristics are rule-of-thumb strategies—such as playing chess defensively—that are based on past successes in similar situations. (p. 214)

a., b., & c. These are all algorithms.

9. **a.** is the answer. Sultan suddenly arrived at a novel solution to his problem, thus displaying apparent insight. (p. 214)

b. Sultan did not randomly try various strategies of reaching the fruit; he demonstrated the "light bulb" reaction that is the hallmark of insight.

c. Functional fixedness is an *impediment* to problem solving. Sultan obviously solved his problem.

d. An algorithm is a step-by-step procedure for solving a problem.

10. **c.** is the answer. Your conclusion is based on sex stereotypes, that is, athletic ability and participation are for you more *representative* of boys. Your conclusion is by no means necessarily right, however, especially since the Smiths have four daughters and only one son. (p. 216)

a. The confirmation bias is the tendency to look for information that confirms one's preconception.

b. The availability heuristic involves judging the probability of an event in terms of how readily it comes to mind.

d. Belief perseverance is the tendency to cling to beliefs, even when the evidence has shown that they are wrong.

11. **c.** is the answer. Children are biologically prepared to learn language as they and their caregivers interact. (p. 224)

a. This is Skinner's position.

b. No psychologist, including Chomsky, believes that language is entirely a product of biological maturation.

d. Although language acquisition is not completely understood, research has shed sufficient light on it to render it less than a complete mystery.

12. **b.** is the answer. The evidence that absence of a term for a color does not affect ability to perceive the color challenges the idea that language always shapes thought. (p. 227)

a. & d. These findings would not be relevant to the linguistic relativity hypothesis, which addresses the relationship between language and thought.

c. This finding is in keeping with the linguistic relativity hypothesis.

13. **c.** is the answer. The generic pronoun *he* evidently tends, for both adults and children, to conjure up images of males. (p. 228)

14. **c.** is the answer. If we divide 9, the measured mental age, by 6, the chronological age, and multiply the result by 100, we obtain 150. (p. 231)

15. **b.** is the answer. (p. 233)

a. & d. These answers refer to a test's validity.

c. This answer refers to a test's reliability.

16. **c.** is the answer. Heritability is a measure of the extent to which a trait's variation within a group of people can be attributed to heredity. (p. 240)

a. & b. Heritability is *not* a measure of how much of an *individual's* behavior is inherited, nor of the relative contribution of genes from that person's mother and father. The heritability of any trait depends on the context, or environment, in which that trait is being studied.

17. **d.** is the answer. Up to an IQ of about 120, there is a positive correlation between IQ and creativity. But beyond this point the correlation disappears, indicating that factors other than intelligence are also involved. (p. 238)

a. The ability to think imaginatively and intelligence are *both* components of creativity.

b. Creativity, the capacity to produce ideas that are novel and valuable, is related to and depends in part on intelligence but cannot be considered simply a kind of intelligence.

c. Beyond an IQ score of about 120 there is no correlation between IQ scores and creativity.

18. **a.** is the answer. An exam for a professional license is intended to measure whether you have gained the overall knowledge and skill to practice the profession. (p. 230)

b. The test measures general skills, not a specific one.

c. & d. Aptitude tests are designed to predict ability to learn a new skill; the licensing test is administered to determine whether the individual has already achieved the basic skills.

19. **d.** is the answer. That savants excel in one area but are intellectually retarded in others suggests that there are multiple intelligences. (p. 237)

a. The ability to adapt *defines* the capacity we call intelligence.

b. Mental retardation is an indicator of the *range* of human intelligence.

c. A general intelligence factor was hypothesized by Spearman to underlie each specific factor of intelligent behavior, but its existence is controversial and remains to be proved.

20. **a.** is the answer. Identical twins who live apart have the same genetic makeup but different environments; if their scores are more similar than those of fraternal twins, with their somewhat different genetic makeups, raised together, this is evidence for the role of heredity. (pp. 239–240)

b. Since fraternal twins are no more genetically

alike than ordinary siblings, this could not provide evidence for the role of heredity.

c. That twins raised together have more similar scores than twins raised apart provides evidence of the role of environment.

d. As both sets of correlations are weak, little evidence is provided either for or against the role of heredity.

21. **c.** is the answer. Recent estimates are generally in the range of 50 to 60 percent. (p. 240)

22. **a.** is the answer. If everyone has nearly the same heredity, then heritability—the variation in a trait attributable to heredity—must be low. If individuals within a group come from very similar environments, environmental differences cannot account for variation in a trait; heritability, therefore, must be high. (p. 241)

23. **d.** is the answer. (p. 234)

a. g is Spearman's term for "general intelligence"; there is no such thing as a "g curve."

b. There is no such thing as a "'standardization curve."

c. A bimodal curve is one having two (bi-) modes, or averages. The normal curve has only one mode.

Matching Items

1. h (p. 231)	**5.** k (p. 232)	**9.** d (p. 234)
2. g (p. 238)	**6.** a (p. 230)	**10.** j (p. 219)
3. f (p. 217)	**7.** b (p. 230)	**11.** c (p. 234)
4. i (p. 237)	**8.** e (p. 231)	**12.** l (p. 215)

PROGRESS TEST 2

Multiple-Choice Questions

1. **d.** is the answer. These are all basic principles of learning and language development. (p. 224)

2. **d.** is the answer. Syntax is one of the fundamental aspects of language, and chimps seem unable, for example, to use word order to convey differences in meaning. (p. 226)

a. & c. Chimps' use of sign language demonstrates both the use of symbols and the acquisition of fairly sizable vocabularies.

b. No psychologist would require the use of speech as evidence of language; significantly, all the research and arguments focus on what chimps are and are not able to do in acquiring *other* facets of language.

3. **b.** is the answer. Both are rule-of-thumb strategies that allow us to make quick judgments. (pp. 216–218)

a. & d. Confirmation bias and fixation are obstacles to problem solving. In the first, we look for

solutions that confirm our bias. In the second, we tend to repeat solutions that have worked in the past and are unable to conceive of other possible solutions.

c. Algorithms are methodical strategies that guarantee a solution to a particular problem.

4. **d.** is the answer. If we use the availability heuristic, we base judgments on the availability of information in our memories, and more vivid information is often the most readily available. (pp. 217–218)

5. **a.** is the answer. (p. 219)

b. & c. These may very well occur, but they do not define belief perseverance.

d. This is the confirmation bias.

6. **d.** is the answer. Chomsky believes that the inborn capacity for language acquisition must be activated by exposure to language. And in fact, children raised in isolation will *not* begin to speak spontaneously. (pp. 224–225)

7. **d.** is the answer. The availability heuristic is the judgmental strategy that estimates the likelihood of events in terms of how readily they come to mind, and the most vivid information is often the most readily available. (pp. 217–218)

8. **b.** is the answer. Follow the directions precisely and you can't miss! (p. 214)

a. A prototype is the best example of a concept.

c. & d. Heuristics are rules of thumb that help solve problems but, in contrast to a recipe that is followed precisely, do not guarantee success.

9. **b.** is the answer. (p. 228)

a. Researchers do not make a distinction between "real" and other thinking, nor do they consider nonlinguistic thinking less valid than linguistic thinking.

c. As indicated by several studies cited in the textbook, this is not true.

d. Only b is true.

10. **c.** is the answer. French compulsory education laws brought more children into the school system, and the government didn't want to rely on teachers' subjective judgments to determine which children would require special help. (p. 231)

a. & b. Binet's test was intended for children, and Binet specifically rejected the idea that his test measured inborn intelligence, which is an abstract capacity that cannot be quantified.

d. This was not a purpose of the test, which dealt with children in the school system.

11. **b.** is the answer. (p. 231)

12. **c.** is the answer. (p. 232)

a. This is William Stern's original formula for the intelligence quotient.

b. & d. Neither of these formulas is used to compute IQ in current intelligence tests.

13. **c.** is the answer. Enrichment led to dramatic results and thereby testified to the importance of environmental factors. (p. 241)

a. & d. The study involved neither IQ tests nor comparisons with control groups.

b. The children showed a dramatic positive response.

14. **b.** is the answer. A standardization group provides a representative comparison for the trait being measured by a test. Since this test will measure musical aptitude in North American children, the standardization group should be limited to North American children but include children of all degrees of musical aptitude. (p. 233)

15. **d.** is the answer. Sternberg and Wagner distinguish among academic intelligence, as measured by IQ tests, practical intelligence, which is involved in everyday life and tasks, such as managerial work, and creative intelligence. (p. 237)

a. & b. Verbal and performance intelligence are both measured by standard IQ tests like the WAIS and would be included in Sternberg and Wagner's academic intelligence.

c. Academic intelligence refers to skills assessed by IQ tests, practical intelligence to skills required for everyday tasks and, often, for occupational success.

16. **c.** is the answer. (p. 236)

a. Performance ability and intellectual ability are separate traits.

b. This has been argued by some, but certainly not most, experts.

d. Although many experts believe that there are multiple intelligences, this would not be the same thing as diverse acquired skills.

17. **a.** is the answer. (p. 231)

18. **b.** is the answer. (p. 230)

c. & d. Reliability and validity are characteristics of good tests.

19. **c.** is the answer. (pp. 238–242)

a. & b. Studies of twins, family members, and adopted children point to a significant hereditary contribution to IQ scores. These same studies, plus others comparing children reared in neglectful or enriched environments, indicate that life experiences also significantly influence test performance.

d. Although the issue of how intelligence should be defined is controversial, IQ tests generally have very high predictive validity.

True-False Items

1. True (p. 215)
2. True (p. 214)
3. False (p. 219)
4. True (p. 214)
5. False (p. 228)
6. True (p. 232)
7. False (p. 234)
8. False (p. 240)
9. False (p. 232)
10. False (p. 240)

KEY TERMS

1. A **concept** is a mental grouping, or category, of similar things. (p. 212)

2. A **prototype** is the best example of a particular category. (p. 213)

Example: A robin, but not a goose, is a prototypical bird; an apple, but not a tomato, is a prototypical fruit.

3. An **algorithm** is a methodical problem-solving strategy that, while sometimes slow, guarantees success. (p. 214)

Example: Algorithms may abound in areas such as mathematics. But, for most of life's everyday problems, there are no **algorithms**.

4. A **heuristic** is any problem-solving strategy based on rules-of-thumb and/or past experience. Although heuristics are more efficient than algorithms, they do not guarantee success and sometimes even impede problem solving. (p. 214)

5. **Insight** is a sudden and often creative solution to a problem. Insight may often follow an unsuccessful episode of trial and error. (p. 214)

6. The **confirmation bias** is an obstacle to problem solving in which people seek information that validates their beliefs. (p. 215)

Example: **Confirmation bias** can often be observed in politicians as they automatically, yet unintentionally, interpret ambiguous statistics as supporting their ideas and proposals.

7. **Fixation** is an inability to approach a problem in a new way. (p. 215)

8. **Functional fixedness** is a type of fixation in which a person can think of things only in terms of their usual functions. (p. 215)

Example: In a creativity test that requires using a pair of pliers as supports for a small board, subjects' **functional fixedness** might prevent them from thinking of pliers as anything other than tools for grasping.

9. The **representativeness heuristic** is the tendency

to judge the likelihood of things in terms of how well they conform to one's prototypes. (p. 216)

Example: The diagnostic process of an experienced doctor provides a good example of the **representativeness heuristic**. The likelihood of a patient's having a particular disease is based on how closely his or her symptoms correspond to the prototypical symptoms for that disease.

10. The **availability heuristic** is based on estimating the probability of certain events in terms of how readily they come to mind. (p. 217)

    Example: In attempting to convince legislators to adopt their viewpoints, lobbyists take advantage of the **availability heuristic**: In-person arguments are more persuasive than written correspondence because, later, they tend to come more readily to mind.

11. Another obstacle to problem solving, the **overconfidence phenomenon** refers to the tendency to overestimate the accuracy of one's beliefs. (p. 219)

12. **Framing** refers to variations in the way an issue or question is posed. These variations can affect people's perception of the issue or answer to the question. (p. 219)

13. **Belief perseverance** is the tendency for people to cling to a particular belief even after the information that led to the formation of the belief is discredited. (pp. 219–220)

14. **Language** refers to words and how we combine them to communicate meaning. (p. 222)

15. The **babbling stage** of speech development, which begins at about 4 months, is characterized by the spontaneous utterance of speech sounds. During the babbling stage, children the world over sound alike. (p. 223)

16. Between 1 and 2 years of age children speak mostly in single words; they are therefore in the **one-word stage** of linguistic development. (p. 223)

17. Beginning about age 2, children are in the **two-word stage** and speak mostly in two-word sentences. (p. 223)

18. **Telegraphic speech** is the economical, telegram-like speech of children in the two-word stage. Utterances consist mostly of nouns and verbs; however, words occur in the correct order, showing that the child has learned some of the language's syntactic rules. (p. 223)

19. The **linguistic relativity hypothesis** is Benjamin Whorf's proposal that language influences the way we think. (p. 227)

20. **Aptitude tests** are designed to predict future performance. They measure your capacity to learn new information, rather than measuring what you already know. (p. 230)

21. **Achievement tests** measure a person's current knowledge. (p. 230)

22. A concept introduced by Binet, **mental age** is the chronological age that most typically corresponds to a given level of performance. (p. 230)

23. The **Stanford-Binet** is Lewis Terman's widely used revision of Binet's original intelligence test. (p. 231)

24. The **intelligence quotient**, or **IQ**, was defined originally as the ratio of mental age to chronological age multiplied by 100. Contemporary tests of intelligence assign an **IQ** score of 100 to the average performance for a given age and define other scores as deviations from this average. (p. 231)

25. The **Wechsler Adult Intelligence Scale (WAIS)** is the most widely used intelligence test. It is individually administered, contains eleven subtests, and yields separate verbal and performance IQ scores, as well as an overall score. (p. 232)

26. **Standardization** is the process of defining meaningful scores on a test by administering it to a large representative sample of people. (p. 233)

27. The **normal curve** is bell-shaped and represents the distribution (frequency of occurrence) of many traits, such as IQ scores. The curve is symmetrical, with most scores near the average and fewer near the extremes. (p. 234)

28. **Reliability** is the extent to which a test produces consistent results. (p. 234)

    Memory aid: If someone is **reliable**, he or she can be depended on. A reliable test is one that can be depended on to produce consistent measurements.

29. **Validity** is the degree to which a test measures what it is supposed to measure or predicts what it is supposed to predict. (p. 234)

30. The two criteria that designate **mental retardation** are an IQ below 70 and difficulty adapting to the normal demands of independent living. Approximately 1 percent of the population satisfies both these criteria. (p. 235)

31. A common cause of severe retardation, **Down syndrome** is usually the result of an extra chromosome in the person's genetic makeup. (p. 235)

32. Most experts define **intelligence** as the capacity for goal-directed adaptive behavior. (p. 236)

33. A **savant syndrome** is a condition in which a retarded person possesses one exceptional ability, for example, in music, drawing, or mathematics. (p. 237)

34. **General intelligence**, or **g** factor, underlies each of the more specific intelligence clusters identified through factor analysis. (p. 238)

    Example: Although people often have special abilities, people who score high on one factor typically score higher than average on other factors. This commonality, according to Spearman, is the **general intelligence** factor.

35. Although many definitions of **creativity** have been proposed, most experts agree that it refers to an ability to generate novel and valuable ideas. People with high IQs may or may not be creative, which indicates that intelligence is only one component of **creativity**. (p. 238)

36. **Heritability** is the amount of variation in a trait that is attributable to genetic factors. Current estimates place the **heritability** of intelligence at about 50 to 60 percent. (p. 240)

Answers to cube root questions on page 138 are 22 and 51.

Chapter 9 | Motivation

Chapter Overview

Perhaps no topic is more fundamental to psychology than motivation—the study of forces that energize and direct our behavior. Chapter 9 discusses various concepts of motivation and looks closely at three motives: hunger, sex, and achievement. Research on hunger points to the interplay between physiological and psychological (internal and external) factors in motivation. Sexual motivation in men and women is triggered less by physiological factors and more by external incentives. Achievement motivation, in particular, demonstrates that a drive-reduction theory is of limited usefulness in explaining human behavior: Although this motivation serves no apparent physiological need, it may be extremely forceful nonetheless.

Guided Study

The textbook chapter should be studied one section at a time. Before you read, preview each section by skimming it, noting headings and boldface items. Then read the appropriate section objectives from the following outline. Keep these objectives in mind, and as you read the chapter section, search for the information that will enable you to meet each objective. Once you have finished a section write out answers for its objectives.

Concepts of Motivation (pp. 248–250)

1. Define motivation and discuss the role of biological states and external incentives in motivated behavior.

2. Describe Maslow's hierarchy of needs.

Hunger (pp. 251–256)

3. Discuss the basis of hunger in terms of both physiology and external incentives.

Sexual Motivation (pp. 257–267)

4. Discuss human sexual behavior, including common practices, adolescent sexuality, and the human sexual response cycle.

5. Discuss the basis of sexual motivation in terms of both internal physiology and external incentives.

6. Describe research findings on the nature and dynamics of sexual orientation.

7. Discuss the place of values in sexual research and education.

Achievement Motivation (pp. 267–273)

8. Describe the nature and origin of achievement motivation.

9. Distinguish between extrinsic and intrinsic achievement motivation and identify factors that encourage each type.

10. Discuss how managers can create a motivated, productive, and satisfied workforce and contrast various leadership styles.

Chapter Review

When you have finished reading the chapter, use the material that follows to review it. Complete the fill-in sentences and answer the essay items in complete sentences. As you proceed, evaluate your performance for each chapter section by consulting the answer key at the end of this chapter. Do not continue with the next section until you've understood each answer. If you need to, review or reread the appropriate chapter section in the textbook before continuing.

1. To motivate is to _____ behavior and _____ it toward goals.

Concepts of Motivation (pp. 248–250)

2. As a result of Darwin's influence, there was an increasing focus on the role of _____ forces in behavior.

3. A rigid, biologically determined behavior that is characteristic of a species is called a(n) _____.

Discuss why instinct theory failed as an explanation of human behavior.

4. According to another view of motivation, organisms may experience a deprivation, or _____, which creates a state of arousal, or _____.

5. The aim of drive reduction is to maintain a constant internal state, called _____.

6. The cognitive perspective spurred the realization that behavior is often not so much pushed by our drives as it is pulled by _____ in the environment.

7. Starting from the idea that some needs take precedence over others, Maslow constructed a(n) _____ of needs.

8. According to Maslow, the _____ needs are the most pressing, whereas the highest-order needs relate to _____-_____.

Hunger (pp. 251–256)

9. Ancel Keys observed that men became preoccupied with thoughts of food when their food intake was severely restricted. This finding _____ (was/was not) consistent with Maslow's need hierarchy.

10. Cannon and Washburn's experiment using a balloon indicated that there is an association between hunger and _____ _____.

11. When an animal has had its stomach removed, hunger _____ (does/does not) continue.

12. Feelings of hunger are decreased when _____ is injected into the bloodstream. Blood sugar is lowered, and hunger increased, when _____ is injected.

13. Taste preferences for sweet and salt are _____ (genetic/learned).

14. Carbohydrates boost levels of the neurotransmitter _____, which _____ (calms/arouses) the body.

15. The brain area that plays a role in hunger and other bodily maintenance functions is the _____. Animals will begin eating when the _____ is electrically stimulated. When this region is destroyed, hunger _____ (increases/decreases). Animals will stop eating when the _____ _____ is stimulated. When this area is destroyed, animals _____ (overeat/undereat).

16. The weight level that an individual's body is programmed to stay at is referred to as the body's _____ _____. A person whose weight goes beyond this level will tend to feel _____ (more/less) hungry than usual.

17. The rate of energy expenditure in the body is the _____ rate. When food intake is reduced, the body compensates by _____ (raising/lowering) this rate.

18. People whose eating is more affected by food stimuli than by internal cues are known as _____. Rodin found that such individuals showed a particularly marked increase in blood _____ level when confronted with the sight, smell, and sound of a steak being grilled.

Sexual Motivation (pp. 257–267)

19. In the 1940s and 1950s, a biologist named _____ surveyed the sexual practices of thousands of men and women. One of his major findings was that there _____ (was/was not) great diversity in "normal" sexual behavior.

Give four reasons why adolescents often fail to use contraceptives.

20. The two researchers who identified a four-stage sexual response cycle are _____ and _____. In order, the stages of the cycle are the _____ phase, the _____ phase, _____, and the _____ phase.

21. During resolution, males experience a _____ _____, during which they are not capable of another orgasm.

22. In most mammals, females are sexually receptive only during ovulation, when the hormone _____ has peaked.

23. The importance of the hormone _____ to male sexual arousal is confirmed by the fact that sexual interest declines in animals if their _____ are removed.

24. Normal hormonal fluctuations in humans have _____ (little/significant) effect on sexual motivation.

25. The region of the brain through which hormones help trigger sexual arousal is the _____.

26. Studies by Heiman and other researchers have shown that erotic stimuli _____ (are/are not) as arousing for women as for men.

Explain some of the possible harmful consequences of sexually explicit material.

27. The importance of the brain in sexual motivation is indicated by the fact that people who, because of injury, have no genital sensation _____ (do/do not) feel sexual desire.

28. A person's sexual attraction to the same or opposite sex is referred to as _____. A person's sense of being female or male is referred to as his or her _____ _____.

29. Historically, _____ (virtually all/a slight majority) of the world's cultures have been predominantly heterosexual.

30. Studies in Western Europe and the United States indicate that approximately _____ percent of men and _____ percent of women are exclusively homosexual.

31. A person's sexual orientation _____ (does/does not) appear to be voluntarily chosen.

32. Childhood events and family relationships _____ (are/are not) important factors in determining a person's sexual orientation.

33. Sex hormone levels _____ (do/do not) predict sexual orientation.

34. Homosexuality _____ (does/ does not) involve a fear of the other sex that leads people to direct their sexual desires toward members of their own sex.

35. As children, most homosexuals _____ (were/were not) sexually victimized.

Explain why many experts feel that the study of sex cannot and should not be free of values.

Achievement Motivation (pp. 267–273)

36. The drive theory of motivation is contradicted by the existence of many behaviors that appear to satisfy no apparent biological _____.

37. Psychologists Murray, McClelland, and Atkinson studied achievement motivation by having people create _____ about ambiguous pictures.

38. In experiments, individuals who chose extremely difficult tasks tended to have a _____ (low/high) need for achievement.

39. In terms of performance in school and on intelligence tests, children who are firstborn do slightly _____ (better/worse) than later born children. Other studies have shown that firstborn children tend to be _____ (more/less) socially relaxed and popular.

40. Motivation to perform a behavior for its own sake is referred to as _____. Motivation based on external rewards and punishments is called _____ _____.

Of the two, _____ _____ appears to be more successful in fueling achievement.

41. Spence and Helmreich found that people who tend to achieve the most are oriented toward

_____ and hard _____ while being _____ (high/low) in competitiveness.

42. Studies have shown that rewards lower intrinsic motivation when they are used to _____ but raise it when they are used to _____.

Discuss effective management in terms of the different leadership styles.

43. Managers who are directive and well-organized and who focus on specific goals are said to employ a _____ style of leadership. More democratic managers who aim to build teamwork and mediate conflicts in the workforce employ the _____ style of leadership.

44. In experiments, women tended to excel at _____ leadership, while men tended to excel at _____ leadership.

45. McGregor refers to managers who assume that workers are basically lazy and motivated only by money as _____ managers. Managers who assume that people are intrinsically motivated in their work are referred to as _____ managers.

FOCUS ON PSYCHOLOGY:
Motivation for Listening to Rock Music

Many motivation researchers now believe that motivated behavior involves three basic components: learning, cognition, and biology. The word "component" implies that each factor influences the behavior in question and is, in turn, influenced by the other factors.

Motivation researcher Robert Franken offers an example of the components approach in explaining why people enjoy listening to rock music. Franken begins with the assumption that cognitive processes obviously play a role in the appreciation of music. We enjoy new songs not only for their lyrics, but also because they involve novel melodies, rhythms, and combinations of voices and instruments. The motivating properties of curiosity and the reinforcing value of novel stimuli are both well-documented in humans.

Learning also plays a significant role in the enjoyment of music. Our taste in music can be attributed, at least in part, to past musical exposure and reinforcement. We are more likely to enjoy music that has been associated with feelings of well-being, for example, than music that has been associated with less desirable psychological states.

For many of us, music may serve as a conditioned stimulus. It can, for example, elicit emotional memories as classically conditioned responses. Hearing a song that was popular during our youth, for example, we may vividly re-experience feelings of well-being, self-confidence, or rebelliousness, if the song was at one time associated with these emotions. Perhaps the clearest example of music as a conditioned stimulus is the fact that people often play particular pieces of music to trigger specific moods.

The role of the biological component in listening to rock music is less obvious than that of learning or cognition, but no less significant. For many listeners, rock music is best appreciated when played very loud. Indeed, live rock music is often played at loudness levels in excess of 100 decibels. Sounds louder than approximately 80 decibels produce a number of physiological changes in the body, including arousal of the reticular activating system, stimulation of the cortex of the brain, and the outpouring of stress hormones and neurotransmitters that accompany the "fight-or-flight" reaction of the autonomic nervous system.

Numerous studies have shown that moderate increases in arousal are pleasurable. Higher levels of arousal, although not always pleasurable, have been shown to intensify prevailing emotions. It may be, therefore, that listening to loud rock music is at least partially motivated by a desire to experience increased arousal. And, if the listener is already in a good mood —perhaps enjoying the company of friends at a concert or party—the increased arousal associated with loud music may enhance the good mood.

Franken's example strongly suggests that motivation involves the interaction of biological, learned, and cognitive factors. The pleasure derived from the moderate increases in arousal associated with listening to music is evidence for the biological component. Yet, as Franken notes, "The fact that people listen to rock music when they could more readily obtain the same arousal level by running around the block indicates that something more is involved. Obviously the structure of the music and the associations it elicits are important factors in the total reaction to it. Somehow all these factors interact to produce a particular sensation. The joining together—or, more precisely, the pooling—of motivation is a fascinating thing to note about human behavior."

Source: Franken, R. E. (1988). *Human Motivation* (2nd ed.). Pacific Grove, California: Brooks/Cole, 44–47.

Progress Test 1

Multiple-Choice Questions

Circle your answers to the following questions and check them with the answer key at the end of this chapter. If your answer is incorrect, read the answer key explanation for why it is incorrect and then consult the appropriate pages of the text to understand the correct answer.

1. Motivation is best understood as a state that:
   a. reduces a drive.
   b. aims at satisfying a biological need.
   c. energizes an organism to act.
   d. energizes and directs behavior.

2. Which of the following is a difference between a drive and a need?
   a. Needs are learned; drives are inherited.
   b. Needs are physiological states; drives are psychological states.
   c. Drives are generally stronger than needs.
   d. Needs are generally stronger than drives.

3. One problem with drive-reduction theory is that:
   a. because some motivated behaviors do not seem to be based on physiological needs, they cannot be explained in terms of drive reduction.
   b. it fails to explain any human motivation.
   c. it cannot account for homeostasis.
   d. it does not explain the hunger drive.

4. Which of the following needs are at the top of Maslow's hierarchy?
   a. physiological needs
   b. safety needs
   c. belongingness needs
   d. self-actualization needs

5. Injections of insulin will:
   a. lower blood sugar and trigger hunger.
   b. raise blood sugar and trigger hunger.
   c. lower blood sugar and trigger satiety.
   d. raise blood sugar and trigger satiety.

6. Electrical stimulation of the lateral hypothalamus will cause:
   a. an animal to begin eating.
   b. an animal to stop eating.
   c. an animal to become obese.
   d. an animal to begin copulating.

7. Rodin found that, in response to the sight and smell of a steak being grilled:
   a. overweight people had a greater insulin response than people of normal weight.
   b. people of normal weight had a greater insulin response than overweight people.
   c. externals had a greater insulin response than internals.
   d. internals had a greater insulin response than externals.

8. The correct order of the stages of Masters and Johnson's sexual response cycle is:
   a. plateau; excitement; orgasm; resolution.
   b. excitement; plateau; orgasm; resolution.
   c. excitement; orgasm; resolution; refractory.
   d. plateau; excitement; orgasm; refractory.

9. Few human behaviors are sufficiently automatic to qualify as:
   a. needs.
   b. drives.
   c. instincts.
   d. gender-typed behaviors.

10. At the local factory, the boss began rewarding the most productive workers with special recognition pins. This practice illustrates the use of:
   a. incentives.
   b. drives.
   c. intrinsic motivation.
   d. work-mastery orientation.

11. In his study of men on a semistarvation diet, Keys found that:
   a. the metabolic rate of the subjects increased.
   b. the subjects eventually lost interest in food.
   c. the subjects became obsessed with food.
   d. the subjects' behavior directly contradicted predictions made by Maslow's hierarchy.

12. Lucille has been sticking to a strict diet but can't seem to lose weight. What is the most likely explanation of her difficulty?
   a. Her body has a very low set point.
   b. Her prediet weight was near her body's set point.
   c. Her weight problem is actually caused by an underlying eating disorder.
   d. Lucille is an "external."

13. It has been said that the body's major sex organ is the brain. With regard to sex education:
   a. transmission of value-free information about the wide range of sexual behaviors should be the primary focus of the educator.
   b. transmission of technical knowledge about the biological act should be the classroom focus,

free from the personal values and attitudes of researchers, teachers, and students.

c. the home, not the school, should be the focus of all instruction about reproductive behavior.

d. attitudes, values, and morals cannot be divorced from the biological aspects of sexuality.

14. A course that Janice wants very much to take is being offered by three instructors. Janice opts for an instructor with a reputation for being moderately difficult over one perceived as impossibly difficult and another viewed as very easy. It is most likely that Janice's choice reflects her:

Matching Items

Match each term with its definition or description.

Terms

_____ 1. intrinsic motivation
_____ 2. set point
_____ 3. task leadership
_____ 4. theory X manager
_____ 5. extrinsic motivation
_____ 6. estrogen
_____ 7. homeostasis
_____ 8. sexual orientation
_____ 9. social leadership
_____ 10. incentive
_____ 11. theory Y manager

Progress Test 2

Progress Test 2 should be completed during a final chapter review. Do this test after you thoroughly understand the correct answers for the Chapter Review and Progress Test 1.

Multiple-Choice Questions

1. Sexual motivation in women is most influenced by:
   a. the level of progesterone.
   b. the level of estrogen.
   c. the phase of the menstrual cycle.
   d. social and psychological factors.

2. Which of the following tends to foster a high need for achievement?
   a. the frequent use of extrinsic controls on behavior
   b. encouraging young children to remain dependent
   c. the use of punishment for failures
   d. rewards that provide feedback

a. being a later born child.
b. having a low need for achievement.
c. having a high need for achievement.
d. having a high level of extrinsic motivation.

15. To increase employee motivation and productivity, industrial/organizational psychologists advise managers to:
   a. adopt a task leadership style.
   b. adopt a social leadership style.
   c. instill competitiveness in each employee.
   d. deal with employees according to their individual motives.

Definitions

a. a hormone secreted more by females than males
b. the body's tendency to maintain an optimum internal state
c. an environmental stimulus that motivates behavior
d. a person's attraction to members of a particular sex
e. the motivation to perform a behavior for its own sake
f. a desire to perform a behavior due to promised rewards
g. a leadership style that builds teamwork
h. a leader who assumes workers are motivated primarily by extrinsic means
i. a leader who assumes that workers are motivated intrinsically
j. a goal-oriented leadership style
k. the body's weight-maintenance setting

3. Which of the following is true concerning the relationship between birth order and achievement?
   a. Firstborn children tend to do better on various measures of academic achievement.
   b. Later born children tend to do better on various measures of academic achievement.
   c. Later born children tend to be more intrinsically motivated to achieve; firstborn children tend to be more extrinsically motivated.
   d. Compared to later born children, firstborn children are more competitive but have a lower work-mastery orientation.

4. The brain area that when stimulated suppresses eating is the:
   a. lateral hypothalamus.
   b. ventromedial hypothalamus.
   c. lateral thalamus.
   d. ventromedial thalamus.

5. Nancy decided to take introductory psychology because she has always been interested in human

behavior. Jack enrolled in the same course because he thought it would be easy. Nancy's behavior was motivated by _____; Jack's by _____.

a. extrinsic motivation; intrinsic motivation
b. intrinsic motivation; extrinsic motivation
c. drives; incentives
d. incentives; drives

6. Which of the following statements concerning homosexuality is true?
a. Homosexuals have abnormal hormone levels.
b. As children, most homosexuals were molested by an adult homosexual.
c. Homosexuals had a domineering opposite-sex parent.
d. The basis for sexual orientation is largely unknown.

7. According to Maslow's theory:
a. the most basic motives are based on physiological needs.
b. needs are satisfied in a specified order.
c. the highest motives relate to self-actualization.
d. all of the above are true.

8. Which of the following is inconsistent with the drive-reduction theory of motivation?
a. When an individual's body temperature drops below 98.6 degrees Fahrenheit, blood vessels constrict to conserve warmth.
b. A person is driven to seek a drink when his or her cellular water level drops below its optimum point.
c. Monkeys will work puzzles even if not given a food reward.
d. A person becomes hungry when body weight falls below its biological set point.

9. Which of the following is true of the relationship between competitiveness and a work-mastery orientation?
a. Work-mastery orientation and competitiveness are positively correlated, so individuals who are high in one are high in the other.
b. People tend to be motivated either by competitiveness or by work-mastery, so few individuals are high in both.
c. Among those who have a high work-mastery orientation, less competitive individuals achieve more.
d. Among those who have a low work-mastery orientation, less competitive individuals achieve more.

10. Whether a person is heterosexual, homosexual, or bisexual is an indication of his or her:
a. gender identity.

b. sexual response cycle.
c. sexual orientation.
d. sexual identity.

11. For as long as she has been the plant manager, Juanita has welcomed input from employees and has delegated authority. Bill, in managing his department, takes a more authoritarian, iron-fisted approach. Juanita's style is one of _____ leadership, whereas Bill's is one of _____ leadership.
a. task; social   c. theory X; theory Y
b. social; task   d. theory Y; theory X

12. The power of external stimuli in sexual motivation is illustrated in Julia Heiman's experiment, which recorded subjects' responses to various romantic, erotic, or neutral audio tapes. Which of the following was among the findings?
a. The women were more aroused by the romantic tape; the men were more aroused by the sexually explicit tape.
b. The sexually experienced subjects reported greater arousal when the tape depicted a sexual encounter in which a woman is overpowered by a man and enjoys being dominated.
c. Whereas the men's physical arousal was both obvious and consistent with their verbal reports, the women's verbal reports did not correspond very directly with their measured physical arousal.
d. Both men and women found the most sexually explicit tape in the series both dehumanizing and unarousing.

13. According to Masters and Johnson, the sexual response of males is most likely to differ from that of females during:
a. the excitement phase.   c. orgasm.
b. the plateau phase.   d. the resolution phase.

14. In animals, destruction of the lateral hypothalamus results in _____, whereas destruction of the ventromedial hypothalamus results in _____.
a. overeating; loss of hunger
b. loss of hunger; overeating
c. an elevated set point; a lowered set point
d. increased thirst; loss of thirst

15. Why do people with a high need for achievement prefer tasks of moderate difficulty?
a. They are afraid of failing at more difficult tasks.
b. They want to avoid the embarrassment of failing at easy tasks.
c. Moderately difficult tasks present an attainable goal in which success is attributable to their own skill.

d. They have high extrinsic motivation.

16. Beginning with the most fundamental needs, which of the following represents the correct sequence of needs in the hierarchy described by Maslow?

a. safety; physiological; esteem; love; self-fulfillment

b. safety; physiological; love; esteem; self-fulfillment

c. physiological; safety; esteem; love; self-fulfillment

d. physiological; safety; love; esteem; self-fulfillment

17. Hunger is to food deprivation as _____ is to _____.

a. drive; need   **c.** incentive; need
b. need; drive   **d.** incentive; drive

True-False Items

Indicate whether each item is true or false by placing *T* or *F* in the blank next to the item.

_____ **1.** Most sexually active teenagers do not use contraception consistently.

_____ **2.** According to Masters and Johnson, only males experience a plateau period in the cycle of sexual arousal.

_____ **3.** Testosterone affects the sexual arousal of the male only.

_____ **4.** Unlike men, women tend not to be aroused by sexually explicit material.

_____ **5.** All taste preferences are conditioned.

_____ **6.** Later born children tend to be more social and more popular than firstborn children.

_____ **7.** An injection of insulin increases blood glucose levels and triggers hunger.

_____ **8.** Theory Y managers often welcome employee participation in decision making.

_____ **9.** Intrinsic motivation fuels achievement more than does extrinsic motivation.

_____ **10.** One's sexual orientation is not voluntarily chosen.

Key Terms

Using your own words, write a brief definition or explanation of each of the following terms.

1. motivation

2. instinct

3. need

4. drive

5. homeostasis

6. incentive

7. hierarchy of needs

8. glucose

9. insulin

10. lateral hypothalamus (LH)

11. ventromedial hypothalamus (VMH)

12. set point

13. metabolic rate

14. anorexia nervosa

15. bulimia nervosa

16. sexual response cycle

17. refractory period

18. estrogen

19. sexual orientation

20. gender identity

21. achievement motivation

22. intrinsic motivation

23. extrinsic motivation

24. task leadership

25. social leadership

26. theory X

27. theory Y

Answers
CHAPTER REVIEW
1. energize; direct
2. biological
3. instinct

According to instinct theory, any human behavior could be regarded as an instinct. The only evidence for each such "instinct" was the behavior used to identify it. Thus, instinct theory offered only circular explanation; it labeled behaviors but did not explain them.

4. need; drive
5. homeostasis
6. incentives
7. hierarchy
8. physiological; self-actualization
9. was
10. stomach contractions
11. does
12. glucose; insulin
13. genetic
14. serotonin; calms
15. hypothalamus; lateral hypothalamus; decreases; ventromedial hypothalamus; overeat
16. set point; less
17. metabolic; lowering
18. externals; insulin
19. Kinsey; was

Ignorance regarding safe and risky times of the menstrual cycle and lack of birth control planning due to guilt about sex are two factors related to failure to use contraception. A third is a failure to communicate effectively with parents, partners, and peers regarding birth control. Fourth, use of alcohol may cloud judgment by depressing brain centers that control inhibition and self-awareness.

20. Masters; Johnson; excitement; plateau; orgasm; resolution
21. refractory period
22. estrogen
23. testosterone; testes
24. little
25. hypothalamus
26. are

Erotic material may lead people to devalue their partners and relationships. It may create unrealistic expectations and as a result make people feel sexually inadequate. Material that is both sexually explicit and violent may promote violent behavior toward women.

27. do
28. sexual orientation; gender identity
29. virtually all
30. 4; 1
31. does not

32. are not
33. do not
34. does not
35. were not

Because the words we use to describe behavior often reflect our values, sex research can never be value free. When sexual information is taught apart from a context of human values, students may get the message that intercourse is merely a biological act of recreation. Sex education that places equal emphasis on respect for oneself and for one's friends and lovers can resolve for adolescents and for adults questions about when to "just say no" to sexual intimacy.

36. need
37. stories
38. low
39. better; less
40. intrinsic motivation; extrinsic motivation; intrinsic motivation
41. mastery; work; low
42. control; inform

Because effective leadership styles vary with the situation and the person, managers are advised to assess individual employees' motives and adjust their management styles accordingly. Setting clear, challenging goals and giving feedback to employees both stimulate achievement. Also, some people are better suited to one or the other leadership style.

43. task; social
44. social; task
45. theory X; theory Y

PROGRESS TEST 1

Multiple-Choice Questions

1. **d.** is the answer. (p. 247)

   a. & b. Although motivation is often aimed at reducing drives and satisfying biological needs, this is by no means always the case, as achievement motivation illustrates.

   c. Motivated behavior is not only energized but also directed at a goal.

2. **b.** is the answer. A drive is the psychological consequence of a physiological need. (p. 249)

   a. Needs are unlearned states of deprivation.

   c. & d. Since needs are physical and drives psychological, their strengths cannot be compared directly.

3. **a.** is the answer. The curiosity of a child or a scientist is an example of behavior apparently moti-

vated by something other than a physiological need. (pp. 249–250)

b. & d. Some behaviors, such as thirst and hunger, *are* partially explained by drive reduction.

c. Drive reduction is directly based on the principle of homeostasis.

4. **d.** is the answer. The other needs mentioned were for Maslow more fundamental than self-actualization. (p. 250)

5. **a.** is the answer. Insulin injections increase hunger directly and also indirectly by lowering blood sugar, or glucose. It is glucose injections, as in d., that would raise blood sugar and increase satiety. (p. 253)

6. **a.** is the answer. This area of the hypothalamus seems to elevate hunger. (p. 253)

b. Stimulating the ventromedial hypothalamus has this effect.

c. Destroying the ventromedial hypothalamus has this effect.

d. The hypothalamus *is* involved in sexual motivation, but not in this way.

7. **c.** is the answer. Externals, those whose eating is especially triggered by food stimuli, showed a greater insulin response than did internals. (p. 256)

a. & b. The greater insulin response occurred in people who were especially sensitive to external cues, regardless of whether they were overweight.

d. Blood insulin levels rose less in internal subjects.

8. **b.** is the answer. (p. 259)

9. **c.** is the answer. (p. 249)

a. & b. Needs and drives are biologically based states that stimulate behaviors but are not themselves behaviors.

d. Gender-typed behaviors are learned behaviors that are traditionally masculine or feminine.

10. **a.** is the answer. The pins are an external stimulus that can motivate behavior. (p. 250)

b. Drives are states of arousal that arise from physiological needs.

c. Intrinsic motivation is the desire to perform a behavior for its own sake; external incentives are unnecessary.

d. A work-mastery orientation is characteristic of people who are intrinsically motivated.

11. **c.** is the answer. The deprived subjects focused on food almost to the exclusion of anything else. (p. 251)

a. In order to conserve energy, the men's metabolic rate actually *decreased.*

b. & d. Far from losing interest in food, the subjects came to care only about food—a finding consistent with Maslow's hierarchy, in which physiological needs are at the base.

12. **b.** is the answer. The body acts to defend its set point, or the weight to which it is predisposed. If Lucille was already near her set point, weight loss would prove difficult. (p. 254)

a. If the weight level to which her body is predisposed is low, weight loss upon dieting should *not* be difficult.

c. The eating disorders relate to eating behaviors and psychological factors and would not explain a difficulty with weight loss.

d. Externals might have greater problems losing weight, since they tend to respond to food stimuli, but this can't be the explanation in Lucille's case, since she has been sticking to her diet.

13. **d.** is the answer. Sex is much more than just a biological act and its study therefore inherently involves values, attitudes, and morals, which should thus be discussed openly. (p. 266)

14. **c.** is the answer. Individuals with a high need for achievement tend to choose moderately difficult tasks, at which they can succeed if they work. (p. 268)

a. The choice described is characteristic of those with a high need for achievement, which in turn tends to be more characteristic of firstborn than of later born children.

b. People with a low need for achievement might be more likely to prefer either the easy or the very difficult course.

d. That she chooses the course because it interests her implies that she is *intrinsically* motivated.

15. **d.** is the answer. As different people are motivated by different things, to increase motivation and thus productivity, managers are advised to learn what motivates individual employees and to challenge and reward them accordingly. (p. 272)

a. & b. The most effective leadership style will depend on the situation.

c. This might be an effective strategy with some, but not all, employees.

Matching Items

1. e (p. 269)	**5.** f (p. 269)	**9.** g (p. 272)
2. k (p. 254)	**6.** a (p. 261)	**10.** c (p. 250)
3. j (p. 272)	**7.** b (p. 249)	**11.** i (p. 272)
4. h (p. 272)	**8.** d (p. 263)	

PROGRESS TEST 2

Multiple-Choice Questions

1. **d.** is the answer. In contrast to the sexual behavior of animals, which is largely controlled by hormones, sexual motivation is primarily influenced by social and psychological factors. (p. 266)

2. **d.** is the answer. If used to inform rather than to control, rewards can increase intrinsic motivation and the need for achievement. (pp. 267–269)

   a., b., & c. Each of these has been shown to *discourage* the development of intrinsic motivation.

3. **a.** is the answer. The differences found between firstborn and later born children are in measures of achievement, with firstborn children doing slightly better than their siblings in grades, intelligence tests, and school admissions. (p. 269)

   b. Later born children tend to be more socially relaxed and popular.

   c. & d. Firstborn and later born children do not differ in their competitiveness, work-mastery orientation, or intrinsic motivation.

4. **b.** is the answer. (p. 253)

   a. Stimulation of the lateral hypothalamus triggers eating.

   c. & d. The thalamus is a sensory relay station; stimulation of it has no effect on eating.

5. **b.** is the answer. Wanting to do something for its own sake is intrinsic motivation; wanting to do something for a reward (in this case, presumably, a high grade) is extrinsic motivation. (pp. 269–270)

   a. The opposite is true, since Nancy was motivated to take the course for its own sake, whereas Jack was evidently motivated by the likelihood of a reward in the form of a good grade.

   c. & d. A good grade, such as the one Jack is expecting, is an incentive. Drives, however, are aroused states that result from physical deprivation; they are not involved in this example.

6. **d.** is the answer. Researchers have not been able to find any clear differences, psychological or otherwise, between homosexuals and heterosexuals. Thus the basis for sexual orientation remains unknown. (pp. 263–264)

7. **d.** is the answer. (p. 250)

8. **c.** is the answer. Such behavior, presumably motivated by curiosity rather than any biological need, is inconsistent with a drive-reduction theory of motivation. (pp. 249–250)

   a., b., d. Each of these examples is consistent with a drive-reduction theory of motivation.

9. **c.** is the answer. (p. 269)

a. & b. People may or may not be both competitive and oriented toward work mastery.

   d. Among those who have a low work-mastery orientation, less competitive people achieve less.

10. **c.** is the answer. (p. 263)

    a. Gender identity is the individual's sense of being male or female.

    b. The sexual response cycle applies to everyone, independent of sexual orientation.

    d. This is not a term used by sex researchers.

11. **b.** is the answer. (p. 272)

    a. Managers such as Bill, who are more directive, excel at task leadership.

    c. & d. Theories X and Y have to do with whether managers believe employees are motivated extrinsically (theory X) or intrinsically (theory Y).

12. **c.** is the answer. (p. 262)

13. **d.** is the answer. During the resolution phase males experience a refractory period. (p. 260)

    a., b., & c. The male and female responses are very similar in each of these phases.

14. **b.** is the answer. (p. 253)

    a. These effects are the reverse of what takes place.

    c. If anything, set point is lowered by destruction of the lateral hypothalamus and raised by destruction of the ventromedial hypothalamus.

    d. These effects do not occur.

15. **c.** is the answer. (p. 268)

16. **d.** is the answer. (p. 250)

17. **a.** is the answer. Hunger is the drive that arises in response to the need of food deprivation. (p. 249)

    b. Hunger is a drive, or psychological state of arousal; food deprivation is a physical need.

    c. & d. Incentives are positive or negative environmental stimuli that motivate behavior.

True-False Items

1. True (p. 258) 5. False (p. 253) 8. True (p. 272)
2. False (p. 259) 6. True (p. 269) 9. True (p. 269)
3. False (p. 261) 7. False (p. 252) 10. True (p. 263)
4. False (p. 262)

KEY TERMS

1. **Motivation** is a force, internal or external, that energizes and directs behavior. (p. 247)

   Example: A classic debate in the study of **motivation** concerns whether behavior is more pushed from within by biological drives or pulled from without by incentives.

2. An **instinct** is a stereotyped behavior pattern that is rigid, characteristic of an entire species, and innate. (p. 249)

3. A **need** is a state of deprivation that arouses a drive that will reduce the deprivation. (p. 249)

4. A **drive** is an energized state that arises from an underlying need. (p. 249)

5. **Homeostasis** refers to the body's tendency to maintain a constant, and optimum, internal state. (p. 249)

6. An **incentive** is an environmental stimulus that motivates behavior by "pulling" it from without. (p. 250)
   Example: Under the company's employee **incentive** plan, low absenteeism was rewarded with bonus pay.

7. Maslow's **hierarchy of needs** proposes that human motives may be ranked from the basic, physiological level through higher level needs for safety, esteem, and self-fulfillment, and that until they are satisfied, the more basic needs are more compelling than the higher level ones. (p. 250)

8. **Glucose**, or blood sugar, is the major source of energy for the body. Elevating the level of glucose in the body will reduce hunger. (p. 252)

9. **Insulin** is a hormone that helps the body convert glucose into fat. Elevating the level of insulin in the body will trigger hunger. (p. 252)

10. The **lateral hypothalamus (LH)** triggers eating when electrically stimulated and, when destroyed, causes an animal to stop eating. Normal neural activity in the LH brings on feelings of hunger. (p. 253)

11. The **ventromedial hypothalamus (VMH)** causes an animal to stop eating, while its destruction causes an animal to overeat. (p. 253)

12. **Set point** is an individual's regulated weight level, which is maintained by adjusting food intake and energy output. (p. 254)

13. **Metabolic rate** is the body's rate of energy expenditure. (p. 254)

14. **Anorexia nervosa** is an eating disorder, most common in adolescent females, in which a person restricts food intake to become significantly underweight and yet still feels fat. (p. 255)

15. **Bulimia nervosa** is an eating disorder characterized by repeated "binge-purge" episodes of overeating followed by vomiting or laxative use. (p. 255)

16. The **sexual response cycle** described by Masters and Johnson consists of four stages of bodily reaction: excitement, plateau, orgasm, and resolution. (p. 259)

Example: Perhaps the most important result of Masters and Johnson's study of the **sexual response cycle** is the finding that except for the resolution phase, males and females have very similar responses.

17. The **refractory period** is a resting period after orgasm, during which a male cannot be aroused to another orgasm. (p. 260)

18. **Estrogen** is a sex hormone secreted in greater amounts by females than by males. In mammals other than humans, estrogen levels peak during ovulation and trigger sexual drive. (p. 261)

19. **Sexual orientation** refers to a person's attraction to members of either the same or the opposite sex. (p. 263)
    Example: Although theories of the origins of **sexual orientation** abound, few conclusions exist, other than that one's orientation does not seem to be a voluntary choice.

20. **Gender identity** is the individual's sense of being male or female. (p. 263)

21. **Achievement motivation** is the degree to which a person is motivated internally by a desire for significant accomplishment and attaining a high standard. (p. 267)

22. **Intrinsic motivation** is the desire to perform a behavior for its own sake, rather than for some external reason. (p. 269)
    Memory aid: *Intrinsic* means "internal": A person who is **intrinsically** motivated is motivated from within.

23. **Extrinsic motivation** is the desire to perform a behavior in order to obtain a reward or avoid a punishment. (p. 269)
    Memory aid: *Extrinsic* means "external": A person who is **extrinsically** motivated is motivated by some outside factor.

24. Managers who excel at **task leadership** are goal-oriented, often directive leaders, who are particularly effective at keeping a group on its mission. (p. 272)

25. Managers who excel at **social leadership** have a democratic style that builds a sense of teamwork among the members of a group. (p. 272)

26. **Theory X** managers assume that employees are basically lazy, extrinsically motivated, and require constant supervision. (p. 272)

27. **Theory Y** managers assume that employees are intrinsically motivated by the need to demonstrate their competence and creativity. Theory Y managers tend to give employees greater control over their work and input in company decision making. (p. 272).

Chapter 10 | Emotion

Chapter Overview

Emotions are responses of the whole individual, involving physiological arousal, expressive behavior, and conscious feelings and thoughts. Chapter 10 examines each of these components in detail, particularly as they relate to three specific emotions: fear, anger, and happiness. In addition, the chapter discusses several theoretical controversies concerning the relationship and sequence of the components of emotion. Primary among these are whether body response to a stimulus causes the emotion that is felt and whether thinking is necessary to and must precede the experience of emotion.

Guided Study

The textbook chapter should be studied one section at a time. Before you read, preview each section by skimming it, noting headings and boldface items. Then read the appropriate section objectives from the following outline. Keep these objectives in mind, and as you read the chapter section, search for the information that will enable you to meet each objective. Once you have finished a section, write out answers for its objectives.

The Physiology of Emotion (pp. 277–280)

1. Identify the three components of emotion and describe the physiological changes that occur during emotional arousal, including the relationship between arousal and performance.

2. Discuss the research findings on the relationship between bodily states and specific emotions and discuss the effectiveness of the polygraph in detecting lies.

Expressing Emotion (pp. 281–284)

3. Discuss the extent to which nonverbal expressions of emotion are universally understood and describe the effects of facial expressions on emotion.

Experiencing Emotion (pp. 285–293)

4. Discuss the significance of biological and environmental factors in the acquisition of fear and explain how specific fears may be adaptive.

5. Discuss the catharsis hypothesis and identify some of the advantages and disadvantages of openly expressing anger.

6. Identify some potential causes and consequences of happiness and discuss reasons for the relativity of happiness.

Theories of Emotion (pp. 293–297)

7. Contrast the James-Lange and Cannon-Bard theories of emotion.

8. Describe Schachter's two-factor theory of emotion and discuss evidence suggesting that some emotional reactions involve no conscious thought.

1. Of all the species, _____ are the most emotional.

2. Three aspects of any emotion are

_____ _____,

_____ _____, and

_____ _____.

The Physiology of Emotion (pp. 277–280)

3. Describe the major physiological changes that each of the following undergoes during emotional arousal:
   a. heart: _____
   b. muscles: _____
   c. liver: _____
   d. breathing: _____
   e. digestion: _____
   f. pupils: _____
   g. blood: _____

4. The responses of arousal are activated by the _____ nervous system. In response to its signal, the _____ glands release the hormones _____ and _____, which increase heart rate, blood pressure, and blood sugar levels.

5. When the need for arousal has passed, the body is calmed through activation of the _____ nervous system.

Explain the relationship between performance and arousal.

Chapter Review

When you have finished reading the chapter, use the material that follows to review it. Complete the fill-in sentences and answer the essay items in complete sentences. As you proceed, evaluate your performance for each chapter section by consulting the answer key at the end of this chapter. Do not continue with the next section until you've understood each answer. If you need to, review or re-read the appropriate chapter section in the textbook before continuing.

6. The various emotions are associated with _____ (similar/different) forms of physiological arousal.

7. Generally, psychologists _____ (believe/do not believe) that different patterns of brain activity underlie different emotions.

8. The technical name for the "lie detector" is the _____.

Explain how lie detectors supposedly indicate whether a person is lying.

9. By and large, experts _____ (agree/do not agree) that lie detector tests are highly accurate.

10. Those who criticize lie detectors feel that the tests are particularly likely to err in the case of the _____ (innocent/guilty), because different emotions all register as

    _____.

11. A test that assesses a suspect's knowledge of details of a crime that only the guilty person should know is the _____

    _____ _____.

Expressing Emotion (pp. 281–284)

12. Emotions may be communicated in words and/or through bodily expressions, referred to as _____ communication.

13. Women are generally _____ (better/worse) than men at detecting nonverbal signs of emotion.

14. Gestures have _____ (the same/different) meanings in different cultures.

15. Studies of adults indicate that in different cultures facial expressions have

    _____ (the same/different) meanings. Studies of children indicate that the meaning of their facial expressions

    _____ (varies/does not vary) across cultures.

16. Darwin believed that human emotional expressions _____(were/were not) an important factor in the survival of our species.

17. Darwin also believed that when an emotion is accompanied by an outward facial expression,

the emotion is _____ (intensified/diminished).

18. In one study, students who were induced to smile _____ (found/did not find) cartoons more humorous.

19. Ekman and colleagues found that imitating emotional facial expressions resulted in

    _____ changes characteristic of emotional arousal.

20. Studies have found that imitating another person's facial expressions _____ (leads/does not lead) to greater empathy with that person's feelings.

Experiencing Emotion (pp. 285–293)

21. Fear can by and large be seen as a(n)

    _____ (adaptive/maladaptive) response.

22. Most human fears are acquired through

    _____.

Explain why researchers believe that some fears are biologically predisposed.

23. People differ _____ (little/ significantly) in their level of fearfulness.

24. Averill has found that most people become angry several times per _____.

25. According to one theory, expressing pent-up emotion is adaptive. This is the

    _____ hypothesis.

26. Psychologists have found that when anger has been provoked, retaliation may have a calming effect under certain circumstances. List these circumstances below.

    a. _____

    b. _____

    c. _____

Identify some of the potential problems of unchecked anger.

27. List two suggestions offered by experts for handling one's anger.

    a. _____

    b. _____

28. Psychologists have consistently found that people become more willing to help others when they themselves are _____.

29. After experiencing tragedy, people generally _____ (regain/do not regain) their previous degree of happiness.

30. Since the 1950s, spendable income has doubled; personal happiness has _____ (increased/decreased/remained unchanged).

31. The idea that happiness is relative to one's most recent experience is stated by the

    _____ - _____

    phenomenon.

Explain how this phenomenon accounts for the fact that, for some people, material desires can never be satisfied.

32. The principle that one's happiness is relative to others' is known as _____

    _____.

33. (Box) The idea that "every emotion triggers its opposite" is the basis of the _____-_____ theory of emotion. According to this theory, the opposing emotion is most intense immediately _____ (before/after) an emotion-arousing event. With repeated experience of the event, the primary

emotion becomes _____ (weaker/stronger) and the opposing emotion becomes _____ (weaker/stronger).

34. List six factors that have been shown to be positively correlated with feelings of happiness.

    _____   _____

    _____   _____

    _____   _____

35. List six factors that are evidently unrelated to happiness.

    _____   _____

    _____   _____

    _____   _____

Theories of Emotion (pp. 293–297)

36. According to the James-Lange theory, emotional states _____ (precede/follow) bodily arousal.

Describe two problems that Walter Cannon identified with the James-Lange theory.

37. Cannon proposed that emotional stimuli in the environment are routed simultaneously to the _____, which results in awareness of the emotion, and to the _____ nervous system, which causes the body's reaction. Because another scientist concurrently proposed similar ideas, this theory has come to be known as the

    _____-_____

    theory.

38. For victims of spinal cord injuries who have lost all feeling below the neck, the intensity of emotions tends to _____. This result supports the _____- _____ theory of emotion.

39. The two-factor theory of emotion proposes that emotion has two components: _____

arousal and a _____ label. This theory was proposed by

_____.

40. Schachter and Singer found that physically aroused subjects told that an injection would cause arousal _____ (did/did not) become emotional in response to an accomplice's aroused behavior. Physically aroused subjects not expecting arousal _____ (did/did not) become emotional in response to the accomplice's behavior.

41. Psychologist Robert Zajonc believes that the feeling of emotion _____ (can/cannot) precede our cognitive labeling of that emotion.

42. The researcher who disagrees with Zajonc and argues that most emotions require cognitive processing is _____.

Express some general conclusions that can be drawn about cognition and emotion.

FOCUS ON PSYCHOLOGY:
Does Unhappiness Run in Families?

Researchers investigating human emotions have recently come to the surprising conclusion that happiness (a subjective sense of well-being) and unhappiness are separate feelings, rather than opposite endpoints on one emotional continuum. Edward Diener, psychology professor at the University of Illinois, believes that the two emotions can exist simultaneously in each of us, much as we can have mixed or conflicting feelings about a partner in a close relationship.

Evidence for the independence of happiness and unhappiness comes from research showing that while a predisposition toward sadness may be inherited, happiness is more situationally controlled. In one study, researchers at the University of Southern California measured levels of happiness and unhappiness in more than 100 pairs of twins, as well as in several generations of other families. They found that family members were much more similar in level of unhappiness than in level of happiness. Furthermore, identical twins were more similar than fraternal twins, but *only in levels of unhappiness*. These results suggest that sadness, or unhappiness, may run in families, while happiness is more a matter of personal control and environmental influence.

In another study, researchers at the University of Minnesota compared the personalities of identical twins who had been raised together with those who had not. Twins who had grown up together had much more similar levels of happiness than did twins who had been raised apart. In terms of unhappiness, however, twins raised together were no more similar than twins raised separately.

Science writer Diane Swanbrow believes these findings offer useful clues to people wishing to live happier lives. Because happiness and unhappiness are independent emotions, "changing or avoiding things that make you miserable may well make you less miserable but probably won't make you any happier." Instead, Swanbrow suggests, you should focus on what makes you happy and do those things. In one experiment, people were asked to spend more time doing things they enjoyed for one month. At the end of the month, average happiness levels increased significantly as compared with happiness levels of control subjects, who did not change their monthly activities.

Although psychologists have only recently begun to investigate happiness, their initial findings are important to all of us. By planning to be happy, making the pursuit of a happy life a priority, and making time to do the things that make us happy, each of us can discover that whatever our emotional heritage, happiness is something attainable and under our control.

Source: Swanbrow, D. (1989, July-August). The paradox of happiness. *Psychology Today*, 37–39.

Progress Test 1

Multiple-Choice Questions

Circle your answers to the following questions and check them with the answer key at the end of this chapter. If your answer is incorrect, read the answer key explanation for why it is incorrect and then consult the appropriate pages of the text to understand the correct answer.

1. Which of the following is correct regarding the relationship between arousal and performance?
   a. Generally, performance is optimal when arousal is low.
   b. Generally, performance is optimal when arousal is high.

c. On easy tasks, performance is optimal when arousal is low.

d. On easy tasks, performance is optimal when arousal is high.

2. Which division of the nervous system is especially involved in bringing about emotional arousal?

   a. somatic nervous system
   b. peripheral nervous system
   c. sympathetic nervous system
   d. parasympathetic nervous system

3. Concerning emotions and their accompanying bodily responses, which of the following appears to be true?

   a. Each emotion has its own bodily response and underlying brain activity.
   b. All emotions involve the same bodily response as a result of the same underlying brain activity.
   c. Many emotions involve similar bodily responses but have different underlying brain activity.
   d. All emotions have the same underlying brain activity but different bodily responses.

4. The Cannon-Bard theory of emotion states that:

   a. emotions have two ingredients: physical arousal and a cognitive label.
   b. the conscious experience of an emotion occurs at the same time as the body's physical reaction.
   c. emotional experiences are based on an awareness of bodily responses to an emotion-arousing stimulus.
   d. emotional ups and downs tend to balance in the long run.

5. Electrical stimulation of which brain region can produce terror or rage in cats?

   a. limbic system   c. cortex
   b. hypothalamus   d. cerebellum

6. You're on your way to school to take a big exam. Suddenly, on noticing that your pulse is racing and that you are sweating, you feel nervous. With which theory of emotion is this experience most consistent?

   a. Cannon-Bard theory
   b. James-Lange theory
   c. the optimum arousal principle
   d. adaptation-level phenomenon

7. Which of the following was *not* raised as a criticism of the James-Lange theory of emotion?

   a. Bodily responses are too similar to trigger the various emotions.
   b. Emotional reactions occur before bodily responses can take place.
   c. The cognitive activity of the cortex plays a role in the emotions we experience.

d. People with spinal cord injuries at the neck typically experience less emotion.

8. Current estimates are that the polygraph is inaccurate approximately _____ of the time.

   a. three-fourths   c. one-third
   b. one-half   d. one-tenth

9. In the Schachter-Singer experiment, which subjects reported feeling an emotional change in the presence of the experimenter's highly emotional confederate?

   a. those receiving adrenaline and expecting to feel physical arousal
   b. those receiving a placebo and expecting to feel physical arousal
   c. those receiving adrenaline but not expecting to feel physical arousal
   d. those receiving a placebo and not expecting to feel physical arousal

10. Which of the following is true?

    a. People with more education tend to be happier.
    b. Highly intelligent people tend to be happier.
    c. Women tend to be happier than men.
    d. People who are socially outgoing or who exercise regularly tend to be happier.

11. Catharsis will be most effective in reducing anger toward another person if:

    a. you wait until you are no longer angry before confronting the person.
    b. the target of your anger is someone you feel has power over you.
    c. your anger is directed specifically toward the person who angered you.
    d. the other person is able to retaliate by also expressing anger.

12. Emotions are:

    a. physiological reactions.
    b. behavioral expressions.
    c. conscious feelings.
    d. all of the above.

13. Law enforcement officials sometimes use a lie detector to assess a suspect's responses to details of the crime believed to be known only to the perpetrator. This is known as the:

    a. inductive approach.
    b. deductive approach.
    c. guilty knowledge test.
    d. screening examination.

14. Research on nonverbal communication has revealed that:

    a. it is easy to hide your emotions by controlling your facial expressions.

b. facial expressions tend to be the same the world over, while gestures vary from culture to culture.

c. most authentic expressions last between 7 and 10 seconds.

d. most gestures have universal meanings; facial expressions vary from culture to culture.

15. Expressing anger can be adaptive when you:

a. retaliate immediately.

b. have first rehearsed all the reasons for your anger in your mind.

c. count to ten, then blow off steam.

d. first wait until the anger subsides, then deal with the situation in a civil manner.

16. Research indicates that a person is most likely to be helpful to others if he or she:

a. is feeling guilty about something.

b. is happy.

c. recently received help from another person.

d. recently offered help to another person.

17. When Professor Simon acquired a spacious new office, he was overjoyed. Six months later, however, he was taking the office for granted. Which of the following is illustrated by his behavior?

a. the relative deprivation principle

b. the adaptation-level phenomenon

c. the opponent-process theory

d. the optimum arousal principle

18. (Box) Research supporting the opponent-process theory suggests that:

a. the price of pleasure is pain.

b. with repetition a task that arouses fear will become more tolerable.

c. suffering can pay emotional dividends.

d. all of the above.

Matching Items

Match each definition or description with the appropriate term.

Definitions

_____ 1. the tendency to react to changes on the basis of recent experience

_____ 2. we are sad because we cry

_____ 3. emotional release

_____ 4. the tendency to evaluate our situation negatively against that of other people

_____ 5. the reason emotions may balance in the short run

_____ 6. emotions consist of both physical arousal and a cognitive label

_____ 7. an emotion-arousing stimulus triggers cognitive and bodily responses simultaneously

_____ 8. the division of the nervous system that calms the body following arousal

_____ 9. the division of the nervous system that activates arousal

_____ 10. a device that measures the physiological correlates of emotion

Terms

a. adaptation-level phenomenon

b. opponent-process theory

c. two-factor theory

d. catharsis

e. sympathetic nervous system

f. James-Lange theory

g. polygraph

h. Cannon-Bard theory

i. parasympathetic nervous system

j. relative deprivation principle

Progress Test 2

Progress Test 2 should be completed during a final chapter review. Do so after you thoroughly understand the correct answers for the Chapter Review and Progress Test 1.

Multiple-Choice Questions

1. After Brenda scolded her brother because he forgot to pick her up from school as he had promised, the physical arousal that had accompanied her anger diminished. Which division of her nervous system mediated her physical *relaxation*?

a. sympathetic division
b. parasympathetic division
c. somatic division
d. peripheral nervous system

2. Schachter's two-factor theory emphasizes that emotion involves both:
   a. the sympathetic and parasympathetic divisions of the nervous system.
   b. verbal and nonverbal expression.
   c. physical arousal and a cognitive label.
   d. universal and culture-specific aspects.

3. Dermer found that students who had seen others worse off felt greater satisfaction with their own lives; this is the principle of:
   a. relative deprivation.   c. behavioral contrast.
   b. adaptation level.   d. catharsis.

4. Which theory of emotion emphasizes the simultaneous experience of bodily response and emotional feeling?
   a. James-Lange theory   c. two-factor theory
   b. Cannon-Bard theory   d. adaptation–level theory

5. Two years ago Maria was in an automobile accident in which her spinal cord was severed, leaving her paralyzed from her neck down. Today Maria finds that she experiences emotions less intensely than she did before her accident. This tends to support which theory of emotion?
   a. James-Lange theory
   b. Cannon-Bard theory
   c. relative deprivation theory
   d. adaptation-level theory

6. The polygraph measures:
   a. lying.
   b. brain rhythms.
   c. chemical changes in the body.
   d. physiological indexes of arousal.

7. (Box) According to the opponent-process theory, as an emotion is repeatedly experienced:
   a. the primary emotional experience becomes stronger.
   b. the opposing emotional experience becomes weaker.
   c. both a. and b. occur.
   d. the primary emotional experience becomes weaker; the opposing emotional experience becomes stronger.

8. Which of the following is true?
   a. Gestures are universal; facial expressions, culture specific.
   b. Facial expressions are universal; gestures, culture specific.
   c. Both gestures and facial expressions are universal.
   d. Both gestures and facial expressions are culture specific.

9. Which theory of emotion implies that every emotion is associated with a unique physiological reaction?
   a. James-Lange theory
   b. Cannon-Bard theory
   c. two-factor theory
   d. adaptation–level theory

10. For which of the following fears do humans appear biologically prepared?
    a. fear of electricity   c. fear of thunder
    b. fear of cliffs   d. fear of flying

11. Concerning the catharsis hypothesis, which of the following is true?
    a. Expressing anger can be temporarily calming if it does not leave one feeling guilty or anxious.
    b. The arousal that accompanies unexpressed anger never dissipates.
    c. Expressing one's anger always calms one down.
    d. Psychologists agree that under no circumstances is catharsis beneficial.

12. In an emergency situation, emotional arousal will result in:
    a. increased rate of respiration.
    b. increased blood sugar.
    c. a slowing of digestion.
    d. all of the above.

13. A relatively high level of arousal would be most likely to facilitate:
    a. remembering the lines of a play.
    b. shooting free throws in basketball.
    c. sprinting 100 meters.
    d. taking a final exam in introductory psychology.

14. Several studies have shown that physical arousal can intensify just about any emotion. For example, when people who have been physically aroused by exercise are insulted, they often misattribute their arousal to the insult. This finding illustrates the importance of:
    a. cognitive labels of arousal in the conscious experience of emotions.
    b. a minimum level of arousal in triggering emotional experiences.
    c. the simultaneous occurrence of physical arousal and cognitive labeling in emotional experience.
    d. all of the above.

15. Psychologist David Lykken is opposed to the use of lie detectors because:

    a. they represent an invasion of privacy and could easily be used for unethical purposes.
    b. there are often serious discrepancies among the various indicators such as perspiration and heart rate.
    c. the polygraph cannot distinguish the various possible causes of arousal.
    d. it is accurate only about 50 percent of the time.

16. The candidate stepped before the hostile audience, panic written all over his face. It is likely that the candidate's facial expression caused him to experience:

    a. a lessening of his fear.
    b. an intensification of his fear.
    c. a surge of digestive enzymes in his body.
    d. increased body temperature.

17. Which of these factors have researchers *not* found to correlate with happiness?

    a. a satisfying marriage or other love relationship
    b. high self-esteem
    c. religious faith
    d. intelligence

18. After hitting a grand-slam home run, Mike noticed that his heart was pounding and concluded that he was ecstatic. Later that evening, after nearly having a collision while driving on the freeway, Mike again noticed that his heart was pounding. That he interpreted this reaction as fear, rather than as ecstasy, can best be explained by which theory?

    a. the James-Lange theory
    b. the Cannon-Bard theory
    c. the adaptation–level theory
    d. the two-factor theory

True-False Items

Indicate whether each statement is true or false by placing *T* or *F* in the blank next to the item.

_____ 1. For easy tasks, the optimal level of arousal is higher than for difficult tasks.

_____ 2. Men are generally better than women at detecting nonverbal emotional expression.

_____ 3. The sympathetic nervous system triggers physiological arousal during an emotion.

_____ 4. The adrenal glands produce the hormones epinephrine and norepinephrine.

_____ 5. When one imitates an emotional facial expression, the body may experience physiological changes characteristic of that emotion.

_____ 6. Paraplegics who have lost sensation only in their lower bodies experience a considerable decrease in the intensity of their emotions.

_____ 7. Wealthy people tend to be much happier than middle-income people.

_____ 8. Physical arousal can intensify emotion.

_____ 9. All emotions involve conscious thinking.

_____ 10. According to the two-factor theory, emotions are labeled cognitively before physical arousal occurs.

Key Terms

Using your own words, write a brief definition or explanation of each of the following terms.

1. emotion

2. polygraph

3. catharsis

4. adaptation-level phenomenon

5. opponent-process theory

6. relative deprivation

7. James-Lange theory

8. Cannon-Bard theory

9. two-factor theory

Answers

CHAPTER REVIEW

1. humans

2. physiological arousal; expressive behavior; conscious experience

3. a. Heart rate increases.
   b. Muscles become tense.
   c. The liver releases sugar into the bloodstream.
   d. Breathing rate increases.
   e. Digestion slows down.
   f. Pupils dilate.
   g. Blood tends to clot more rapidly.

4. sympathetic; adrenal; adrenaline (epinephrine); noradrenaline (norepinephrine)

5. parasympathetic

Our performance on a task is usually best when arousal is moderate. However, the difficulty of the task affects optimum arousal level. A relatively high level of arousal is best on easy tasks; a relatively low level of arousal is best on difficult tasks.

6. similar

7. believe

8. polygraph

The polygraph measures several of the physiological responses that accompany emotion, such as changes in breathing, pulse rate, blood pressure, and perspiration. The assumption is that lying is stressful, so a person who is lying will become physically aroused.

9. do not agree

10. innocent; arousal

11. guilty knowledge test

12. nonverbal

13. better

14. different

15. the same; does not vary

16. were

17. intensified

18. found

19. physiological

20. leads

21. adaptive

22. learning (conditioning)

The fact that humans quickly learn and slowly unlearn to fear snakes, spiders, and cliffs—fears that were presumably very useful to our ancestors—suggests that these are biologically predisposed fears that develop with little or no learning.

23. significantly

24. week

25. catharsis

26. a. Retaliation must be directed against the person who provoked the anger.
    b. Retaliation must be justifiable.
    c. The target of the retaliation must not be someone who is intimidating.

One problem with frequently being angry is that anger also breeds more anger, in part because it may trigger retaliation. Expressing anger can also magnify anger.

27. a. Wait to calm down.
    b. Deal with anger in a civil way that promotes reconciliation rather than retaliation.

28. happy

29. regain

30. remained unchanged

31. adaptation-level

If we acquire new possessions, we feel an initial surge of pleasure. But we then adapt to having these new possessions, come to see them as normal, and require other things to give us another surge of happiness.

32. relative deprivation

33. opponent-process; after; weaker; stronger

34. high self-esteem; satisfying marriage or other love relationship; meaningful religious faith; outgoing personality; good sleeping habits; regular exercise; employment

35. age; race; gender; education; intelligence; parenthood

36. follow

Cannon argued that the body's responses were not sufficiently distinct to trigger the various different emotions and, furthermore, that physiological changes occur too slowly to trigger sudden emotion.

37. cortex; sympathetic; Cannon-Bard

38. diminish; James-Lange

39. physiological; cognitive; Schachter

40. did not; did

41. can

42. Lazarus

It seems that some emotional responses—especially simple likes, dislikes, and fears—involve no conscious thinking. Other emotions are greatly affected by our interpretations, memories, and expectations.

PROGRESS TEST 1

Multiple-Choice Questions

1. **d.** is the answer. Generally speaking, performance is optimal when arousal is moderate; for easy tasks, however, performance is optimal when arousal is high. For difficult tasks, performance is optimal when arousal is low. (p. 278)

2. **c.** is the answer. (p. 278)

   a. The somatic division of the peripheral nervous system carries sensory and motor signals to and from the CNS.

   b. The peripheral nervous system is too general an answer, since it includes sympathetic *and* parasympathetic divisions, as well as the somatic division.

   d. The parasympathetic nervous system restores the body to its unaroused state.

3. **c.** is the answer. Although many emotions have the same general bodily arousal, resulting from activation of the sympathetic nervous system, they appear to be associated with different brain regions and different patterns of brain activity. (pp. 278–279)

4. **b.** is the answer. (p. 294)

   a. This expresses the two-factor theory.

   c. This expresses the James-Lange theory.

   d. This expresses the opponent-process theory.

5. **a.** is the answer. (pp. 278–279)

   b. The hypothalamus is involved in eating, thirst, and sexual motivation.

   c. The cortex is the center of higher cognitive functions, such as memory and thinking.

   d. The cerebellum is involved in motor coordination.

6. **b.** is the answer. The James-Lange theory proposes that the experienced emotion is an aware-

ness of a prior bodily response: Your pulse races, and so you feel nervous. (p. 294)

   a. According to the Cannon-Bard theory, your body's reaction would occur simultaneously with, rather than before, your experience of the emotion.

   c. The optimum arousal principle does not *explain* your physiological state. Rather, it deals with what your arousal *should be* under these conditions.

   d. The adaptation-level principle concerns our tendency to judge stimuli on the basis of recent experience.

7. **d.** is the answer. The finding that people whose brains can't sense bodily responses experience considerably less emotion in fact supports the James-Lange theory, which claims that experienced emotion follows from bodily responses. (p. 294)

   a., b., & c. All these statements go counter to the theory's claim that experienced emotion is essentially just an awareness of a bodily response.

8. **c.** is the answer. (p. 280)

9. **c.** is the answer. Subjects who received adrenaline without an explanation felt arousal and, moreover, experienced this arousal as whatever emotion the experimental confederate in the room with them was displaying. (p. 296)

   a. Adrenaline recipients who expected arousal attributed their arousal to the drug and reported no emotional change in reaction to the confederate's behavior.

   b. & d. In addition to the two groups discussed in the text, the experiment involved placebo recipients; these subjects were not physically aroused and did not experience an emotional change.

10. **d.** is the answer. Education level, intelligence, and gender seem unrelated to happiness. (p. 292)

11. **c.** is the answer. (p. 287)

    a. This would not be an example of catharsis, since catharsis involves releasing, rather than suppressing, aggressive energy.

    b. Expressions of anger in such a situation tend to cause the person anxiety and thus not to be effective.

    d. One of the dangers of expressing anger is that it will lead to retaliation and an escalation of anger.

12. **d.** is the answer. These are the three components of emotions identified in the textbook. (p. 277)

13. **c.** is the answer. If the suspect becomes physically aroused while answering questions about details only the perpetrator of the crime could know, it is presumed that he or she committed the crime. (p. 280)

14. **b.** is the answer. (p. 282)

a. The opposite is true; relevant facial muscles are hard to control voluntarily.

c. Authentic facial expressions tend to fade within 5 seconds.

d. Facial expressions are generally universal; many gestures vary from culture to culture.

15. **d.** is the answer. (p. 287)

a. Venting anger immediately may lead one to say things one later regrets and/or may lead to retaliation by the other person.

b. Going over the reasons for one's anger merely prolongs the emotion.

c. Counting to ten *may* give you a chance to calm down, but "blowing off steam" may work you up again.

16. **b.** is the answer. (p. 288)

a., c., & d. Research studies have not found these factors to be related to altruistic behavior.

17. **b.** is the answer. Professor Simon's judgment of his office is affected by his recent experience: when that experience was of a smaller office, his new office seemed terrific; now, however, it no longer does. (p. 289)

a. Relative deprivation is the sense that one is better or worse off than those with whom one compares oneself.

c. This is the theory that every emotion triggers an opposing emotion.

d. This is the principle that there is an inverse relationship between the difficulty of a task and the optimum level of arousal.

18. **d.** is the answer. According to the theory, with repeated stimulations the primary emotion becomes weaker and the opponent emotion becomes stronger. (p. 290)

Matching Items

1. a (p. 289)
2. f (p. 294)
3. d (p. 287)
4. j (p. 291)
5. b (p. 290)
6. c (p. 295)
7. h (p. 294)
8. i (p. 278)
9. e (p. 278)
10. g (p. 279)

PROGRESS TEST 2

Multiple-Choice Questions

1. **b.** is the answer. The parasympathetic division is involved in calming arousal. (p. 278)

a. The sympathetic division is active during states of arousal and hence would *not* be active in the situation described.

c. The somatic division is involved in transmitting sensory information and controlling skeletal muscles; it is not involved in arousing and calming the body.

d. This answer is too general, since the peripheral nervous system includes not only the parasympathetic division but also the sympathetic division and the somatic division.

2. **c.** is the answer. According to Schachter, the two factors in emotion are (1) bodily arousal and (2) conscious interpretation of the arousal. (p. 295)

3. **a.** is the answer. The principle of relative deprivation states that happiness is relative to others' attainments. This helps explain why those who are relatively well off tend to be slightly more satisfied than the relatively poor, with whom the better-off can compare themselves. (p. 291)

b. Adaptation level is the tendency for our judgments to be relative to our prior experience.

c. This phenomenon has nothing to do with the interpretation of emotion.

d. Catharsis is an emotional release; it has nothing to do with interpreting others' emotions.

4. **b.** is the answer. (p. 294)

a. The James-Lange theory states that the experience of an emotion is an awareness of one's physical response to an emotion-arousing stimulus.

c. The two-factor theory states that to experience emotion one must be physically aroused *and* attribute the arousal to an emotional cause.

d. Adaptation level has nothing to do with the original experience of emotion.

5. **a.** is the answer. According to the James-Lange theory, Maria's emotions should be greatly diminished since her brain is unable to sense physical arousal. (p. 294)

b. Cannon and Bard would expect Maria to experience emotions normally because they believed that the experiencing of emotions occurs separately from bodily responses.

c. & d. The relative-deprivation and adaptation-level theories make no particular prediction regarding the importance of physical arousal in the conscious experience of emotion.

6. **d.** is the answer. No device can literally measure lying. The polygraph measures breathing, pulse rate, blood pressure, and perspiration for changes indicative of physiological arousal. (p. 279)

7. **d.** is the answer. (p. 290)

8. **b.** is the answer. Whereas the meanings of gestures vary from culture to culture, facial expressions seem to have the same meanings around the world. (pp. 282–283)

9. a. is the answer. If, as the theory claims, emotions are triggered by physiological reactions, then each emotion must be associated with a unique physiological reaction. (p. 294)

b. According to the Cannon-Bard theory, the same general bodily response accompanies many emotions.

c. The two-factor theory states that the cognitive interpretation of a general state of physical arousal determines different emotions.

d. The adaptation level does not deal with physiological reactions.

10. b. is the answer. The fears for which humans seem biologically prepared are fears that probably were useful to our ancestors, such as fear of cliffs. (p. 286)

11. a. is the answer. (p. 287)

b. In fact, the opposite is true. Any emotional arousal will simmer down if you wait long enough.

c. Catharsis often magnifies anger, escalates arguments, and leads to retaliation.

d. When counterattack is justified and can be directed at the offender, catharsis may be helpful.

12. d. is the answer. (p. 277)

13. c. is the answer. Easy or well-rehearsed tasks, such as sprinting, are best performed when arousal is high; more difficult tasks are best performed when arousal is lower. (p. 278)

14. a. is the answer. That physical arousal can be misattributed demonstrates that it is the cognitive interpretation of arousal, rather than the intensity or specific nature of the body's arousal, that determines the conscious experience of emotions. (pp. 296–297)

b. & c. The findings of these studies do not indicate that a minimum level of arousal is necessary for an emotional experience nor that applying a cognitive label must be simultaneous with arousal, rather than following it.

15. c. is the answer. As heightened arousal may reflect feelings of anxiety or irritation, rather than of guilt, the polygraph, which simply measures arousal, may easily err. (p. 280)

a. Misuse and invasion of privacy are valid issues, but Lykken primarily objects to use of lie detectors because of their inaccuracy.

b. Although there are discrepancies on the various measures of arousal, this was not what Lykken objected to.

d. The lie detector errs about one-third of the time.

16. b. is the answer. Expressions may have the effect of amplifying the associated emotions. (p. 284)

a. Laboratory studies have shown that facial expressions intensify emotions.

c. Arousal of the sympathetic nervous system, such as occurs when one is afraid, slows digestive function.

d. Increased body temperature accompanies anger but not fear.

17. d. is the answer. (p. 292)

18. d. is the answer. According to the two-factor theory, it is cognitive interpretation of the same general physiological arousal that distinguishes the two emotions. (p. 294)

a. According to the James-Lange theory, if the same physical arousal occurred in the two instances, the same emotions should result.

b. The Cannon-Bard theory argues that conscious awareness of an emotion and bodily reaction occur at the same time.

c. The adaptation–level theory has no relevance to the example.

True-False Items

1. True (p. 278)
2. False (p. 282)
3. True (p. 278)
4. True (p. 278)
5. True (p. 284)

6. False (p. 295)
7. False (p. 292)
8. True (pp. 295–296)
9. False (p. 297)
10. False (p. 295)

KEY TERMS

1. **Emotion** is a response of the whole organism involving three components: (1) physical arousal, (2) expressive reactions, and (3) conscious experience. (p. 277)

   Example: The major theories of **emotion** differ on the issue of the relative importance of physiological and cognitive factors.

2. The **polygraph**, or lie detector, is a device that measures physical arousal of the sympathetic nervous system. (p. 279)

   Example: Psychologist David Lykken opposes the use of the **polygraph** on the grounds that as it simply detects increased arousal, it cannot distinguish between feelings of guilt and those of anxiety or irritation.

3. **Catharsis** is emotional release; according to the catharsis hypothesis, by expressing our anger, we can reduce it. (p. 287)

4. The **adaptation-level phenomenon** refers to our tendency to judge things relative to our prior experience. (p. 289)

5. The **opponent-process theory** states that every emotion triggers an opposing emotion. Once the

opposing emotion is activated, there is a diminishing of the initial emotion's intensity. This theory helps explain why our emotional ups and downs tend to balance and provides a useful explanation of the dilemma of the substance abuser. (p. 290)

6. The principle of **relative deprivation** states that we judge our situation in relation to what we perceive other people's situations to be. (p. 291)

   Example: The concept of **relative deprivation** helps explain why the relatively well-off tend to be somewhat more satisfied with life than the relatively poor.

7. The **James-Lange theory** states that emotional experiences are based on an awareness of bodily responses to emotion-arousing stimuli: a stimulus triggers bodily responses that in turn trigger the experienced emotion. (p. 294)

8. The **Cannon-Bard theory** states that the conscious experience of an emotion occurs at the same time as the body's physical reaction. (p. 294)

9. The **two-factor theory** theory of emotion proposes that emotions have two ingredients: physical arousal and a cognitive label. Thus, physical arousal is a necessary, but not a sufficient, component of emotional change. For an emotion to be experienced, arousal must be attributed to an emotional cause. (p. 295)

Chapter 11 | Personality

Chapter Overview

Personality refers to each individual's relatively distinctive and consistent pattern of thinking, feeling, and acting. Chapter 11 examines four perspectives on personality. The psychoanalytic theory emphasizes the unconscious and irrational aspects of personality. The trait theory led to advances in techniques for evaluating and describing personality. The humanistic theory draws attention to the concept of self and to human potential for healthy growth. The social-cognitive perspective emphasizes the effects of our interactions with the environment. The text first describes and then evaluates the contributions and shortcomings of each perspective.

Guided Study

The textbook chapter should be studied one section at a time. Before you read, preview each section by skimming it, noting headings and boldface items. Then read the appropriate section objectives from the following outline. Keep these objectives in mind, and as you read the chapter section, search for the information that will enable you to meet each objective. Once you have finished a section, write out answers for its objectives.

1. Define "personality."

The Psychoanalytic Perspective (pp. 302–311)

2. Explain how Freud's treatment of psychological disorders led to his study of the unconscious.

3. Describe Freud's views of personality structure, development, and dynamics.

4. Discuss the major ideas of the neo-Freudians.

5. Explain how projective tests are used to assess personality and describe research findings regarding their validity and reliability.

6. Evaluate the psychoanalytic perspective.

The Social-Cognitive Perspective (pp. 322–329)

11. Describe the social-cognitive perspective and explain the meaning of reciprocal determinism.

The Trait Perspective (pp. 311–316)

7. Discuss trait theories of personality and identify the assessment techniques associated with this perspective.

12. Discuss research findings on personal control.

13. Describe how social-cognitive researchers study behavior and evaluate this perspective on personality.

8. Evaluate the trait perspective on personality and describe research findings regarding the consistency of behavior over time and across situations.

Chapter Review

When you have finished reading the chapter, use the material that follows to review it. Complete the fill-in sentences and answer the essay items in complete sentences. As you proceed, evaluate your performance for each chapter section by consulting the answer key at the end of this chapter. Do not continue with the next section until you've understood each answer. If you need to, review or reread the appropriate chapter section in the textbook before continuing.

The Humanistic Perspective (pp. 317–322)

9. Describe the humanistic perspective on personality and discuss the basic ideas of Maslow and Rogers.

1. An individual's relatively distinctive and consistent ways of thinking, feeling, and acting constitute that individual's _____.

2. The four major perspectives on personality discussed in this chapter are the

_____, _____,

_____, and _____-

_____ theories.

10. Evaluate the humanistic perspective and describe recent research findings.

The Psychoanalytic Perspective (pp. 302–311)

3. The psychoanalytic perspective on personality was proposed by _____

_____.

4. According to this theory, the mind is like an iceberg in that many of a person's thoughts, wishes, and feelings are hidden in a large _____ region. Some of the thoughts in this region can be retrieved at will into consciousness; these thoughts are said to be _____. Many of the memories of this region, however, are blocked, or _____, from consciousness.

5. The technique used by Freud, in which the patient relaxes and says whatever comes to mind, is called _____ _____.

6. Freud called his technique for exposing painful unconscious memories, _____.

7. Freud believed that a person's unconscious wishes are often reflected in his or her _____ and in slips of the tongue or pen.

8. According to Freud, personality consists of three structures: the _____, the _____, and the _____.

9. The id is a reservoir of energy that is primarily _____ (conscious/unconscious) and operates according to the _____ principle.

10. The ego develops _____ (before/after) the id and consists of perceptions, thoughts, and memories that are mostly _____ (conscious/ unconscious). The ego operates according to the _____ principle.

Explain why the ego is considered the "executive" of personality.

11. The personality structure that reflects moral values is the _____.

12. A person with a _____ (strong/weak) superego may be self-indulgent; one with an unusually _____ (strong/weak) superego may be continually guilt-ridden.

13. According to Freud, personality is formed as the child passes through a series of _____ stages.

14. The first stage is the _____ stage, which takes place during the first 18 months of life. During this stage, the id's energies are focused on behaviors such as _____.

15. The second stage is the _____ stage, which lasts from about age _____ months to _____ years.

16. The third stage is the _____ stage, which lasts roughly from ages _____ to _____. During this stage the id's energies are focused on the _____. Freud also believed that during this stage children develop sexual desires for the _____ (same/ opposite)-sex parent. Freud referred to these feelings as the _____ _____ in boys and the _____ _____ in girls.

Explain how this complex of feelings is resolved through the process of identification.

17. During the next stage, sexual feelings are repressed: this phase is called the _____ period and lasts until adolescence.

18. The final stage of development is called the
_____ stage.

19. According to Freud, it is possible for a person's development to become blocked in any of the stages; in such an instance, the person is said to be _____.

20. The ego attempts to protect itself against anxiety through the use of _____ _____. The process underlying each of these mechanisms is _____.

21. Dealing with anxiety by returning to an earlier stage of development is called _____.

22. When a person reacts in a manner opposite that of his or her true feelings, _____

_____ is said to have occurred.

23. When a person attributes his or her own feelings to another person, _____ has occurred.

24. When a person offers a false, self-justifying explanation for his or her actions, _____ has occurred.

25. When impulses are directed toward an object other than the one that caused arousal, _____ has occurred.

26. When unacceptable impulses are channeled into socially acceptable activities, _____ has occurred.

Matching Items

Match each defense mechanism in the following list with the proper example of its manifestation.

Defense Mechanisms

_____ 1. displacement
_____ 2. projection
_____ 3. reaction formation
_____ 4. rationalization
_____ 5. regression
_____ 6. sublimation

Manifestations

a. nail biting or thumb sucking in an anxiety-producing situation
b. artistic achievements through which unacceptable urges may somehow be expressed
c. over-zealous crusaders against "immoral behaviors," who don't want to acknowledge their own sexual desires
d. saying you drink "just to be sociable" when in reality you have a drinking problem
e. thinking someone hates you when in reality you hate that person
f. a child who is angry at his parents and vents this anger on the family pet, a less threatening target

27. Defense mechanisms are _____ (conscious/unconscious) processes.

28. The theorists who established their own, modified versions of psychoanalytic theory are called _____. These theories typically place _____ (more/less) emphasis on the conscious mind than Freud did.

Briefly summarize how each of the following theorists departed from Freud.

a. Adler and Horney _____

_____

b. Jung _____

_____

29. Henry Murray introduced the personality assessment technique called the

_____ _____

Test.

30. Tests such as the TAT, which provide subjects with ambiguous stimuli for interpretation, are called _____ tests. The most widely used of these tests is the

_____, in which subjects are shown a series of _____.

Generally, these tests appear to have

_____ (little/significant)

validity.

31. Recent researchers primarily perceive the unconscious not as the site of instinctual urges, but as where _____ is processed without awareness.

Give several examples of Freudian ideas that are *not* widely accepted by contemporary psychologists.

32. Criticism of psychoanalysis as a scientific theory centers on the fact that it provides after-the-fact explanations and does not offer

_____ _____ .

The Trait Perspective (pp. 311–316)

33. Gordon Allport developed trait theory, which defines personality in terms of people's characteristic _____ and conscious _____ .

34. Trait theorists are generally less interested in _____ (explaining/describing) behavior than they are in _____ (explaining/describing) it.

35. Sheldon identified three body types: the jolly _____ type, the bold _____ type, and the high-strung _____ type.

36. A statistical procedure that identifies clusters of basic traits is _____

_____ .

37. The Eysencks believe that two personality dimensions are fundamental: _____ -_____ and emotional _____ -_____ .

More recently, researchers have arrived at a cluster of five factors that seem to describe the major features of personality. List and briefly describe the "Big Five."

a. _____

b. _____

c. _____

d. _____

e. _____

38. Questionnaires that categorize personality traits are called _____ _____ .
The most widely used of all personality tests is the _____ _____

_____ _____ .

This test was developed by testing a large pool of items and selecting those that differentiated particular individuals; in other words, the test was _____ derived.

39. Human behavior is influenced both by our inner _____ and by the external _____ .

40. Research, for example, on children's propensity to cheat, indicates that people's behavior on different occasions is generally quite _____ (variable/consistent).

41. An individual's score on a personality test _____ (is/is not) very predictive of his or her behavior in any given situation.

Write a sentence defending trait theory against the criticism that people seem not to have clear, consistent personalities.

The Humanistic Perspective (pp. 317–322)

42. Two influential theories of humanistic psychology were proposed by _____ and _____ .

43. According to Maslow, humans are motivated by needs that are organized into a _____ . Maslow refers to the process of fulfilling one's potential as

_____ -_____ .

List some of the characteristics Maslow associated with those who fulfilled their potential.

44. According to Rogers, a person nurtures growth in a relationship by being _____, _____, and _____.

45. In Rogers' theory, _____ _____ refers to an accepting attitude toward another person despite his or her failings.

46. For both Maslow and Rogers, an important feature of personality is how an individual perceives himself or herself; this is the person's _____-_____.

State three criticisms that have been made of humanistic psychology.

47. Since the 1940s, research on the self has greatly _____ (increased/decreased).

48. According to the humanists, personality development hinges on our feelings of inner worth, or _____-_____. People who feel good about themselves are relatively _____ (dependent on/independent of) outside pressures, while people who fall short of their ideals are more prone to _____ and _____.

49. Research has shown that most people tend to have _____ (low/high) self-esteem.

50. The tendency of people to perceive themselves favorably is called the _____-_____ bias.

51. Responsibility for success is generally accepted _____ (more/less) readily than responsibility for failure.

52. Most people perceive their own behavior and

traits as being _____ (above/below) average.

The Social-Cognitive Perspective (pp. 322–329)

53. Social-cognitive theorists focus on how the individual and the _____ interact. One such theorist is _____.

54. Social-cognitive theorists propose that personality is shaped by the mutual influence of our _____, _____ factors, and _____ factors. This is the principle of _____ _____.

Describe three different ways in which the environment and personality interact.

55. Individuals who believe that they control their own destinies are said to perceive an _____ _____ _____ _____. Individuals who believe that their fate is determined by outside forces are said to perceive an _____ _____ _____ _____.

56. Seligman found that exposure to inescapable punishment produced a passive resignation in behavior, which he called _____.

57. People become happier when they are given _____ (more/less) control over what happens to them.

Describe two criticisms that have been made of the social-cognitive perspective.

List the major contributions of each perspective to our understanding of personality.

a. Psychoanalytic _____

_____

b. Trait _____

_____

c. Humanistic _____

_____

d. Social-cognitive _____

_____

FOCUS ON PSYCHOLOGY:
Personality Over the Life Span

Do personalities change significantly over the life span? Many people think so, but this may be a result of their tendency to overestimate changes in personality. In one study that showed this to be the case, a group of college students rated themselves on several personality traits. Twenty-five years later, they rated themselves again, not only as they saw their current personalities, but also as they thought they had been during college. Only the *original* college rating and the current rating were similar; there was little similarity between how people remembered themselves as having been during college and either their current ratings or their original ratings as college students. These results support the idea that there is an underlying consistency to personality, a consistency that people often underestimate.

In another study, the personality traits of 2,000 men, who ranged in age from their 20s to their 90s, were compared several times over a ten-year period. Three personality dimensions remained stable over the course of the longitudinal study: *neuroticism* (the tendency toward feelings of anxiety, worry, and depression); *extraversion* (the tendency to be outgoing, active, and assertive); and *openness* (the tendency to be receptive to new ideas and experiences).

Compared with those who scored low on neuroticism, men who scored high on this dimension consistently tended to complain more about their health, were more likely to be heavy drinkers and smokers, more often reported financial and sexual problems, and were generally dissatisfied with life.

Men who scored high on extraversion were happier, showed stronger signs of well-being, and were more likely to seek out jobs dealing with other people than men who scored low on this dimension. With the exception of a tendency to become less independent with age, the extraverted men also demonstrated stable personality traits throughout adulthood.

Compared with those who scored low on openness, those who scored high on this dimension also tended to score high on aesthetic and theoretical values, had above-average IQ scores, and were more likely to change jobs, have "eventful" lives, and experience both positive and negative emotions with greater intensity.

Although the stability of personality remains a controversial issue, these results suggest that certain core personality traits remain stable throughout life — unless there are sudden, critical breaks in the continuity of a person's life situation. As developmental psychologist Kathleen Berger notes, "Anxious, neurotic people are likely to be so throughout life. Similarly, the very outgoing college student is likely to be, in middle age, the kind of person who speaks to everyone at work, who spends a lot of time interacting with friends, family members, and neighbors, and who is likely to be involved in community activities. . . ."

Berger suggests three reasons for the apparent consistency in personality. First, there is evidence that some aspects of temperament, such as reactivity, emotionality, and sociability, are probably inherited. Second, numerous studies have shown that the experiences of childhood have a long-lasting impact on personality. Growing up in an affectionate and supportive family, for example, seems to foster openness and a tendency toward extraversion. Third, choices made in early adulthood regarding career, marriage, and friends, often reinforce already established personality traits.

Sources: Berger, K. S., & Straub, R. O. (1989). *Instructor's resource manual for use with the developing person through the life span* (2nd ed.). New York: Worth Publishers, Inc., pp. 388–389.

Berger, K. S. (1988). *The developing person through the life span* (2nd ed.). New York: Worth Publishers, Inc., pp. 515–517.

McCrae, R. R., & Costa, P. T. (1987). Validation of the five factor model of personality across instruments and observers. *Journal of Personality and Social Psychology, 52,* 81–90.

Progress Test 1

Multiple-Choice Questions

Circle your answers to the following questions and check them with the answer key at the end of this chapter. If your answer is incorrect, read the answer key explanation for why it is incorrect and then consult the appropriate pages of the text to understand the correct answer.

1. How is personality defined in your text?
   a. as the set of personal attitudes that characterizes a person
   b. as an individual's relatively distinctive and consistent ways of thinking, feeling, and acting
   c. as a predictable set of responses to environmental stimuli
   d. as an unpredictable set of responses to environmental stimuli

2. Which of the following places the greatest emphasis on the unconscious mind?

   a. the humanistic perspective
   b. the social-cognitive perspective
   c. the trait perspective
   d. the psychoanalytic perspective

3. Which of the following is the correct order of psychosexual stages proposed by Freud?

   a. oral stage; anal stage; phallic stage; latency period; genital stage
   b. anal stage; oral stage; phallic stage; latency period; genital stage
   c. oral stage; anal stage; genital stage; latency period; phallic stage
   d. anal stage; oral stage; genital stage; latency period; phallic stage

4. According to Freud, defense mechanisms are methods of reducing:

   a. anger.   **c.** anxiety.
   b. fear.   **d.** lust.

5. Tests that provide ambiguous stimuli the subject must interpret are called:

   a. personality tests.
   b. personality inventories.
   c. subjective scales.
   d. projective tests.

6. Neo-Freudians such as Adler and Horney believed that:

   a. Freud placed too great an emphasis on the conscious mind.
   b. Freud placed too great an emphasis on sexual and aggressive instincts.
   c. the years of childhood were more important in the formation of personality than Freud had indicated.
   d. Freud's ideas about the id, ego, and superego as personality structures were incorrect.

7. Bill is muscular and physically strong. Sheldon would classify him as a(n):

   a. endomorphic type.   **c.** ectomorphic type.
   b. mesomorphic type.   **d.** dysmorphic type.

8. Which two dimensions of personality have the Eysencks emphasized?

   a. extraversion-introversion and emotional stability-instability
   b. internal-external locus of control and extraversion-introversion
   c. internal-external locus of control and emotional stability-instability
   d. sociable-retiring and self-disciplined–weak-willed

9. With regard to personality, it appears that:

   a. there is little consistency of behavior from one situation to the next and little consistency of traits over the life span.
   b. there is little consistency of behavior from one situation to the next but significant consistency of traits over the life span.
   c. there is significant consistency of behavior from one situation to the next but little consistency of traits over the life span.
   d. there is significant consistency of behavior from one situation to the next and significant consistency of traits over the life span.

10. The humanistic perspective on personality:

    a. emphasizes the driving force of unconscious motivations in personality.
    b. emphasizes the growth potential of "healthy" individuals.
    c. emphasizes the importance of interaction with the environment in shaping personality.
    d. describes personality in terms of scores on various personality scales.

11. According to Rogers, three conditions are necessary to promote growth in personality. These are:

    a. honesty, sincerity, and empathy.
    b. high self-esteem, honesty, and empathy.
    c. genuineness, acceptance, and empathy.
    d. high self-esteem, acceptance, and honesty.

12. Regarding the self-serving bias, humanistic psychologists have emphasized that self-affirming thinking:

    a. is generally maladaptive to the individual because it distorts reality by overinflating self-esteem.
    b. is generally adaptive to the individual because it maintains self-confidence and minimizes depression.
    c. tends to prevent the individual from viewing others with compassion and understanding.
    d. tends *not* to characterize people who have experienced unconditional positive regard.

13. Which of Freud's ideas would *not* be accepted by most contemporary psychologists?

    a. Development is essentially fixed in childhood.
    b. Sexuality is a potent drive in humans.
    c. The mind is an iceberg with consciousness being only the tip.
    d. Repression can be the cause of forgetting.

14. A psychoanalyst would characterize a person who is impulsive and self-indulgent as possessing a strong _____ and a weak _____.

    a. id and ego; superego   **c.** ego; superego
    b. id; ego and superego   **d.** id; superego

15. Projective tests such as the Rorschach inkblot test have been criticized because:

   a. their scoring system is too rigid and leads to unfair labeling.
   b. they were standardized with unrepresentative samples.
   c. they have low reliability and low validity.
   d. it is easy for people to fake answers in order to appear healthy.

16. A major criticism of trait theory is that it:

   a. places too great an emphasis on early childhood experiences.
   b. overestimates the consistency of behavior in different situations.
   c. underestimates the importance of heredity in personality development.
   d. places too great an emphasis on positive traits.

17. For humanistic psychologists, many of our attitudes and behaviors are ultimately shaped by whether our _____ is _____ or _____.

   a. ego; strong; weak
   b. locus of control; internal; external
   c. personality structure; introverted; extraverted
   d. self-concept; positive; negative

18. Because Ramona identifies with her politically conservative parents, she chose to enroll in a conservative college. After four years in this environment, Ramona's politics have become even more conservative. Which perspective best accounts for the mutual influences of Ramona's upbringing, choice of school, and political viewpoint?

   a. psychoanalytic perspective
   b. trait perspective
   c. humanistic perspective
   d. social-cognitive perspective

19. Which of the following is a major criticism of the social-cognitive perspective?

   a. It focuses too much on early childhood experiences.
   b. It focuses too little on the inner traits of a person.
   c. It provides descriptions but not explanations.
   d. It lacks appropriate assessment techniques.

Matching Items

Match each of the definitions or descriptions with the appropriate term.

Definitions

_____ 1. redirecting impulses to a less threatening object
_____ 2. test consisting of a series of inkblots
_____ 3. the conscious executive of personality
_____ 4. personality inventory
_____ 5. disguising an impulse by imputing it to another person
_____ 6. switching an unacceptable impulse into its opposite
_____ 7. the unconscious repository of instinctual drives
_____ 8. redirecting impulses into a more socially acceptable channel
_____ 9. personality structure that corresponds to a person's conscience
_____ 10. providing self-justifying explanations for an action
_____ 11. a projective test consisting of a set of ambiguous pictures

Terms

   a. id
   b. ego
   c. superego
   d. reaction formation
   e. rationalization
   f. displacement
   g. sublimation
   h. projection
   i. TAT
   j. Rorschach
   k. MMPI

Progress Test 2

Progress Test 2 should be completed during a final chapter review. Do this test after you thoroughly understand the correct answers for the Chapter Review and Progress Test 1.

Multiple-Choice Questions

1. Jill has a biting, sarcastic manner. According to Freud:

   a. she is projecting her anxiety onto others.

b. she is probably fixed in the oral stage of development.

c. she is probably fixed in the anal stage of development.

d. she is displacing her anxiety onto others.

2. James attributes his failing grade in chemistry to an unfair final exam. His attitude exemplifies:

    a. the Barnum effect.

    b. unconditional positive regard.

    c. the self-serving bias.

    d. reciprocal determinism.

3. In high school Britta and Debbie were best friends. They thought they were a lot alike, and so did everyone else who knew them. After high school they went on to very different colleges, careers, and life courses. Now, at their twenty-fifth reunion, the two are shocked at how little they have in common. Bandura would suggest that their differences reflect the interactive effects of environment, personality, and behavior—effects he refers to as:

    a. reciprocal determinism.

    b. reaction formation.

    c. identification.

    d. external locus of control.

4. Seligman has found that humans and animals who are exposed to aversive events they cannot escape may develop:

    a. an internal locus of control.

    b. an external locus of control.

    c. learned helplessness.

    d. neurotic anxiety.

5. According to Freud, a person who is overzealous in campaigning against pornography may be displaying:

    a. sublimation.   **c.** rationalization.

    b. displacement.   **d.** reaction formation.

6. The Minnesota Multiphasic Personality Inventory (MMPI) is:

    a. a projective personality test.

    b. a personality test that is empirically derived and objective.

    c. a personality test developed mainly to assess job applicants.

    d. a personality test used primarily to assess locus of control.

7. Trait theory attempts to:

    a. show how development of personality is a life-long process.

    b. describe and classify people in terms of their predispositions to behave in certain ways.

    c. determine which traits are most conducive to individual self-actualization.

    d. explain how behavior is shaped by the interaction between traits and the environment.

8. Which of the following statements is true?

    a. People with an internal locus of control achieve more in school.

    b. "Externals" are better able to cope with stress than "internals."

    c. "Internals" are less independent than "externals."

    d. All of the above are true.

9. Which of the following statements about self-esteem is *not* correct?

    a. People with low self-esteem tend to be negative about others.

    b. People with high self-esteem are less prone to drug addiction.

    c. People with low self-esteem tend to be non-conformists.

    d. People with high self-esteem suffer less from insomnia and ulcers.

10. The Oedipus and Electra complexes have their roots in the:

    a. anal stage.   **c.** phallic stage.

    b. latency stage.   **d.** genital stage.

11. Which of the following is a common criticism of the humanistic perspective?

    a. Its concepts are vague and subjective.

    b. The emphasis on the self encourages selfishness in individuals.

    c. Humanism fails to appreciate the reality of evil in human behavior.

    d. All of the above are common criticisms of humanism.

12. In studying personality, a social-cognitive theorist would most likely make use of:

    a. personality inventories.

    b. projective tests.

    c. observations of behavior in different situations.

    d. factor analyses.

13. A major difference between the psychoanalytic and trait perspectives is that:

    a. trait theory defines personality in terms of behavior; psychoanalytic theory, in terms of its underlying dynamics.

    b. trait theory describes behavior but does not attempt to explain it.

    c. psychoanalytic theory emphasizes the origins of personality in childhood sexuality.

    d. all of the above are differences.

14. A statistical technique that can be used to identify clusters of basic personality traits is:

    a. the MMPI.

b. the personality inventory.

c. factor analysis.

d. free association.

15. The "Big Five" personality factors are:

   a. emotional stability, openness, introversion, sociability, locus of control.

   b. neuroticism, extraversion, openness, emotional stability, sensitivity.

   c. neuroticism, gregariousness, extraversion, impulsiveness, conscientiousness.

   d. emotional stability, extraversion, openness, agreeableness, conscientiousness.

16. Randy "lives for the moment," squandering his paycheck as soon as he receives it. According to Freud, Randy's behavior is dominated by the:

   a. id.   **c.** superego.

   b. ego.   **d.** self-serving bias.

17. According to Freud, _____ is the process by which children incorporate their parents' values into their _____.

   a. reaction formation; superegos

   b. reaction formation; egos

   c. identification; superegos

   d. identification; egos

Matching Items

Match each term with the appropriate definition or description.

Terms

_____ **1.** projective test

_____ **2.** unconditional positive regard

_____ **3.** collective unconscious

_____ **4.** reality principle

_____ **5.** internal locus of control

_____ **6.** pleasure principle

_____ **7.** external locus of control

_____ **8.** reciprocal determinism

_____ **9.** personality inventory

_____ **10.** Oedipus complex

_____ **11.** preconscious

Definitions

a. the id's demand for immediate gratification

b. the child's sexual desires toward the opposite-sex parent

c. information that is retrievable but currently not in conscious awareness

d. the belief that one's fate is determined by outside forces

e. questionnaire used to assess personality traits

f. the two-way interactions of behavior with personal and environmental factors

g. personality test that provides ambiguous stimuli

h. the repository of universal memories, proposed by Jung

i. an attitude of total acceptance toward another person

j. the process by which the ego seeks to gratify impulses of the id in nondestructive ways

k. the belief that one controls one's own fate

KEY TERMS

Using your own words, write a brief definition or explanation of each of the following terms.

1. personality

2. unconscious

3. preconscious

4. free association

5. psychoanalysis

6. id

7. pleasure principle

8. ego

9. reality principle

10. superego

11. psychosexual stages

12. oral stage

13. anal stage

14. phallic stage

15. Oedipus complex

16. identification

17. latency period

18. genital stage

19. fixation

20. defense mechanisms

21. repression

22. regression

23. reaction formation

24. projection

25. rationalization

26. displacement

27. sublimation

28. collective unconscious

29. projective tests

30. Thematic Apperception Test (TAT)

31. Rorschach inkblot test

32. traits

33. trait theory

34. personality inventories

35. Minnesota Multiphasic Personality Inventory (MMPI)

36. empirically derived test

37. self-actualization

38. unconditional positive regard

39. empathy

40. self-concept

41. self-esteem

42. self-serving bias

43. social-cognitive perspective

44. reciprocal determinism

45. external locus of control

46. internal locus of control

47. learned helplessness

48. Barnum effect

Answers
CHAPTER REVIEW

1. personality
2. psychoanalytic; trait; humanistic; social-cognitive
3. Sigmund Freud

4. unconscious; preconscious; repressed
5. free association
6. psychoanalysis
7. dreams
8. id; ego; superego
9. unconscious; pleasure
10. after; conscious; reality

The ego is considered the executive of personality because it directs our actions as it intervenes among the impulsive demands of the id, the reality of the external world, and the ideals of the superego.

11. superego
12. weak; strong
13. psychosexual
14. oral; sucking (also biting, chewing)
15. anal; 18; 3
16. phallic; 3; 6; genitals; opposite; Oedipus complex; Electra complex

Children eventually cope with their feelings for the opposite-sex parent by repressing them and by identifying with the rival (same-sex) parent. Through this process children incorporate many of their parents' values, thereby strengthening the superego.

17. latency
18. genital
19. fixated
20. defense mechanisms; repression
21. regression
22. reaction formation
23. projection
24. rationalization
25. displacement
26. sublimation

Matching Items

1. f   3. c   5. a
2. e   4. d   6. b

27. unconscious
28. neo-Freudians; more

    a. Adler and Horney emphasized the social, rather than the sexual, tensions of childhood.
    b. Jung emphasized an inherited collective unconscious.

29. Thematic Apperception
30. projective; Rorschach; inkblots; little
31. information

Psychologists today do not widely accept Freud's ideas

that conscience and gender identity are formed by res- olution of the Oedipus (or the Electra) complex, that dreams are disguised wish fulfillments, that women have weak superegos, that repression is the main cause of memory loss, and that the unconscious mainly con- tains unacceptable desires and repressed memories.

32. testable hypotheses (or predictions)

33. behaviors; motives

34. explaining; describing

35. endomorph; mesomorph; ectomorph

36. factor analysis

37. extraversion-introversion; stability-instability
   a. Emotional stability: calm vs. worrying; secure vs. insecure
   b. Extraversion: sociable vs. retiring
   c. Openness: preference for variety vs. routine
   d. Agreeableness: soft-hearted vs. ruthless
   e. Conscientiousness: self-disciplined vs. weak- willed

38. personality inventories; Minnesota Multiphasic Personality Inventory; empirically

39. traits (or dispositions); situation (or environment)

40. variable

41. is not

At any given moment a person's behavior is power- fully influenced by the immediate situation, so that it may appear that the person does not have a consistent personality. But averaged over many situations a per- son's outgoingness, happiness, and carelessness, for instance, are more predictable.

42. Maslow; Rogers

43. hierarchy; self-actualization

For Maslow, such people were self-aware, self-accept- ing, open, spontaneous, loving, and caring, secure, and problem-centered rather than self-centered.

44. genuine; accepting; empathic

45. unconditional positive regard

46. self-concept

Humanistic psychology is criticized for being vague and subjective, for encouraging self-indulgence and selfishness, and for failing to appreciate the capacity of humans for evil.

47. increased

48. self-esteem; independent of; anxiety; depression

49. high

50. self-serving

51. more

52. above

53. environment; Bandura

54. behaviors; personal/cognitive; environmental; re- ciprocal determinism

Different people choose different environments based partly on their dispositions. Our personality shapes how we interpret and react to events. It also helps create the situations to which we react.

55. internal locus of control; external locus of control

56. learned helplessness

57. more

One criticism is that the theory offers only after-the- fact explanations and thus can "explain" anything. Another is that the theory has overemphasized situa- tional influences to the neglect of inner traits.

   a. The psychoanalytic perspective has drawn at- tention to the unconscious and irrational aspects of personality.
   b. The trait perspective has systematically de- scribed and measured important components of personality.
   c. The humanistic perspective emphasizes the healthy potential of personality and the impor- tance of our sense of self.
   d. The social-cognitive perspective emphasizes that we always act in a particular situational context.

PROGRESS TEST 1

Multiple-Choice Questions

1. **b.** is the answer. Personality is defined as patterns of response—of thinking, feeling, and acting— that are relatively consistent across a variety of situations. (p. 301)

2. **d.** is the answer. (p. 302)
   a. & b. Conscious processes are the focus of these perspectives.
   c. The trait perspective focuses on description of behaviors.

3. **a.** is the answer. (p. 304)

4. **c.** is the answer. According to Freud, defense mechanisms reduce anxiety unconsciously, by dis- guising one's threatening impulses. (p. 305)
   a., b., & d. Unlike these specific emotions, anxiety need not be focused. Defense mechanisms help us cope when we are unsettled but are not sure why.

5. **d.** is the answer. They are so called because the individual supposedly projects his or her feelings into the ambiguous test stimuli. (p. 308)
   a. Not all personality tests provide ambiguous stimuli.

b. Personality inventories are objective tests such as the MMPI.

c. There are no such tests.

6. **b.** is the answer. (p. 307)

a. According to most neo-Freudians, Freud placed too great an emphasis on the *unconscious* mind.

c. Freud placed great emphasis on early childhood, and the neo-Freudians basically agreed with him. Differences were in the direction of placing *less* emphasis on childhood, based on the idea that development is a lifelong process.

d. The neo-Freudians basically agreed with Freud regarding this aspect of the psychoanalytic perspective.

7. **b.** is the answer. (p. 312)

a. Endomorphs are overweight.

c. Ectomorphs are thin.

d. This is not one of Sheldon's types.

8. **a.** is the answer. (p. 313)

b. & c. Locus of control is emphasized by the social-cognitive perspective.

d. Sociable-retiring describes their extraversion-introversion dimension, but self-disciplined–weak-willed is one aspect of the "big five" factors described by other researchers.

9. **b.** is the answer. Studies have shown that people do not act with predictable consistency from one situation to the next. But, over a number of situations, consistent patterns emerge, and this basic consistency of traits persists over the life span. (pp. 315–316)

10. **b.** is the answer. (p. 317)

a. This is true of the psychoanalytic perspective.

c. This is true of the social-cognitive perspective.

d. This is true of the trait perspective.

11. **c.** is the answer. (p. 318)

12. **b.** is the answer. Humanistic psychologists emphasize that for the individual, self-affirming thinking is generally adaptive (therefore, not a.); such thinking maintains self-confidence, minimizes depression, and enables us to view others with compassion and understanding (therefore, not c.); unconditional positive regard tends to *promote* self-esteem and thus self-affirming thinking (therefore, not d.). (p. 321)

13. **a.** is the answer. Developmental research indicates that development is lifelong. (p. 307)

b., c., & d. To varying degrees, research has partially supported these Freudian ideas.

14. **d.** is the answer. Impulsiveness is the mark of a strong id; self-indulgence is the mark of a weak superego. Because the ego serves to mediate the demands of id, superego, and the outside world, its strength or weakness is judged by its decision-making ability, not by the character of the decision—so it is not relevant to the question asked. (pp. 303–304)

15. **c.** is the answer. As scoring is largely subjective and the tests have not been very successful in predicting behavior, their reliability and validity have been called into question. (p. 308)

a. & d. These are untrue.

b. Unlike empirically derived personality tests, projective tests are not standardized.

16. **b.** is the answer. In doing so it underestimates the influence of the environment. (pp. 315–316)

a. The trait perspective does not emphasize early childhood experiences.

c. This criticism is unlikely since trait theory does not seek to explain personality development.

d. Trait theory does not look on traits as being "positive" or "negative."

17. **d.** is the answer. (p. 318)

a. & c. Personality structure, of which the ego is a part, is a concern of the psychoanalytic perspective. Introversion and extraversion are dimensions in the Eysencks' trait theory.

b. Locus of control is a major focus of the social-cognitive perspective.

18. **d.** is the answer. The social-cognitive perspective emphasizes the reciprocal influences between people and their situations. In this example, Ramona's parents (situational factor) helped shape her political beliefs (internal factor), which influenced her choice of colleges (situational factor), and created an environment that fostered her predisposed political attitudes. (pp. 322–329)

19. **b.** is the answer. The social-cognitive theory has been accused of putting so much emphasis on the situation that inner traits are neglected. (p. 328)

a. Such a criticism has been made of the psychoanalytic perspective but is not relevant to the social-cognitive perspective.

c. Such a criticism might be more relevant to the trait perspective; the social-cognitive perspective offers an explanation in the form of reciprocal determinism.

d. There are assessment techniques appropriate to the theory, namely, questionnaires and observations of behavior in situations.

Matching Items

1. f (p. 306)   5. h (p. 306)   9. c (p. 304)
2. j (p. 308)   6. d (p. 306)   10. e (p. 306)
3. b (p. 303)   7. a (p. 303)   11. i (p. 308)
4. k (p. 314)   8. g (p. 306)

PROGRESS TEST 2

Multiple-Choice Questions

1. **b.** is the answer. Sarcasm is said to be an attempt to deny the passive dependence characteristic of the oral stage. (p. 305)

    a. A person who is projecting attributes his or her own feelings to others.

    c. Such a person might be either messy and disorganized or highly controlled and compulsively neat.

    d. Displacement involves diverting aggressive impulses onto a more acceptable object than that which aroused them.

2. **c.** is the answer. (p. 321)

    a. The Barnum effect is our tendency to accept general and favorable characterizations as specifically and accurately describing us.

    b. Unconditional positive regard is an attitude of total acceptance directed toward others.

    d. Reciprocal determinism refers to the mutual influences among personality, environment, and behavior.

3. **a.** is the answer. Reciprocal determinism refers to the mutual influences among personal factors, environmental factors, and behavior. (p. 323)

    b. Reaction formation is a Freudian defense mechanism in which one switches an unacceptable impulse into its opposite.

    c. Identification is the process by which, according to Freud, children incorporate parental values into their developing superegos.

    d. External locus of control is Rotter's term for the perception that one's fate is determined by outside forces.

4. **c.** is the answer. In such situations, passive resignation, called learned helplessness, develops. (p. 324)

    a. This refers to the belief that one controls one's fate; the circumstances described lead to precisely the opposite belief.

    b. External locus of control is Rotter's term for the perception that one's fate is determined by outside forces.

    d. Seligman did not specify that neurotic anxiety occurs.

5. **d.** is the answer. The ego unconsciously makes unacceptable impulses look like their opposites. The person vehemently crusading against pornography would be moved by sexual desires he or she found unacceptable. (p. 306)

    a. Sublimation refers to transforming unacceptable impulses into socially valued behaviors.

    b. Displacement refers to diverting aggressive or sexual impulses toward an object other than the one responsible for the impulses.

    c. To rationalize is to generate inaccurate, self-justifying explanations for our actions.

6. **b.** is the answer. The MMPI was developed by selecting from many items those that differentiated between the groups of interest; hence it was empirically derived. That it is an objective test is shown by the fact that it can be scored by computer. (p. 314)

    a. Projective tests present ambiguous stimuli such as inkblots or drawings for people to interpret; the MMPI is a questionnaire.

    c. Although sometimes used to assess job applicants, the MMPI was developed to assess emotionally troubled people.

    d. The MMPI does not focus on locus of control but, rather, measures various aspects of personality.

7. **b.** is the answer. Trait theory attempts to describe behavior and not to develop explanations or applications. The emphasis is more on consistency than on change. (p. 312)

8. **a.** is the answer. "Internals," those with a sense of personal control, have been shown to achieve more in school. Relative to externals, they also cope better with stress and are more independent. (p. 324)

9. **c.** is the answer. In actuality, people with *high* self-esteem are generally more independent of pressures to conform. (p. 320)

10. **c.** is the answer. (p. 305)

11. **d.** is the answer. (pp. 319–320)

12. **c.** is the answer. In keeping with their emphasis on interactions between people and situations, social-cognitive theorists would most likely make use of observations of behavior in relevant situations. (p. 322)

    a. & d. Personality inventories and factor analyses would more likely be used by a trait theorist.

    b. Projective tests would more likely be used by a

psychologist working within the psychoanalytic perspective.

13. **d.** is the answer. Trait theory defines personality in terms of behavior and is therefore interested in describing behavior; psychoanalytic theory defines personality as the dynamics underlying behavior and therefore is interested in explaining behavior in terms of these dynamics. (pp. 311–312)

14. **c.** is the answer. (p. 312)

a. & b. The MMPI is a personality inventory, and personality inventories are questionnaires, not statistical techniques.

d. Free association is the psychoanalytic method of exploring the unconscious in which the person says whatever comes to mind.

15. **d.** is the answer. (p. 313)

16. **a.** is the answer. Operating according to the pleasure principle, the id's impulses, unless checked by the ego, might lead to such behavior. (p. 303)

b. The ego is the rational part of personality that mediates between the demands of the id and superego and reality. If the ego dominates, such pleasure-seeking behavior is unlikely.

c. The superego is the conscience of personality; if it is dominant, such pleasure-seeking behavior is unlikely.

d. The self-serving bias is the tendency of people to perceive themselves favorably; it is not related to Freud's theory.

17. **c.** is the answer. (p. 305)

a. & b. Reaction formation is the defense mechanism by which people transform unacceptable impulses into their opposites.

d. It is the superego, rather than the ego, that represents parental values.

Matching Items

1. g (p. 308)
2. i (p. 318)
3. h (p. 307)
4. j (p. 303)
5. k (p. 324)
6. a (p. 303)
7. d (p. 324)
8. f (p. 323)
9. e (p. 313)
10. b (p. 305)
11. c (p. 302)

KEY TERMS

1. **Personality** is an individual's relatively distinctive and consistent pattern of thinking, feeling, and acting. (p. 301)

2. In Freud's theory, the **unconscious** is the repository of thoughts, wishes, feelings, and memories of which we are unaware. (p. 302)

   Example: According to Freud, much of the content of the **unconscious** is so threatening and unacceptable that it is repressed from awareness.

3. In Freud's theory, the **preconscious** area is a region of the unconscious that contains material that is retrievable at will into conscious awareness. (p. 302)

   Example: The Freudian notion of a **preconscious** is similar to the concept of long-term memory: material is accessible but not currently in our awareness.

4. **Free association** is the Freudian technique in which the person is encouraged to say whatever comes to mind as a means of exploring the unconscious. (p. 302)

5. In Freud's theory, **psychoanalysis** refers to the analysis of the tensions within a patient's unconscious, using methods such as free association. (p. 303)

6. In Freud's theory, the **id** is the system of personality consisting of instinctual drives for survival, reproduction, and aggression, that supplies psychic energy to personality. (p. 303)

7. In Freud's theory, the **pleasure principle** refers to the id's demands for immediate gratification. (p. 303)

   Example: Governed only by the id, the newborn infant demands immediate gratification of its physical needs according to the **pleasure principle**.

8. In psychoanalytic theory, the **ego** is the conscious division of personality that attempts to mediate between the demands of the id and superego and reality. (p. 303)

9. The **reality principle** refers to the ego's tendency to gratify the desires of the id in ways that are realistic. (p. 303)

   Example: Operating according to the **reality principle**, the ego "referees" the continual battle between the pleasure-seeking demands of the id and the voice of conscience of the superego.

10. In Freud's theory, the **superego** is the division of personality that contains the conscience and develops by incorporating the perceived moral standards of society. (p. 304)

    Example: If a person has an overdeveloped **superego**, he or she might have a very rigid lifestyle and yet be continually guilt ridden.

11. Freud's **psychosexual stages** are developmental periods during which the id's pleasure-seeking energies are focused on different erogenous zones. (p. 304)

    Example: Freud's analysis of his patients' problems led to his conclusion that personality is fixed early in life as children pass through a series of **psychosexual stages**.

12. During the **oral stage**, which lasts throughout the first 18 months of life, pleasure centers on activities of the mouth. (p. 304)

13. The **anal stage**, lasting from 18 months to 3 years, shifts the source of gratification to bowel and bladder retention and elimination. (p. 304)

14. During the **phallic stage**, from 3 to 6 years, the genitals become the pleasure zone. (p. 304)

15. According to Freud, children in the phallic stage develop a collection of feelings, known as the **Oedipus complex**, that center on sexual attraction to the opposite-sex parent and the resentment of the same-sex parent. In girls, it is sometimes called the Electra complex. (p. 305)

    Example: According to Freud, resolution of the **Oedipus complex** occurs as the child represses his or her feelings of hatred and identifies with the parent of the same sex.

16. In Freud's theory, **identification** is the process by which the child's superego develops and incorporates the parents' values. Freud saw identification as crucial, not only to resolution of the Oedipus complex, but also to the development of gender identity. (p. 305)

17. During the **latency period**, from about age 6 to puberty, sexual impulses are dormant. (p. 305)

    Memory aid: Something that is **latent** exists but is not manifesting itself.

18. At puberty the repressed sexual feelings of the latency stage give way to the **genital stage** and the maturation of sexual interests. (p. 305)

19. In Freud's theory, **fixation** occurs when development becomes arrested in an immature psychosexual stage. (p. 305)

    Example: The "odd couple," consisting of one compulsively neat and one messy roommate, represents two manifestations of **fixation** in the anal stage.

20. In Freud's theory, **defense mechanisms** are the ego's methods of unconsciously protecting itself against anxiety by distorting reality. (p. 305)

21. The basis of all defense mechanisms, **repression** is the unconscious exclusion of painful impulses from the conscious mind. Repression is an example of motivated forgetting: one "forgets" what one really does not wish to remember. (p. 306)

22. **Regression** is the defense mechanism in which the person reverts to a less mature pattern of behavior. (p. 306)

    Example: One defense mechanism that people sometimes use during frustrating arguments is to storm away—a classic example of **regressing** to an immature behavior pattern.

23. **Reaction formation** is the defense mechanism in which the ego converts unacceptable feelings into their opposites. (p. 306)

    Memory aid: Social reformers often protest *too* vehemently. Their critics then cite their over*reaction* as an example of **reaction formation**.

24. In psychoanalytic theory, **projection** is the unconscious attribution of one's own unacceptable feelings, attitudes, or desires to others. (p. 306)

    Memory aid: To project is to thrust outward. **Projection** is an example of thrusting one's own feelings outward to another person.

25. **Rationalization** is the defense mechanism in which one devises self-satisfying but incorrect reasons for one's behavior. (p. 306)

    Example: A student who flunks out of school because of not studying may engage in **rationalization** by claiming that all along he or she had wanted to be out in the "real world" anyway.

26. **Displacement** is the defense mechanism in which an impulse is shifted to an object other than the one that originally aroused the impulse. (p. 306)

    Example: An employee who is angry at his or her boss might **displace** this anger onto a subordinate or some other safe target.

27. **Sublimation** is the defense mechanism in which an instinctual impulse is modified in a socially acceptable manner. (p. 306)

    Memory aid: **Sublimate** and *sublime* derive from the same Latin root, meaning "to raise, uplift, or ennoble; of high spiritual, moral, or intellectual value."

28. The **collective unconscious** is Jung's concept of an inherited unconscious shared by all people and deriving from our early ancestors' universal experiences. (p. 307)

29. **Projective tests**, such as the TAT and Rorschach, present ambiguous stimuli onto which people supposedly *project* their own inner feelings. (p. 308)

    Example: A major criticism of **projective tests** is that the interpretations of a subject's responses are, like the test stimuli themselves, ambiguous.

30. The **Thematic Apperception Test (TAT)** is a projective test that consists of ambiguous pictures about which people are asked to make up stories. (p. 308)

31. The **Rorschach inkblot test**, the most widely used projective test, consists of ten inkblots that people are asked to interpret. (p. 308)

32. **Traits** are people's characteristic predispositions to act in certain ways. (p. 312)

    Example: Five **traits** that describe the major features of personality are emotional stability, extraversion, openness, agreeableness, and conscientiousness.

33. **Trait theory** seeks to describe personality in terms of behavioral predispositions; it focuses on description rather than explanation. (p. 312)

34. **Personality inventories**, associated with the trait perspective, are questionnaires used to assess personality traits. (p. 313)

    Memory aid: Just as a shopkeeper takes inventory of stock, a **personality inventory** takes stock of a person's traits.

35. Consisting of ten clinical scales, the **Minnesota Multiphasic Personality Inventory (MMPI)** is the most widely used personality inventory. (p. 314)

36. An **empirically derived test** is one developed by testing many items to see which best distinguishes between groups of interest. (p. 314)

    Example: The MMPI is an **empirically derived test**, since the questions chosen for it were those that best differentiated groups of interest, namely, "normal" and disordered people.

37. In Maslow's theory, **self-actualization** describes the process of fulfilling one's potential and becoming spontaneous, loving, creative, and self-accepting. Self-actualization is at the very top of Maslow's need hierarchy and therefore becomes active only after the more basic physical and psychological needs have been met. (p. 317)

38. **Unconditional positive regard** is, according to Rogers, an attitude of total acceptance and one of the three conditions essential to a "growth-promoting" climate. (p. 318)

    Memory aid: The phrase is really self-defining. Feelings of *positive regard* toward another person are offered *unconditionally*, that is, with no qualifications.

39. **Empathy** is the ability to understand and feel the emotions of another person. (p. 318).

40. **Self-concept** refers to one's personal awareness of "who I am." In the humanistic perspective, self-concept is a central feature of personality; life happiness is significantly affected by whether the self-concept is positive or negative. (p. 318)

41. In humanistic psychology, **self-esteem** refers to an individual's sense of self-worth. (p. 320)

42. The **self-serving bias** is the tendency to perceive oneself favorably. (p. 321)

    Example: The pervasiveness of the **self-serving bias** is indicated by the fact that most people tend to see themselves as relatively superior on just about every ability and personality dimension.

43. The **social-cognitive perspective** applies the principles of cognition and social learning to personality and emphasizes the reciprocal influences of personality and environment. (p. 322)

44. According to the social-cognitive perspective, personality is shaped through **reciprocal determinism**, or the interaction among situations, thoughts and feelings, and behaviors. (p. 323)

45. **External locus of control** is the belief that one's fate is determined by forces not under personal control. (p. 324)

46. **Internal locus of control** is the belief that to a great extent one controls one's own destiny. (p. 324)

47. **Learned helplessness** is the passive resignation and perceived lack of control that a person or animal develops from repeated exposure to inescapable aversive events. (p. 324)

    Example: Following repeated exposure to inescapable shock, Seligman's dogs developed **learned helplessness**; later, when they could escape simply by jumping a hurdle, they failed to do so.

48. The **Barnum effect** is our tendency to accept as applying to us personality descriptions that are general and favorable, such as those we read in horoscopes. (p. 327)

Chapter 12 | Psychological Disorders

Chapter Overview

Although there is no clear-cut line between normal and abnormal behavior, we can characterize as abnormal those behaviors that are atypical, disturbing, maladaptive, and unjustifiable. Chapter 12 discusses types of anxiety, somatoform, dissociative, mood, schizophrenic, and personality disorders, as classified by the *Diagnostic and Statistical Manual of Mental Disorders* (DSM-III-R). Although this classification system follows a medical model, in which disorders are classified as illnesses, the chapter discusses psychological as well as physiological factors. Thus, psychoanalytic theory, social-cognitive theory, and other psychological perspectives are drawn on when relevant. The chapter concludes with a discussion of the advantages and problems connected with the use of diagnostic labels.

Your major task in this chapter is to learn about psychological disorders, their various subtypes, characteristics, and their possible causes. Since the material to be learned is extensive, it may be helpful to rehearse it by mentally completing the Chapter Review several times.

Guided Study

The textbook chapter should be studied one section at a time. Before you read, preview each section by skimming it, noting headings and boldface items. Then read the appropriate section objectives from the following outline. Keep these objectives in mind, and as you read the chapter section, search for the information that will enable you to meet each objective. Once you have finished a section, write out answers for its objectives.

Perspectives on Psychological Disorders (pp. 333–339)

1. List the criteria for judging whether behavior is disordered.

2. Discuss the different perspectives on psychological disorders.

3. Describe the system used to classify psychological disorders and explain the reasons for its development.

Anxiety Disorders (pp. 339–343)

4. Describe the various anxiety disorders and discuss their possible causes.

Somatoform Disorders (p. 343)

5. Describe the somatoform disorders and identify their common characteristic.

Dissociative Disorders (pp. 344–346)

6. Describe the dissociative disorders and discuss the various explanations for their occurrence.

Mood Disorders (pp. 346–352)

7. Describe the mood disorders and discuss the alternative explanations for their occurrence.

Schizophrenia Disorders (pp. 353–358)

8. Describe the various forms and symptoms of schizophrenia disorders and discuss research on the causes of schizophrenia.

Personality Disorders (pp. 358–359)

9. Describe the nature of personality disorders and the specific characteristics of the antisocial personality disorder.

Labeling People: The Power of Preconceptions (pp. 359–361)

10. Discuss the controversy surrounding the use of diagnostic labels.

Chapter Review

When you have finished reading the chapter, use the material that follows to review it. Complete the fill-in sentences and answer the essay items in complete sentences. As you proceed, evaluate your performance for each chapter section by consulting the answer key at the end of this chapter. Do not continue with the next section until you've understood each answer. If you need to, review or reread the appropriate chapter section in the textbook before continuing.

Perspectives on Psychological Disorders (pp. 333–339)

1. In order to be classified as disordered, behavior must be _____, _____, _____, and _____. This definition emphasizes that standards of acceptability for behavior are _____ (constant/variable).

2. The view that psychological disorders are diseases is the basis of the _____ model. One of the first reformers to advocate this position and call for providing more humane living conditions for the mentally ill was

_____.

3. Psychiatrist Thomas Szasz has argued against this model, which emphasizes mental health and mental illness, on the grounds that psychological disorders are not defined medically, but rather

_____.

4. Freud's theory is _____ (consistent/inconsistent) with the idea that behavior disorders are internal sicknesses.

Summarize the viewpoint of those who disagree with the medical model.

5. The most widely used system for classifying psychological disorders is the American Psychiatric Association manual commonly known by its abbreviation, _____.

6. The reliability of diagnoses made under DSM-III-R has been improved because the current manual bases diagnoses on _____ (objective/subjective) criteria.

Anxiety Disorders (pp. 339–343)

7. When a person tends to feel anxious for no apparent reason, he or she is diagnosed as suffering from a _____

_____ disorder.

8. In generalized anxiety disorder, the body reacts physiologically with arousal of the

_____ nervous system. In some instances the anxiety of this disorder may intensify dramatically and be accompanied by trembling or fainting; this is called a(n)

_____ _____.

The psychoanalytic interpretation of this type of disorder is that the ego's _____

_____ are weak.

9. The anxiety response probably

_____ (is/is not) genetically influenced. Learning theorists, drawing on

research in which rats are given unpredictable shocks, view anxiety as a response to feelings of

_____.

10. When a person has an irrational fear of a specific object or situation, the diagnosis is a(n) _____ disorder.

Contrast the psychoanalytic and learning theory explanations of phobias.

11. When a person cannot control repetitive thoughts and actions, a(n) _____-

_____ disorder is diagnosed.

12. PET scans of persons with obsessive-compulsive disorder often show elevated metabolic activity in the _____ lobe of the

_____ hemisphere of the brain.

13. Compulsive acts are typically exaggerations of behaviors that were important in our

_____ _____.

Examples of such acts include _____

_____.

Somatoform Disorders (p. 343)

14. When a distressing symptom is expressed bodily, as in vomiting, dizziness, or blurred vision, the diagnosis is a(n) _____ disorder.

15. Freud believed that the _____ disorder resulted when anxiety was transformed into a very specific physical symptom. Today, this disorder is relatively _____ (rare/common).

16. When normal aches and pains are interpreted as serious illnesses, the person is said to suffer from

_____.

Dissociative Disorders (pp. 344–346)

17. In dissociative disorders, _____

_____ becomes dissociated, or

_____, from previous

memories, thoughts, and feelings. These disorders are relatively _____ (common/uncommon).

18. A person who experiences a sudden loss of memory is suffering from _____. If the loss of memory has occurred in response to intolerable stress, the person is said to have

_____ _____.

19. Such memory loss is usually for _____ (all/selective) memories.

20. When an individual not only loses memory but also runs away, that person is said to be in a _____ state.

21. A person who develops two or more distinct personalities is suffering from a(n)

_____ _____

disorder.

22. Nicolas Spanos has argued that such people may merely be playing different _____.

Mood Disorders (pp. 346–352)

23. The mood disorders are characterized by _____ extremes.

24. When a person experiences prolonged depression with no discernible cause, the disorder is called

_____ _____.

25. Research suggests that major depression will be suffered at some time by approximately _____ percent of men; for women, the projected incidence is _____ (higher/lower).

26. The possible signs of depression include _____

_____

_____.

27. When a person's mood alternates between depression and the hyperactive state of

_____, a _____

disorder is diagnosed.

28. The bipolar disorder occurs in approximately _____ percent of men and women.

29. Depressed persons usually _____ (can/cannot) recover without therapy.

30. It usually _____ (is/is not) the case that a depressive episode has been triggered by a stressful event.

State the psychoanalytic explanation of depression.

31. Mood disorders _____ (tend/ do not tend) to run in families.

32. Certain types of depression may be caused by _____ (high/low) levels of

_____ or _____, two neurotransmitters.

33. Aaron Beck has suggested that depression may be linked with beliefs that are _____-

_____. Such beliefs, in turn, might be linked to _____

_____, the feeling that can arise when the individual repeatedly experiences uncontrollable aversive events.

Describe how depressed people differ from others in their explanations of failure and how such explanations tend to feed depression.

34. A depressed person tends to elicit social _____ (empathy/rejection).

Outline the vicious cycle of depression.

Schizophrenia Disorders (pp. 353–358)

35. *Schizophrenia*, or "split-mind," refers not to a split personality but rather to a split from

    _____ .

36. Three manifestations of schizophrenia are disorganized _____, disturbed _____, and inappropriate _____ and _____.

37. The time of life during which schizophrenia typically emerges is _____.

38. The distorted, false beliefs of schizophrenics are called _____.

Matching Items

Match each type of schizophrenia with its symptoms

Types

_____ 1. Disorganized
_____ 2. Catatonic
_____ 3. Paranoid
_____ 4. Undifferentiated
_____ 5. Residual

42. The brain tissue of schizophrenia patients has been found to have an abnormally high density of receptors for the neurotransmitter _____. Drugs that block these receptors have been found to _____ (increase/decrease) schizophrenic behaviors.

43. Brain scans have shown that many people suffering from schizophrenia have a shrinkage of brain tissue or abnormal patterns of brain activity in the _____ lobes. People with schizophrenia also tend to have a reduced quantity of an enzyme that converts _____ into norepinephrine.

44. Twin and adoption studies _____ (support/do not support) the contention that heredity plays a role in schizophrenia.

45. It appears that for schizophrenia to develop there must be both a _____ predisposition and some _____ trigger.

39. Many psychologists attribute the disorganized thinking of schizophrenia to a breakdown in the capacity for _____

    _____ .

40. The disturbed perceptions of people suffering from schizophrenia may take the form of _____, which usually are _____ (visual/auditory).

41. The term *schizophrenia* describes a _____ (single disorder/cluster of disorders).

Symptoms

a. delusions of grandeur or prosecution
b. bizarre physical movements
c. delusions, hallucinations, and other symptoms typical of schizophrenia, but not neatly fitting any one type
d. minor symptoms of schizophrenia that linger after a serious episode
e. incoherent speech and inappropriate emotions

List several of the warning signs of schizophrenia in high-risk children.

Personality Disorders (pp. 358–359)

46. Personality disorders exist when an individual has character traits that are enduring and

    _____ .

47. An individual who seems to have no conscience, lies, steals, is generally irresponsible, and may be criminal is said to have a(n) _____ personality. Previously, this person was labeled a(n) _____.

48. When awaiting electric shocks, antisocial persons show _____ (more/less)

arousal of the autonomic nervous system than do control subjects.

Labeling People: The Power of Preconceptions
(pp. 359–361)

49. Studies have shown that labeling has
_____ (little/a significant)
effect on our interpretation of individuals and their behavior.

Outline the pros and cons of labeling psychological disorders.

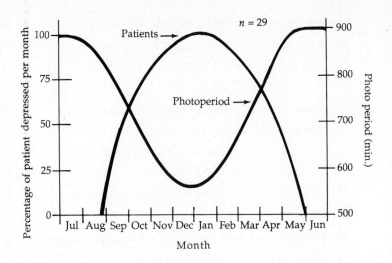

FOCUS ON PSYCHOLOGY:
Seasonal Affective Disorder (SAD)

A new category may soon need to be added to the bipolar family of psychological disorders. Persons with seasonal affective disorder, dubbed "SAD" for short, experience months of depression that begin each year in October or November and gradually give way to a more normal, occasionally manic mood as spring and summer approach. During the winter, SAD victims complain of loss of energy, sadness or hopelessness, and a desire to withdraw socially. Other symptoms include oversleeping and eating and a drop in sexual arousal.

Depressive episodes among SAD patients are closely linked to the average temperature and number of hours of sunlight per day, as shown in the figure on this page. So strong are these relationships that when SAD patients travel south during the winter their depression often eases, returning to full intensity only when they come back to northern climes.

Although the prevalence of SAD is unknown, researchers at the National Institutes of Mental Health estimate that approximately 20 percent of the population experiences marked mood swings as the seasons change. Women suffering from SAD outnumber men four to one, and the disorder has been identified in children as well as adults.

Several biological factors have been linked to SAD. In one study, nearly 75 percent of SAD patients were discovered to have relatives who also suffered from affective disorders, suggesting a possible genetic component to the disorder. Another study found that the hormone prolactin reached abnormally high levels during the winter depressions of those with SAD, suggesting a possible biochemical factor as well.

Some people apparently suffer a reverse form of SAD, experiencing depression during the spring and summer and an elevation in mood during winter. Although the basic symptoms are the same for both types of SAD, other evidence indicates that the reverse SAD pattern may involve a more serious form of depression. For example, suicide rates typically peak during the spring. Similarly, psychiatric hospital admissions for the most serious forms of depression peak in the spring.

Although much further research is needed, experts believe that it may be possible to prevent seasonal mood swings by manipulating environmental factors such as temperature and hours of daylight. In one treatment program, patients are exposed to bright, white "growlights" placed in key locations in their homes and set to artificially lengthen the daylight hours. Relief following this type of treatment often occurs within days.

Although anyone with serious depression should consult a doctor, people who feel mild SAD symptoms are advised to increase their exposure to available sunlight during the gray days of winter. Because the timing, rather than total hours, of light exposure seems to be critical, they should focus on the morning hours. Taking early morning walks and avoiding the urge to hibernate during winter are two steps sufferers of seasonal mood swings are advised to try.

Sources: Rosenhan, D. L., & Seligman, M. E. P. (1989). *Abnormal Psychology* (2nd ed.). New York: W. W. Norton, 354–355.

Adelmann, P. (1988, Feb. 26). Moods Swing by Season. *Detroit Free Press*, 3B.

Progress Test 1

Multiple-Choice Questions

Circle your answers to the following questions and check them with the answer key at the end of this chapter. If your answer is incorrect, read the answer key explanation for why it is incorrect and then consult the appropriate pages of the text to understand the correct answer.

1. Amnesia, fugue state, and multiple personality are all examples of:
   a. anxiety disorders.
   b. mood disorders.
   c. somatoform disorders.
   d. dissociative disorders.

2. Joe has an intense, irrational fear of snakes. He is suffering from a(n):
   a. generalized anxiety disorder.
   b. obsessive-compulsive disorder.
   c. phobic disorder.
   d. somatoform disorder.

3. Most mental health workers today take the view that disordered behaviors:
   a. are usually genetically triggered.
   b. are organic diseases.
   c. arise from the interaction of nature and nurture.
   d. are the product of learning.

4. While mountain climbing Jack saw his best friend killed by an avalanche. Jack himself was found months later, hundreds of miles away. On questioning, he claimed to be another person and, indeed, appeared to have no knowledge about any aspect of his former life. Most likely, Jack was suffering from:
   a. a fugue state.
   b. the conversion disorder.
   c. a multiple personality disorder.
   d. psychogenic amnesia.

5. Which of the following is the most pervasive of the psychological disorders?
   a. depression
   b. schizophrenia
   c. hypochondriasis
   d. generalized anxiety disorder

6. Which of the following is *not* true concerning depression?
   a. Depression is more common in females than in males.
   b. Most depressive episodes appear not to be preceded by any particular factor or event.
   c. Most depressive episodes last less than 3 months.

d. Most people recover from depression without professional therapy.

7. Which of the following is *not* true regarding schizophrenia?
   a. It affects men and women about equally.
   b. It occurs more frequently in the lower socioeconomic classes.
   c. It occurs more frequently in industrialized countries.
   d. It usually appears during adolescence or early adulthood.

8. Schizophrenia that involves bizarre physical movements is called:
   a. disorganized.   c. paranoid.
   b. catatonic.   d. undifferentiated.

9. The effect of drugs that block receptors for dopamine is to:
   a. alleviate schizophrenic symptoms.
   b. alleviate depression.
   c. increase schizophrenic symptoms.
   d. increase depression.

10. Bob has never been able to keep a job. He's been in and out of jail for charges such as theft, sexual assault, and spouse abuse—and he shows no remorse for his behavior. Bob would most likely be diagnosed as having:
    a. a multiple personality.
    b. disorganized schizophrenia.
    c. undifferentiated schizophrenia.
    d. an antisocial personality.

11. Behavior is classified as disordered when it is:
    a. atypical.   d. disturbing.
    b. maladaptive.   e. all of the above.
    c. unjustifiable.

12. Julio's psychologist believes that Julio's fear of heights can be traced to a conditioned fear he developed after falling from a ladder. This explanation reflects a _____ perspective.
    a. medical   c. social-cognitive
    b. psychoanalytic   d. learning

13. According to the social-cognitive perspective, a person who experiences unexpected aversive events may develop helplessness and manifest:
    a. an obsessive-compulsive disorder.
    b. a dissociative disorder.
    c. a personality disorder.
    d. a mood disorder.

14. Before he can begin studying, Rashid must arrange his books, pencils, paper, and other items on his desk, so that they are "just so." The campus coun-

selor suggests that Rashid's compulsive behavior may help alleviate his anxiety about failing in school, which reinforces the compulsive actions. This explanation of obsessive-compulsive behavior is most consistent with which perspective?

a. learning
b. psychoanalytic
c. humanistic
d. social-cognitive

15. According to psychoanalytic theory, internalized anger is likely to result in:

a. learned helplessness.
b. the self-serving bias.
c. weak ego-defense mechanisms.
d. depression.

16. When expecting to be electrically shocked, people with an antisocial disorder, as compared to normal people, show:

a. less fear and greater arousal of the autonomic nervous system.

b. less fear and less autonomic arousal.
c. greater fear and greater autonomic arousal.
d. greater fear and less autonomic arousal.

17. Hearing voices would be a(n) _____; believing that you are Napoleon would be a(n) _____.

a. obsession; compulsion
b. compulsion; obsession
c. delusion; hallucination
d. hallucination; delusion

18. In treating depression, a psychiatrist would probably prescribe a drug that would:

a. increase levels of acetylcholine.
b. decrease levels of dopamine.
c. increase levels of norepinephrine.
d. decrease levels of serotonin.

Matching Items

Match each term with the appropriate definition or description.

Terms

_____ 1. fugue
_____ 2. psychogenic amnesia
_____ 3. mood disorder
_____ 4. dissociative disorders
_____ 5. mania
_____ 6. obsessive-compulsive disorder
_____ 7. schizophrenia
_____ 8. somatoform disorder
_____ 9. panic attack
_____ 10. hypochondriasis

Definitions

a. a psychological disorder of emotional extremes
b. an extremely elevated mood
c. a disorder in which symptoms take a bodily form
d. a dissociative disorder in which the person experiences a loss of memory following severe psychological stress
e. a sudden escalation of anxiety often accompanied by a sensation of choking or other physical symptoms
f. a dissociative disorder in which the person flees from home and identity
g. a disorder in which normal physical sensations are misinterpreted as symptoms of a disease
h. disorders such as fugue, amnesia, or multiple personality
i. a group of disorders marked by disorganized thinking, disturbed perceptions, and inappropriate emotions
j. a disorder characterized by repetitive thoughts and actions

Progress Test 2

Progress Test 2 should be completed during a final chapter review. Do this test after you thoroughly understand the correct answers for the Chapter Review and Progress Test 1.

Multiple-Choice Questions

1. Which of the following is true concerning abnormal behavior?

a. Definitions of abnormal behavior are culture dependent.
b. A behavior cannot be defined as abnormal unless it is considered harmful to society.
c. Abnormal behavior can be defined as any behavior that is atypical.
d. Definitions of abnormal behavior are based on physiological factors.

2. According to the psychoanalytic perspective, phobias are:

   a. conditioned fears.
   b. displaced responses to incompletely repressed impulses.
   c. biological predispositions.
   d. manifestations of self-defeating thoughts.

3. Your textbook suggests that the disorganized thoughts of people with schizophrenia may be attributed to a breakdown in:

   a. selective attention.   c. motivation.
   b. memory storage.   d. memory retrieval.

4. The most widely used system of classifying and describing disordered behavior is:

   a. *The Diagnostic and Statistical Manual of Mental Disorders (Third Edition — Revised).*
   b. *The World Health Organization's International Classification of Diseases.*
   c. *The Mental Measurements Yearbook.*
   d. *The Psychiatric Reference Book.*

5. Sharon is continually tense, jittery, and apprehensive for no specific reason. She would probably be diagnosed as suffering a(n):

   a. phobic disorder.
   b. conversion disorder.
   c. obsessive-compulsive disorder.
   d. generalized anxiety disorder.

6. Jason is so preoccupied with staying clean that he showers as many as ten times each day. Jason would be diagnosed as suffering from a(n):

   a. somatoform disorder.
   b. conversion disorder.
   c. personality disorder.
   d. obsessive-compulsive disorder.

7. Which of the following statements concerning the labeling of disordered behaviors is *not* true?

   a. Labels interfere with effective treatment of psychological disorders.
   b. Labels promote research studies of psychological disorders.
   c. Labels may create preconceptions that bias people's perceptions.
   d. Labels may influence behavior by creating self-fulfilling prophecies.

8. Lee is convinced that the eyestrain he feels after a day of working at his computer is caused by a detached retina. Although several doctors have assured him that he is fine, Lee continues to worry. His behavior is an example of:

   a. a conversion disorder.
   b. schizophrenia.
   c. a panic attack.
   d. hypochondriasis.

9. Which neurotransmitter is present in overabundant amounts during the manic phase of bipolar depression?

   a. dopamine   c. epinephrine
   b. serotonin   d. norepinephrine

10. Psychiatrist Thomas Szasz has argued that:

    a. the medical model has played a valuable role in shaping the therapeutic process.
    b. psychological disorders will not be truly treatable until the underlying biochemical mechanisms are identified.
    c. the medical model errs in viewing psychological disorders as diseases.
    d. disordered behavior typically results from stress, and treatment must therefore aim at alleviating stress.

11. If a person experiences blindness, paralysis, or some other physical ailment for which no physiological cause can be found, the diagnosis would be:

    a. hypochondriasis.
    b. a conversion disorder.
    c. panic attack.
    d. schizophrenia.

12. Both the medical model and the psychoanalytic model:

    a. have in recent years been in large part discredited.
    b. view psychological disorders as sicknesses that are diagnosable and treatable.
    c. emphasize the role of physiological factors in disorders over that of psychological factors.
    d. emphasize all of the above.

13. Sandy was referred to a psychiatrist after she was arrested for disorderly behavior in a restaurant. Claiming that she heard a voice commanding her to warn others that eating was harmful, Sandy attempted to convince others not to eat. The psychiatrist found that Sandy's thinking and speech were often fragmented and incoherent. In addition, Sandy has an unreasonable fear that someone is "out to get her" and consequently trusts no one. Her condition is most indicative of:

    a. paranoid schizophrenia.
    b. catatonic schizophrenia.
    c. undifferentiated schizophrenia.
    d. residual schizophrenia.

14. The early warning signs of schizophrenia, based on studies of high-risk children, include all *but* which of the following?

    a. having a severely schizophrenic mother
    b. having been separated from parents
    c. having a short attention span
    d. having matured physically at a very early age

15. Irene occasionally experiences unpredictable episodes of intense dread accompanied by chest pain and a sensation of smothering. Since her experiences have no apparent cause, they would probably be classified as examples of:
    a. residual schizophrenia.
    b. hysteria.
    c. hypochondriasis.
    d. panic attack.

16. Social-cognitive theorists believe that depression is linked with:
    a. negative moods.
    b. maladaptive explanations of failure.
    c. self-defeating beliefs.
    d. all of the above.

17. Most schizophrenic hallucinations involve the sense of:
    a. smell.   c. hearing.
    b. vision.   d. touch.

18. Among the following, which is generally accepted as a possible cause of schizophrenia?
    a. an excess of endorphins in the brain
    b. being a twin
    c. extensive learned helplessness
    d. a genetic predisposition

Matching Items

Match each term with the appropriate definition or description.

Terms

_____ 1. multiple personality
_____ 2. hallucinations
_____ 3. paranoid
_____ 4. conversion disorder
_____ 5. antisocial personality
_____ 6. undifferentiated
_____ 7. residual
_____ 8. bipolar disorder
_____ 9. delusions
_____ 10. catatonic
_____ 11. disorganized

Definitions

a. a type of schizophrenia characterized by false beliefs of grandeur or persecution
b. minor symptoms of schizophrenia that linger after a more serious episode
c. an individual who seems to have no conscience
d. a type of schizophrenia characterized by bizarre physical movements
e. false beliefs that may accompany psychological disorders
f. sensory experiences in the absence of sensory stimulation
g. a type of schizophrenia characterized by incoherent speech and inappropriate emotions
h. a type of dissociative disorder
i. a type of schizophrenia with symptoms that are not confined to any one of the other types
j. a type of mood disorder
k. a type of somatoform disorder

Key Terms

Using your own words, write a brief definition or explanation of each of the following terms.

1. psychological disorder

2. medical model

3. insanity

4. DSM-III-R

5. anxiety disorders

14. amnesia

6. generalized anxiety disorder

15. fugue

7. panic attack

16. multiple personality disorder

8. phobic disorder

17. mood disorders

9. obsessive-compulsive disorder

18. major depression

10. somatoform disorders

19. bipolar disorder

11. conversion disorder

20. mania

12. hypochondriasis

21. schizophrenia

13. dissociative disorders

22. delusions

23. personality disorders

24. antisocial personality

Answers

CHAPTER REVIEW

1. atypical; disturbing; maladaptive; unjustifiable; variable

2. medical; Pinel

3. socially

4. consistent

Critics of the medical model maintain that disorders are caused by psychological as well as physical factors. They contend that *all* behavior arises from the interaction of nature and nurture. Therefore, abnormal behavior cannot be viewed simply as an internal "sickness."

5. DSM-III-R.

6. objective

7. generalized anxiety

8. autonomic; panic attack; defense mechanisms

9. is; helplessness

10. phobic

The psychoanalytic explanation is that phobias represent incompletely repressed impulses over which the person is anxious. When repression is incomplete, the anxiety is displaced onto the phobic stimulus. The learning explanation is that phobias are conditioned fears. Since avoiding the feared situation reduces anxiety, the phobic behavior is reinforced.

11. obsessive-compulsive

12. frontal; left

13. species' survival; grooming, cleaning, maintaining order, checking territorial boundaries

14. somatoform

15. conversion; rare

16. hypochondriasis

17. conscious awareness; separated; uncommon

18. amnesia; psychogenic amnesia

19. selective

20. fugue

21. multiple personality

22. roles

23. emotional

24. major depression

25. 5 to 10; higher

26. poor appetite; insomnia; lethargy; feelings of worthlessness; loss of interest in family, friends, and activities

27. mania; bipolar

28. 1

29. can

30. is

The psychoanalytic perspective suggests that adulthood depression can be triggered by losses that evoke feelings associated with earlier, childhood losses, feelings that include anger. Since this anger is unacceptable to the superego, the emotion is turned inward and takes the form of depression.

31. tend

32. low; norepinephrine; serotonin

33. self-defeating; learned helplessness

Depressed people are more likely than others to explain failures or bad events in terms that are *stable* (it's going to last forever), *global* (it will affect everything), and *internal* (it's my fault). Such explanations lead to feelings of hopelessness, which in turn feed depression.

34. rejection

Depression is often brought on by stressful experiences. Depressed people brood over such experiences with maladaptive explanations that produce self-blame and amplify their depression, which in turn triggers other symptoms of depression. In addition, being withdrawn and complaining tends to elicit more social rejection and other negative experiences.

35. reality

36. thinking; perceptions; emotions; actions

37. adolescence or early adulthood

38. delusions

39. selective attention

40. hallucinations; auditory

41. cluster of disorders

Matching Items

1. e   3. a   5. d
2. b   4. c

42. dopamine; decrease

43. frontal; dopamine

44. support

45. genetic; psychological

Such signs may include severe, long-lasting schizophrenia in the mother; complications at birth; separation from parents; short attention span and poor coordination; and behavioral problems at school.

46. maladaptive

47. antisocial; psychopath or sociopath

48. less

49. a significant

Psychological labels may be arbitrary. They can create preconceptions that can bias our perceptions and interpretations and can affect people's self-images. Moreover, labels can even change reality, by serving as self-fulfilling prophecies. Despite these drawbacks, labels are useful in describing, treating, and researching the causes of psychological disorders.

PROGRESS TEST 1

Multiple-Choice Questions

1. **d.** is the answer. In each of these disorders a person's conscious awareness becomes dissociated, or separated, from previous memories, thoughts, and feelings. (p. 344)

2. **c.** is the answer. An intense fear of a specific object is a phobia. (p. 341)

   a. His fear is *focused* on a specific object, not generalized.

   b. In this disorder a person is troubled by repetitive thoughts and actions.

   d. In this disorder there is a bodily symptom that has no apparent physical cause.

3. **c.** is the answer. Most clinicians agree that psychological disorders may be caused by both psychological (**d.**) and physical factors (**a.** and **b.**). (p. 336)

4. **a.** is the answer. A fugue involves totally fleeing one's identity and home. (p. 344)

   b. A conversion disorder is diagnosed when a psychological problem is expressed in a bodily symptom.

   c. In a multiple personality disorder, two or more personalities exist simultaneously, which is not the case in the example.

   d. Psychogenic amnesia is generally a selective forgetting; it does not involve physical flight or total loss of identity.

5. **a.** is the answer. Depression is the most pervasive disorder; according to some estimates, at least 25 percent of us will experience at least one depressive episode. (pp. 346–348)

6. **b.** is the answer. Usually, depression is preceded by a stressful event related to work, marriage, or a close relationship. (p. 348)

7. **c.** is the answer. The incidence of schizophrenia does not vary significantly from country to country. (p. 353)

8. **b.** is the answer. (p. 355)

   a. In disorganized schizophrenia the person exhibits incoherent speech and inappropriate emotion.

   c. In paranoid schizophrenia the person has delusions of persecution or grandeur.

   d. Undifferentiated schizophrenia is diagnosed when symptoms do not easily fit one of the other categories.

9. **a.** is the answer. (p. 356)

   b. & d. Thus far, it is norepinephrine and serotonin that have been implicated in depression and bipolar disorder.

   c. Schizophrenia has been associated with an excess of dopamine receptors. Blocking them alleviates schizophrenia symptoms rather than increasing them.

10. **d.** is the answer. Repeated wrongdoing, aggressive behavior, and lack of remorse are part of the pattern associated with the antisocial personality disorder, which may also include marital problems and inability to keep a job. (p. 359)

    a. Although multiple personalities may involve an aggressive personality, there is nothing in the example to indicate a dissociation.

    b. & c. Bob's behavior does not include the disorganized thinking and disturbed perceptions typical of schizophrenia.

11. **e.** is the answer. Behavior is considered disordered when it is atypical, maladaptive, unjustifiable, and disturbing. (p. 335)

12. **d.** is the answer. In the learning perspective, a phobia, such as Julio's, is seen as a conditioned fear. (p. 340)

    a. Because the fear is focused on a specific stimulus, the medical model does not easily account for the phobic disorder. In any event, it would presumably offer an internal, biological explanation.

    b. The psychoanalytic view of phobias is that they represent incompletely repressed anxieties that are displaced onto the feared object.

    c. The social-cognitive perspective emphasizes a person's conscious, cognitive processes, not reflexive conditioned responses.

13. **d.** is the answer. Learned helplessness may lead to self-defeating beliefs, which in turn are linked with depression, a mood disorder. (p. 350)

14. **a.** is the answer. According to the learning view, compulsive behaviors are reinforced because they reduce the anxiety created by obsessive thoughts. Rashid's obsession concerns failing, and his desk-arranging compulsive behaviors apparently help him control these thoughts. (p. 343)

b. According to the psychoanalytic view, obsessive thoughts are a symbolic representation of forbidden impulses. These thoughts may prompt the person to perform compulsive acts that counter these impulses.

c. & d. The textbook does not offer explanations of obsessive-compulsive behavior based on the humanistic and social-cognitive perspectives. Presumably, however, these explanations would emphasize growth-blocking difficulties in the person's environment (humanistic perspective) and the reciprocal influences of personality and environment (social-cognitive perspective), rather than symbolic expressions of forbidden impulses.

15. **d.** is the answer. When a loss evokes feelings of anger toward others, associated with an earlier loss, such anger is unacceptable to the superego and is turned against the self. This internalized anger results in depression. (p. 349)

a. Explanations in terms of learned helplessness would be offered by the social-cognitive perspective.

b. The self-serving bias is not discussed in terms of its relationship to depression.

c. This is the psychoanalytic explanation of anxiety.

16. **b.** is the answer. Those with antisocial personality disorders show less autonomic arousal in such situations, and emotions, such as fear, are tied to arousal. (p. 359)

17. **d.** is the answer. Hallucinations are false sensory experiences; delusions are false beliefs. (pp. 353–354)

a. & b. Obsessions are repetitive and unwanted thoughts. Compulsions are repetitive behaviors.

18. **c.** is the answer. Drugs that relieve depression tend to increase norepinephrine. (p. 350)

a. Acetylcholine is a neurotransmitter involved in muscle contractions.

b. It is in certain types of schizophrenia that decreasing dopamine levels is known to be helpful. Although researchers are investigating a possible role for dopamine in depression, answers have not yet been obtained.

d. On the contrary, it appears that a particular type of depression may be related to low levels of serotonin.

Matching Items

1. f (p. 344)	**5.** b (p. 348)	**8.** c (p. 343)
2. d (p. 344)	**6.** j (p. 342)	**9.** e (p. 340)
3. a (p. 346)	**7.** i (p. 353)	**10.** g (p. 343)
4. h (p. 344)		

PROGRESS TEST 2

Multiple-Choice Questions

1. **a.** is the answer. Different cultures have different standards for behaviors that are considered acceptable and normal. (p. 334)

b. Some abnormal behaviors are simply maladaptive for the individual.

c. Many individuals who are atypical, such as Olympic gold medalists, are not considered abnormal. There are other criteria that must be met in order for behavior to be considered abnormal.

d. Although physiological factors play a role in the various disorders, they do not define abnormal behavior. Rather, behavior is said to be abnormal if it is atypical, disturbing, maladaptive, and unjustifiable.

2. **b.** is the answer. (p. 341)

a. This answer reflects the learning perspective.

c. Although certain phobias are biologically predisposed, this could not fully explain phobias, nor is it the explanation offered by psychoanalytic theory.

d. Social-cognitive theorists propose self-defeating thoughts as a cause of depression.

3. **a.** is the answer. Schizophrenics are easily distracted by irrelevant stimuli, evidently because of a breakdown in the capacity for selective attention. (p. 353)

4. **a.** is the answer. (p. 338)

5. **d.** is the answer. (p. 340)

a. In the phobic disorder, anxiety is focused on a specific object.

b. In conversion disorders, anxiety is manifested in physical symptoms.

c. The obsessive-compulsive disorder is characterized by repetitive and unwanted thoughts and/or actions.

6. **d.** is the answer. Jason is obsessed with cleanliness and, as a result, has developed a compulsion to shower. (p. 342)

a. & b. These are disorders in which the symptoms take the form of physical symptoms.

c. This disorder is characterized by maladaptive character traits.

7. **a.** is the answer. In fact, just the opposite is true. Labels are useful in promoting effective treatment of psychological disorders. (pp. 359–360)

8. **d.** is the answer. Lee is interpreting a normal sensation as a disease symptom. (p. 343)

   a. In a conversion disorder, a genuine physical ailment is exhibited.

   b. Schizophrenia is not characterized by such fears of illness.

   c. In a panic attack, the person has a sudden escalation of anxiety.

9. **d.** is the answer. In bipolar disorder, norepinephrine appears overabundant during mania and in short supply during depression. (p. 350)

   a. There is an overabundance of dopamine receptors in some schizophrenics.

   b. There is a shortage of serotonin in a certain type of depression.

   c. Epinephrine has not been implicated in psychological disorders.

10. **c.** is the answer. Szasz believes that psychological disorders are problems in living and that treating them as medically defined diseases is wrong and has negative consequences. (pp. 335–336)

11. **b.** is the answer. (p. 343)

   a. In hypochondriasis, the person believes there is something physically wrong when nothing is.

   c. A panic attack is a generalized anxiety disorder in which the person experiences an episode of intense dread.

   d. Schizophrenia is characterized by disorganized thinking, disturbing perceptions, and inappropriate emotions and actions.

12. **b.** is the answer. (p. 343)

   a. This isn't the case; in fact, the medical model has gained credibility from recent discoveries of genetic and biochemical links to some disorders.

   c. The psychoanalytic perspective tends to place equal, if not more, emphasis on psychological factors.

13. **c.** is the answer. Because Sandy experiences hallucinations (hearing voices), delusions (fearing someone is "out to get her"), and incoherence —characteristics typical of several types of schizophrenia—she would most likely be diagnosed as suffering undifferentiated schizophrenia. (p. 355)

   a. Paranoid schizophrenia is characterized by delusions of persecution or grandeur, but is typically not accompanied by the other symptoms mentioned.

   b. Catatonic schizophrenia is characterized by bizarre physical movements.

   d. Residual schizophrenia is characterized by minor symptoms of schizophrenia that linger after a major disorder; Sandy's symptoms are apparently much more serious.

14. **d.** is the answer. There is no evidence that early physical maturation is an early warning sign of schizophrenia. (pp. 356–358)

15. **d.** is the answer. These symptoms are characteristic of a panic attack, which is an episode of heightened anxiety. (p. 340)

   a. Baseless physical symptoms rarely play a role in residual schizophrenia.

   b. This is an older, Freudian term for somatoform disorders.

   c. In hypochondriasis, normal aches and pains are falsely interpreted as illness.

16. **d.** is the answer. (pp. 350–352)

17. **c.** is the answer. (p. 354)

18. **d.** is the answer. Risk for schizophrenia increases for individuals who are related to a schizophrenia victim, and the greater the genetic relatedness, the greater the risk. (pp. 356–357)

   a. Schizophrenia victims have an overabundance of the neurotransmitter dopamine, not endorphins.

   b. Being a twin is, in itself, irrelevant to developing schizophrenia.

   c. Although helplessness has been suggested by social-cognitive theorists as a cause of self-defeating depressive behaviors, it has not been suggested as a cause of schizophrenia.

Matching Items

1. h (p. 344)	**5.** c (p. 359)	**9.** e (p. 353)
2. f (p. 354)	**6.** i (p. 355)	**10.** d (p. 355)
3. a (p. 355)	**7.** b (p. 355)	**11.** g (p. 355)
4. k (p. 343)	**8.** j (p. 346)	

KEY TERMS

1. In order to be classified as a **psychological disorder**, behavior must be atypical, disturbing, maladaptive, and unjustifiable. (p. 335)

2. The **medical model** holds that psychological disorders are illnesses that can be diagnosed and treated using traditional methods of medicine and psychiatry. (p. 335)

3. **Insanity** is a legal term for unsoundness of mind such that a person committing a crime does not understand the wrongness of the act. (p. 335)

Example: **Insanity** is an all-or-none legal description, whereas psychological disorders have many degrees and are rarely clear-cut.

4. **DSM-III-R** is a short name for the American Psychiatric Association's *Diagnostic and Statistical Manual of Mental Disorders (Third Edition – Revised)*, which provides a widely used system of classifying psychological disorders. The revised DSM-III-R bases diagnosis less on subjective assessment and more on observable behavior, to improve reliability. (p. 338)

5. **Anxiety disorders** involve distressing, persistent anxiety and/or maladaptive behavior in response to such anxiety. (p. 339)

6. In the **generalized anxiety disorder**, the person is continually tense, apprehensive, and in a state of autonomic arousal for no apparent reason. (pp. 339–340)

7. A **panic attack** is an episode of intense dread accompanied by chest pain, dizziness, or fainting. Panic attacks are essentially an escalation of the anxiety associated with generalized anxiety disorder. (p. 340)

8. The **phobic disorder** is an anxiety disorder in which a person is irrationally afraid of a specific object or situation. (pp. 341–342)

   Example: Many **phobias** may actually be classically conditioned fears: the new irrational fear remains even though the conditioning experience may have long since been forgotten.

9. The **obsessive-compulsive disorder** is an anxiety disorder in which the person experiences uncontrollable and repetitive thoughts (obsessions) and actions (compulsions). (pp. 342–343)

10. In a **somatoform disorder** there are physical symptoms but no apparent physical cause. (p. 343)

    Memory aid: *Somatic* means "bodily." A **somatoform disorder** is one in which the disorder appears in bodily form.

11. The **conversion disorder** is a somatoform disorder in which there are very specific physical symptoms (e.g., paralysis, blindness, or inability to swallow) with no apparent physiological cause. (p. 343)

    Memory aid: The **conversion disorder** is so named because Freud believed that in this disorder anxiety was *converted* into bodily symptoms.

12. **Hypochondriasis** is the somatoform disorder in which a person interprets normal aches and pains as symptoms of disease. (p. 343)

13. The **dissociative disorders** involve a separation of conscious awareness from one's previous memories, thoughts, and feelings. (p. 344)

Memory aid: To dissociate is to separate or pull apart. In the **dissociative disorder** a person becomes dissociated from his or her memories and identity.

14. **Amnesia** is a selective loss of memory. Amnesia may be caused by illness or head injuries, but the dissociative disorder, psychogenic amnesia, is usually precipitated by extreme stress. (p. 344)

15. **Fugue** is a dissociative disorder in which forgetting occurs and the person physically runs away from home and identity. (p. 344)

    Memory aid: *Fugue* and *fugitive* both derive from the same Latin root, meaning "to flee."

16. The **multiple personality disorder** is a dissociative disorder in which a person exhibits two or more personalities. (pp. 344–345)

    Example: A common pattern in the **multiple personality disorder** is for one personality to be rather inhibited and shy while the second is more impulsive and uninhibited.

17. The **mood disorders** are characterized by emotional extremes. (p. 346)

18. **Major depression** is the mood disorder that occurs when a person exhibits the passive, resigned, and self-defeating thoughts and behaviors of depression for more than a 2-week period and for no discernible reason. Because of its relative frequency, depression has been called the "common cold" of psychological disorders. (p. 346)

19. The **bipolar disorder** is the mood disorder in which a person alternates between depression and the euphoria of a manic state. (p. 346)

    Memory aid: *Bipolar* means having two poles, that is, two opposite qualities. In the **bipolar disorder**, the opposing states are mania and depression.

20. **Mania** is the euphoric, hyperactive state that alternates with depression in the bipolar disorder. (p. 348)

21. **Schizophrenia** refers to the group of disorders whose symptoms may include disorganized thinking, inappropriate emotions, false beliefs or delusions, bizarre movements, and hallucinations. (pp. 353–358)

22. **Delusions** are false beliefs that often are symptoms of schizophrenia and other psychotic disorders. (p. 353)

    Example: The hallmark of paranoid schizophrenia is the **delusion** of persecution suffered by its victims.

23. **Personality disorders** are characterized by enduring maladaptive character traits. These disorders

may, but need not, involve anxiety, depression, or dissociation from reality. (p. 358)

Example: Examples of **personality disorders** include sexual deviations, the "asthenic personality" in which a person has a marked incapacity for enjoyment, and the "explosive personality," characterized by outbursts of verbal or physical aggressiveness.

24. The **antisocial personality** is a personality disorder in which the person is aggressive, ruthless, and shows no signs of a conscience that would inhibit wrongdoing. (p. 359)

Example: Once called sociopaths or psychopaths, those with **antisocial personalities** are emotionally flat persons who express little remorse over violating others' rights.

Chapter 13 | Therapy

Chapter Overview

Chapter 13 discusses the major psychotherapies and biomedical therapies for maladaptive behaviors. The various psychotherapies all derive from the psychological perspectives discussed earlier, namely, the psychoanalytic, humanistic, behavioristic, and cognitive perspectives. The chapter groups the therapies by perspective but also emphasizes the common threads that run through all. In evaluating the therapies, the chapter points out that, although people who are untreated often improve, those receiving psychotherapy tend to improve somewhat more, regardless of the type of therapy they receive.

The biomedical therapies discussed are psychosurgery, which is seldom used; electroconvulsive therapy; and drug therapies. By far the most important of the biomedical therapies, drug therapies are being used in the treatment of psychotic, anxiety, and mood disorders.

But the origins of problems often lie beyond the individual, and the chapter concludes by discussing the need to prevent psychological disorders by focusing on the conditions that cause them.

Guided Study

The textbook chapter should be studied one section at a time. Before you read, preview each section by skimming it, noting headings and boldface items. Then read the appropriate section objectives from the following outline. Keep these objectives in mind, and as you read the chapter section, search for the information that will enable you to meet each objective. Once you have finished a section, write out answers for its objectives.

The Psychological Therapies (pp. 366–385)

1. Discuss the aims and methods of psychoanalysis and explain the critics' concerns with this form of therapy.

2. Identify the basic themes of humanistic therapies and describe Rogers' person-centered approach.

3. Discuss the application of humanistic principles in group and family therapies.

4. Identify the basic assumptions of behavior therapy and discuss the classical conditioning techniques.

5. Describe behavior modification and explain the critics' concerns with this technique.

6. Describe the cognitive therapies and discuss their goals.

7. Discuss the findings regarding the effectiveness of the psychotherapies.

8. Discuss the commonalities among psychotherapies.

The Biomedical Therapies (pp. 385–388)

9. Describe the use of psychosurgery and electroconvulsive therapy in the treatment of psychological disorders.

10. Identify the common forms of drug therapy.

Preventing Psychological Disorders (pp. 388–389)

11. Explain the rationale of preventive mental health programs.

Chapter Review

When you have finished reading the chapter, use the material that follows to review it. Complete the fill-in sentences and answer the essay items in complete sentences. As you proceed, evaluate your performance for each chapter section by consulting the answer key at the end of this chapter. Do not continue with the next section until you've understood each answer. If you need to, review or reread the appropriate chapter section in the textbook before continuing.

1. Therapies are divided into two types:

_____ and _____

therapies.

The Psychological Therapies (pp. 366–385)

2. Psychological therapy is more commonly called

_____.

3. Therapists who blend several psychotherapy techniques are referred to as _____.

4. The major psychotherapies are based on four perspectives: the _____,

_____, _____,

and _____ perspectives.

Describe the aims of psychoanalysis.

5. Freud's technique in which a client says whatever comes to mind, is called

_____ _____ .

6. When, in the course of therapy, a person omits shameful or embarrassing material, _____ is occurring. Insight is facilitated by the analyst's _____ of the meaning of such omissions, of dreams, and other information revealed during therapy sessions.

7. Freud referred to the hidden meaning of a dream as its _____

_____ .

8. When strong feelings, similar to those experienced in other important relationships, are developed toward the therapist, _____ has occurred.

Outline the criticisms that have been made of psychoanalysis.

9. Humanistic therapies attempt to help people meet their potential for _____-

_____ .

List several ways that humanistic therapy differs from psychoanalysis.

10. The humanistic therapy based on Rogers' theory is called _____-_____ therapy. It is so named because the therapist _____ (interprets/does not interpret) the person's problems.

11. In order to promote growth in clients, humanistic therapists exhibit _____,

_____, and _____ .

12. Rogers' technique of restating and clarifying what a person is saying is called

_____ _____ .

List several advantages of group therapy.

13. "T-groups" refer to groups of individuals participating in _____ training.

14. Rogers and other therapists developed a form of intensive group therapy known as the _____ group.

15. One type of group interaction that focuses on the social context in which the individual exists is _____ _____ .

Contrast the assumptions of the behavior therapies with those of psychoanalysis and humanistic therapy.

16. One type of behavior therapy is based on the principles of _____

_____, as developed in Pavlov's experiments. The technique in which a new, incompatible response is substituted for a maladaptive one is called _____.
Two examples of this technique are

_____ _____

and _____ _____ .

17. The technique of systematic desensitization has been most fully developed by the therapist _____. The assumption behind this technique is that one cannot simultaneously be _____ and relaxed.

18. The first step in systematic desensitization is the construction of a(n) _____ of anxiety-arousing stimuli. The second step

involves training in _____. In the final step, the person is trained to associate the _____ state with the _____-arousing stimuli.

19. In aversive conditioning the therapist attempts to substitute a _____ (positive/ negative) response for one that is currently _____ (positive/negative). In this technique, unwanted behaviors become associated with _____ consequences.

20. Therapies that influence behavior by controlling its consequences are called _____ _____. Such therapies are based on principles of _____ conditioning.

21. One application of this form of therapy to institutional settings is the _____ _____, in which desired behaviors are rewarded.

Outline two criticisms of behavior modification.

22. Behavior therapies are generally most successful with problems that are _____ (specific/generalized).

23. Therapists who teach people more constructive ways of thinking are using _____ therapy.

24. The therapy technique that attempts to eliminate irrational thinking is _____- _____ therapy. The creator of this technique is _____. A related technique developed by Aaron Beck attempts to reverse the negative attitudes associated with _____ by helping people see their irrationalities.

25. In contrast to earlier times, most therapy today

_____ (is/is not) provided by psychiatrists.

26. A majority of psychotherapy clients express _____ (satisfaction/ dissatisfaction) with their therapy.

Give three reasons that clients' perceptions of the effectiveness of psychotherapy are potentially misleading.

27. The debate over the effectiveness of psychotherapy began with a study by _____; it showed that the rate of improvement for those who received therapy _____ (was/was not) higher than the rate for those who did not.

28. Overall, statistical analyses indicate that psychotherapy is _____ (somewhat effective/ineffective).

29. As a rule, psychotherapy is most effective with problems that are _____ (specific/nonspecific).

30. Comparisons of the effectiveness of different forms of therapy reveal _____ (clear/no clear) differences.

31. With phobias, compulsions, and other specific behavior problems, _____ _____ therapies have been the most effective. For depression, the _____ therapies have been the most successful.

Relate the three benefits provided by all forms of psychotherapy.

32. The beneficial effect of a person's belief in treatment is called the _____ _____.

33. Several studies found that treatment for mild problems offered by paraprofessionals _____ (is/is not) as effective as that offered by professional therapists.

The Biomedical Therapies (pp. 385–388)

34. The biomedical therapy in which a portion of brain tissue is removed or destroyed is called _____.

35. In the 1930s, Moniz developed an operation called the _____. In this technique, the _____ lobes of the brain are disconnected from the rest of the brain.

36. Today, most psychosurgery has been replaced by the use of _____ or some other form of treatment.

37. The therapeutic technique in which the patient receives an electric shock to the brain is referred to as _____ therapy, abbreviated as _____.

38. ECT is most often used with patients suffering from severe _____. One theory of how this treatment works suggests that it causes an increase in the neurotransmitter _____.

39. The most widely used biomedical treatments are the _____ therapies.

40. When neither the subjects nor those assessing them are aware of which condition a given individual is in, a _____-_____ experiment is being conducted.

41. One effect of _____ drugs is to decrease responsiveness to irrelevant stimuli in patients suffering from _____. Such drugs do so by blocking the receptor sites for the neurotransmitter _____.

42. Valium and Librium are classified as _____ drugs. These drugs

depress activity in the _____ _____ _____.

43. Drugs that are prescribed to alleviate depression are called _____ drugs. These drugs work by increasing levels of the neurotransmitters _____ and _____.

44. In order to stabilize the mood swings in bipolar disorder, the drug _____ is often prescribed.

Preventing Psychological Disorders (pp. 388–389)

45. Unlike psychotherapists and biomedical therapists, who focus on treatment of the _____, psychologists who practice preventive mental health believe that it is necessary to work on changing _____ conditions.

FOCUS ON PSYCHOLOGY:
Job-Related Psychotherapy

In his classic book, *A General Introduction to Psychoanalysis*, Sigmund Freud wrote that a healthy adult was one who could love and work. While Freud focused on issues more closely related to love than work, contemporary psychotherapists are finding that the nature of their clients' jobs is an increasingly important factor in their psychological well-being.

Many research studies have demonstrated the importance of work. Researchers have found, for example, that people who are out of work often feel depressed and empty. And, when people are asked what they would do if they suddenly became millionaires, more than 80 percent say they would continue to work at their regular jobs (Berger, 1988). As psychologist Douglas LaBier, author of *Modern Madness: The Emotional Fallout of Success*, puts it, increasingly for many of us "career and identity are inextricably bound up: Indeed they are almost equivalent."

Evidence for this career-identity merger comes from research showing that troubled behavior, including depression, anxiety, and drug abuse, is often a reaction to difficulties at work rather than a symptom of an underlying personality disorder. Other evidence comes from the trend toward occupational specialization among psychotherapists. According to science writer Ronni Sandroff, "Work–proud dentists, police officers, middle managers, tennis champions, stockbrokers and other professionals have begun searching for therapists who talk their language and appreciate the tremendous importance of work in their lives."

Specialization exemplifies the spirit of eclectic therapy discussed in the text: Some forms of therapy are more effective than others for certain problems and, apparently, for certain professions. Stress-management techniques such as relaxation training, biofeedback, and counterconditioning—all types of behavior therapy—have proven especially beneficial in treating stress-related problems. One New York therapist, for example, specializes in treating stress-related hypertension and headaches in corporate executives whose complaints have been diagnosed as psychophysiological.

Performance enhancement, also a form of behavior therapy, has been especially successful with clients in sales and business management. Originally developed by sports psychologists, performance enhancement helps people to attain "peak performance" in their events, or jobs, through visualization and rehearsal of critical situations and the application of other behavior modification techniques.

Traditional psychoanalysis seems to be most effective with artists, actors and actresses, writers, and people in the helping professions (including psychotherapy). Through free association, dream analysis, and therapist interpretation, such clients are able to deeply probe their problems and gain insight into their causes.

Group therapy is another technique that is becoming popular with therapists who are also occupational specialists. With this approach people employed in the same line of work are able to confront their problems together. Not only may they be able to help each other, but they are also better able than outsiders to empathize with the troubled individual.

As our identities and well-being become even more closely connected with our work, the trend toward occupational specialization in psychotherapy can certainly be expected to continue. The healthy adult may become the one who can love and work and find the right therapist for his or her profession should troubled times arise.

Sources: Berger, K. S. (1988). *The developing person through the life span* (2nd ed.). New York: Worth Publishers Inc., p. 449.

Sarnoff, R. (1989, July/August). Is your job driving you crazy? *Psychology Today*, pp. 41–45.

Progress Test 1

Multiple-Choice Questions

Circle your answers to the following questions and check them with the answer key at the end of this chapter. If your answer is incorrect, read the answer key explanation for why it is incorrect and then consult the appropriate pages of the text to understand the correct answer.

1. Electroconvulsive therapy is most useful in the treatment of:
   a. schizophrenia.   c. personality disorders.
   b. depression.   d. anxiety disorders.

2. During his session of psychoanalysis, Jamal hesitates while describing a highly embarrassing thought. In the psychoanalytic framework, this is an example of a(n):
   a. transference.   c. mental repression.
   b. insight.   d. resistance.

3. During her sessions of psychoanalysis, Jane has developed strong feelings of hatred for her therapist. The analyst believes that Jane is showing _____ of her feelings toward her father.
   a. projection   c. sublimation
   b. resistance   d. transference

4. Which of the following is *not* a common criticism of psychoanalysis?
   a. It could discourage women from developing to their full potential.
   b. It provides interpretations that are hard to disprove.
   c. It is generally a very expensive process.
   d. It gives therapists too much control over patients.

5. Which of the following is *not* necessarily an advantage of group therapies over individual therapies?
   a. They tend to take less time for the therapist.
   b. They tend to cost less money for the client.
   c. They are more effective.
   d. They allow the client to test new behaviors in a social context.

6. Which biomedical therapy is *least* likely to be practiced today?
   a. psychosurgery
   b. electroconvulsive therapy
   c. drug therapy
   d. counterconditioning

7. The effectiveness of psychotherapy has been assessed both through clients' perspectives and through controlled research studies. What have such assessments found?
   a. Clients' perceptions and controlled studies alike strongly affirm the effectiveness of psychotherapy.
   b. Whereas clients' perceptions strongly affirm the effectiveness of psychotherapy, studies point to more modest results.
   c. Whereas studies strongly affirm the effectiveness of psychotherapy, many clients feel dissatisfied with their progress.

d. Clients' perceptions and controlled studies alike paint a very mixed picture of the effectiveness of psychotherapy.

8. The results of statistical analysis of the effectiveness of different psychotherapies reveal that:

    a. no single type of therapy is consistently superior.

    b. behavior therapies are most effective in treating specific problems, such as phobias.

    c. cognitive therapies are most effective in treating depressed emotions.

    d. all of the above are true.

9. The antipsychotic drugs appear to produce their effects by blocking the receptor sites for:

    a. dopamine.   c. norepinephrine.

    b. epinephrine.   d. serotonin.

10. Psychologists who advocate a _____ approach to mental health believe that many psychological disorders could be prevented by changing the disturbed individual's _____.

    a. biomedical; diet

    b. family; behavior

    c. humanistic; feelings

    d. preventive; environment

11. An eclectic psychotherapist is one who:

    a. takes a nondirective approach in helping clients solve their problems.

    b. views psychological disorders as usually stemming from one cause, such as a biological abnormality.

    c. uses one particular technique, such as psychoanalysis or behavior modification, in treating disorders.

    d. uses a variety of techniques, depending on the client and the problem.

12. Because Jim's therapist attempts to help him by offering genuineness, acceptance, and empathy, she is probably practicing:

    a. psychoanalysis.

    b. behavior therapy.

    c. counterconditioning.

    d. person-centered therapy.

13. To help Sam quit smoking, his therapist blew a hot blast of smoke into Sam's face each time Sam inhaled. Which technique is the therapist using?

    a. rational-emotive therapy

    b. behavior modification

    c. systematic desensitization

    d. aversive conditioning

14. The operant conditioning technique in which desired behaviors are rewarded with points or poker chips that can later be exchanged for various rewards is called:

    a. counterconditioning.

    b. systematic desensitization.

    c. token economy.

    d. rational-emotive therapy.

15. After Darnel dropped a pass in an important football game, he became depressed and vowed to quit the team because of his athletic incompetence. The campus psychologist challenged his illogical reasoning and pointed out that Darnel's "incompetence" had earned him an athletic scholarship. The psychologist's response was most typical of a _____ therapist.

    a. biomedical   c. person-centered

    b. psychoanalytic   d. rational-emotive

16. A person can derive benefits from psychotherapy simply by believing in it. This illustrates the importance of:

    a. active listening.

    b. the placebo effect.

    c. the transference effect.

    d. interpretation.

17. Seth enters therapy to talk about some issues that have been upsetting him. The therapist prescribes some medication to help him. The therapist is most likely a:

    a. psychologist.

    b. psychiatrist.

    c. psychiatric social worker.

    d. clinical social worker.

Matching Items

Match each term with the appropriate definition or description.

Terms

_____ **1.** cognitive therapy
_____ **2.** behavior therapy
_____ **3.** systematic desensitization
_____ **4.** rational-emotive therapy
_____ **5.** person-centered therapy
_____ **6.** aversive conditioning
_____ **7.** psychoanalysis
_____ **8.** family therapy
_____ **9.** biomedical therapy
_____ **10.** counterconditioning

Definitions

a. associates unwanted behavior with unpleasant experiences
b. associates a relaxed state with anxiety-arousing stimuli
c. emphasizes the social context of psychological disorders
d. attempts to eliminate irrational thinking through a confrontational approach
e. category of therapies that teach people more adaptive ways of thinking and acting
f. therapy developed by Carl Rogers
g. therapy based on Freud's theory of personality
h. treatment with psychosurgery, electroconvulsive therapy, or drugs
i. classical conditioning procedure in which new responses are conditioned to stimuli that trigger unwanted behaviors
j. category of therapies based on learning principles derived from classical and operant conditioning

Progress Test 2

Progress Test 2 should be completed during a final chapter review. Do this test after you thoroughly understand the correct answers for the Chapter Review and Progress Test 1.

Multiple-Choice Questions

1. Carl Rogers was a _____ therapist who was the creator of _____ therapy.
   a. behavior; desensitization
   b. psychoanalytic; insight
   c. humanistic; person-centered
   d. cognitive; rational-emotive

2. Using techniques of classical conditioning to develop an association between unwanted behavior and an unpleasant experience is known as:
   a. aversive conditioning.
   b. systematic desensitization.
   c. transference.
   d. electroconvulsive therapy.

3. Which type of psychotherapy emphasizes the individual's inherent potential for self-fulfillment?
   a. behavior therapy   **c.** humanistic therapy
   b. psychoanalysis   **d.** biomedical therapy

4. Which type of psychotherapy focuses on changing symptoms rather than on the client's responsibility?
   a. behavior therapy   **c.** humanistic therapy
   b. cognitive therapy   **d.** psychoanalysis

5. The technique of counterconditioning is based on principles of:
   a. observational learning.
   b. classical conditioning.
   c. operant conditioning.
   d. behavior modification.

6. In which of the following does the client learn to associate a relaxed state with a hierarchy of anxiety-arousing situations?
   a. rational-emotive therapy
   b. cognitive therapy
   c. counterconditioning
   d. systematic desensitization

7. Principles of operant conditioning underlie the techniques of:
   a. behavior modification.
   b. counterconditioning.
   c. systematic desensitization.
   d. rational-emotive therapy.

8. Which of the following is *not* a common criticism of behavior therapy?
   a. Clients may not develop intrinsic motivation for their new behaviors.
   b. Behavior control is unethical.
   c. Although one symptom may be eliminated, another may replace it unless the underlying problem is treated.
   d. All of the above are criticisms of behavior therapy.

9. Which type of therapy focuses on eliminating irrational thinking?
   a. family therapy
   b. person-centered therapy
   c. rational-emotive therapy
   d. behavior therapy

10. Antidepressant drugs are believed to work by affecting one or more of all the following neurotransmitters *except*:
    a. dopamine.   c. norepinephrine.
    b. serotonin.   d. acetylcholine.

11. Which of the following is the drug most commonly used to treat the bipolar disorder?
    a. Valium   c. Librium
    b. serotonin   d. lithium

12. The most widely prescribed drugs in biomedical therapy are the:
    a. antianxiety drugs.   c. antidepressant drugs.
    b. antipsychotic drugs. d. amphetamines.

13. Neither Dr. Cunningham nor her patients knows whether the patients are in the experimental or the control group of an experiment testing the effects of a new antipsychotic drug. The researchers are using the _____ procedure.
    a. placebo   c. double-blind
    b. within subjects   d. single-blind

14. Although Moniz won the Nobel prize for developing the lobotomy procedure, the technique is not widely used today because:
    a. it produces a lethargic, immature personality.
    b. it is irreversible.
    c. calming drugs became available in the 1950s.
    d. of all the above reasons.

15. A statistical analysis of research studies comparing the effectiveness of professional therapists with paraprofessionals found that:

Matching Items

Match each term with the appropriate definition or description.

Terms

_____ 1. active listening
_____ 2. token economy
_____ 3. placebo effect
_____ 4. lobotomy
_____ 5. lithium
_____ 6. eclectic therapy
_____ 7. encounter group
_____ 8. double-blind procedure
_____ 9. Valium
_____ 10. free association

a. the professionals were much more effective than the paraprofessionals.
b. the paraprofessionals were much more effective than the professionals.
c. except in treating depression, the paraprofessionals were about as effective as the professionals.
d. the paraprofessionals were about as effective as the professionals.

16. Among the common ingredients of the psychotherapies is:
    a. the offer of a therapeutic relationship.
    b. the expectation among clients that the therapy will prove helpful.
    c. the chance to develop a fresh perspective on oneself and the world.
    d. all of these.

17. Of the following therapists, who would be most likely to interpret a person's psychological problems in terms of repressed impulses?
    a. a behavior therapist
    b. a cognitive therapist
    c. a humanistic therapist
    d. a psychoanalyst

18. One reason that aversive conditioning may only be temporarily effective is that:
    a. for ethical reasons, therapists cannot use sufficiently intense unconditioned stimuli to sustain classical conditioning.
    b. patients are often unable to become sufficiently relaxed for conditioning to take place.
    c. patients know that outside the therapist's office they can engage in the undesirable behavior without fear of aversive consequences.
    d. most conditioned responses are elicited by many nonspecific stimuli and it is impossible to countercondition them all.

Definitions

a. type of psychosurgery
b. therapy based on a blend of techniques
c. antidepressant drug
d. empathic technique based on person-centered therapy
e. the beneficial effect of a person's expecting that treatment will be effective
f. antianxiety drug
g. technique of psychoanalytic therapy
h. an operant conditioning procedure
i. a group therapy emphasizing the social sensitivity of participants
j. experimental procedure in which both the patient and staff are unaware of a patient's treatment condition

Key Terms

Using your own words, write a brief definition or explanation of each of the following terms.

1. psychotherapy

2. eclectic

3. psychoanalysis

4. resistance

5. interpretation

6. transference

7. person-centered therapy

8. active listening

9. encounter groups

10. family therapy

11. behavior therapy

12. counterconditioning

13. systematic desensitization

14. aversive conditioning

15. behavior modification

16. token economy

17. cognitive therapy

18. rational-emotive therapy

19. placebo effect

20. psychosurgery

21. lobotomy

22. electroconvulsive therapy (ECT)

23. double-blind procedure

24. lithium

Answers

CHAPTER REVIEW

1. psychological; biomedical
2. psychotherapy
3. eclectic
4. psychoanalytic; humanistic; behavioral; cognitive

Starting from the assumption that psychological problems are caused by repressed unconscious conflicts that develop during childhood, psychoanalysis aims to bring these feelings into conscious awareness and help the person work through them.

5. free association
6. resistance; interpretation
7. latent content
8. transference

Psychoanalysis has been criticized as being impossible to prove or disprove. Psychoanalysis is criticized for being a lengthy and expensive process that only the relatively well-off can afford. Finally, psychoanalysis has been criticized for rationalizing the oppression of women.

9. self-fulfillment

Unlike psychoanalysis, humanistic therapy is focused on the present instead of the past, on conscious rather than unconscious processes, on promoting growth and fulfillment instead of curing illness, and on helping clients take immediate responsibility for their feelings and actions rather than on uncovering the obstacles to doing so.

10. person-centered; does not interpret
11. genuineness; acceptance; empathy
12. active listening

Group therapy saves therapists time and clients money. The social context of group therapy allows people to discover that others have similar problems and to try out new ways of behaving.

13. sensitivity
14. encounter
15. family therapy

Whereas psychoanalysis and humanistic therapies assume that problems diminish as self-awareness grows, behavior therapists doubt that self-awareness is the key. Instead of looking for the inner cause of unwanted behavior, behavior therapy applies learning principles to directly attack the unwanted behavior itself.

16. classical conditioning; counterconditioning; systematic desensitization; aversive conditioning
17. Wolpe; anxious
18. hierarchy; relaxation; relaxed; anxiety
19. negative; positive; aversive
20. behavior modification; operant
21. token economy

Critics say that since behavior modification depends on extrinsic rewards, once the person leaves the conditioning environment, the appropriate behaviors may soon disappear. Second, critics question whether it is ethical for a therapist to exercise so much control over another's behavior.

22. specific

23. cognitive

24. rational-emotive; Ellis; depression

25. is not

26. satisfaction

People often enter therapy during times of crisis, so when the crisis passes, they may incorrectly attribute improvement to therapy. Clients may also exaggerate the effectiveness of therapy in order to self-justify the time and money they put into it. Finally, because clients generally like their therapists, they tend to view therapy favorably.

27. Eysenck; was not

28. somewhat effective

29. specific

30. no clear

31. behavioral conditioning; cognitive

First, psychotherapy enables people to believe that things can and will get better. Second, therapy offers people a plausible explanation of problems and alternative ways of responding. Third, therapy establishes an empathic, trusting relationship between client and therapist.

32. placebo effect

33. is

34. psychosurgery

35. lobotomy; frontal

36. drugs

37. electroconvulsive; ECT

38. depression; norepinephrine

39. drug

40. double-blind

41. antipsychotic; schizophrenia; dopamine

42. antianxiety; central nervous system

43. antidepressant; norepinephrine; serotonin

44. lithium

45. individual; environmental (or social)

PROGRESS TEST 1

Multiple-Choice Questions

1. **b.** is the answer. Although no one is sure how ECT works, one possible explanation is that it triggers an increased release of norepinephrine, the neurotransmitter that elevates mood. (p. 386)

2. **d.** is the answer. Resistances are blocks in the flow of free association that hint at underlying anxiety. (p. 367)

a. Transference is attribution by a patient of feelings from other relationships to his or her analyst.

b. The goal of psychoanalysis is for patients to gain insight into their feelings.

c. Although such hesitation may well involve material that has been repressed, the hesitation itself is a resistance.

3. **d.** is the answer. An important element of the psychoanalytic process, transference involves the patient's developing toward the therapist feelings that were experienced in important early relationships but repressed. (p. 367)

a. Projection is a defense mechanism in which a person imputes his or her own feelings onto someone else.

b. Resistances are blocks in the flow of free association that indicate repressed material.

c. Sublimation is a defense mechanism in which a person channels unacceptable impulses into socially desirable activities.

4. **d.** is the answer. This is not among the criticisms commonly made of psychoanalysis. (It would more likely be made of behavior therapies.) (p. 367)

5. **c.** is the answer. Statistical analysis of the relative effectiveness of different therapies reveals no clear winner; the other factors mentioned are advantages of group therapies. (pp. 370–371)

6. **a.** is the answer. The fact that its effects are irreversible makes psychosurgery a drastic procedure, and with advances in drug therapies, psychosurgery was largely abandoned. (p. 385)

b. ECT is still widely used as a treatment of major depression.

c. Drug therapy is the *most* widely used biomedical therapy.

d. Counterconditioning is not a biomedical therapy.

7. **b.** is the answer. Clients' testimonials regarding psychotherapy are generally very positive. The research, in contrast, seems to show that therapy is only *somewhat* effective. (pp. 381–383)

8. **d.** is the answer. (p. 382)

9. **a.** is the answer. By occupying receptor sites for dopamine, these drugs block its activity and reduce its production. (p. 387)

10. **d.** is the answer. (p. 389)

11. **d.** is the answer. Today, half of all psychotherapists describe themselves as eclectic—as using a blend of therapies. (p. 366)

a. An eclectic therapist may use a nondirective

approach with certain behaviors; however, a more directive approach might be chosen for other clients and problems.

b. In fact, just the opposite is true. Eclectic therapists generally view disorders as stemming from many influences.

c. Eclectic therapists, in contrast to this example, use a combination of treatments.

12. **d.** is the answer. According to Rogers' person-centered therapy, genuineness, acceptance, and empathy on the part of the therapist are crucial if the client is to move toward self-fulfillment. (pp. 369–370)

a. Psychoanalysts are much more directive in providing interpretations of clients' problems than are humanistic therapists.

b. & c. Behavior therapists as well as those using the classical conditioning technique of counterconditioning, focus on modifying the behavior symptoms of psychological problems.

13. **d.** is the answer. Aversive conditioning is the classical conditioning technique in which a positive response is replaced by a negative response. (In this example, the UCS is the hot blast of smoke, the CS is the taste of the cigarette as it is inhaled, and the intended CR is aversion to cigarettes.) (p. 374)

a. Rational-emotive therapy is a confrontational cognitive therapy.

b. Behavior modification applies the principles of operant conditioning and thus, in contrast to the example, uses reinforcements.

c. Systematic desensitization is used to help people overcome specific anxieties.

14. **c.** is the answer. (p. 375)

a. & b. Counterconditioning is the replacement of an undesired response with a desired one by means of aversive conditioning or systematic desensitization.

d. Rational-emotive therapy is a cognitive approach that challenges people's self-defeating attitudes.

15. **d.** is answer. Because the psychologist is challenging Darnel's illogical, self-defeating attitude, this response is most typical of rational-emotive therapy. (pp. 376–377)

a. Biomedical therapists view troubled behavior as biologically rooted and therefore use therapies that alter the functioning of the nervous system.

b. Psychoanalysts focus on helping patients gain self-insight into previously repressed feelings.

c. Person-centered therapists attempt to facilitate clients' growth by offering a genuine, accepting, empathic environment.

16. **b.** is the answer. (p. 384)

a. A feature of Carl Rogers' therapy, active listening is an empathic technique in which the therapist echoes, restates, and clarifies clients' statements.

c. Transference is the psychoanalytic phenomenon in which a client transfers feelings from other relationships onto his or her analyst.

d. Interpretation is the psychoanalytic procedure through which the analyst helps the client become aware of resistances and understand their meaning.

17. **b.** is the answer. Psychiatrists are physicians who specialize in treating psychological disorders. As doctors they can prescribe medications. (p. 366)

a., c., & d. These professionals cannot prescribe drugs.

Matching Items

1. e (p. 376)	**5.** f (p. 369)	**8.** c (p. 371)
2. j (pp. 372–375)	**6.** a (p. 374)	**9.** h (p. 385)
3. b (p. 372)	**7.** g (p. 366)	**10.** i (p. 372)
4. d (p. 376)		

PROGRESS TEST 2

Multiple-Choice Questions

1. **c.** is the answer. (p. 369)

a. This answer would be a correct description of J. Wolpe.

b. There is no such thing as insight therapy.

d. This answer would be a correct description of A. Ellis.

2. **a.** is the answer. (p. 374)

b. In desensitization the client's relaxed state is associated with a hierarchy of anxiety-provoking stimuli.

c. Transference refers to a patient's transferring of feelings from other relationships onto his or her psychoanalyst.

d. Electroconvulsive therapy is a biomedical shock treatment.

3. **c.** is the answer. (p. 368)

a. Behavior therapy focuses on behavior, not self-awareness.

b. Psychoanalysis focuses on bringing repressed feelings into awareness.

d. Biomedical therapy focuses on physical treatment through drugs, ECT, or psychosurgery.

4. a. is the answer. For behavior therapy, the symptoms themselves are the problems. (p. 372)

b. Cognitive therapy teaches people to think and act in more adaptive ways.

c. Humanistic therapy promotes growth and self-fulfillment by providing an empathic, genuine, and accepting environment.

d. Psychoanalytic therapy focuses on uncovering and interpreting repressed feelings.

5. b. is the answer. In counterconditioning an established CS, which triggers an undesirable CR, is paired with a new UCS in order to condition a new, and more adaptive, CR. (p. 372)

a. As indicated by its name, counterconditioning is a form of conditioning; it does not involve learning by observation.

c. & d. The principles of operant conditioning are the basis of behavior modification, which in contrast to counterconditioning, involves use of reinforcements.

6. d. is the answer. (p. 372)

a. This is a confrontational therapy aimed at teaching people to think and act in more adaptive ways.

b. Cognitive therapies emphasize changing clients' self-defeating attitudes and assumptions.

c. Counterconditioning is a general term, including not only systematic desensitization, in which a hierarchy of fears is desensitized, but also other techniques, such as aversive conditioning.

7. a. is the answer. (p. 375)

b. & c. These techniques are based on classical conditioning.

d. This is a type of cognitive therapy.

8. d. is the answer. (pp. 372–375)

9. c. is the answer. (p. 376)

a. Whereas cognitive therapies, such as rational-emotive therapy, focus on irrational thought patterns, group therapies such as family therapy are more concerned with the social environment of the client.

b. In this humanistic therapy, the therapist facilitates a client's growth by offering a genuine, accepting, and empathic environment.

d. Behavior therapy concentrates on modifying the actual symptoms of psychological problems.

10. d. is the answer. (p. 388)

11. d. is the answer. Lithium works as a mood stabilizer. (p. 388)

a. & c. Valium and Librium are antianxiety drugs.

b. Serotonin is a neurotransmitter whose availability is increased by the use of antidepressant drugs.

12. a. is the answer. Antianxiety drugs are among the most heavily prescribed of all drugs. (p. 388)

13. c. is the answer. (p. 387)

a. There is no such procedure.

b. In this design there is only a single research group. Since the experiment is using both an experimental group and a control group, this answer is incorrect.

d. This answer would be correct if the experimenter but not the subjects knew which condition was in effect.

14. d. is the answer. (p. 385)

15. d. is the answer. Even when dealing with seriously depressed adults, the paraprofessionals were as effective as the professionals. (p. 384)

16. d. is the answer. (p. 387)

17. d. is the answer. A key aim of psychoanalysis is to unearth and understand repressed impulses. (p. 366)

a. & c. Behavior and humanistic therapists focus on the present rather than the past.

a. & b. Behavior and cognitive therapists avoid concepts such as *repression* and *unconscious*.

18. c. is the answer. Although aversive conditioning may work in the short run, the person's ability to discriminate between the situation in which the aversive conditioning occurs and other situations can limit the treatment's effectiveness. (p. 374)

a., b., & d. These were not offered in the textbook as limitations of the effectiveness of aversive conditioning.

Matching Items

1. d (p. 369)   **5.** c (p. 388)   **8.** j (p. 387)
2. h (p. 375)   **6.** b (p. 366)   **9.** f (p. 388)
3. e (p. 384)   **7.** i (p. 370)   **10.** g (p. 366)
4. a (p. 385)

KEY TERMS

1. Psychotherapy is the psychological treatment of mental and emotional problems, based on the interaction between therapist and client. (p. 366)

Example: Four major **psychotherapies** are the psychoanalytic, humanistic, behavior, and cognitive therapies.

2. Eclectic psychotherapists are not locked into one form of psychotherapy, but draw on whatever combination seems best suited to a client's needs. (p. 366)

Example: The **eclectic** approach in psychotherapy is much more common today than in the past, when therapists were more likely to practice only one approach.

3. **Psychoanalysis**, the therapy developed by Freud, attempts to give clients self-insight by bringing into awareness and interpreting previously repressed feelings. (p. 366)

Example: The tools of the **psychoanalyst** include free association, the analysis of dreams, and the interpretation of repressed impulses.

4. **Resistance** is the psychoanalytic term for the blocking from consciousness of anxiety-provoking memories. Hesitation during free association may reflect resistance. (p. 367)

5. **Interpretation** is the psychoanalytic term for the analyst's helping the client to understand resistances and other aspects of behavior, so that the client may gain deeper insights. (p. 367)

6. **Transference** is the psychoanalytic term for a patient's attributing to the analyst emotions from other relationships. (p. 367)

Example: Perhaps the best example of **transference** in psychoanalysis is when patients transfer long-repressed feelings about their parents to the analyst.

7. **Person-centered therapy** is a humanistic therapy developed by Rogers, in which growth and self-awareness are facilitated in an environment that offers genuineness, acceptance, and empathy. (p. 369)

8. **Active listening** is a nondirective technique of person-centered therapy, in which the listener echoes, restates, clarifies, but does not interpret, clients' remarks. (p. 369)

9. **Encounter groups** provide a form of group therapy in which people discuss problems and feelings in a very open way; as a result, exchanges are often characterized by strong emotions and even confrontations. (p. 370)

10. **Family therapy** views problem behavior as partially engendered by the client's family system and environment. Therapy therefore focuses on relationships and problems among the various members of the family. (p. 371)

Example: A school psychologist who felt that a student's behavioral problems in the classroom reflected difficulties in the home environment might recommend counseling with a **family therapist**.

11. **Behavior therapy** is therapy that applies principles of operant or classical conditioning to the treatment of problem behaviors. (pp. 372–375)

Example: One criticism of **behavior therapy** is that it treats only the symptoms, rather than the causes, of problems. Critics fear that such treatment may merely result in the substitution of one symptom of the problem for another.

12. **Counterconditioning** is a technique of behavior therapy in which new responses are classically conditioned to stimuli that elicit unwanted behaviors. (p. 372)

13. **Systematic desensitization** is a type of counterconditioning in which a state of relaxation is classically conditioned to a hierarchy of anxiety-provoking stimuli. (p. 372)

Memory aid: This is a form of counterconditioning in which sensitive, anxiety-triggering stimuli are desensitized in a progressive, or *systematic*, fashion.

14. **Aversive conditioning** is a form of counterconditioning in which an unpleasant response becomes conditioned to an unwanted behavior. (p. 374)

Example: **Aversive conditioning** has been tried with limited success for treating alcoholism, smoking, and certain sexual deviations.

15. **Behavior modification** refers to any technique of psychotherapy that is based on operant conditioning. Thus, behavior modification typically involves shaping behavior by giving and withholding rewards. (p. 375)

16. A **token economy** is a situation in which desirable behaviors are promoted in people by rewarding them with tokens, or secondary reinforcers, which can be exchanged for privileges or treats. For the most part, token economies are used in hospitals, schools, and other institutional settings. (p. 375)

17. **Cognitive therapy** focuses on teaching people new and more adaptive ways of thinking and acting. The therapy is based on the idea that our feelings and responses to events are strongly influenced by our thinking, or cognition. (pp. 376–379)

18. **Rational-emotive therapy** is a confrontational therapy that maintains that irrational thinking is the cause of many psychological problems. (p. 376)

19. The **placebo effect** refers to the beneficial effect of a person's belief that a treatment will be helpful. (p. 384)

20. **Psychosurgery** is a biomedical therapy that attempts to change behavior by removing or destroying brain tissue. Since drug therapy became widely available in the 1950s, psychosurgery has been infrequently used. (p. 385)

21. Once used to control violent patients, the **lobotomy** is a form of psychosurgery in which the

nerves linking the emotion centers of the brain to the frontal lobes are severed. (p. 385)

22. In **electroconvulsive therapy (ECT)**, a biomedical therapy often used to treat major depression, electric shock is passed through the brain. ECT may work by increasing the availability of norepinephrine, the neurotransmitter that elevates mood. (p. 386)

23. The **double-blind procedure** is a technique of experimentation, often used in drug evaluation studies, in which neither the patient nor the hospital staff knows which treatment the patient is receiving. In this way, the biases that could come from staff and subject expectancies are avoided. (p. 387)

24. **Lithium** is an antidepressant drug that is commonly used to stabilize the manic-depressive mood swings of the bipolar disorder. (p. 388)

Chapter 14 | Stress and Health

Chapter Overview

Behavioral factors play a major role in maintaining health and causing illness. The effort to understand this role more fully has led to the emergence of the interdisciplinary field of *behavioral medicine*. The field is notable for its "systems theory" perspective: illness is assumed to result, not from a single cause, but from the interactions of various systems. The subfield of health psychology focuses on systems within the domain of psychology.

Chapter 14 addresses key topics in health psychology. First and foremost is stress—its nature and its effects on the body. Second, the chapter examines stress management through exercise, relaxation, social support, and biofeedback. The chapter concludes by looking at ways of modifying illness-related behaviors, including smoking, nutrition, and obesity.

Guided Study

The textbook chapter should be studied one section at a time. Before you read, preview each section by skimming it, noting headings and boldface items. Then read the appropriate section objectives from the following outline. Keep these objectives in mind, and as you read the chapter section, search for the information that will enable you to meet each objective. Once you have finished a section, write out answers for its objectives.

1. Explain the "systems theory" perspective of behavioral medicine and identify the major concerns of health psychology.

Stress and Illness (pp. 394–405)

2. Describe the body's response to stress and discuss research findings on the health consequences of stressful life events.

3. Discuss the factors that influence our vulnerability to stress.

4. Discuss the role of stress in coronary heart disease and contrast Type A and Type B personalities.

5. Describe how stress affects the body's immune system.

6. Discuss the role of stress in cancer and whether the immune system can be conditioned.

Promoting Health (pp. 406–422)

7. Identify and discuss different strategies for coping with stress.

8. Explain why people smoke and discuss ways of preventing and reducing this health hazard.

9. Discuss the relationship between nutrition and physical well-being and describe the research findings on obesity and weight control.

Chapter Review

When you have finished reading the chapter, use the material that follows to review it. Complete the fill-in sentences and answer the essay items in complete sentences. As you proceed, evaluate your performance for each chapter section by consulting the answer key at the end of this chapter. Do not continue with the next section until you've understood each answer. If you need to, review or reread the appropriate chapter section in the textbook before continuing.

1. Today, half the mortality from the ten leading causes of death can be traced to people's _____.

2. The four leading causes of serious illness and death in the United States are _____, _____, _____, and _____.

3. List several of the behaviors that have been linked to the leading causes of death. _____ _____

4. The new field that integrates psychological and medical knowledge relevant to health and disease is _____ _____.

Explain the "systems theory" of illness and how it differs from the traditional medical view.

5. The subfield of psychology related to behavioral medicine is called _____ psychology.

Stress and Illness (pp. 394–405)

6. The process by which we perceive environmental events as threatening or challenging and respond accordingly is called _____.

7. In the 1920s, physiologist Walter _____ began studying the effect of stress on the body. He discovered that the hormones _____ and _____ are released into the bloodstream in response to stress. This and other bodily changes to stress are mediated by the _____ nervous system.

8. More recently, physiologists have discovered that stress also triggers release of the hormone _____.

9. In studying animals' reactions to stressors, Selye repeatedly found similar physiological effects which he labelled the _____ _____.

10. During the first phase of the GAS—the
_____ reaction—the person is
in a state of shock due to the sudden arousal of
the _____ nervous system.

11. This is followed by the stage of
_____, in which the body's
resources are mobilized to cope with the stressor.

12. If stress continues, the person enters the stage of
_____. During this stage a
person is _____ (more/less)
vulnerable to disease.

13. In one study of catastrophic events, it was found
that following the eruption of Mount Saint
Helens there was an increase in the number of
_____
_____.

14. Research studies have found that people who
have recently been widowed, fired, or divorced
are _____ (more/no more)
vulnerable to illness than other people.

15. One source of everyday stress is being pulled by
two attractive but incompatible goals; this is the
_____-_____
conflict. Being forced to choose between two
undesirable alternatives is an example of an
_____-_____
conflict. When one is both attracted and repelled
by the same goal the _____-
_____ conflict is operating.

16. People are more likely to suffer ill health if they
perceive a loss of _____ over
their lives. People who have an
_____ attitude are *less* likely
than others to suffer ill health.

17. In animals and humans, sudden lack of control
is followed by a drop in immune responses and a
rise in the levels of _____
_____.

18. The leading cause of death in North America is
_____ _____
_____. List several risk factors
for developing this condition. _____
_____

19. Taken together, these factors _____
(account/do not account) for most instances of
heart disease.

20. Friedman and Rosenman discovered that tax
accountants experience an increase in blood
_____ level and blood-
_____ speed during tax season.

Friedman and Rosenman's subsequent study grouped
people into Type A and Type B personalities. Characterize these types and indicate the difference that
emerged between them over the course of this 9-year
study.

21. Recent research _____ (has/
has not) consistently shown that Type A
behaviors lead to heart attacks. The Type A
characteristic that is most strongly linked with
coronary heart disease is _____.

22. When a person is angered, blood flow is diverted
away from the internal organs, including the
liver, which is responsible for removing
_____ and fat from the blood.
This finding may explain why _____
(Type A/Type B) persons have elevated levels of
these substances in the blood.

23. In _____ illnesses, physical
symptoms are not associated with any known
_____ disorder, but appear to
be linked to _____. Examples
of such illnesses are certain forms of
_____, _____,
and _____.

24. The body's system of fighting disease is the
_____ system. This system
includes two types of white blood cells: the
_____ _____,
which fight bacterial infections, and the
_____ _____,
which, for example, attack foreign substances.

25. When stress increases the levels of epinephrine, norepinephrine, and cortisol, there is a(n) _____ (increase/decrease) in the number of lymphocyte cells. This results in a(n) _____ (increase/decrease) in disease resistance.

Characterize the link between stress and cancer.

26. Experiments by Ader and Cohen demonstrate that the functioning of the body's immune system _____ (can/cannot) be affected by conditioning.

Promoting Health (pp. 406–422)

27. Sustained exercise that increases heart and lung fitness is known as _____ exercise. Experiments _____ (have/have not) been able to demonstrate conclusively that such exercise reduces stress, anxiety, and depression.

28. A system for recording a physiological response and providing information concerning it is called _____. The instruments used in this system _____ (provide/do not provide) the individual with a means of controlling physiological responses.

29. Lowered blood pressure and strengthened immune defenses have been found to be characteristic of people who regularly practice _____.

30. Meyer Friedman found that modifying Type A behavior in a group of heart attack survivors _____ (reduced/did not significantly reduce) the rate of recurrence of heart attacks.

31. Researchers have found that life events may be less stressful for people who have a good sense of _____.

32. Another buffer against the effects of stress is _____ support.

33. Combat veterans and victims of sexual assault may suffer haunting memories, social withdrawal, anxiety or depression, and other symptoms of _____ _____ _____.

Summarize the potential effects of stress and the factors that explain why some people are better able than others to cope with stress.

34. Advocates of behavioral medicine believe that creating programs to _____ disease by promoting healthy life-styles will result in lower health-care costs than will focusing only on _____ existing diseases.

35. Thirty percent of cancer and heart disease deaths in the United States are linked to _____.

Explain when and why, according to social-cognitive theory, people start smoking.

36. Why people continue to smoke seems to have less to do with _____ (social/physiological) factors than with _____ (social/physiological) factors.

37. By terminating an aversive state, smoking provides a person with a powerful _____ reinforcer. In addition, nicotine triggers the release of epinephrine and norepinephrine, which increase _____, and of

neurotransmitters that reduce _____.
For these reasons, most programs to help
people quit smoking _____
(are/are not) very effective in the long run.

38. A study found that junior high students who
were taught to cope with peer pressure and
advertisements for smoking were
_____ (more/less) likely to
begin smoking than were students in a control
group.

39. Certain foods may affect mood and behavior by
influencing the formation of specific
_____.

40. A relaxed state may be facilitated by eating
certain _____, which increase
the amount of tryptophan that the brain receives
and can thus be used for synthesizing the
neurotransmitter _____.
Concentration and alertness, in contrast, may be
improved by meals that are low in
_____ but have a high
_____ content.

41. People with high blood pressure tend to have a
higher-than-normal intake of _____
but a lower-than-normal intake of
_____. Certain forms of cancer
have been linked with diets that are high in
_____.

42. A person is said to be obese when he or she is
_____ percent or more
overweight.

Cite some of the ways in which obesity is a threat to
physical and psychological health.

43. The energy equivalent of a pound of fat is
approximately _____ calories.
The immediate determinant of body fat is the
size and number of _____

_____ one has. This number
is, in turn, determined by several factors,
including _____.

44. The size of fat cells _____
(can/cannot) be decreased by dieting; the
number of fat cells _____
(can/cannot) be decreased by dieting.

45. Fat tissue has a _____ (higher/
lower) metabolic rate than lean tissue. The result
is that fat tissue requires _____
(more/less) food energy to maintain.

46. Obese persons who are dieting tend to be more
responsive than others to external food cues and,
as a result, may secrete more _____,
which triggers hunger.

Explain why, metabolically, many obese people find it
so difficult to become and stay thin.

Explain whether heredity plays no role, some role, or
an exclusive role in causing obesity, and cite evidence
to support your answer.

47. Most obese persons who lose weight
_____ (gain/do not gain) it
back.

FOCUS ON PSYCHOLOGY:
Job-related Stress: Who's in Charge Here?

It's almost a cliché: If you are an ambitious manager,
chief executive officer, or professional, you are a prime
candidate for heart disease. The psychological stresses
of decision making and being "in charge" presumably
cause this dismal prognosis. A recent public health
study contradicts this widespread belief by demonstrating that employees nearer to the *bottom* of the

corporate ladder may be under even greater psychological stress than those at the top.

Industrial sociologist Robert Karasek and his colleagues evaluated the nature of the jobs held by more than 4,800 male heart attack victims. The jobs were scored according to several criteria, including how physically and psychologically demanding they were and the degree of decision-making power exerted by the workers who held them. Surprisingly, the researchers found that most of the heart attack victims had not been employed in managerial positions or professional occupations; rather, they tended to be assembly-line workers, cooks, waiters, and laborers, for example. In fact, the rate of heart attacks among employees in such occupations was nearly three times that of those employed in managerial jobs.

According to the researchers, the stress of lower-echelon jobs is more than merely physical: "Job demands are potential sources of stress," they explain, "but how much freedom a worker has in deciding how to meet those demands will determine if they actually produce stress." Clearly, there are significant differences in the level of job control exerted by workers at the top and those at the bottom. Science writer Valerie Adler notes that in comparison to professionals such as doctors and lawyers, who have control over almost everything they do, low-status workers typically have little or no control over their work methods, schedules, or co-workers. This lack of control is a major factor in creating stress, and thus heart disease.

Although there have been fewer studies on the relationship between job stress and heart disease in women, Adler notes that the available evidence supports the low-control, high-stress hypothesis. The ongoing Framingham Heart Study, for example, has found that women having low-control clerical jobs have twice the incidence of heart disease as compared with women whose jobs give them substantial personal control.

The results of these studies are consistent with the textbook discussion of the relationship between perceived control and stress. People who perceive that they have little control over their lives tend to suffer greater health problems. Even among laboratory rats, "subordinate" rats that receive uncontrollable electric shocks are more likely to develop ulcers than "executives" that control whether they, and the subordinates, are shocked.

These findings paint a rather bleak picture for workers who have little control over their jobs. There is hope, however. To reduce job-related stress, workers should try to become involved in whatever ways they can. For example, by discussing work conditions and procedures with management and other workers, they will increase their feelings of involvement and control

—and this might even produce improved work conditions. The perception of control alone, even if not completely accurate, may help workers cope with the stresses of low-control jobs.

Sources: Adler, V. (1989, April). Little control = lots of stress. *Psychology Today*, 18–19.

Karsek, R., Theorell, T., Schwartz, J. E., Schnall, P. L., Pieper, C. F., & Michela, J. L. (1988, August). Job characteristics in relation to the prevalence of myocardial infarction in the US health examination survey and the health and nutrition examination survey. *American Journal of Public Health*, 78, 910–918.

Progress Test 1

Circle your answers to the following questions and check them with the answer key at the end of this chapter. If your answer is incorrect, read the answer key explanation for why it is incorrect and then consult the appropriate pages of the text to understand the correct answer.

1. Behavioral and medical knowledge about factors influencing health form the basis of the field of:
   a. health psychology.
   b. holistic medicine.
   c. behavioral medicine.
   d. osteopathic medicine.

2. The stress hormones epinephrine and norepinephrine are released by the _____ gland, in response to stimulation by the _____ branch of the nervous system.
   a. pituitary; sympathetic
   b. pituitary; parasympathetic
   c. adrenal; sympathetic
   d. adrenal; parasympathetic

3. During which stage of the general adaptation syndrome is a person especially vulnerable to disease?
   a. alarm reaction
   b. stage of resistance
   c. stage of exhaustion
   d. stage of adaptation

4. The leading cause of death in North America is:
   a. lung cancer.
   b. AIDS.
   c. coronary heart disease.
   d. alcohol-related accidents.

5. Researchers Friedman and Rosenman refer to individuals who are very time-conscious, supermotivated, verbally aggressive, and easily angered as:
   a. ulcer-prone personalities.
   b. cancer-prone personalities.
   c. Type A.
   d. Type B.

6. Genuine illnesses that are caused by stress are called _____ illnesses.
   a. psychophysiological
   b. hypochondriacal
   c. psychogenic
   d. psychotropic

7. Stress has been demonstrated to place a person at increased risk of:
   a. cancer.
   b. tuberculosis.
   c. viral infections.
   d. all of the above.

8. Which of the following is *not* necessarily a reason obese people have trouble losing weight?
   a. Fat tissue has a lower metabolic rate than lean tissue.
   b. Obese people are more responsive to external cues.
   c. Obese people have a stronger insulin reaction to external cues.
   d. Obese people tend to lack willpower.

9. In one experiment, both "executive" rats and "subordinate" rats received identical electric shocks, the only difference being whether the shocks could be _____. The results showed that _____ rats were most likely to develop ulcers.
   a. predicted; subordinate
   b. predicted; executive
   c. controlled; executive
   d. controlled; subordinate

10. Studies have demonstrated that meals that are high in _____ promote relaxation because they raise levels of _____.
    a. carbohydrates; serotonin
    b. carbohydrates; cortisol
    c. protein; serotonin
    d. protein; cortisol

11. A study in which people were asked to confide troubling feelings to an experimenter found that subjects typically:
    a. were not truthful in reporting feelings and events.
    b. experienced a sustained increase in blood pressure until the experiment was finished.
    c. became physiologically more relaxed after confiding their problem.
    d. denied having any problems.

12. Research suggests that _____ influences often lead a person to start smoking, while _____ influences are more important in explaining why people continue to smoke.
    a. biological; social
    b. social; biological
    c. biological; cognitive
    d. cognitive; biological

13. After an initial rapid weight loss, a person on a diet loses weight much more slowly. This slowdown occurs because:
    a. most of the initial weight loss is simply water.
    b. when a person diets, metabolism decreases.
    c. people begin to "cheat" on their diets.
    d. insulin levels tend to increase with reduced food intake.

14. Which of the following was *not* mentioned in the text as a potential health benefit of exercise?
    a. Exercise can increase ability to cope with stress.
    b. Exercise can lower blood pressure.
    c. Exercise can reduce depression and anxiety.
    d. Exercise improves functioning of the immune system.

15. The "systems theory" perspective emphasizes:
    a. social factors in health and illness.
    b. psychological factors in health and illness.
    c. biological factors in health and illness.
    d. the interaction of social, psychological, and biological factors in health and illness.

Matching Items

Match each term with the appropriate definition or description.

Terms

_____ 1. aerobic exercise
_____ 2. coronary heart disease
_____ 3. stress
_____ 4. lymphocytes
_____ 5. psychophysiological illness
_____ 6. behavioral medicine
_____ 7. general adaptation syndrome
_____ 8. Type A
_____ 9. Type B
_____ 10. biofeedback
_____ 11. health psychology

Definitions

a. disease- and infection-fighting cells of the immune system
b. interdisciplinary field that treats disease and promotes health
c. process by which people appraise and respond to challenging events
d. anger- and coronary-disease-prone personality
e. easygoing, relaxed personality
f. sustained exercise that increases heart and lung fitness
g. electronic system for recording heart rate, blood pressure, or muscle tension
h. stages of bodily adaptation to stress
i. "mind-body" disorder often linked with stress
j. leading cause of death in the United States
k. field concerned with how health and illness are influenced by emotions, stress, personality, and life-style

Progress Test 2

Progress Test 2 should be completed during a final chapter review. Do so after you thoroughly understand the correct answers for the Chapter Review and Progress Test 1.

1. The field of health psychology is concerned with:
   a. the prevention of illness.
   b. the promotion of health.
   c. the effects of stress.
   d. all of the above.

2. In order, the sequence of stages in the general adaptation syndrome is:
   a. alarm reaction, stage of resistance, stage of exhaustion.
   b. stage of resistance, alarm reaction, stage of exhaustion.
   c. stage of exhaustion, stage of resistance, alarm reaction.
   d. alarm reaction, stage of exhaustion, stage of resistance.

3. Researchers have found that individuals who suppress their anger are especially prone to:
   a. ulcers.   c. stroke.
   b. hypertension.   d. cancer.

4. Virginia can't decide whether to spend winter break on a Caribbean cruise or skiing with her friends. Virginia's dilemma is an example of:
   a. an approach-approach conflict.
   b. an approach-avoidance conflict.
   c. an avoidance-avoidance conflict.
   d. none of the above.

5. According to the textbook, one-half of all deaths from the ten leading causes of death in the United States can be attributed to:
   a. stress.   c. nutrition.
   b. obesity.   d. behavior.

6. The disease- and infection-fighting cells of the immune system are:
   a. B lymphocytes.   c. both a. and b.
   b. T lymphocytes.   d. antigens.

7. One effect of stress on the body is to:
   a. suppress the immune system.
   b. facilitate the immune system response.
   c. increase disease resistance.
   d. increase the proliferation of B and T lymphocytes.

8. According to the textbook, the single most beneficial change in a person's behavior, from the point of view of health, would be:
   a. to stop abusing alcohol and drugs.
   b. to begin a daily vigorous exercise regime.
   c. to go on a diet that is low in fat intake and high in fiber intake.
   d. to stop smoking.

9. In response to uncontrollable shock, levels of stress hormones _____ and immune responses are _____.
   a. decrease; suppressed   c. decrease; increased
   b. increase; suppressed   d. increase; increased

10. Ricardo has an important psychology exam in the afternoon. In an effort to improve his concentra-

tion and alertness, Ricardo orders a lunch that is high in _____ and low in

_____.

    a. carbohydrates; protein
    b. carbohydrates; fat
    c. protein; carbohydrates
    d. protein; fat

11. The component of Type A behavior that is the most predictive of coronary disease is:
    a. time urgency.   **c.** high motivation.
    b. competitiveness.   **d.** anger.

12. Which of the following is true concerning smoking treatment programs?
    a. Most are effective in the long run.
    b. Hypnosis is more effective than behavior modification.
    c. Treatment programs are more effective with women than with men.
    d. Most participants eventually resume smoking.

13. During biofeedback training:
    a. a subject is given sensory feedback for a subtle bodily response.
    b. biological functions controlled by the autonomic nervous system may come under conscious control.
    c. the accompanying relaxation is much the same as that produced by other, simpler methods of relaxation.
    d. all of the above occur.

14. Research on obesity indicates that:
    a. pound for pound, fat tissue requires more calories to maintain than lean tissue.
    b. once fat cells are acquired they are never lost, no matter how severely one diets.
    c. one pound of weight is lost for every 3500-calorie reduction in diet.
    d. compared to normal-weight persons, those who are obese secrete less insulin (which suppresses appetite) in response to external food cues.

15. Relaxation is the most effective technique for preventing:
    a. alcoholism.
    b. a stressful environment.
    c. smoking.
    d. a repeat heart attack.

16. Which of the following was offered in the textbook as a reason people continue to smoke?
    a. Social pressure from peers is strong.
    b. Cigarettes provide powerful negative reinforcers.
    c. Regular use of nicotine impairs the brain's ability to produce neurotransmitters such as serotonin.

    d. Most adults who smoke don't really want to quit.

True-False Items

Indicate whether each statement is true or false by placing *T* or *F* in the blank next to the item.

_____ 1. Most obese people who lose weight eventually gain it back.

_____ 2. Stressors tend to increase activity in the immune system and in this way make people more vulnerable to illness.

_____ 3. Diet has not been linked to cancer.

_____ 4. Optimists generally are healthier than pessimists.

_____ 5. The single most important factor in causing obesity is heredity.

_____ 6. An approach-avoidance conflict occurs when a person is both attracted and repelled by the same goal.

_____ 7. "Executive" rats that can control shock are more likely to develop ulcers than "subordinate" rats that cannot.

_____ 8. Type A persons tend to have excess cholesterol and fat in their bloodstream.

_____ 9. Chronic stress can lead to ulcers, headaches, and hypertension.

_____ 10. People with few social and community ties are more likely to die prematurely than are those with many social ties.

Key Terms

Using your own words, write a brief definition or explanation of each of the following terms.

1. behavioral medicine

2. health psychology

3. stress

4. general adaptation syndrome (GAS)

5. coronary heart disease

6. Type A

7. Type B

8. psychophysiological illnesses

9. lymphocytes

10. aerobic exercise

11. biofeedback

12. obesity

Answers
CHAPTER REVIEW

1. behavior
2. heart disease; cancer; stroke; accidents
3. cigarette smoking, alcohol abuse, maladaptive responses to stress, insufficient exercise, use of illicit drugs, poor nutrition
4. behavioral medicine

Behavioral medicine's "systems theory" maintains that illness results from the interaction of biological, psychological, and social systems within which a person exists. This contrasts with traditional efforts to link specific diseases to single causes, such as genes, germs, or emotions.

5. health
6. stress
7. Cannon; epinephrine, or adrenaline; norepinephrine, or noradrenaline; sympathetic
8. cortisol
9. general adaptation syndrome (GAS)
10. alarm; sympathetic
11. resistance
12. exhaustion; more
13. emergency room visits, deaths, stress-related health complaints
14. more
15. approach-approach; avoidance-avoidance; approach-avoidance
16. control; optimistic
17. stress hormones
18. coronary heart disease; smoking, obesity, family history, high fat diet, physical inactivity, elevated blood pressure and cholesterol
19. do not account
20. cholesterol; clotting

Type A people were competitive, hard-driving, supermotivated, impatient, verbally aggressive, and easily angered. Type B people were more relaxed and easygoing. Heart attack victims over the course of the study came overwhelmingly from the Type A group.

21. has not; the tendency to become angry (or negative emotions, or an aggressively reactive temperament)
22. cholesterol; Type A
23. psychophysiological; physical; stress; hypertension; ulcers; headaches
24. immune; B lymphocytes; T lymphocytes
25. decrease; decrease

Stress can affect the spread of cancer by weakening the body's defenses against malignant cells. When rodents were inoculated with tumor cells, tumors developed sooner in those that were also exposed to uncontrollable stress. Stress does not cause cancer, however; nor can relaxation prevent it.

26. can

27. aerobic; have

28. biofeedback; do not provide

29. relaxation

30. reduced

31. humor

32. social

33. posttraumatic stress disorder

Stressful events are potentially debilitating. Stress may contribute to heart disease and to a variety of psychophysiological illnesses. It can also weaken the immune system, making the person more vulnerable to disease. Since the effects of stress depend largely on one's response, personality differences are a major factor in differential ability to cope with stress. Furthermore, the negative impacts of stress can be buffered by a healthy life-style and by the social support of friends and family, or increased where these factors are lacking.

34. prevent; treating

35. smoking

Those who smoke usually begin during adolescence if their friends, parents, and siblings are smokers. Because adolescent smokers tend to be perceived by other teenagers as tough and sociable, self-conscious adolescents may begin to emulate these models in order to receive the social rewards of peer acceptance.

36. social; physiological

37. negative; alertness; anxiety and sensitivity to pain; are not

38. less

39. neurotransmitters

40. carbohydrates; serotonin; carbohydrates; protein

41. salt; calcium; fat

42. 20

Obesity increases one's risk of diabetes, high blood pressure and heart disease, gallstones, arthritis, and certain types of cancer. It negatively affects self-image and the perceptions of others, particularly if the excess weight is seen as the fault of the individual.

43. 3500; fat cells; genetic predisposition, early childhood eating patterns, and adult overeating

44. can; cannot

45. lower; less

46. insulin

Obese persons have higher set-point weights than nonobese persons. During a diet, metabolic rate drops to defend the set-point weight. The dieter therefore finds it hard to progress beyond an initial weight loss. When the diet is concluded, the lowered metabolic rate continues, so that relatively small amounts of food may prove fattening. Also, some people have lower metabolic rates than others.

Heredity plays some role, but not an exclusive role, in determining obesity. Adoption and twin studies both provide evidence for the role of heredity. Yet the weight resemblance between identical twins is less in females than males, suggesting that social pressure can also play a role. Moreover, heredity cannot explain the fact that obesity is much more common in lower-class than upper-class women, more common among Americans than Japanese or Europeans, and more common today than at the beginning of the century.

47. gain

PROGRESS TEST 1

Multiple-Choice Questions

1. **c.** is the answer. (p. 393)

   a. Health psychology is a subfield within behavioral medicine.

   b. Holistic medicine is an older term that refers to medical practitioners who take more of an interdisciplinary approach to treating disorders.

   d. Osteopathy is a medical therapy that emphasizes manipulative techniques for correcting physical problems.

2. **c.** is the answer. (p. 395)

   a. The pituitary does not produce stress hormones.

   b. The pituitary does not produce stress hormones nor is the parasympathetic division involved in arousal.

   d. The parasympathetic nervous system is the calming, rather than the arousing, division of the autonomic system.

3. **c.** is the answer. The body's continued resistance to a stressor may eventually lead to exhaustion and increased vulnerability. (p. 396)

   a. & b. During these stages the body's defensive mechanisms are at peak function.

   d. This is not a stage of the GAS.

4. **c.** is the answer. Coronary heart disease is the leading cause of death in North America; it is followed by (all) cancer, stroke, and accidents (of whatever source). AIDS has not yet become one of the four leading causes of deaths in North America among the general population. (p. 400)

5. **c.** is the answer. (p. 401)

a. & b. Researchers have not identified such personality types.

d. Individuals who are more easygoing are labeled Type B.

6. **a.** is the answer. (p. 402)

b. Hypochondriacs think something is wrong with them, but nothing physical can be detected.

c. *Psychogenic* means "originating in the mind." One's reaction to stress *is* partially psychological, but this term is not used to refer to stress-related illness.

d. There is no such term.

7. **d.** is the answer. Because stress depresses the immune system, stressed individuals are prone to all of these conditions. (p. 403)

8. **d.** is the answer. Most researchers today discount the idea that people are obese because they lack willpower. (p. 421)

a., b., & c. Each of these is a reason why obese people may have difficulty losing weight.

9. **d.** is the answer. (p. 399)

10. **a.** is the answer. Certain high-carbohydrate foods raise the levels of serotonin, which facilitates relaxation by increasing the amount of tryptophan reaching the brain. (pp. 414–415)

b. Cortisol is a stress hormone and hence not related either to carbohydrates or to relaxation.

c. & d. Meals that are high in protein promote alertness.

11. **c.** is the answer. The finding that talking about grief leads to better health makes a lot of sense in light of this physiological finding. (p. 410)

a., b., & d. The study by Pennebaker did not find these to be true.

12. **b.** is the answer. People generally *start* smoking in adolescence in order to gain peer acceptance; they continue smoking primarily because they have become addicted to nicotine. Thus, the factors that motivate people to start smoking are best described as social, while the factors that explain continued smoking are mainly biological. (pp. 412–413)

13. **b.** is the answer. Following the initial weight loss, metabolism drops as the body attempts to defend its set-point weight. This drop in metabolism means that eating an amount that once produced a loss in weight may now actually result in weight gain. (p. 417)

14. **d.** is the answer. Regular aerobic exercise has been shown to increase ability to cope with stress, lower blood pressure, and reduce depression and anxi-

ety. The textbook does not cite evidence that exercise enhances immune function. (pp. 406–407)

15. **d.** is the answer. The systems theory approach, which underlies behavioral medicine, emphasizes that health and illness depend on the interaction of biological, psychological, and social systems. (p. 393)

Matching Items

1. f (p. 406)
2. j (p. 400)
3. c (p. 394)
4. a (p. 403)
5. i (p. 402)
6. b (p. 393)
7. h (p. 395)
8. d (p. 401)
9. e (p. 401)
10. g (p. 407)
11. k (p. 394)

PROGRESS TEST 2

Multiple-Choice Questions

1. **d.** is the answer. This chapter deals with the topics of health psychology, namely, preventing illness by developing better ways to cope with stress, and promoting health, for example, through nutrition and weight control. (p. 394)

2. **a.** is the answer. (p. 396)

3. **b.** is the answer. People who suppress their anger are prone to hypertension. (p. 402)

a., c., & d. Suppression of anger has not specifically been linked to these conditions.

4. **a.** is the answer. This is an example of choosing between two desirable, but incompatible, goals. (p. 398)

b. This conflict occurs when a person is both attracted and repelled by the same goal.

c. This conflict occurs when a person must choose between two undesirable alternatives.

5. **d.** is the answer. Behaviors that contribute to the leading causes of mortality include smoking, excessive alcohol consumption, maladpative responses to stress, nonadherence to doctors' instructions, insufficient exercise, use of illicit drugs, and poor nutrition. (p. 393)

6. **c.** is the answer. B lymphocytes fight bacterial infections; T lymphocytes attack cancer cells, viruses, and foreign substances. (p. 403)

d. Antigens are substances that cause the production of antibodies when they are introduced into the body.

7. **a.** is the answer. A variety of studies have shown that stress depresses the immune system, increasing the risk and potential severity of many diseases. (p. 403)

8. **d.** is the answer. Approximately 30 percent of all cancer deaths and 30 percent or more of the deaths caused by heart disease in the United States are linked with cigarette smoking. (p. 412)

a., b., & c. Although each of these is an important factor in health promotion, cigarette smoking is the *largest* preventable cause of illness and death.

9. **b.** is the answer. Both human and animal studies indicate that uncontrollable negative events trigger an outpouring of stress hormones and a drop in immune responses. (p. 403)

10. **c.** is the answer. High-protein foods seem to improve alertness, whereas high-carbohydrate foods seem to promote relaxation. (pp. 414–415)

11. **d.** is the answer. The crucial characteristic of Type A behavior seems to be a tendency to react with negative emotions, especially anger; other aspects of Type A behavior appear not to predict heart disease, and some appear to be helpful to the individual. (p. 401)

12. **d.** is the answer. No particular treatment seems to stand out in terms of effectiveness. Two-thirds of the people who quit smoking in such programs eventually return to the habit. (p. 413)

13. **d.** is the answer. In biofeedback training, subjects are given sensory feedback about autonomic responses. Although biofeedback may promote relaxation, its benefits may be no greater than those produced by simpler, and less expensive, methods. (pp. 407–408)

14. **b.** is the answer. Fat cells may change in size as a person gains or loses weight, but their number never decreases. (p. 417)

a. In fact, because of its lower metabolic rate, fat tissue can be maintained on *fewer* calories.

c. Because metabolism slows as food intake is restricted, a 3500-calorie reduction may not reduce weight by one pound.

d. In fact, just the opposite is true. In response to external cues, obese people secrete *more* insulin. Furthermore, insulin *triggers hunger*, rather than suppressing it.

15. **d.** is the answer. Friedman's subjects who received counseling on relaxation experienced half as many repeat heart attacks as did a control group. Relaxation may help one to cope with a stressful environment, but it will not prevent it. (p. 409)

16. **b.** is the answer. By alleviating the aversive physiological state of nicotine withdrawal, cigarettes act as negative reinforcers. (p. 413)

a. This is one explanation of why adolescents *start* smoking.

c. There is no evidence that this occurs.

d. Most smokers would like to quit smoking.

True – False Items

1. True (p. 420)
2. False (p. 403)
3. False (p. 415)
4. True (p. 399)
5. False (p. 418)
6. True (p. 398)
7. False (p. 399)
8. True (p. 401)
9. True (p. 398)
10. True (p. 410)

KEY TERMS

1. **Behavioral medicine** is the interdisciplinary health field that integrates and applies biological, psychological, and sociological knowledge to the treatment of disease and the promotion of health. (p. 393)

   Example: Because the leading causes of death today are related to stress and life-style factors, the field of **behavioral medicine** has grown rapidly.

2. **Health psychology** is a new branch of psychology that studies how health and illness are influenced by emotions, stress, personality, life-style, and other psychological factors. (p. 394)

3. **Stress** refers to the psychological and physiological processes by which people evaluate and react to stressors, or events they perceive as threatening or challenging. (p. 394)

4. The **general adaptation syndrome (GAS)** is the three-stage sequence of bodily reaction to stress outlined by Hans Selye. (p. 395)

   Example: According to Selye, during the final stage of the **general adaptation syndrome**, the stage of exhaustion, people become more vulnerable to "diseases of adaptation" such as hypertension, ulcers, and coronary heart disease.

5. The leading cause of death in the United States today, **coronary heart disease** results from the narrowing of the coronary arteries and the subsequent reduction in blood and oxygen supply to the heart muscle. (p. 400)

6. **Type A** personality is the coronary-prone behavior pattern of hard-driving, impatient, verbally aggressive, and anger-prone people. (p. 401)

7. **Type B** personality is the coronary-resistant behavior pattern of easygoing people. (p. 401)

8. A **psychophysiological illness** is any genuine illness, such as hypertension, ulcers, and headaches, that is apparently linked to stress, rather than caused by a physical disorder. (p. 402)

   Memory aid: Psycho- refers to mind; *physiological* refers to body; a **psychophysiological illness** is a mind-body disorder.

9. **Lymphocytes** are the white blood cells of the immune system that fight infections, viruses, and foreign substances in the body. (p. 403)

Memory aid: *B* **lymphocytes** fight *b*acteria. *T* **lymphocytes** attack cancer cells, viruses, and other bodily in*t*ruders.

10. **Aerobic exercise** is any sustained activity, such as running, swimming, or cycling, that promotes heart and lung fitness and may help alleviate depression and anxiety. (p. 406)

11. **Biofeedback** refers to a system that provides external sensory feedback on an internal physiological state. (pp. 407–408)

Memory aid: A **biofeedback** device, such as a brain-wave trainer, provides auditory or visual *feedback* about *bio*logical responses.

12. **Obesity** is a surplus of body fat that causes one to be 20 percent or more above the optimum for one's sex, height, and build. (p. 416)

Chapter 15 | Social Behavior

Chapter Overview

Chapter 15 explores three aspects of social behavior: social thinking, social influence, and social relations. Research in these areas has helped us to understand how we think about, influence, and relate to one another.

The first section, social thinking, focuses on beliefs and attitudes—on how we interpret others' behavior (attribution theory) and on how our attitudes and actions relate. With regard to the latter, cognitive dissonance theory suggests that when our behaviors conflict with our attitudes, the discomfort that results leads us to modify our attitudes.

The social influence section deals with conformity, compliance, group interaction, and minority influence. The social principles that emerge from the research discussed help us to understand how we are influenced by the various groups to which we belong.

The last section focuses on some polarities of social relations: aggression and altruism, prejudice and attraction, conflict and peacemaking. The section concludes with a discussion of the social traps that engender conflict, along with techniques that have been shown to promote conflict resolution between groups —techniques that foster cooperation, communication, and conciliation.

There is not a great deal of terminology for you to learn in this chapter. Your primary task is to absorb the findings of the many research studies discussed. You should find this chapter interesting, since it explores topics of considerable relevance to your everyday life.

Guided Study

The textbook chapter should be studied one section at a time. Before you read, preview each section by skimming it, noting headings and boldface items. Then read the appropriate section objectives from the following outline. Keep these objectives in mind, and as you read the chapter section, search for the information that will enable you to meet each objective. Once you have finished a section, write out answers for its objectives.

Social Thinking (pp. 425–429)

1. Explain attribution theory and discuss how the explanations we provide for people's behavior often lead us to underestimate the importance of social influence.

2. Define attitude and identify the conditions under which attitudes predict behavior.

3. Describe how actions influence attitudes and explain how cognitive dissonance theory accounts for this phenomenon.

Social Influence (pp. 430–439)

4. Describe the results of experiments on conformity and obedience and distinguish between normative and informational social influence.

5. Discuss how the presence of others may produce social facilitation, social loafing, or deindividuation.

6. Describe group polarization and show how it can be a source of groupthink.

7. Explain how a minority can influence the majority.

Social Relations (pp. 440–460)

8. Describe the roles of social inequalities, ingroup bias and scapegoating in prejudice.

9. Discuss the cognitive roots and consequences of stereotypes.

10. Describe the impact of biology, unpleasant events, and learning experiences on aggressive behavior.

11. Discuss the effects of television violence and pornographic films on viewers.

12. Identify the determinants of social attraction and distinguish between passionate and companionate love.

13. Describe and explain the "bystander effect."

14. Describe social traps and mirror-image perceptions and explain how they fuel conflict.

15. Discuss effective ways of resolving conflict.

Chapter Review

When you have finished reading the chapter, use the material that follows to review it. Complete the fill-in sentences and answer the essay items in complete sentences. As you proceed, evaluate your performance for each chapter section by consulting the answer key at the end of this chapter. Do not continue with the next section until you've understood each answer. If you need to, review or reread the appropriate chapter section in the textbook before continuing.

1. Social psychologists are concerned with three aspects of behavior: (a) _____ _____, our beliefs and attitudes and their relationship to behavior; (b) _____ _____, the impact of others' behavior on our own; and (c) _____ _____, the ways in which we interact with others, including peacemaking, aggression, and love.

Social Thinking (pp. 425–429)

2. In the 1950s, a theory of how people explain others' behavior was proposed by _____. This theory, known as _____ _____, suggests that people attribute others' behavior either to internal causes, or their _____, or to external causes, or the _____.

3. Most people tend to _____

(overestimate/underestimate) the extent to which people's actions are influenced by social situations. This tendency is called the

_____ _____

_____.

4. Beliefs and feelings that predispose our responses are called _____.

5. The many research studies on attitudes and actions conducted during the 1960s _____ (challenged/supported) the common assumption that our actions are guided by our attitudes.

List three conditions under which our attitudes do predict our actions; give examples.

6. Attitudes that come to mind quickly are _____ (more/less) likely to guide behavior than those that do not.

7. A set of behaviors expected of someone in a given social position is called a(n) _____.

8. Taking on a set of behaviors, or acting in a certain way, generally _____ (changes/does not change) people's attitudes.

9. When people are induced to perform actions that go against their true attitudes, these attitudes are often _____ (strengthened/ weakened).

10. According to _____ _____ theory, thoughts and feelings change because people are motivated to justify actions that could otherwise seem hypocritical. This theory was proposed by _____.

11. Dissonance theory predicts that people induced (without coercion) to behave contrary to their true attitudes will be motivated to reduce the resulting _____ by changing their _____.

Social Influence (pp. 430–439)

12. The term that refers to the tendency to adjust one's behavior to coincide with an assumed group standard is _____.

13. The psychologist who studied the effects of group pressure on conformity is

_____.

14. In this study, when the opinion of other group members was contradicted by objective evidence, subjects _____ (were/were not) willing to conform to the group opinion.

Identify several conditions that were found to promote conformity.

15. One reason that people comply with social pressure is to gain approval or avoid rejection; this is called _____

_____ _____.

Rules for accepted and expected behavior are called _____.

16. Another reason people comply is that they have genuinely been influenced by what they have learned from others; this type of influence is called _____

_____ _____.

17. The classic social psychology studies of obedience were conducted by _____. When ordered by the experimenter to electrically shock the "learner," most subjects in these studies _____ (complied/refused).

Describe the conditions under which obedience was greatest in these experiments.

18. When subjects were asked to administer the test while another person delivered the shocks, compliance was _____ (reduced/increased).

19. People who are working simultaneously on the same noncompetitive task are called

_____.

20. The tendency to perform a task better when other people are present is called

_____ _____.

Explain how and why this tendency is affected by the difficulty of the task.

21. Researchers have found that the reactions of people in crowded situations are often _____ (lessened/amplified).

22. Ingham found that people worked _____ (harder/less hard) in a team tug-of-war than they had in an individual contest. This phenomenon has been called

_____ _____.

23. The feeling of anonymity and loss of restraint that an individual may develop when in a group is called _____.

24. Over time, the initial differences between groups usually _____ (increase/ decrease). This phenomenon is called

_____ _____.

25. When the desire for group harmony overrides realistic thinking in individuals, the phenomenon known as _____ has occurred.

Identify some psychological factors that promote this phenomenon and steps that leaders can take to prevent it.

26. Although social influence on behavior is extensive, it is important to remember that the power of the situation, or _____ control, interacts with the power of the individual, or _____ control.

27. A minority opinion will have most success in swaying the majority if it takes a stance that is _____ (unswerving/flexible).

Social Relations (pp. 440–460)

28. A(n) _____ and _____ attitude toward a group is called prejudice. Prejudice involves generalized beliefs known as _____, as well as predispositions to actions that are _____.

29. For those with money, power, and prestige, prejudice often serves as a means of _____ social inequalities.

30. Prejudice is also fostered by _____ _____, a tendency to favor groups to which one belongs.

31. People who have experienced failure are _____ (more/less) likely to criticize another person.

32. That prejudice derives from attempts to blame others for one's frustration is proposed by the _____ theory.

33. Research suggests that prejudice may also derive from _____, the process by which we attempt to simplify our world by classifying people into groups. One by-product of this process is that people tend to _____ (overestimate/ underestimate) the similarity of those within a group.

34. Another factor that fosters the formation of group stereotypes is the tendency to _____ from vivid or memorable cases.

35. The belief that people get what they deserve— that the good are rewarded and the bad punished—is expressed in the _____ - _____ phenomenon.

36. Aggressive behavior is defined by the textbook as: _____ _____.

37. One theorist who proposed that aggression is instinctive is _____. Today most psychologists _____ (believe/do not believe) that human aggression is instinctive.

38. In humans, aggressiveness _____ (varies/does not vary) greatly from culture to culture.

39. That there are genetic influences on aggression can be shown by the fact that many species of animals have been _____ for aggressiveness.

40. In humans and animals, aggression is activated and inhibited by _____ systems, which are in turn influenced by _____ and other substances in the blood.

41. One drug that reduces a person's natural restraints against aggression is _____.

42. Violent criminals tend to have higher than average levels of the hormone _____. Drugs that diminish testosterone levels _____ (are/are not) effective in reducing aggression.

43. According to the _____ - _____ theory, inability to achieve a goal leads to anger, which can generate aggression.

44. Aggressive behavior can be learned through direct _____, as shown by the fact that people use aggression where they've found it pays, and through _____ of others.

45. The average American household has the television on _____ hours a day. Violence on television appears to promote aggressive behavior as a result of four factors: the excitement of television causes _____; seeing violence triggers _____ related to violence; TV violence erodes viewers' _____; and viewers tend to _____ behaviors they have seen.

Comment on the impression of women that pornography frequently conveys and the effects this impression has on attitudes and behavior.

Summarize the findings of the Donnerstein and Linz study on the effects of violent pornography ("slasher" movies) on attitudes toward rape.

46. When other studies looked instead at *nonviolent* pornography, it was found that attitudes toward rape (as reflected in the length of sentence recommended for a convicted rapist) _____ (were/were not) affected.

47. Correlational studies of pornography and aggression _____ (generally/do not generally) show a relationship between availability of pornography and incidence of rape.

48. Most rapes _____ (are/are not) reported. About 1 in every _____ women reported having been raped.

49. A prerequisite for, and perhaps the most powerful predictor of, attraction is _____.

50. When people are repeatedly exposed to unfamiliar stimuli, their liking of the stimuli _____ (increases/decreases). This phenomenon is called the _____ _____ effect.

51. Our first impression of another person is most influenced by the person's _____.

52. List several of the characteristics that physically attractive people are judged to possess.
_____
_____

53. A person's attractiveness _____ (is/is not) strongly related to his or her self-esteem.

54. Relationships in which the partners are very similar are _____ (more/less) likely to last.

55. Compared to strangers, friends and couples are more likely to share _____.

Explain what a reward theory of attraction is and how it can account for the three predictors of liking — proximity, attractiveness, and similarity.

56. Hatfield has distinguished two types of love: _____ love and _____ love.

57. According to the two-factor theory, emotions have two components: physical _____ and a _____ label.

58. When college men were placed in an aroused state, their feelings toward an attractive woman _____ (were/were not) more positive than those of men who had not been aroused.

59. Companionate love is promoted by _____—mutual sharing and giving by both partners. Another key ingredient of loving relationships is the revealing of intimate aspects of ourselves through _____.

60. An unselfish regard for the welfare of others is called _____.

61. According to Darley and Latané, people will help only if a three-stage decision-making process is completed: Bystanders must first _____ the incident, then _____ it as an emergency, and finally _____ _____ for helping.

62. In one experiment involving a simulated physical emergency, subjects overheard a seizure victim calling for help. Those who thought others were hearing the same plea were _____ (more/less) likely to call for help than those who thought no one else was aware of the emergency.

63. In a series of staged emergencies, Latané and Darley found that a bystander was _____ (more/less) likely to help if other bystanders were present. This phenomenon has been called the _____ _____.

Identify the circumstances in which a person is most likely to offer help during an emergency.

64. A perceived incompatibility of actions, goals, or ideas is called _____.

65. Two destructive social processes that contribute to many conflicts are _____ and _____ perceptions.

66. When the "non-zero-sum game" is played, most people fall into the social trap by mistrusting the other player and pursuing their own _____-_____.

Give an example of a real-life situation involving a social trap.

Explain how mirror-image perceptions extend the arms race.

67. Several psychological tendencies foster the arms race. First, leaders, like other people, tend to accept credit for good deeds but not blame for bad deeds, a phenomenon called the _____-_____. Second, each country tends to attribute the other's actions to an aggressive disposition, an example of the _____ _____. Preconceived attitudes, or _____, also contribute to the problem, as does the _____ which emerges within each nation as like-minded groups of leaders interact.

68. Conflict resolution is most likely in situations characterized by _____, _____, and _____.

69. In most situations, establishing contact between two conflicting groups _____ (is/is not) sufficient to resolve conflict.

70. In Sherif's study, two conflicting groups of

campers were able to resolve their conflicts by working together on projects in which they shared _____ goals.

71. Osgood has advocated a strategy of conciliation called GRIT, which stands for

_____ and _____

_____ in _____-

reduction. The key to this method is each side's offering of a small _____

gesture in order to increase mutual trust and cooperation.

FOCUS ON PSYCHOLOGY:
Games that Promote Cooperation

Social psychologists believe that many conflicts arise from destructive social processes, such as social traps. Social traps are situations in which conflicting parties become caught in mutually destructive behavior by not trusting each other and pursuing their individual interests.

Computer systems engineer Gerald Rabow suggests that the roots of social traps may lie in the games children are taught to play—games adults continue to play throughout their careers and personal lives. Football, basketball, and most board games engender "zero-sum" (ZS) thinking: When one player wins, the other loses. In such games, according to Rabow, "Any positive score by one side is in effect a negative score by the other; hence the name, zero sum." As adults, zero-sum thinking is evident whenever our actions are guided by the attitude that we lose if someone else wins.

Rabow believes that if children and adults learn to play games that promote cooperation, they might later avoid conflicts and reach better solutions to problems. These would be "non-zero-sum" (NZS) games, since "opposing" sides could both benefit from cooperation because the net score need not equal zero.

Rabow suggests that many familiar ZS games can be made into NZS versions in which cooperation, as well as competition, would be rewarded. In the traditional word game Scrabble, for example, players score points by forming words from letter tiles placed on a special game board. The game winner is the player with the highest score. Good strategy therefore includes not only forming high-scoring words to increase one's own point total, but also making it difficult for the other player to score.

The NZS version of Scrabble retains the central features of ZS Scrabble—players still try to form high-scoring words—but eliminates the benefits of obstructing the other player's scoring opportunities. Instead, the objective becomes to score as many points as possible, regardless of the other player's score. All players can in effect "win" by scoring more points than their previous personal bests. All players therefore benefit from high scores by inducing cooperative play from one another. In addition to promoting cooperation, the NZS version of the game has the advantage of placing even greater emphasis than regular Scrabble on word skills.

Rabow also believes that many team games can be converted into challenging and enjoyable NZS versions that retain most of the regular rules but do more to promote cooperation among players. In NZS basketball, for example, each player receives the conventional one to three points for making a basket, minus one-fifth the number of points scored by the other team during the time that player is in the game. The net result is that while the combined score of the two teams equals zero, each player receives an individual point total that can be compared with that of other players. As in regular basketball, NZS players must cooperate with team members in overcoming the other team's defense so scoring is possible at all. In the NZS version of the game, however, the focus of competition is shifted from team scoring to individual scoring. Since there are no team victories, coaches and players can focus on teaching and player skill development rather than on making sure the team wins. Younger and less-skilled players can get equal playing time, since there is no pressure on coaches to keep their top scorers in the game to ensure a win.

Rabow believes that many other common games can be converted into NZS games and that entirely new ones can easily be devised. The dynamics of NZS play, involving both cooperation and competition among players, should make the games enjoyable both to play and to watch. "And the new skills that they simulate can be useful in the real NZS world," says Rabow. "The strategies that successful players evolve may even provide some useful insights into solving real-world problems."

Source: Rabow, Gerald (1988, January). The cooperative edge. *Psychology Today*, 54–58.

Progress Test 1

Multiple-Choice Questions

Circle your answers to the following questions and check them with the answer key at the end of this chapter. If your answer is incorrect, read the answer key explanation for why it is incorrect and then consult the appropriate pages of the text to understand the correct answer.

1. Which of the following best exemplifies the fundamental attribution error?
   a. the tendency of political liberals to blame poverty on the individual's circumstances
   b. the feeling people have of being "different" when in another culture
   c. people's tendency to think well of actors who play appealing roles
   d. people's tendency to emphasize the situational context when explaining others' behavior

2. In Stanley Milgram's study of obedience it was found that:
   a. most subjects refused to shock the learner even once.
   b. most subjects complied with the experiment until the "learner" first indicated pain.
   c. most subjects complied with the experiment until the "learner" began screaming in agony.
   d. most subjects complied with all the demands of the experiment.

3. According to the cognitive dissonance theory, dissonance is most likely to occur when:
   a. a person's behavior is not based on strongly held attitudes.
   b. two people have conflicting attitudes and find themselves in disagreement.
   c. an individual does something that is personally disagreeable.
   d. an individual is coerced into doing something that he or she does not want to do.

4. Which of the following statements about groups is true?
   a. Groups are almost never swayed by minority opinions.
   b. Group polarization is most likely to occur when group members frequently disagree with one another.
   c. Groupthink provides the consensus needed for effective decision-making.
   d. A group that is like-minded will probably not change its opinions through discussion.

5. In Asch's studies of conformity, conformity increased when:
   a. the group had three or more people.
   b. the group had high status.
   c. individuals were made to feel insecure.
   d. all of the above increased conformity.

6. One reason that people comply with social pressure is to avoid rejection or gain approval; this is called:
   a. informational social influence.
   b. the fundamental attribution error.
   c. normative social influence.
   d. deindividuation.

7. Which of the following would most likely be subject to social facilitation?
   a. running quickly around a track
   b. proofreading a page for spelling errors
   c. typing a letter with accuracy
   d. playing a difficult piece on a musical instrument

8. The phenomenon in which individuals lose their identity and relinquish normal restraints when part of a group is called:
   a. groupthink.   c. group polarization.
   b. cognitive dissonance.   d. deindividuation.

9. Which of the following is important in promoting conformity in individuals?
   a. whether an individual's behavior will be observed by others in the group
   b. whether the individual is male or female
   c. the size of the room a group is meeting in
   d. the age of the members of the group

10. Jane and Sandy were best friends as freshmen. Jane joined a sorority; Sandy didn't. By the end of their college careers, they find that they have less in common with each other than with the other members of their respective circles. Which of the following phenomena most likely explains their feelings?
    a. group polarization   c. deindividuation
    b. groupthink   d. cognitive dissonance

11. Subjects in Asch's line-judgment experiment conformed to the group standard when their judgments were observed by others but not when they were made in private. This tendency to conform in public demonstrates:
    a. social facilitation.
    b. social loafing.
    c. informational social influence.
    d. normative social influence.

12. Which of the following is most likely to promote groupthink?
    a. The group's leader does not take a firm stance on an issue.
    b. A minority faction holds to its position.
    c. The group consults with various experts.
    d. Group polarization is evident.

13. Aggression is defined as behavior that:
    a. hurts another person.
    b. intends to hurt another person.
    c. is hostile, passionate, and produces physical injury.
    d. has all of the above characteristics.

14. Findings from cross-cultural studies of aggression suggest that:
    a. aggression is not a human instinct.
    b. aggression is just one instinct among many.

c. aggression is instinctive but shaped by learning.

d. aggression is the most important of the human instincts.

15. A positive correlation has been found between aggressive tendencies and levels of the hormone:

a. estrogen.

b. adrenaline.

c. noradrenaline.

d. testosterone.

16. Research studies of the effects of pornography have indicated that the tendency of viewers to misperceive normal sexuality, devalue their partners, and trivialize rape:

a. is increased by exposure to pornography.

b. is not changed after exposure to pornography.

c. is decreased in men by exposure to pornography.

d. is decreased in both men and women by exposure to pornography.

17. Increasing the number of people that are present during an emergency tends to:

a. increase the likelihood that people will cooperate in rendering assistance.

b. decrease the empathy that people feel for the victim.

c. increase the role that social norms governing helping will play.

d. decrease the likelihood that anyone will help.

18. Social traps are situations in which:

a. conflicting parties realize that they have shared goals, the attainment of which requires their mutual cooperation.

b. conflicting parties have similar, and generally negative, views of one another.

c. conflicting parties each pursue their self-interest and become caught in mutually destructive behavior.

d. two conflicting groups meet face to face in an effort to resolve their differences.

19. Which of the following was *not* mentioned in the textbook's discussion of the roots of prejudice?

a. people's tendency to overestimate the similarity of people within groups

b. people's tendency to assume that exceptional, or especially memorable individuals, are unlike the majority of members of a group

c. people's tendency to assume that the world is just and that people get what they deserve

d. people's tendency to discriminate against those they view as "outsiders"

20. The tendency of people to assume that those who suffer deserve their fate is expressed in the:

a. just-world phenomenon.

b. phenomenon of ingroup bias.

c. fundamental attribution error.

d. phenomenon of deindividuation.

21. The mere exposure effect demonstrates that:

a. familiarity breeds contempt.

b. opposites attract.

c. birds of a feather flock together.

d. familiarity breeds fondness.

22. In one experiment, college men were physically aroused and then introduced to an attractive woman. Compared to men who had not been aroused, these men:

a. reported more positive feelings toward the woman.

b. reported more negative feelings toward the woman.

c. were more likely to feel that the woman was "out of their league" in terms of attractiveness.

d. focused more on the woman's attractiveness and less on her intelligence and personality.

23. The deep affection that is felt in long-lasting relationships is called _____ love; this feeling is fostered in relationships in which:

a. passionate; there is equity between the partners.

b. passionate; traditional roles are maintained.

c. companionate; there is equity between the partners.

d. companionate; traditional roles are maintained.

24. Which of the following is associated with an increased tendency of a bystander to offer help in an emergency situation?

a. being in a good mood

b. having recently needed help and not received it

c. observing someone refusing to offer help

d. being a female

25. Which of the following strategies would be most likely to foster positive feelings between two conflicting groups?

a. Take steps to reduce the likelihood of social traps.

b. Separate the groups from each other so that tensions will diminish.

c. Have one representative from each group visit the other and field questions.

d. Have the groups work on a superordinate goal.

26. Which of the following best expresses the relationship between aversive events and aggression?

a. Only aversive stimuli that produce frustration increase anger.

b. Aversive stimuli increase hostility in males but not females.

c. Foul odors, heat, smoke, and other aversive stimuli can provoke hostility.

d. Only aversive stimuli that block our attempts to achieve some goal arouse hostility.

27. Which of the following would be the best advice to give parents who are concerned about the effects of television violence on their children?

   a. "Don't worry, there is in fact little solid evidence that viewing violence actually leads to violence."

   b. "Limit television watching and discuss the programs with your children."

   c. "Allow children to watch a few extremely violent programs so that they will see the absurdity of television's portrayal of the world."

   d. "Ban all television viewing."

Matching Items

Match each term with its definition or description.

Terms

_____   1. social facilitation
_____   2. social loafing
_____   3. norms
_____   4. roles
_____   5. normative social influence
_____   6. informational social influence
_____   7. group polarization
_____   8. coactors
_____   9. attribution
_____   10. altruism
_____   11. ingroup bias
_____   12. mere exposure effect
_____   13. mirror-image perceptions
_____   14. companionate love
_____   15. passionate love
_____   16. stereotype
_____   17. prejudice
_____   18. scapegoat theory
_____   19. frustration-aggression theory

Definitions

a. a causal explanation for someone's behavior
b. people working at the same task at the same time
c. people work less hard in a group
d. performance is improved by an audience
e. a set of social expectations for a position
f. the effect of social approval or disapproval
g. rules for acceptable behavior
h. group discussion enhances prevailing tendencies
i. accepting others' opinions about something
j. the theory that blocked goals generate aggression
k. the tendency to favor one's own group
l. an unjustifiable attitude toward a group
m. the similar views parties in conflict have of each other
n. repeated exposure to stimuli increases liking of them
o. an overgeneralized belief about a group
p. unselfish regard for others
q. a state of intense emotional absorption in another
r. deep and enduring affectionate attachment to another
s. the theory that prejudice provides an outlet for anger

Progress Test 2

Progress Test 2 should be completed during a final chapter review. Do this test after you thoroughly understand the correct answers for the Chapter Review and Progress Test 1.

Multiple-Choice Questions

1. The board members of Acme Truck Company are so afraid of going against the chairman's ideas and breaking the "team spirit" that they often conceal their true opinions; this group is a victim of:

   a. group polarization.
   b. cognitive dissonance.
   c. informational social influence.
   d. groupthink.

2. When subjects in an experiment were told that a woman to whom they would be speaking had been instructed to act in a friendly or unfriendly way, most of them subsequently attributed her behavior to:

   a. the situation.
   b. both the situation and her personal disposition.
   c. her personal disposition.
   d. their own skill or lack of skill in a social situation.

3. José is the student member on the college board of trustees. At the first meeting, he wants to disagree with the others on several issues but in each case decides to say nothing. Studies on conformity suggest all of the following as factors in José's not speaking up *except* that:

   a. the board is a large group.
   b. the board is prestigious and most of its members are well known.
   c. the board members are already aware that José

and the student body disagree with them on these issues.

    d. because this is the first meeting José has attended, he feels insecure and not fully competent.

4. After Marilyn Monroe committed suicide, there was an increase in suicides in the United States. This has been attributed to the social influence of:

    a. conformity.   **c.** compliance.

    b. suggestibility.   **d.** all of the above.

5. An army captain orders a village destroyed. As the soldiers are unaccustomed to attacking civilian targets, there is some concern about whether they will comply. Which of the following would promote the greatest compliance?

    a. Orders are given immediately prior to the time fixed for the attack.

    b. A decision is made to launch the attack by air.

    c. Reinforcements are sent in to assist in the attack.

    d. When several soldiers balk at the orders, they are severely reprimanded in front of the others.

6. Maria recently heard a speech calling for a ban on aerosol sprays that endanger the earth's ozone layer. Maria's subsequent decision to stop using aerosol sprays is an example of:

    a. informational social influence.

    b. normative social influence.

    c. conformity.

    d. social facilitation.

7. Which of the following is true?

    a. Attitudes and actions rarely correspond.

    b. Attitudes predict behavior about half of the time.

    c. Attitudes are excellent predictors of behavior.

    d. Attitudes predict behavior under certain conditions.

8. When Lynn first joined the sorority she felt awkward during rituals and sorority functions. After having been in this role for some time she will probably:

    a. experience an increase in awkwardness.

    b. continue to feel awkward but learn to hide these feelings.

    c. begin to resent the group.

    d. begin to adopt her role and feel more comfortable.

9. Which of the following situations should produce the greatest cognitive dissonance?

    a. A soldier is forced to carry out orders he finds disagreeable.

    b. A student who loves animals has to dissect a cat in order to pass biology.

    c. As part of an experiment, a subject is directed to deliver shock to another person.

    d. A student volunteers to debate an issue, taking the side he personally disagrees with.

10. An individual may work harder when alone than as a member of a group. This phenomenon is called:

    a. social loafing.   **c.** deindividuation.

    b. social facilitation.   **d.** group polarization.

11. Which of the following most accurately states the effects of crowding on behavior?

    a. Crowding makes people irritable.

    b. Crowding sometimes intensifies people's reactions.

    c. Crowding promotes altruistic behavior.

    d. Crowding usually weakens the intensity of people's reactions.

12. Research has found that for a minority to succeed in swaying a majority, the minority must:

    a. make up a sizable portion of the group.

    b. express its position as consistently as possible.

    c. express its position in the most extreme terms possible.

    d. be able to convince a key leader of the majority.

13. Professor Washington's students did very poorly on the last exam. The tendency to make the fundamental attribution error might lead Professor Washington to conclude that the class did poorly because:

    a. the test was unfair.

    b. not enough time was given for completing the test.

    c. they were distracted by some social function on campus.

    d. they were unmotivated.

14. Which of the following conclusions did Milgram derive from his studies of obedience?

    a. Even ordinary people, without any particular hostility, can become agents in a destructive process.

    b. Most people are able, under the proper circumstances, to suppress their natural aggressiveness.

    c. The need to be accepted by others is a powerful motivating force.

    d. All of the above.

15. Which of the following best summarizes the relative importance of personal control and social control of our behavior?

    a. Situational influences on behavior generally are much greater than personal influences.

    b. Situational influences on behavior generally are slightly greater than personal influences.

c. Personal influences on behavior generally are much greater than situational influences.

d. Situational influences and personal influences interact in determining our behavior.

16. Which of the following pairs of individuals would be considered "coactors?"

a. debaters on opposing teams

b. two members of an audience watching a play

c. the pitcher and batter during a baseball game

d. psychology lab partners collecting data during an experiment

17. Which theorist argued that aggression was a manifestation of a person's "death instinct" redirected toward another person?

a. Heider   c. Asch

b. Freud   d. Skinner

18. The fact that certain animals have been bred for aggressiveness suggests that:

a. aggressive behavior may have a genetic basis.

b. aggressive behavior is primarily a learned rather than a genetically determined behavior.

c. aggressive behavior cannot be increased through breeding.

d. both b. and c. are true.

19. Regarding the influence of alcohol and testosterone on aggressive behavior, which of the following is true?

a. Consumption of alcohol increases aggressive behavior; raising testosterone levels reduces aggressive behavior.

b. Consumption of alcohol reduces aggressive behavior; raising testosterone levels increases aggressive behavior.

c. Consumption of alcohol and raising testosterone levels both promote aggressive behavior.

d. Consumption of alcohol and raising testosterone levels both reduce aggressive behavior.

20. Research studies have shown that frequent exposure to sexually explicit films:

a. may promote increased acceptance of promiscuity.

b. diminishes the attitude that rape is a serious crime.

c. may lead individuals to devalue their partners.

d. may produce all of the above effects.

21. Research studies indicate that in an emergency situation the presence of others often:

a. prevents people from even noticing the situation.

b. prevents people from interpreting an unusual event as an emergency.

c. prevents people from assuming responsibility for assisting.

d. leads to all of the above.

22. People with power and status may become prejudiced as a result of the tendency:

a. to justify the social inequalities between themselves and others.

b. of those with less status and power to be resentful toward them.

c. of those with less status and power to appear less capable.

d. to feel proud and boastful of their achievements.

23. Based on the tendency of people to categorize information, which of the following stereotypes would Juan, a 65-year-old political liberal and fitness enthusiast, be most likely to have?

a. "People who exercise regularly are very extraverted."

b. "All political liberals are advocates of a reduced defense budget."

c. "Young people today have no sense of responsibility."

d. "Older people are lazy."

24. Which of the following factors is the most powerful predictor of friendship?

a. similarity in age

b. common racial and religious background

c. similarity in physical attractiveness

d. physical proximity

25. Ahmad and Monique are on a blind date. Which of the following factors will probably be most influential in determining whether they like each other?

a. their personalities

b. their beliefs

c. their social skills

d. their physical attractiveness

26. Ever since their cabin lost the camp softball competition, the campers have become increasingly hostile toward one camper, blaming her for every problem in the cabin. This behavior is best explained in terms of:

a. the ingroup bias.

b. prejudice.

c. the scapegoat theory.

d. cognitive dissonance theory.

27. Opening her mail, Joan discovers a romantic greeting card from her boyfriend. According to the two-factor theory, she is likely to feel the most intense romantic feelings if she has just:

a. completed her daily run.

b. finished reading a chapter in her psychology textbook.

c. awakened from a nap.

d. finished eating lunch.

28. After waiting in line for an hour to buy concert tickets, Teresa is told that the concert is sold out. In

her anger she pounds her fist on the ticket counter, frightening the clerk. Teresa's behavior is best explained by the:

a. scapegoat theory.

b. cognitive dissonance theory.

c. just-world phenomenon.

d. frustration-aggression theory.

29. Which of the following best exemplifies GRIT?

a. The fact that two sides in a conflict have great respect for each other's strength prevents further escalation of the problem.

b. The two sides engage in a series of reciprocated conciliatory acts.

c. The two sides agree to have their differences settled by a neutral, third-part mediator.

d. The two sides engage in cooperation in those areas where shared goals are possible.

30. Mr. and Mrs. Samuels are constantly fighting, and each perceives the other as hard-headed and insensitive. Their conflict is being fueled by:

a. self-disclosure.

b. stereotypes.

c. mirror-image perceptions.

d. equity.

31. Most researchers agree that:

a. television violence leads to aggression.

b. although there is a correlation between television watching and aggressiveness, it's impossible to establish causation.

c. paradoxically, watching excessive television violence ultimately diminishes an individual's aggressive tendencies.

d. television violence is too unreal to promote aggression in viewers.

32. Students at State University are convinced that their school is better than any other; this most directly illustrates:

a. an ingroup bias.

b. prejudice and discrimination.

c. the scapegoat effect.

d. the fundamental attribution error.

33. After having read the chapter, which of the following is best borne out by research?

a. Birds of a feather flock together.

b. Opposites attract.

c. Familiarity breeds contempt.

d. Absence makes the heart grow fonder.

True-False Items

Indicate whether each statement is true or false by placing *T* or *F* in the blank next to the item.

_____ 1. When explaining another's behavior, we tend to underestimate situational influences.

_____ 2. Self disclosure in a relationship promotes companionate love.

_____ 3. An individual is more likely to conform when the rest of the group is unanimous.

_____ 4. The tendency of people to conform is influenced by the culture in which they were socialized.

_____ 5. Companionate love is not as enduring as passionate love.

_____ 6. Counter-attitudinal behavior (acting contrary to our beliefs) often leads to attitude change.

_____ 7. Viewers of violent pornography are more likely to act aggressively when provoked.

_____ 8. Group polarization tends to prevent groupthink from occurring.

_____ 9. Crowded conditions usually subdue people's reactions.

_____ 10. When individuals lose their sense of identity in a group, they often become more uninhibited.

Key Terms

Using your own words, write a brief definition or explanation of each of the following terms.

1. attribution theory

2. fundamental attribution error

3. attitudes

4. role

5. cognitive dissonance theory

6. conformity

7. normative social influence

8. norms

9. informational social influence

10. coactor

11. social facilitation

12. social loafing

13. deindividuation

14. group polarization

15. groupthink

16. prejudice

17. stereotype

18. ingroup bias

19. scapegoat theory

20. just-world phenomenon

21. aggression

22. frustration-aggression theory

23. mere exposure effect

24. passionate love

25. companionate love

26. equity

27. self-disclosure

28. altruism

29. bystander effect

30. conflict

31. social traps

32. mirror-image perceptions

33. superordinate goals

34. GRIT

Answers

CHAPTER REVIEW

1. social thinking; social influence; social relations
2. Heider; attribution theory; dispositions; situations
3. underestimate; fundamental attribution error
4. attitudes
5. challenged

Attitudes predict actions when other influences on the attitudes and actions are minimized, when the attitude is specifically relevant to the behavior, and when we are especially aware of our attitudes. Thus, our attitudes are more likely to predict behavior when we are not attempting to adjust our behavior to please others, when we are in familiar situations in which we don't have to stop and think about our attitudes, and when the attitude pertains to a specific behavior, such as purchasing a product or casting a vote.

6. more
7. role
8. changes
9. weakened
10. cognitive dissonance; Festinger
11. dissonance; attitudes
12. conformity
13. Asch
14. were

Conformity is promoted when people feel insecure, when they are in larger groups, when the group is unanimous and of high status, when no prior commitment has been made, when behavior will be observed, and when people have been socialized in a culture that encourages respect for social standards.

15. normative social influence; norms

16. informational social influence

17. Milgram; complied

Obedience was highest when the experimenter was nearby and was perceived as a legitimate authority supported by a prestigious institution, when the victim was depersonalized or at a distance, and when there was no role model for defiance.

18. increased

19. coactors

20. social facilitation

Social facilitation of tasks occurs with simple or well-learned tasks but not with tasks that are difficult or not yet mastered. When observed by others, people become aroused. Arousal facilitates the most likely response—the correct one on an easy task, an incorrect one on a difficult task.

21. amplified

22. less hard; social loafing

23. deindividuation

24. increase; group polarization

25. groupthink

Groupthink is promoted by the psychological tendencies of conformity, self-justification, group polarization, and the desire for group harmony. Groupthink can be prevented when the leader welcomes dissenting opinions, invites criticism, and encourages critical thinking.

26. social; personal

27. unswerving

28. unjustified; negative; stereotypes; discriminatory

29. justifying (rationalizing)

30. ingroup bias

31. more

32. scapegoat

33. categorization; overestimate

34. overgeneralize

35. just-world

36. any physical or verbal behavior intended to hurt or destroy

37. Freud; do not believe

38. varies

39. bred

40. neural; hormones

41. alcohol

42. testosterone; are

43. frustration-aggression

44. rewards; observation (or imitation)

45. 7; arousal; ideas; inhibitions; imitate

Pornography tends to portray women as enjoying being the victims of sexual aggression, and this perception increases the acceptance of coercion in sexual relationships.

The Donnerstein and Linz study found that after viewing violent pornography for several days, men were more likely, on seeing a reenacted rape trial, to blame the victim and downplay her injuries.

46. were

47. generally

48. are not; 5

49. proximity

50. increases; mere exposure

51. appearance

52. Attractive people are perceived as happier, more sensitive, more successful, and more socially skilled.

53. is not

54. more

55. common attitudes, beliefs, and interests, religion, race, intelligence, smoking behavior, economic status, age

Reward theories of attraction say that we are attracted to, and continue relationships with, those people whose behavior provides us with more benefits than costs. Proximity makes it easy to enjoy the benefits of friendship at little cost, attractiveness is pleasing, and similarity is reinforcing to us.

56. passionate; companionate

57. arousal; cognitive

58. were

59. equity; self-disclosure

60. altruism

61. notice; interpret; assume responsibility

62. less

63. less; bystander effect

People are most likely to help someone when they have just observed someone else being helpful; when they are not in a hurry; when the victim appears to need and deserve help; when they are in some way similar to the victim; when in a small town; when feeling guilty; when not preoccupied; and when in a good mood.

64. conflict

65. social traps; mirror-image

66. self-interests

One such situation involves the person who refuses to conserve energy by turning down thermostats, car-pooling, and recycling, because of the personal inconvenience of doing so. In this example, by falling into the social trap of thinking that one person's efforts to conserve don't matter, the person pursues individual interests and the energy status of the community at large is diminished.

As we see them—untrustworthy, evil, and aggressive—so they see us. Each side sees its weapons as defensive, and the other side's as aggressive.

67. self-serving bias; fundamental attribution error; sterotypes; groupthink

68. cooperation; communication; conciliation

69. is not

70. superordinate

71. Graduated; Reciprocated Initiatives; Tension; concilatory

PROGRESS TEST 1

Multiple-Choice Questions

1. **c.** is the answer. The fundamental attribution error is our tendency to think of people's behaviors as reflecting their personality and to overlook the influence of situational or social factors. In an extreme case, we tend to think of actors as "good" or "bad" people, according to their roles, and forget that they're just following a script. (p. 426)

2. **d.** is the answer. In Milgram's initial experiments, about 65 percent of the subjects fully complied with the experiment. (pp. 432–434)

3. **c.** is the answer. Cognitive dissonance is the tension we feel when we are aware of a discrepancy between our thoughts and actions, as would occur when we do something we find distasteful. (p. 429)

   a. Dissonance requires strongly held attitudes, which must be perceived as not fitting behavior.

   b. Dissonance is a personal cognitive process.

   d. In such a situation the person is less likely to experience dissonance, since the action can be attributed to "having no choice."

4. **d.** is the answer. In such groups, discussion usually strengthens prevailing opinion; this phenomenon is known as group polarization. (p. 437)

   a. Minority opinions, especially if consistently and firmly stated, can sway the majority in a group.

   b. Group polarization, or the strengthening of a group's prevailing tendencies, is most likely in groups where members agree.

   c. When groupthink occurs, there is so much consensus that decision-making becomes less effective.

5. **d.** is the answer. (p. 431)

6. **c.** is the answer. (p. 432)

   a. Informational social influence results from accepting the opinions of others about a situation one is unsure of.

   b. The fundamental attribution error is the tendency to underestimate situational influences on the behavior of others.

   d. Deindividuation is the loss of self-consciousness that sometimes occurs to individuals in groups.

7. **a.** is the answer. Social facilitation, or better performance in the presence of others, occurs for easy tasks but not for more difficult ones. For tasks such as proofreading, typing, or playing an instrument, the arousal resulting from the presence of others can lead to mistakes. (pp. 435–436)

8. **d.** is the answer. (p. 437)

   a. Groupthink refers to the mode of thinking that occurs when the desire for group harmony overrides realistic and critical thinking.

   b. Cognitive dissonance refers to the discomfort a person feels when two thoughts (which include the knowledge of our *behavior*) are inconsistent.

   c. Group polarization refers to the enhancement of a group's prevailing tendency over time.

9. **a.** is the answer. As Solomon Asch's experiments demonstrated, individuals are more likely to conform when they are being observed by others in the group. The other factors were not discussed in the text and probably would not promote conformity. (p. 431)

10. **a.** is the answer. Group polarization means that the tendencies within a group—and therefore the differences among groups—grow stronger over time. Thus the differences between the sorority and nonsorority students have increased, and Jane and Sandy are aware of having little in common. (p. 437)

    b. Groupthink is the tendency for realistic decision-making to disintegrate when the desire for group harmony is strong.

    c. Deindividuation is the loss of self-consciousness and restraint that sometimes occurs when one is part of a group.

    d. Cognitive dissonance refers to the feeling of discomfort that occurs when one's beliefs and behaviors conflict.

11. **d.** is the answer. Normative social influence refers to influence on behavior that comes from a desire to look good to others. Subjects who were observed conformed because they didn't want to look like oddballs. (p. 432)

a. Social facilitation is the better or faster performance of tasks that occurs in the presence of others.

b. Social loafing is the tendency for individual effort to be diminished when one is part of a group working toward a common goal.

c. Informational social influence is the tendency of individuals to accept the opinions of others, especially in situations where they themselves are unsure.

12. **d.** is the answer. Group polarization, or the enhancement of a group's prevailing attitudes, promotes groupthink, that is, disintegration of critical thinking. (p. 437)

a. Groupthink is more likely when a leader is highly in favor of an idea, which may make members reluctant to disagree.

b. A strong minority faction would probably have the opposite effect, in that it would diminish group harmony while promoting critical thinking.

c. Consulting with experts would discourage groupthink by exposing the group to other opinions.

13. **b.** is the answer. Aggression is any behavior, physical or verbal, that is intended to hurt or destroy. (p. 442)

a. A person may accidentally be hurt in a nonaggressive incident; and aggression does not necessarily prove hurtful.

c. Verbal behavior, which does not result in physical injury, is also aggressive. Moreover, acts of aggression may be cool and calculated, rather than hostile and passionate.

14. **a.** is the answer. The very wide variations in aggressiveness from culture to culture indicate that aggression cannot be considered an instinct, or unlearned, universal characteristic of the species. (p. 443)

15. **d.** is the answer. (p. 443)

16. **a.** is the answer. (pp. 446–447)

17. **d.** is the answer. This phenomenon is known as the bystander effect. (p. 455)

a. This answer is incorrect since individuals are less likely to render assistance at all if others are present.

b. Although people are less likely to assume the responsibility of helping, this does not mean they experience decreased empathy.

c. This answer is incorrect since norms such as the social responsibility norm encourage helping others, yet people are less likely to help with others around.

18. **c.** is the answer. Social traps foster conflict in that

two parties, by pursuing their self-interests, create a result that neither group wants. (p. 456)

a. As Sherif's studies demonstrated, the possession of shared or superordinate goals tends to reduce conflict between groups.

b. This is an example of mirror-image perceptions, which foster conflict along with social traps.

d. Face-to-face confrontations between conflicting parties generally do not reduce conflict, nor are they social traps.

19. **b.** is the answer. In fact, people tend to overgeneralize from vivid cases, rather than assume that they are unusual. (p. 442)

a., c., & d. Each of these is an example of a cognitive (a. & c.) or a social root (d.) of prejudice.

20. **a.** is the answer. (p. 442)

b. Ingroup bias is the tendency of people to favor their own group.

c. The fundamental attribution error is the tendency of people to underestimate situational influences when observing the behavior of other people.

d. Deindividuation refers to the loss of self-awareness that sometimes occurs in group situations.

21. **d.** is the answer. Being repeatedly exposed to novel stimuli increases our liking for them. (p. 450)

a. For the most part, the opposite is true.

b. & c. The mere exposure effect concerns our tendency to develop likings on the basis, not of similarities or differences, but simply of familiarity, or repeated exposure.

22. **a.** is the answer. This result supports the two-factor theory of emotion and passionate attraction, according to which arousal from any source can facilitate an emotion, depending on how we label the arousal. (pp. 452–453)

23. **c.** is the answer. Deep affection is typical of companionate love, rather than passionate love, and is promoted by equity, whereas traditional roles may be characterized by the dominance of one sex. (p. 453)

24. **a.** is the answer. (p. 455)

b. & c. These factors would most likely decrease a person's altruistic tendencies.

d. There is no evidence that one sex is more altruistic than the other.

25. **d.** is the answer. Sherif found that hostility between two groups could be dispelled by giving the groups superordinate, or shared, goals. (p. 458)

a. Although reducing the likelihood of social traps might reduce mutually destructive behavior, it would not lead to positive feelings between the groups.

b. Such segregation would likely increase ingroup bias and group polarization, resulting in further group conflict.

c. This might help, or it might increase hostilities; it would not be as helpful a strategy as communication through an outside mediator or, as in d., cooperation toward a superordinate goal.

26. **c.** is the answer. (p. 445)

a. & d. It is now believed that the frustration-aggression effect actually represents the aggression-eliciting effect of any aversive stimulus.

b. There is no documented sex difference in the effect of aversive stimuli on aggression.

27. **b.** is the answer. By limiting the number and types of programs children watch, and by discussing how television's portrayal of violence is unrealistic, parents can minimize the effects of viewing this violence. (p. 446)

a. There is a well-established relationship between viewing television violence and aggressiveness.

c. Doing so would only further desensitize children to violence and promote aggressiveness.

d. This is unrealistic.

Matching Items

1. d (p. 435)	**8.** b (p. 435)	**14.** r (p. 453)
2. c (p. 436)	**9.** a (p. 426)	**15.** q (p. 452)
3. g (p. 432)	**10.** p (p. 453)	**16.** o (p. 440)
4. e (p. 428)	**11.** k (p. 441)	**17.** l (p. 440)
5. f (p. 432)	**12.** n (p. 450)	**18.** s (p. 441)
6. i (p. 432)	**13.** m (p. 457)	**19.** j (p. 445)
7. h (p. 437)		

PROGRESS TEST 2

Multiple-Choice Questions

1. **d.** is the answer. (p. 438)

a. Group polarization refers to the tendency for differences in groups to become accentuated over time. Groupthink often promotes polarization, but the question does not indicate that Acme Truck Company is being compared with another group.

b. Dissonance is the personal discomfort one feels when attitudes and behaviors are discrepant.

c. Informational social influence refers to the tendency to seek the opinions of others when one is unsure about one's own attitudes or behavior.

2. **c.** is the answer. In this example of the fundamental attribution error, even when given the situational explanation for the woman's behavior, stu-

dents ignored it and attributed her behavior to her personal disposition. (p. 426)

3. **c.** is the answer. Known commitment to a view generally tends to work against conformity. In contrast, large group size, prestigiousness of a group, and an individual's feelings of incompetence and insecurity all strengthen the tendency to conform. (p. 431)

4. **b.** is the answer. Although the three concepts are related, it is suggestibility that specifically refers to the tendency to be influenced by or to imitate the behavior of others. Conformity is the tendency to adjust one's behavior to go along with a group standard. Compliance is the tendency to obediently follow the demands of another person. (pp. 430–431)

5. **b.** is the answer. An air attack would depersonalize the villagers, leading to compliance from those who might not comply if they had to destroy the village at close range. The other factors should not promote compliance, which would, if anything, be reduced by the role models for defiance in d. (p. 430)

6. **a.** is the answer. As illustrated by Maria's decision to stop buying aerosol products, informational social influence occurs when people have genuinely been influenced by what they have learned from others. (p. 432)

b. Had Maria's behavior been motivated by the desire to avoid rejection or to gain social approval (which we have no reason to suspect is the case), it would have been an example of normative social influence.

c. Conformity is the tendency to change one's attitudes or behavior to be more in line with a group standard. In this example, Maria is being persuaded by a speech, rather than the behavior of a group.

d. Social facilitation is the improvement in performance of well-learned tasks that may result when one is observed by others.

7. **d.** is the answer. Our attitudes are more likely to guide our actions when other influences are minimal, when there's a specific connection between the two, and when we're aware of the relevant attitude. The presence of other people would more likely be an outside factor that would lessen the likelihood of actions being guided by attitude. (pp. 427–429)

8. **d.** is the answer. Research demonstrates that playing a particular role often leads to adoption of the role. (p. 428)

9. **d.** is the answer. In this situation, the counter-atti-

tudinal behavior is done voluntarily and cannot be attributed to the demands of the situation. (p. 429)

a., b., & c. In these situations, the counter-attitudinal behaviors should not arouse much dissonance, since they can be attributed to the demands of the situation.

10. **a.** is the answer. (p. 436)

b. Social facilitation refers to the improvement in performance that may result when one is observed by others.

c. Deindividuation is the loss of self-awareness that may occur in individual members of a group. Such feelings may foster social loafing, but do not specifically refer to the tendency of individuals to slacken their effort as part of a group.

d. Group polarization refers to the strengthening of prevailing group attitudes that occurs with discussion.

11. **b.** is the answer. (p. 436)

a. & c. Crowding may amplify irritability or altruistic tendencies that are already present. Crowding does not, however, produce these reactions as a general effect.

d. In fact, just the opposite is true. Crowding often intensifies people's reactions.

12. **b.** is the answer. (p. 439)

a., c., & d. These aspects of minority influence were not discussed in the text.

13. **d.** is the answer. The fundamental attribution error refers to the tendency to underestimate situational influences in favor of this type of dispositional attribution when explaining the behavior of other people. (p. 426)

a., b., & c. Each of these is a situational attribution.

14. **a.** is the answer. (pp. 434–435)

15. **d.** is the answer. The textbook emphasizes the ways in which personal and social control interact in influencing behavior. It does not suggest that one factor is more influential than the other. (pp. 435–437)

16. **d.** is the answer. Coactors are people who are simultaneously at work on the same noncompetitive task. Debaters (a.) are obviously engaged in a competitive event, as are a pitcher and a batter (c.), although their tasks are not the same. As part of an audience (b.), one is not engaged in a specific task, competitive or otherwise. (p. 435)

17. **b.** is the answer. (p. 443)

a. & c. Heider originated attribution theory. Asch's research concerned conformity, rather than aggression.

d. Being a behaviorist, Skinner would argue that aggression is a learned behavior.

18. **a.** is the answer. Aggressiveness *can* be increased through selective breeding, which suggests that it is genetically influenced. (p. 443)

19. **c.** is the answer. (p. 443)

20. **d.** is the answer. (pp. 446–447)

21. **d.** is the answer. (p. 455)

22. **a.** is the answer. Such justifications arise as a way to preserve inequalities. The just-world phenomenon presumes that people get what they deserve. According to this view, someone who has less must deserve less. (p. 442)

23. **c.** is the answer. People tend to overestimate the similarity of people within groups other than their own. Thus, Juan is not likely to form stereotypes of fitness enthusiasts (a.), political liberals (b.), or older adults (d.), because these are groups to which he belongs. (p. 442)

24. **d.** is the answer. Because it provides people with an opportunity to meet, proximity is the most powerful predictor of friendship, even though, once a friendship is established, the other factors mentioned become more important. (p. 450)

25. **d.** is the answer. Hundreds of experiments indicate that first impressions are most influenced by physical appearance. (p. 450)

26. **c.** is the answer. The scapegoat theory says that when things go wrong, people look for someone on whom to take out their anger and frustration. (p. 441)

a. Although this is not always true of scapegoats, in this example the campers are venting their frustration on a member of their own cabin group.

b. Prejudice refers to an unjustifiable attitude toward another group.

d. Cognitive dissonance theory concerns the tendency of individuals to alter attitudes that conflict with their actions.

27. **a.** is the answer. According to the two-factor theory, physical arousal can intensify whatever emotion is currently felt. Only in the situation described in a. is Joan likely to be physically aroused. (pp. 452–453)

28. **d.** is the answer. The frustration-aggression theory states that the blocking of an attempt to achieve some goal, in Teresa's case buying concert tickets, creates anger and can generate aggression. (p. 445)

a. & c. Scapegoat theory and the just-world phenomenon are concerned with how prejudice develops; they are therfore irrelevant to Teresa's situation.

b. Cognitive dissonance is aroused when attitudes and actions conflict. There is nothing in this example that indicates Teresa is experiencing such feelings.

29. **b.** is the answer. (p. 458)

a. GRIT is a technique for reducing conflict through a series of conciliatory gestures, not for maintaining the status quo.

c. & d. These measures may help reduce conflict but they are not aspects of GRIT.

30. **c.** is the answer. The couple's similar, and presumably distorted, feelings toward each other fuels their conflict. (p. 457)

a. Self-disclosure, or the sharing of intimate feelings, fosters companionate love.

b. Stereotypes are overgeneralized ideas about groups.

d. Equity refers to the condition in which there is mutual giving and receiving between the partners in a relationship.

31. **a.** is the answer. (pp. 445–446)

b. Although some researchers take this view, the consensus, as expressed by the National Institute of Mental Health and by the American Psychological Association, is that violence on television does lead to aggressive behavior.

c. & d. Most viewers would maintain the opposite.

32. **a.** is the answer. (p. 441)

b. Prejudices are unjustifiable attitudes toward other groups. They may result from an ingroup bias, but are probably not the reason students favor their own university.

c. Scapegoats are individuals or groups toward which prejudice is directed as an outlet for the anger of frustrated individuals or groups.

d. The fundamental attribution error is the tendency to overestimate the impact of personal dispositions upon the behavior of others.

33. **a.** is the answer. Friends and couples are much more likely than randomly paired people to be similar in views, interests, and a range of other factors. (p. 430)

b. The opposite is true.

c. The mere exposure effect demonstrates that familiarity tends to breed fondness.

d. This is unlikely, given the positive effects of proximity and intimacy.

True-False Items

1. True (p. 426)
2. True (p. 453)
3. True (p. 431)
4. True (p. 431)
5. False (p. 453)
6. True (p. 428)
7. True (pp. 447–448)
8. False (pp. 437–438)
9. False (p. 436)
10. True (p. 437)

KEY TERMS

1. **Attribution theory** provides a way of analyzing how we explain others' behavior. We attribute behavior to individuals' dispositions or to their situations. (p. 426)

2. The **fundamental attribution error** is our tendency to underestimate the impact of situations and to overestimate the impact of personal dispositions upon the behavior of others. (p. 426)

   Example: If we meet someone who is withdrawn because of some preoccupation we know nothing about, we're liable to commit the **fundamental attribution error** and **attribute** that person's behavior to shyness or unfriendliness.

3. **Attitudes** are personal beliefs and feelings that may predispose a person to act in particular ways. (p. 427)

4. A **role** is a set of behaviors expected of someone in a particular social position. (p. 428)

5. **Cognitive dissonance** theory refers to the theory that we act to reduce the psychological discomfort we experience when our behavior conflicts with what we think and feel, or more generally, when two of our thoughts conflict—frequently, by changing our attitude rather than our behavior. (p. 429)

   Memory aid: *Dissonance* means disagreeing, or "at variance." **Cognitive dissonance** occurs when two thoughts or cognitions, are at variance with one another.

6. **Conformity** is the tendency to change one's attitudes or behavior to be more in line with a group standard. (p. 430)

   Example: Experiments by Solomon Asch demonstrated that **conformity** is especially likely when a person is made to feel insecure in the presence of a high-status group of three or more people.

7. **Normative social influence** refers to the pressure on individuals to conform in order to avoid rejection or gain social approval. (p. 432)

   Memory aid: *Normative* means "based on a norm, or pattern regarded as typical for a specific group." **Normative social influence** is the pressure groups exert on the individual to be *normal*.

8. **Norms** are social prescriptions, or rules, for expected behavior. (p. 432)

9. **Informational social influence** is the tendency to go along with a group when one is unsure or lacks information. (p. 432)

   Example: **Informational social influence** demonstrates that it is sometimes adaptive to be a conformist, such as when one is unsure about a behavior or opinion and looks to group members for helpful information.

10. A **coactor** is a person who is working simultaneously with you on the same task. (p. 435)

    Memory aid: *Co-* means "together"; **coactors** are people engaged in some action together.

11. **Social facilitation** is the improvement in performance of well-learned tasks that occurs when other people are present. (p. 435)

12. **Social loafing** is the tendency for individual effort to be diminished when one is part of a group working toward a common goal. (p. 436)

13. **Deindividuation** refers to the loss of self-awareness and self-restraint that sometimes occurs in group situations. (p. 437)

    Memory aid: As a prefix, *de-* indicates reversal or undoing. To *de*individuate is to undo one's individuality.

14. **Group polarization** refers to the enhancement of a group's prevailing tendencies over time, which often has the effect of accentuating the group's differences from other groups. (p. 437)

    Memory aid: To *polarize* is to "cause thinking to concentrate about two poles, or contrasting positions."

15. **Groupthink** refers to the unrealistic thought processes and decision-making that occurs within groups when the desire for group harmony becomes paramount. (p. 438)

    Example: The psychological tendencies of self-justification, conformity, and group polarization foster the development of the "team spirit" mentality known as **groupthink**.

16. **Prejudice** is a negative, unjustifiable attitude toward the members of a group. (p. 440)

    Example: There are many social and psychological roots of **prejudice**, including the ingroup bias and the tendency of people to simplify the world through categorization.

17. **Stereotypes** are overgeneralized attitudes about a particular group of people. (p. 440)

18. The **ingroup bias** refers to the tendency of people to look more favorably on the groups to which they belong. (p. 441)

19. The **scapegoat theory** proposes that prejudice arises when people who are frustrated or angry seek a target on which to vent these feelings. (p. 441)

20. The **just-world phenomenon** is the tendency of people to justify social inequities by assuming that the world is fair and people get what they deserve. (p. 442)

    Example: The **just-world phenomenon** is a manifestation of the commonly held belief that good is rewarded and evil punished. The logic is indisputable: "If I am rewarded, I must be good."

21. **Aggression** is physical or verbal action intended to harm someone or destroy. (p. 442)

22. The **frustration-aggression theory** states that aggression is triggered when people become angry because their efforts to achieve a goal have been blocked. (p. 445)

    Example: Researchers have realized that the **frustration-aggression** effect was a more general one in that, not only frustration but many other aversive events, including humidity, hot weather, and foul odors, promote anger.

23. The **mere exposure effect** refers to the fact that repeated exposure to an unfamiliar stimulus increases our liking of it. (p. 450)

    Example: The **mere exposure effect** is one of the many roots of ingroup bias. The more often we are exposed to the "in-group," the more favorable our impression of it.

24. **Passionate love** refers to intense emotional absorption in another, especially at the beginning of a relationship. (p. 452)

25. **Companionate love** refers to a deep, enduring affectionate attachment. (p. 453)

26. **Equity** refers to the condition in which there is mutual giving and receiving between the partners in a relationship. (p. 453)

    Example: Studies indicate that lasting relationships tend to be **equitable** relationships.

27. **Self-disclosure** refers to a person's sharing intimate feelings with another. (p. 453)

28. **Altruism** is unselfish behavior that helps others. (p. 453)

29. The **bystander effect** is the tendency of a person to be less likely to offer help to someone if there are other people present. (p. 455)

    Example: Latané and Darley have argued that the **bystander effect** occurs because with others present, the individual is less likely to notice an incident, identify it as a true emergency, and assume responsibility for helping.

30. **Conflict** is a perceived incompatibility of actions or goals between two individuals or groups. (p. 456)

31. **Social traps** are situations in which individuals or groups become caught up in mutually harmful behavior as each pursues his, her, or its perceived best interests. (p. 456)

32. **Mirror-image perceptions** are the distorted but similar views of one another often held by individuals or groups in conflict. (p. 457)

    Example: Until recently, the **mirror-image percep-** tions of the U.S. and the U.S.S.R., in which each nation viewed the other as diabolical, was a major factor contributing to the arms race.

33. **Superordinate goals** are mutual goals that require the cooperation of individuals or groups otherwise in conflict. (p. 458)

34. **GRIT** (Graduated and Reciprocated Initiatives in Tension-reduction) is a strategy of conflict resolution based on the defusing effect that conciliatory gestures can have on parties in conflict. (p. 458)

Statistical Reasoning in Everyday Life

Chapter Overview

A basic understanding of statistical reasoning has become a necessity in everyday life. Statistics are tools that help the psychologist and layperson to interpret the vast quantities of information they are confronted with on a daily basis. The text appendix discusses how statistics are used to describe data and to generalize from instances.

In studying this chapter you must concentrate on learning a number of procedures and understanding some underlying principles in the science of statistics. The graphic and computational procedures in the section called "Describing Data" include how data are distributed in a sample; measures of central tendency such as the mean, median, mode; variation measures such as the range and standard deviation; and correlation, or the degree to which two variables are related. Most of the conceptual material is then covered in the section called "Generalizing from Instances." You should be able to discuss four important principles concerning populations and samples, as well as the concept of significance in testing differences. The ultimate goal is to make yourself a better consumer of statistical research by improving your critical thinking skills.

Guided Study

The textbook chapter should be studied one section at a time. Before you read, preview each section by skimming it, noting headings and boldface items. Then read the appropriate section objectives from the following outline. Keep these objectives in mind, and as you read the chapter section, search for the information that will enable you to meet each objective. Once you have finished a section, write out answers for its objectives.

Describing Data (pp. 462–469)

1. Explain how frequency distributions, histograms, and percentile ranks are used to describe data.

2. Define the three measures of central tendency and explain how they describe data differently.

3. Define the two measures of variation and describe the normal curve.

4. Explain the correlation coefficient and its importance in assessing relationships between variables and show how such relationships are depicted on a scatterplot.

5. Identify factors that may contribute to illusory correlation and an illusion of control.

Generalizing from Instances (pp. 469–474)

6. Distinguish between a population and a sample and explain the importance of using samples.

7. Discuss four important principles in making generalizations about populations on the basis of samples.

8. Describe how psychologists make inferences about differences between groups.

Chapter Review

When you have finished reading the chapter, use the material that follows to review it. Complete the fill-in sentences and answer the essay items in complete sentences. As you proceed, evaluate your performance for each chapter section by consulting the answer key at the end of this chapter. Do not continue with the next section until you've understood each correct answer. If you need to, review or reread the appropriate chapter section in the textbook before continuing.

Describing Data (pp. 462–469)

1. A table or graph that depicts the number of individual scores occurring at each interval of a range is called a _____.

2. A bar graph that depicts a frequency distribution is called a _____.

3. The percentage of scores in a distribution that fall below an individual score is that score's _____ _____.

4. The three measures of central tendency are the _____, the _____, and the _____.

5. The most frequently occurring score in a distribution is called the _____.

6. The median is the score at the _____ percentile.

7. The mean is computed as the total _____ of scores divided by the _____ of scores.

8. In a symmetrical distribution, the three measures of central tendency are likely to be _____ (similar/different).

9. The measures of variation include the _____ and the _____.

10. The range is computed as the _____.

11. The range provides a(n) _____ (crude/accurate) estimate of variation because it _____ (is/is not) influenced by extreme scores.

12. The standard deviation is a _____ (more accurate/less accurate) measure of variation than the range. Unlike the range, the standard deviation _____ (takes/does not take) into consideration information from each score in the distribution.

13. Give a general definition of the standard deviation.

14. The bell-shaped distribution that often describes large amounts of data is called the

_____ _____.

15. In this distribution, approximately

_____ percent of the individual scores fall within one standard deviation on either side of the mean. Within two standard deviations on either side of the mean fall

_____ percent of the individual scores.

Calculate what a score of 116 on the normally distributed Wechsler IQ test would mean with regard to percentile rank. (Recall that the mean is 100; the standard deviation is ±15 points. Hint: You might find it helpful to first draw the normal curve.)

16. A graph consisting of points that depict the relationship between two sets of scores is called a _____.

17. A measure of the direction and extent of relationship between two sets of scores is called the _____ _____. Numerically, this measure can range from _____ to _____.

18. When there is no relationship at all between two sets of scores, the correlation coefficient is _____. The strongest possible correlation between two sets of scores is either _____ or _____. When the correlation between two sets of scores is negative, as one increases, the other _____.

Cite an example of a positive correlation and a negative correlation. Your examples can be drawn from previous chapters of the textbook or can be based on observations from daily life.
An example of positive correlation is

An example of negative correlation is

19. A correlation that is perceived but doesn't really exist is called _____ _____.

20. When we believe a relationship exists between two things we are most likely to recall instances that _____ (confirm/ disconfirm) our belief.

21. The correlation coefficient _____ (gives/does not give) information about cause-and-effect relationships.

22. That average results are more typical than extreme results is expressed in the phenomenon of _____ _____ _____ _____.

Generalizing from Instances (pp. 469–474)

23. All of the cases in a total group make up a _____.

List four important principles in generalizing from samples to populations.

a. _____

_____

b. _____

_____

c. _____

_____

d. _____

_____

24. People have a tendency to _____ from unrepresentative but vivid cases.

25. A random sample is one in which each person in the population has _____ _____.

26. Small samples provide a _____ (more/less) reliable basis for generalizing than large samples.

27. Averages based on a large number of cases are _____ (more/less) reliable than those based on a few cases.

28. Averages are more reliable when they are based on scores with _____ (high/low) variability.

29. When people perceive little variability in individual instances, they are _____ (more/less) likely to generalize from them.

30. Tests of statistical _____ are used to estimate whether observed differences are reliable, that is, to make sure they are not simply the result of _____ variation.

FOCUS ON PSYCHOLOGY:
Could A Monkey Have Written This?

It has been said that given enough time, a monkey randomly striking the keys of a typewriter could theoretically turn out the great American novel. What is the actual probability of this occurring?

In this study guide there are approximately 200,000 letters, numbers, and spaces. The keyboard of the microcomputer that I used to type it has 63 keys on it. Therefore, at any given point in time, the monkey would have a 1 in 63 chance of striking the correct key. Sounds plausible, you say? To complete the entire study guide, our diligent ape would have to strike the correct key 200,000 times in succession. The probability of this occurring is computed as $1/63 = 0.016$ raised to the power of 200,000. To develop a feeling for how remote this probability is, 0.016 raised to the power of 2 is equal to 0.000256; 0.016 raised to the 20th power is equal to .00000000000000000000000000000000121. Raised to the power of 200,000, the probability is so small that the decimal point is followed by more zeros than there are characters in this entire book.

Source: Suggested by Grasha, A. F. (1963). *Practical Applications of Psychology* (2nd ed.). Boston: Little, Brown.

Progress Test 1

Multiple-Choice Questions

Circle your answers to the following questions and check them with the answer key at the end of this chapter. If your answer is incorrect, read the answer key explanation for why it is incorrect and then consult the appropriate pages of the text to understand the correct answer. Use the page margins if you need extra space for your computations.

1. Jack found that his score on the psychology exam was the highest in his class. His percentile rank for this score is:
   a. 99.
   b. 100.
   c. 95.
   d. This cannot be determined from the information given.

2. What is the mean of the following distribution of scores: 2, 3, 7, 6, 1, 4, 9, 5, 8, 2?
   a. 5   b. 4   c. 4.7   d. 3.7

3. What is the median of the following distribution of scores: 1, 3, 7, 7, 2, 8, 4?
   a. 1   b. 2   c. 3   d. 4

4. What is the mode of the following distribution: 8, 2, 1, 1, 3, 7, 6, 2, 0, 2?
   a. 1   b. 2   c. 3   d. 7

5. Compute the range of the following distribution: 9, 14, 2, 8, 1, 6, 8, 9, 1, 3.
   a. 10   b. 9   c. 8   d. 13

6. If two sets of scores are negatively correlated, it means that:
   a. as one set of scores increases, the other decreases.
   b. as one set of scores increases, the other increases.
   c. there is only a weak relationship between the sets of scores.
   d. there is no relationship at all between the sets of scores.

7. Jane usually averages 175 in bowling. One night her three-game average is 215. Over the next several weeks of bowling, her bowling average will probably:
   a. return to about the level of her average.
   b. continue to increase.
   c. dip down to about 155.
   d. There is no way one can predict what her scores will average.

8. In a normal distribution, what percentage of scores fall between +2 and −2 standard deviations of the mean?
   a. 50 percent
   b. 68 percent
   c. 95 percent
   d. 99.7 percent

9. If height and body weight are positively correlated, which of the following is true?
   a. There is a cause-and-effect relationship between height and weight.
   b. As height increases, weight decreases.
   c. Knowing a person's height, one can predict his or her weight.
   d. None of the above is true.

10. In generalizing from a sample to the population, it is important that:
    a. the sample is representative of the population.
    b. the sample is large.
    c. the scores in the sample have low variability.
    d. all of the above are observed.

11. When a difference between two groups is "statistically significant," this means that:
    a. the difference is statistically real but of little practical significance.
    b. the difference is probably the result of sampling variation.
    c. the difference is not likely to be due to chance variation.
    d. all of the above are true.

12. A listing of the number of scores that occur within each interval of some scale of measurement is called a:
    a. percentile rank.
    b. standard deviation.
    c. frequency distribution.
    d. correlation coefficient.

13. Which of the following is *not* a measure of central tendency?
    a. mean
    b. range
    c. median
    d. mode

14. Which of the following is the measure of central tendency that would be most affected by a few extreme scores?
    a. mean
    b. range
    c. median
    d. mode

15. The football team's punter wants to determine how consistent his punting distances have been during the past season. Which of the following should he compute?
    a. mean
    b. median
    c. mode
    d. standard deviation

16. If the data in a research study tend to be distributed with about two-thirds of the cases falling within 1 standard deviation from the mean and 95 percent within 2 standard deviations, researchers know that their data form a:
    a. frequency distribution.
    b. scatterplot.
    c. normal curve.
    d. histogram.

17. If there is no relationship between two sets of scores, the coefficient of correlation equals:
    a. 0.00
    b. −1.00
    c. +1.00
    d. 0.50

18. Illusory correlation refers to:
    a. the perception that two negatively correlated variables are positively correlated.
    b. the perception of a relationship between two unrelated variables.
    c. an insignificant correlation coefficient.
    d. a correlation coefficient that equals −1.00.

Matching Items

Match each term with the appropriate definition or description.

Terms

_____ 1. histogram
_____ 2. median
_____ 3. population
_____ 4. sample
_____ 5. mode
_____ 6. range
_____ 7. standard deviation
_____ 8. scatterplot
_____ 9. mean
_____ 10. measures of central tendency
_____ 11. measures of variation

Definitions

a. the mean, median, and mode
b. the difference between highest and lowest scores
c. the arithmetic average of a distribution
d. the range and standard deviation
e. all of the cases in a group
f. the most frequently occurring score
g. a subset of scores from a group
h. a bar graph depicting a frequency distribution
i. the middle score in a distribution
j. a graphed cluster of dots depicting the values of two variables
k. the square root of the average squared deviation of scores from the mean

Progress Test 2

Progress Test 2 should be completed during a final chapter review. Do this test after you thoroughly understand the correct answers for the Chapter Review and Progress Test 1.

Multiple-Choice Questions

1. A bar graph that depicts a frequency distribution is called a:
   - **a.** scatterplot.
   - **b.** normal curve.
   - **c.** coefficient plot.
   - **d.** histogram.

2. What is the mean of the following distribution of scores: 2, 5, 8, 10, 11, 4, 6, 9, 1, 4?
   - **a.** 2
   - **b.** 10
   - **c.** 6
   - **d.** 15

3. Which of the following exemplifies regression toward the average?
   - **a.** In his second season of varsity basketball, Edward averaged 5 points more per game than in his first season.
   - **b.** A gambler rolls 5 consecutive "sevens" using her favorite dice.
   - **c.** After earning an unusually low score on the first exam in a class, a "B student" scores much higher on the second exam.
   - **d.** A student who usually earns B's earns grades of A, D, D, and A on the four exams in a class, thus maintaining a B average overall for the class.

4. Which score falls at the fiftieth percentile of a distribution?
   - **a.** mean
   - **b.** median
   - **c.** mode
   - **d.** standard deviation

5. Which statistic is the average amount by which the scores in a distribution vary from the average?
   - **a.** standard deviation
   - **b.** range
   - **c.** median
   - **d.** mode

6. The most frequently occurring score in a distribution is the:
   - **a.** mean.
   - **b.** median.
   - **c.** mode.
   - **d.** range.

7. If scores on an exam have a mean of 50, a standard deviation of 10, and are normally distributed, approximately 95 percent of those taking the exam would be expected to score between:
   - **a.** 45 and 55.
   - **b.** 40 and 60.
   - **c.** 35 and 65.
   - **d.** 30 and 70.

8. Which of the following is the measure of variation that is most affected by extreme scores?
   - **a.** mean
   - **b.** standard deviation
   - **c.** mode
   - **d.** range

9. Which of the following sets of scores would likely be most representative of the population from which it was drawn?
   - **a.** a sample with a relatively large standard deviation
   - **b.** a sample with a relatively small standard deviation
   - **c.** a sample with a relatively large range
   - **d.** a sample with a relatively small range

10. Joe believes that his basketball game is always best when he wears his old gray athletic socks. Joe is a victim of the phenomenon called:
    - **a.** regression toward the average.
    - **b.** the availability heuristic.
    - **c.** illusory correlation.
    - **d.** the gambler's fallacy.

11. If a difference between two samples is *not* statistically significant, which of the following can be concluded?
    - **a.** The difference is probably not a true one.
    - **b.** The difference is probably not reliable.
    - **c.** The difference could be due to sampling variation.
    - **d.** All of the above are true.

12. The first step in constructing a histogram is to create a:
    - **a.** standard deviation.
    - **b.** frequency distribution.
    - **c.** correlation coefficient.
    - **d.** range.

13. Five members of Terry's sorority reported the following individual earnings from their sale of raffle tickets: $6, $3, $8, $6, and $12. In this distribution, the mean is _____ the mode and _____ the median.
    - **a.** equal to; equal to
    - **b.** greater than; equal to
    - **c.** greater than; greater than
    - **d.** equal to; less than

14. Standard deviation is to mode as _____ is to _____.
    - **a.** mean; median
    - **b.** variation; central tendency
    - **c.** median; mean
    - **d.** central tendency; variation

15. In a normal distribution, what percentage of scores fall between −1 and +1 standard deviation units of the mean?
    - **a.** 50 percent
    - **b.** 68 percent
    - **c.** 95 percent
    - **d.** 99.7 percent

16. The precision with which sample statistics reflect population parameters is greater when the sample is:

a. large.
b. characterized by high variability.
c. small in number but consists of vivid cases.
d. statistically significant.

17. During elections, opinion researchers poll selected voters in order to try to gauge overall voter attitudes for or against specific issues and candidates. Pollsters consider all eligible voters the _____ and the selected voters the _____.
   a. sample; representative sample
   b. population; sample
   c. frequency distribution; range
   d. normal distribution; population

18. Which of the following correlation coefficients indicates the strongest relationship between two variables?
   a. −.73   c. 0.00
   b. +.66   d. −.50

19. In six tosses of a coin, which of the following outcomes of heads (H) and tails (T) could not be the result of chance?
   a. HHHTTT
   b. THTHTH
   c. HHHHHH
   d. All of the above could be the result of chance.

True-False Items

Indicate whether each statement is true or false by placing a *T* or *F* in the blank next to the item.

_____ 1. A percentile rank of 60 means that most of the scores in the distribution fall above it.

_____ 2. In almost all distributions, the mean, median, and the mode will be the same.

_____ 3. When a distribution has a few extreme scores, the range is more misleading than the standard deviation.

_____ 4. If increases in the value of variable *x* are accompanied by decreases in the value of variable *y*, the two variables are negatively correlated.

_____ 5. Over time, extreme results tend to fall back toward the average.

_____ 6. If a sample was selected randomly, it cannot be representative of the population from which it was drawn.

_____ 7. The mean is always the most precise measure of central tendency.

_____ 8. Averages that have been derived from scores with low variability are more reliable than those derived from scores that are more variable.

_____ 9. If a difference between two groups is due to sampling variation, it cannot be statistically significant.

_____ 10. Small samples are less reliable than large samples for generalizing to the population.

Key Terms

Using your own words, write a brief definition or explanation of the following terms.

1. frequency distribution

2. histogram

3. percentile rank

4. mode

5. mean

6. median

7. range

8. standard deviation

9. normal curve (normal distribution)

10. scatterplot

11. correlation coefficient

12. illusory correlation

13. regression toward the average

14. population

15. statistical significance

Answers
CHAPTER REVIEW

1. frequency distribution
2. histogram
3. percentile rank

4. mean; median; mode
5. mode
6. 50th
7. sum; number
8. similar
9. range; standard deviation
10. difference between the lowest and highest scores in a distribution
11. crude; is
12. more accurate; takes
13. The standard deviation is a measure of variability of the scores in a distribution. It is computed by squaring the deviation of each score from the mean and finding the square root of their average.
14. normal curve
15. 68; 95

Since the mean equals 100 and the standard deviation is 15 points, a score of 116 is just over one standard deviation unit above the mean. Since 68 percent of the population scores fall within one standard deviation on either side of the mean, 34 percent fall between 0 and +1 standard deviation unit. By definition, 50 percent of the scores fall below the mean. Therefore, a score at or above 115 is higher than that obtained by 84 percent of the population (50 percent + 34 percent = 84 percent).

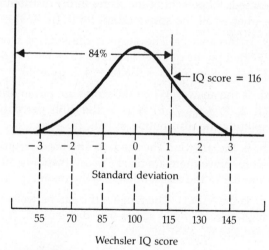

Wechsler IQ score

16. scatterplot
17. correlation coefficient; +1.00; −1.00
18. 0.00; +1.00; −1.00; decreases

An example of a positive correlation is the relationship between air temperature and ice cream sales: as one increases so does the other.

An example of a negative correlation is the relationship between health and the amount of stress a person is under: as stress increases, the odds of good health decrease.

19. illusory correlation

20. confirm

21. does not give

22. regression toward the average

23. population

a. Representative samples are better than biased samples.

b. Random sequences may not look random.

c. Large samples yield more reliable statistics than small samples.

d. Less variable observations are more reliable than highly variable observations.

24. overgeneralize

25. an equal chance of being selected

26. less

27. more

28. low

29. more

30. significance; chance

PROGRESS TEST 1

Multiple-Choice Questions

1. **a.** is the answer. The percentile rank of a score is the percentage of scores in a distribution that a given score exceeds. The highest score in the class exceeds 99 percent of the scores in the distribution —that is, all the scores except itself. (p. 463)

2. **c.** is the answer. The mean is the sum of scores divided by the number of scores. $(2 + 3 + 7 + 6 + 1 + 4 + 9 + 5 + 8 + 2)/10 = 4.7$. (p. 465)

3. **d.** is the answer. When the scores are put in order (1, 2, 3, 4, 7, 7, 8), 4 is at the 50th percentile, splitting the distribution in half. (p. 465)

4. **b.** is the answer. The mode is the most frequent score. Since there are more "twos" than any other number in the distribution, 2 is the mode. (p. 465)

5. **d.** is the answer. The range is the gap between the highest and lowest scores in a distribution. $(14 - 1 = 13.)$ (p. 466)

6. **a.** is the answer. (p. 468)

   b. This situation indicates that the two sets of scores are positively correlated.

   c. Whether a correlation is positive or negative does not indicate the strength of the relationship, but only its direction.

   d. In negative correlations, there *is* a relationship; the correlation is negative because the relationship is an inverse one.

7. **a.** is the answer. Although one cannot predict her

individual scores, over time, Jane's scores will fall close to her average. This is the phenomenon of regression toward the average. (p. 469)

8. **c.** is the answer. (p. 466)

   a. 50 percent of the normal curve falls on either side of its mean.

   b. 68 percent of the scores fall between −1 and +1 standard deviation units.

   d. 99.7 percent fall between −3 and +3 standard deviations.

9. **c.** is the answer. If height and weight are positively correlated, increased height is associated with increased weight. Thus, one can predict a person's weight from his or her height. (p. 467)

   a. Correlation does not imply causality.

   b. This situation depicts a negative correlation between height and weight.

10. **d.** is the answer. (pp. 470–473)

11. **c.** is the answer. (p. 474)

    a. A statistically significant difference may or may not be of practical importance.

    b. This is often the case when a difference is *not* statistically significant.

12. **c.** is the answer. (p. 463)

    a. Percentile rank refers to the percentage of scores in a distribution that a particular score exceeds.

    b. The standard deviation is the average amount by which scores in a distribution differ from the mean of the distribution.

    d. The correlation coefficient is an index of the degree to which two sets of scores are related.

13. **b.** is the answer. The range is a measure of variation. (p. 466)

14. **a.** is the answer. As an average, calculated by adding all scores and dividing by the number of scores, the mean could easily be affected by the inclusion of a few extreme scores. (p. 465)

    b. The range is not a measure of central tendency.

    c. & d. The median and mode give equal weight to all scores; each counts only once and its numerical value is unimportant.

15. **d.** is the answer. A small or large standard deviation indicates whether a distribution is homogeneous or variable. (p. 466)

    a., b., & c. These statistics would not give any information regarding consistency of performance.

16. **c.** is the answer. (p. 466)

    a. A frequency distribution is a listing of the number of scores that occur within each interval of some scale of measurement.

b. A scatterplot is a graph that depicts the nature and degree of relationship between two variables.

d. A histogram is a bar graph that depicts a frequency distribution.

17. **a.** is the answer. (p. 467)

b. & c. These are "perfect" correlations of equal strength.

d. This indicates a much stronger relationship between two sets of scores than does a coefficient of 0.00.

18. **b.** is the answer. (p. 468)

Matching Items

1. h (p. 463)
2. i (p. 465)
3. e (p. 470)
4. g (p. 470)
5. f (p. 465)
6. b (p. 466)
7. k (p. 466)
8. j (p. 467)
9. c (p. 465)
10. a (p. 465)
11. d (p. 466)

PROGRESS TEST 2

Multiple-Choice Questions

1. **d.** is the answer. (p. 463)

a. A scatterplot is a depiction of the nature and degree of relationship between two variables.

b. A normal curve is the symmetrical distribution that describes the frequency of many psychological and physical characteristics in a population.

c. There is no such thing as a coefficient plot.

2. **c.** is the answer. The mean is the sum of the scores divided by the number of scores. (60/10 = 6.) (p. 465)

3. **c.** is the answer. Regression toward the average is the phenomenon that average results are more typical than extreme results. Thus, after an unusual event (the low exam score in this example) things tend to return toward their average level, in this case, the higher score on the second exam. (p. 469)

a. Edward's improved average indicates only that, perhaps as a result of an additional season's experience, he is a better player.

b. Because the probability of rolling 5 consecutive "sevens" is very low, it is to be expected that with subsequent rolls the gambler's "luck" will prove to be atypical and things will tend to return toward their average level. This answer is incorrect, however, because it states only that 5 consecutive "sevens" were rolled.

d. In this example, although the exam grades average to the student's usual grade of B, they all are extreme grades and do not regress toward the average.

4. **b.** is the answer. (p. 465)

a. The mean is the arithmetic average of the scores in a distribution.

c. The mode is the most frequent score in a distribution.

d. The standard deviation is the average deviation of scores from the mean.

5. **a.** is the answer. (p. 466)

b. The range is the difference between the highest and lowest scores in a distribution.

c. The median is the score that falls at the fiftieth percentile.

d. The mode is the most frequent score.

6. **c.** is the answer. (p. 465)

a. The mean is the arithmetic average.

b. The median is the score that splits the distribution in half.

d. The range is the difference between the highest and lowest scores.

7. **d.** is the answer. 95 percent of the scores in a normal distribution fall between 2 standard deviation units below the mean and 2 standard deviation units above the mean. In this example, the test score that corresponds to -2 standard deviation units is $50 - (2 \times 10) = 30$; the score that corresponds to $+2$ standard deviation units is $50 + (2 \times 10) = 70$. (p. 466)

8. **d.** is the answer. Since the range is the difference between the highest and lowest scores, it is by definition affected by extreme scores. (p. 466)

a. & c. The mean and mode are measures of central tendency, not of variation.

b. The standard deviation is less affected than the range because, when it is calculated, the deviation of *every* score from the mean is computed.

9. **b.** is the answer. Averages derived from scores with low variability tend to be more reliable estimates of the populations from which they are drawn. Thus, a. and c. are incorrect. Because the standard deviation is a more accurate estimate of variability than the range, d. is incorrect. (p. 473)

10. **c.** is the answer. A correlation that is perceived but doesn't actually exist, as in the example, is known as an illusory correlation. (p. 468)

a. Regression toward the average is the tendency for extreme scores to fall back toward the average.

b. The availability heuristic is the tendency of people to estimate the likelihood of something in terms of how readily it comes to mind.

d. The gambler's fallacy is the false perception that the probability of a random event is determined by past events.

11. **d.** is the answer. A difference that is statistically significant is a true difference, rather than an apparent difference due to factors such as sampling variation, and it is reliable. (p. 474)

12. **b.** is the answer. A histogram is a bar graph based on a frequency distribution. (p. 463)

13. **c.** is the answer. In this case, the mean, or average (7), is greater than both the mode, or most frequent score (6), and the median, or middle score (6). (p. 465)

14. **b.** is the answer. Just as the standard deviation is a measure of variation, so the mode is a measure of central tendency. (pp. 465–466)

15. **b.** is the answer. (p. 466)

a. 50 percent of the scores in a normal distribution fall on one side of the mean.

c. 95 percent fall between −2 and +2 standard deviations.

d. 99.7 percent fall between −3 and +3 standard deviations.

16. **a.** is the answer. Figures based on larger samples are more reliable. (p. 472)

b. & c. These sample characteristics would tend to lower precision.

d. A test of significance is a determination of the likelihood that an obtained result is real.

17. **b.** is the answer. The whole group of interest, in this case all eligible voters, is the *population*; the subgroup actually polled is the *sample*. (p. 470)

a. Pollsters will work to make their sample conform as closely as possible to the general voting population.

c. & d. A frequency distribution is the listing of scores within each range, while normal distribution refers to one possible shape for the curve.

18. **a.** is the answer. The closer the correlation coefficient is to either +1 or −1, the stronger the relationship between the variables. (p. 467)

19. **d.** is the answer. In such a case, any sequence, no matter how unrandom it may look, can be the result of chance. (p. 474)

True-False Items

1. False (p. 463)	4. True (p. 467)
2. False (p. 465)	5. True (p. 469)
3. True (p. 466)	6. False (p. 470)

7. False (p. 465)	9. True (p. 474)
8. True (p. 466)	10. True (p. 472)

KEY TERMS

1. A **frequency distribution** is a grouping of scores in a distribution into equal-sized intervals. (p. 463)

2. A **histogram** is a bar graph that depicts a frequency distribution. (p. 463)

3. **Percentile rank** is the percentage of scores in a distribution that fall below a particular score. (p. 463)

   Example: A student whose **percentile rank** is 85 has outperformed 85 percent of all students.

4. The **mode** is the most frequent score in a distribution; it is the simplest measure of central tendency to determine. (p. 465)

5. The **mean** is the arithmetic average, the measure of central tendency computed by adding together the scores in a distribution and dividing by the number of scores. (p. 465)

6. The **median**, a measure of central tendency, is the score that falls at the 50th percentile, cutting a distribution in half. (p. 465)

   Example: When the **mean** of a distribution is affected by a few extreme scores, the **median** is the more appropriate measure of central tendency.

7. The **range** is a measure of variation computed as the difference between the highest and lowest scores in a distribution. (p. 466)

8. The **standard deviation** is the average amount by which the scores in a distribution deviate from the mean. Because it is based on every score in the distribution, it is a more precise measure of variation than the range. (p. 466)

9. The **normal curve**, or normal distribution, is the symmetrical curve that describes many types of data, with most scores centering around the mean and progressively fewer scores occurring toward the extremes. (p. 466)

10. A **scatterplot** is a depiction of the relationship between two sets of scores by means of a graphed cluster of dots. (p. 467)

    Example: The extent to which the points in a **scatterplot** fall along a straight line indicates the strength of relationship between two sets of scores. The direction of slope indicates whether the relationship is positive or negative.

11. The **correlation coefficient** is an index of the strength and direction of relationship between two sets of scores. (p. 467)

    Example: When the **correlation coefficient** is positive, the two sets of scores increase together. When it is negative, increases in one set are accompanied by decreases in the other.

12. **Illusory correlation** is the false perception that a correlation exists. (p. 468)

    Example: Superstitious behaviors such as avoiding cracks in the sidewalk, wearing "lucky" clothing, and not walking under ladders exemplify **illusory correlation**, in this case, the illusion that uncontrollable events are correlated with our actions.

13. **Regression toward the average** is the tendency for extreme scores to return back, or regress, toward the average. (p. 469)

    Example: A baseball player who usually bats around .250 may have several exceptional games in which he bats .750 but can then be expected to return to his usual .250 hitting, as a result of **regression toward the average**.

14. A **population** refers to all the members of a group that we are interested in. (p. 470)

    Example: Because it often is not practical to measure every member of the **population**, researchers carefully select and study a representative sample.

15. **Statistical significance** means that an obtained result, such as the difference between the averages for two samples, very likely reflects a real difference rather than sampling variation or chance factors. Tests of statistical significance help researchers decide when they can justifiably generalize from an observed instance. (p. 474)